Indigenous Data So

This book examines how Indigenous Peoples around the world are demanding greater data sovereignty and challenging the ways in which governments have historically used Indigenous data to develop policies and programs.

In the digital age, governments are increasingly dependent on data and data analytics to inform their policies and decision-making. However, Indigenous Peoples have often been the unwilling targets of policy interventions and have had little say over the collection, use and application of data about them, their lands and cultures. At the heart of Indigenous Peoples' demands for change are the enduring aspirations of self-determination over their institutions, resources, knowledge and information systems.

With contributors from Australia, Aotearoa New Zealand, North and South America and Europe, this book offers a rich account of the potential for Indigenous Data Sovereignty to support human flourishing and to protect against the ever-growing threats of data-related risks and harms.

Maggie Walter (Palawa) (PhD, FASSA) is Distinguished Professor of Sociology at the University of Tasmania, Australia. Publishing extensively in the field of Indigenous Data, including *Indigenous Statistics* (with C. Andersen 2013 Routledge), Maggie is a founding member of the Maiam nayri Wingara Indigenous Data Sovereignty Collective and the Global Indigenous Data Alliance.

Tahu Kukutai (Ngāti Tiipa, Ngāti Kinohaku, Te Aupōuri) (PhD) is Professor of Demography at the National Institute of Demographic and Economic Analysis, Aotearoa New Zealand. She co-edited *Indigenous Data Sovereignty: Toward an Agenda* and is a founding member of the Māori Data Sovereignty Network Te Mana Raraunga and the Global Indigenous Data Alliance.

Stephanie Russo Carroll (Ahtna-Native Village of Kluti-Kaah, Sicilian-descent) (DrPH, MPH) is Assistant Professor of Public Health and Associate Director for the Native Nations Institute at the University of Arizona, USA. A researcher active at the nexus of Indigenous governance, the environment, community wellness and data, Stephanie co-founded the US Indigenous Data Sovereignty Network and is a founding member and chair of the Global Indigenous Data Alliance.

Desi Rodriguez-Lonebear (Northern Cheyenne and Chicana) (PhD) is a social demographer who researches the intersection of Indigenous erasure, data and inequality. She is Assistant Professor of Sociology and American Indian Studies at the University of California, Los Angeles. Desi co-founded the US Indigenous Data Sovereignty Network and is a founding member of the Global Indigenous Data Alliance.

Routledge Studies in Indigenous Peoples and Policy

There are an estimated 370 million Indigenous Peoples in over 70 countries worldwide, often facing common issues stemming from colonialism and its ongoing effects. Routledge Studies in Indigenous Peoples and Policy brings together books which explore these concerns, including poverty; health inequalities; loss of land, language and culture; environmental degradation and climate change; intergenerational trauma; and the struggle to have their rights, cultures and communities protected.

Indigenous Peoples across the world are asserting their right to fully participate in policy making that affects their people, their communities, and the natural world, and to have control over their own communities and lands. This book series explores policy issues, reports on policy research, and champions the best examples of methodological approaches. It will explore policy issues from the perspectives of Indigenous Peoples in order to develop evidence-based policy and create policy-making processes that represent Indigenous Peoples and support positive social change.

Human Capital Development and Indigenous Peoples
Nicholas Biddle

Indigenous Knowledges and the Sustainable Development Agenda
Edited by Anders Breidlid and Roy Krøvel

Indigenous Data Sovereignty and Policy
Edited by Maggie Walter, Tahu Kukutai, Stephanie Russo Carroll, and Desi Rodriguez-Lonebear

Indigenous Data Sovereignty and Policy

Edited by Maggie Walter, Tahu Kukutai,
Stephanie Russo Carroll and
Desi Rodriguez-Lonebear

LONDON AND NEW YORK

First published 2021
by Routledge
2 Park Square, Milton Park, Abingdon, Oxon OX14 4RN

and by Routledge
605 Third Avenue, New York, NY 10017

First issued in paperback 2022

Routledge is an imprint of the Taylor & Francis Group, an informa business

© 2021 selection and editorial matter, Maggie Walter, Tahu Kukutai, Stephanie Russo Carroll and Desi Rodriguez-Lonebear; individual chapters, the contributors

The right of Maggie Walter, Tahu Kukutai, Stephanie Russo Carroll, and Desi Rodriguez-Lonebear to be identified as the authors of the editorial material, and of the authors for their individual chapters, has been asserted in accordance with sections 77 and 78 of the Copyright, Designs and Patents Act 1988.

The Open Access version of this book, available at www.taylorfrancis. com, has been made available under a Creative Commons Attribution-Non Commercial-No Derivatives 4.0 license.

Trademark notice: Product or corporate names may be trademarks or registered trademarks, and are used only for identification and explanation without intent to infringe.

Publisher's Note
The publisher has gone to great lengths to ensure the quality of this reprint but points out that some imperfections in the original copies may be apparent.

British Library Cataloguing-in-Publication Data
A catalogue record for this book is available from the British Library

Library of Congress Cataloging-in-Publication Data
Names: Walter, Maggie, editor.
Title: Indigenous data sovereignty and policy/edited by Maggie Walter, Tahu Kukutai, Stephanie Carroll Rainie, and Desi Rodriguez-Lonebear.
Description: Abingdon, Oxon; New York, NY: Routledge, 2021. |
Series: Routledge studies in indigenous peoples and policy | Includes bibliographical references and index. | Identifiers: LCCN 2020020862 (print) | LCCN 2020020863 (ebook) | ISBN 9780367222369 (hardback) | ISBN 9780429273957 (ebook)
Subjects: LCSH: Indigenous peoples–Computer network resources. | Indigenous peoples–Data processing. | Indigenous peoples–Research. | Indigenous peoples–Government policy.
Classification: LCC GN380 .I3456 2021 (print) | LCC GN380 (ebook) | DDC 305.8–dc23
LC record available at https://lccn.loc.gov/2020020862
LC ebook record available at https://lccn.loc.gov/2020020863

ISBN: 978-0-367-56747-7 (pbk)
ISBN: 978-0-367-22236-9 (hbk)
ISBN: 978-0-429-27395-7 (ebk)

DOI: 10.4324/9780429273957

Typeset in Times New Roman
by Deanta Global Publishing Services, Chennai, India

Contents

List of figures and tables   vii
List of contributors   viii

1   Indigenous Data Sovereignty, governance and the link to Indigenous policy   1
MAGGIE WALTER AND STEPHANIE RUSSO CARROLL

2   "Pushing the space": Data sovereignty and self-determination in Aotearoa NZ   21
TAHU KUKUTAI AND DONNA CORMACK

3   The intersection of Indigenous Data Sovereignty and Closing the Gap policy in Australia   36
RAYMOND LOVETT, ROXANNE JONES AND BOBBY MAHER

4   Growing Pueblo data sovereignty   51
MICHELE SUINA AND CARNELL T. CHOSA

5   Indigenous data and policy in Aotearoa New Zealand   62
ANDREW SPORLE, MAUI HUDSON AND KIRI WEST

6   Indigenous self-determination and data governance in the Canadian policy context   81
ROBYN K. ROWE, JULIE R. BULL AND JENNIFER D. WALKER

7   The challenge of Indigenous data in Sweden   99
PER AXELSSON AND CHRISTINA STORM MIENNA

8   Data governance in the Basque Country: Victims and memories of violent conflicts   112
JOXERRAMON BENGOETXEA

9 Indigenous policy and Indigenous data in Mexico: Context, challenges and perspectives 130
OSCAR LUIS FIGUEROA RODRÍGUEZ

10 Indigenous Data Sovereignty: Quechan education data sovereignty 148
JAMESON D. LOPEZ

11 Indigenous Data Sovereignty and the role of universities 157
TENNILLE L. MARLEY

12 Narratives on Indigenous victimhood: Challenges of Indigenous Data Sovereignty in Colombia's transitional setting 169
GUSTAVO ROJAS-PÁEZ AND COLLEEN ALENA O'BRIEN

13 Kaupapa Māori-informed approaches to support data rights and self-determination 187
SARAH-JANE PAINE, DONNA CORMACK, PAPAARANGI REID, RICCI HARRIS AND BRIDGET ROBSON

14 The legal and policy dimensions of Indigenous Data Sovereignty (IDS) 204
REBECCA TSOSIE

15 Embedding systemic change—opportunities and challenges 226
MAGGIE WALTER, STEPHANIE RUSSO CARROLL, TAHU KUKUTAI AND DESI RODRIGUEZ-LONEBEAR

Index 235

Figures and tables

Figures

4.1	Growing Pueblo data sovereignty	52
5.1	Mana-Mahi Framework (source: Te Mana Raraunga 2016)	66
9.1	Ethnicity index in Mexico (ENADID 2006, 2014, 2018)	134
9.2	Map of Mexico Indigenous regions and marginality	136
9.3	Social deprivation indicators 2008–2018 (CONEVAL)	137
9.4	Indigenous data production and use	140

Tables

5.1	Stats NZ engagement with Māori Data Sovereignty-focused events	69
5.2	Assessment questions for Te Mana o te Raraunga Model	72
5.3	Ngā Tikanga Paihere: Ma ngā tikanga e arahina—Be guided by good principles	73
9.1	Criteria to define "Indigenous population" in Mexico's census	132

Contributors

Maggie Walter (Palawa) (PhD, FASSA) is Distinguished Professor of Sociology at the University of Tasmania, Australia. Publishing extensively in the field of Indigenous Data, including *Indigenous Statistics* (with C. Andersen 2013 Routledge), Maggie is a founding member of the Maiam nayri Wingara Indigenous Data Sovereignty Collective and the Global Indigenous Data Alliance.

Tahu Kukutai (Ngāti Tiipa, Ngāti Kinohaku, Te Aupōuri) (PhD) is Professor of Demography at the National Institute of Demographic and Economic Analysis, Aotearoa New Zealand. She co-edited *Indigenous Data Sovereignty: Toward an Agenda* and is a founding member of the Māori Data Sovereignty Network Te Mana Raraunga and the Global Indigenous Data Alliance.

Stephanie Russo Carroll (Ahtna-Native Village of Kluti-Kaah, Sicilian-descent) (DrPH, MPH) is Assistant Professor of Public Health and Associate Director for the Native Nations Institute at the University of Arizona, USA. A researcher active at the nexus of Indigenous governance, the environment, community wellness and data, Stephanie co-founded the US Indigenous Data Sovereignty Network and is a founding member and chair of the Global Indigenous Data Alliance.

Desi Rodriguez-Lonebear (Northern Cheyenne and Chicana) (PhD) is a social demographer who researches the intersection of Indigenous erasure, data and inequality. She is Assistant Professor of Sociology and American Indian Studies at the University of California, Los Angeles. Desi co-founded the US Indigenous Data Sovereignty Network and is a founding member of the Global Indigenous Data Alliance.

Per Axelsson (Swedish) (PhD) is Associate Professor of History at Umeå University, Sweden. He publishes extensively in the fields of Indigenous health and history, medical history and demography, including *Indigenous Peoples and Demography* (with P. Sköld, 2011 Berghahn books).

Joxerramon Bengoetxea (Oiartzun, Euskal Herria) (PhD, Edinburgh) is Professor of Jurisprudence at the University of the Basque Country. He publishes extensively in the fields of sovereignty, multilingualism, transitional justice, EU law, legal reasoning and sustainable development governance. Joxe is a member of the Board of the International Institute for the Sociology of Law, Member of the Basque Arbitration Board and Secretary General of the Basque Council of the European Movement.

Julie Bull (Inuk) (PhD) is an award-winning researcher, ethicist, educator, poet, and spoken-word artist from NunatuKavut, Labrador, Canada. She is an appointed member on the Panel on Research Ethics with Canada's Tri-Agency and holds adjunct professor appointments at Memorial University of Newfoundland and Cape Breton University.

Carnell Chosa (Jemez Pueblo) (PhD) is Co-Founder/Co-Director of the Santa Fe Indian School Leadership Institute (LI) in New Mexico. LI provides research, program development and community planning to New Mexico's tribal peoples. He is Founder/Director of Attach Your Heart Foundation, a working foundation that provides emergency aid to college students and resource support to Pueblo youth-envisioned community development projects.

Donna Cormack (Kāi Tahu, Kati Mamoe) (PhD) is a researcher and teacher with joint positions at the University of Auckland and University of Otago. Her work focuses on the impacts of racism and colonialism on Māori health, Māori Data Sovereignty and critical, decolonial research practices.

Oscar L. Figueroa-Rodríguez (Mestizo) (PhD) is an Associate Researcher Professor at Colegio de Postgraduados, Mexico. His work focuses on design, implementation and evaluation of community-driven development processes in rural settings. He has extensive experience working with Indigenous communities in Southern Mexico. Oscar is a founding member of the Global Indigenous Data Alliance.

Ricci Harris (Ngāti Kahungunu, Ngāi Tahu, Ngāti Raukawa) (MB CHB, MPH, FNZCPHM) is a Public Health Physician and Associate Professor at the Eru Pōmare Māori Health Research Centre, Department of Public Health, University of Otago Wellington. Her research focuses on Māori health and the investigation and elimination of ethnic health inequities in Aotearoa, including the role of racism.

Maui Hudson (Whakatohea) is Associate Professor in the Faculty of Maori and Indigenous Studies at the University of Waikato, New Zealand. Maui is a founding member of the Te Mana Raraunga Maori Data Sovereignty Network and the Global Indigenous Data Alliance.

Roxanne Jones (Palawa) (RN, MPhil (AppEpi)) is a PhD candidate and Research Associate at the Australian National University. Roxy is an Epidemiologist and Registered Nurse with an interest in Aboriginal and Torres Strait Islander child health. Roxy is also a member of the Maiam nayri Wingara Indigenous Data Sovereignty Collective.

Contributors

Jameson D. Lopez (Quechan) (PhD) is Assistant Professor in the Center for the Study of Higher Education at the University of Arizona. He studies Native American education and has expertise in the limitations of collecting and applying quantitative results to Indigenous populations. Most importantly, he is a proud father of two beautiful children Luna and Gordon.

Raymond Lovett (Ngiyampaa) (PhD) is Associate Professor of Epidemiology at the Australian National University. Ray has published across diverse health and well-being issues and has a strong focus on Aboriginal and Torres Strait Islander data sovereignty and governance. Ray is a founding member of the Maiam nayri Wingara Indigenous Data Sovereignty Collective and the Global Indigenous Data Alliance.

Bobby Maher (Yamatji) (PhD candidate) is a research associate at the Australian National University. Bobby is an epidemiologist and has an interest in Social Epidemiology and Evaluation. Bobby is also a member of the Maiam nayri Wingara Indigenous Data Sovereignty Collective and the Global Indigenous Data Alliance.

Tennille Larzelere Marley (Dzil Ligai Sian N'dee—White Mountain Apache) (MPH, PhD) is Assistant Professor of American Indian Studies and a faculty research affiliate with the Southwest Interdisciplinary Research Center. She has extensive experience in community health and research in American Indian communities. Her scholarship includes American Indian health policy, Indigenous Data Sovereignty and determinants of American Indian health.

Colleen Alena O'Brien (non-Indigenous) (PhD) is a postdoctoral researcher at the Jena Center for Reconciliation Studies in Germany, with doctoral training in linguistics at the University of Hawai'i at Mānoa. She works on Indigenous languages in Colombia and Indonesia and is currently making a documentary about the reintegration process of the FARC into civilian society.

Sarah-Jane Paine (Tūhoe) is the Director of the Tōmaiora Research Group at Te Kupenga Hauora Māori, University of Auckland. Her research and teaching are informed by Kaupapa Māori theory and she is particularly interested in the use of quantitative methods to examine mechanisms of Indigenous health inequities across the life course.

Papaarangi Reid (Te Rarawa) is Tumuaki (Deputy Dean Māori) and Professor of Maori Health at the Faculty of Medical and Health Sciences, University of Auckland, New Zealand. She has a passion for equity as a marker of sovereignty and Indigenous rights.

Gustavo Rojas-Páez (non-Indigenous) (MA) is a Lecturer in Legal Theory at Universidad Libre in Bogotá with training in Sociology of Law at IISL, Oñati. His work deals with critical perspectives on Law with an emphasis on structural harm. He is a PhD candidate at University of the Basque Country (EHU) in the doctoral program "Rethinking Globalization: challenges and interdisciplinary solutions".

Contributors xi

Bridget Robson (Ngāti Raukawa) is director of Te Rōpū Rangahau Hauora a Eru Pōmare, a center that promotes a theory-driven approach to understanding and eliminating inequities in health. Her research is primarily quantitative, using kaupapa Māori approaches, including method development that has been influential in public health and Māori health research.

Robyn Rowe (Anishinaabe-kwe with familial roots in Teme-Augama Anishnabai) is a PhD candidate and researcher in Indigenous Health at Laurentian University in Sudbury, Ontario, Canada. She is an emerging leader and advocate for Indigenous Data Sovereignty and a founding member of the Global Indigenous Data Alliance.

Andrew Sporle (Ngāti Apa, Rangitāne, Te Rarawa) is a social researcher with over 25 years' experience developing initiatives in social and health research across the public, private and academic sectors. His current work involves initiating permanent changes to official statistics and research data infrastructure, and practice to increase the impact and accessibility of research and data resources.

Christina Storm Mienna (Sami) (PhD in Medicine, DDS) is Associate Professor, Department of Odontology, at the University of Umeå and Senior Consultant/Specialist in Clinical Oral Physiology, Region Västerbotten, University Hospital of Umeå, Sweden. Her research mainly consists of epidemiological studies in Sami communities in Sweden.

Michele Suina (Cochiti Pueblo) (PhD) is a Program Director at the Albuquerque Area Southwest Tribal Epidemiology Centre with nearly 20 years of experience as a health educator serving Native American communities. Michele is an advocate for tribal control of data and assists Indigenous Data Sovereignty efforts in New Mexico, USA.

Rebecca Tsosie (Yaqui) (JD) is a Regents Professor of Law and Faculty Co-Chair for the Indigenous Peoples' Law and Policy Program at the University of Arizona. She has published widely on the rights of Indigenous Peoples. She is a member of the Arizona and California Bar Associations and serves as an appellate judge for the Fort McDowell Yavapai Nation and the San Carlos Apache Tribe.

Jennifer Walker (Haudenosaunee and a member of Six Nations of the Grand River) (PhD) is Canada Research Chair in Indigenous Health at Laurentian University in Sudbury, Ontario. She advocates for Indigenous data governance throughout her work and is a founding member of the Global Indigenous Data Alliance.

Kiri West is a critical kaupapa Māori researcher in the Māori Studies Department at the University of Auckland. Previously an editor for the multidisciplinary Indigenous *MAI Journal*, Kiri's experience and expertise is vast, including Indigenous studies, data ethics, data sovereignty, consent, sovereignty, sociology, politics, Indigenous studies, theories and methodologies. Her doctoral research centers on Indigenous Data Sovereignty.

1 Indigenous Data Sovereignty, governance and the link to Indigenous policy

Maggie Walter and Stephanie Russo Carroll

Introduction

Across Anglo-colonized nation states, official policy, and the administratively devised strategic actions and programs that flow from that policy, are the predominant ways governments engage with their internal Indigenous Peoples, nations and populations. In the United States, Aotearoa New Zealand, Canada and Australia (referred to as CANZUS countries) (Meyer 2012), without exception, the central feature of this policy is its focus on Indigenous disadvantage and developmental disparity. The vision statements of each country's key Indigenous policy entity highlight this similarity. In the United States, the US Department of the Interior, Indian Affairs (2019) states their mission as: "enhance the quality of life, to promote economic opportunity, and to carry out the responsibility to protect and improve the trust assets of American Indians, Indian tribes, and Alaska Natives". In Australia, the National Indigenous Australians Agency's (2019) Closing the Gap policy framework across health, education and employment targets lists its primary aim as "to improve the lives of Aboriginal and Torres Strait Islander Australians". Indigenous Services Canada proclaim that their vision is "to support and empower Indigenous Peoples to independently deliver services and address the socio-economic conditions in their communities" (Government of Canada 2019) and in Aotearoa New Zealand Te Puni Kōkiri Ministry of Māori Development (2019) states its mission is to "lead public policy for Māori; advise on Government-Māori relationships; provide guidance to government about policies affecting Māori wellbeing; and administer and monitor legislation". All policy frameworks also state, to varying degrees, that they undertake their policy role in collaboration with, and in the interests of, Indigenous Peoples. In practice, these policies lack the actual integration of Indigenous worldviews.

All agencies also reference data as an evidence base for Indigenous policy. These data also display an uncanny sameness. All provide a remarkably similar statistical narrative of Indigenous overrepresentation across the same development indicators of socio-economic, health, education and social disadvantage. Incarceration rate data provide a good example of this phenomenon. In both Canada and Australia, official statistics report that Indigenous People make up a quarter or more of the prison population, despite being less than four percent of the total population of each country (Chartrand 2018). In Aotearoa New Zealand, the data detail that half of those incarcerated are Māori although the Māori population count is around 17 percent of the total Aotearoa population (Department of Corrections 2019). In the United States, the data are disjointed due to the relatively dispersed nature of the criminal justice system, but the pattern is still clear. In Alaska, where 15 percent of the population is Native, 37 percent of the prison population is Alaskan Native or Native American. In South and North Dakota, around 30 percent of those incarcerated are Native American, but the Native population of these states is less than 10 percent of the total ("Native America: A History" 2018).

These numbers and the many other statistics detailing Indigenous societal positioning are not disputed. We know their reality too well. But accepting numerical reality is not the same as accepting the validity of the picture they represent or the policy settings that invariably emerge from these statistics. These pervasive data are not neutral entities. Statistics are human artifacts and in colonizing nation states such numbers applied to Indigenous Peoples have a raced reality (Walter 2010; Walter and Anderson 2013). Their reality emerges not from the mathematically supported analytical techniques they allow but via the social, racial and cultural standpoint of their creators. Data do not make themselves. Data are created and shaped by the assumptive determinations of their makers to collect some data and not others, to interrogate some objects over others and to investigate some variable relationships over others. As per Zuberi and Bonilla-Silva (2008), it is dominant society questions that are hidden behind the cover of claims of objective methodology. Within this, the Indigene remains the object, caught in a numbered bind, viewed through the straitjacketing lens of deficit (Walter and Anderson 2013).

For Indigenous Peoples, the statistics and data themselves per se, are not the problem. From a policy perspective, the far more critical question is how are such numbers deployed and what and whose purposes do they, and their attendant narratives, serve (Walter 2016, 2018)? Our basic contention, here and throughout this book, is that they do not serve our purposes or interests as Indigenous Peoples. With their limited scope, aggregate format, deficit focus and decontextualized framework, this joint data/policy narrative cannot, and does not, yield meaningful portraits of the embodied realities of Indigenous lives (Walter and Suina 2018). As such the social policy framework cannot and does not provide the policy outcomes that Indigenous Peoples across these countries need. Nor does it provide the data that we, as Indigenous Peoples, nations and tribes, need to develop and implement our own policy. The result is a historic and contemporaneous failure of Indigenous-related policy, across fields of policy and across CANZUS countries.

This chapter expands on this central thesis as well as the Indigenous response to nation state data/policy intransigence; Indigenous Data Sovereignty. At its core, Indigenous Data Sovereignty affirms the rights of Indigenous Peoples to control the collection, access, analysis, interpretation, management, dissemination and reuse of Indigenous data (Kukutai and Taylor 2016; Snipp 2016). Indigenous data, born digital or not, is a very broad category, including information, knowledge, specimens, and belongings about Indigenous Peoples or to that which they relate at both the individual and collective levels (Rainie et al. 2019; Lovett et al. 2019). Here, we explore Indigenous Data Sovereignty as a global advocacy movement for Indigenous Peoples and as a growing field of Indigenous scholarship alongside the concept's underpinning policy-related rationales. We also outline the processes of Indigenous data governance, an activating mechanism of Indigenous Data Sovereignty, as a policy response.

Indigenous social policy: a history of failure

In 1858, public concern about destitute Aboriginal people occupying town fringes prompted the New South Wales Colony to hold an inquiry into the welfare of the Natives (Colony of Victoria 1859). The resultant report details the level of intense poverty and unmet need of these survivors of frontier wars, forcibly dislocated from their lands. In 2016, the Australian Productivity Commission, motivated by ongoing concern about Aboriginal inequality, released its seventh biennial report, *Overcoming Indigenous Disadvantage* (SCRGSP 2016). This report series' stated aim is to measure the well-being of Aboriginal and Torres Strait Islander Australians. Again, the data present a picture of deep, unremitting social, economic and health disadvantage, with little or no improvement record from that detailed in earlier reports. Apart from the modernizing of language, these two reports are remarkably similar.

Comparing these two reports highlights that the measuring and recording of Indigenous disadvantage is a long-established bureaucratic response. The resemblance of official documentation in 1858 to that in 2016, and the similarity of the data reproduced, also makes clear that between the first and second inquiries, the "welfare of the Native" is largely unchanged. Despite the more than 150 years of social policy enacted upon Aboriginal and Torres Strait Islander Peoples, as the data indicate, we remain the poorest, sickest, and least educated and employed group in Australia. This Australian example is repeated in other guises across the CANZUS countries. Inquiries such as the 1996 Canadian Royal Commission into Aboriginal Peoples (Government of Canada 2016) or the 1928 Meriam Report from the United States (NARF 2019) all document through data, in great detail, the level and depth of Indigenous disadvantage and the lack of change. To discuss the history of Indigenous policy in Australia, Aotearoa New Zealand, Canada and the United States, therefore, is to discuss the history of an unrelenting repetition of policy failure.

Critiques of poor Indigenous policy outcomes tend to coalesce around two competing positions, both centering Indigenous Peoples. The first emphasizes the lack of connection between the objects of policy (Indigenous People and communities) and policy makers (primarily drawn from the non-Indigenous majority) in terms of interaction, understanding and a corresponding lack of policy self-determination (see Taylor and Hunter 2001). From this position, policy is seen as being imposed on Indigenous Peoples from well-meaning but inadequately equipped policy makers. The remedy is linked to greater Indigenous participation in policy framing and formulation. The other position is developed through the lens of market individualism and points to the perceived failure of individual Indigenous People to take advantage of the opportunities, especially those mandated in policy programs, afforded them by the nation state (see Price 2019). In this positioning, the cause of inequitable Indigenous social and economic positioning is the poor behavior and choices of Indigenous People themselves. The solution is framed in terms of Indigenous People taking greater personal responsibility.

Seeing Indigenous Peoples like a state

Our argument is that neither the lack of self-determination nor poor individual behavior is an adequate explanation for continuing Indigenous policy failure across nation states. Rather, we point to the cross-national patterns inherent in the consistency of the data produced and reproduced, the consistency of policy approaches and the consistency of the failure of that policy. All four nation states, for example, had policies active during the 20th century that sought to assimilate Indigenous populations via the removal of children from their families. The disastrous outcome of these policies has now been laid bare by the Royal Commissions and other formal enquiries held to uncover the harms done (see NTRC 2015; Commonwealth of Australia 1997). Yet, today, in all four nation states, Indigenous children are still far more likely to be removed from their families and placed in state care than non-Indigenous children. In Australia, Aboriginal children are ten times more likely than non-Aboriginal children to be placed in out-of-home care (Dickie 2019); in the United States, the rate is lower but American Indian and Alaskan Native children are 1.6 times more likely to be removed from their biological homes and twice as likely to remain in foster care for over two years (Fostering Together 2019); and in Aotearoa New Zealand, Māori children make up 59 percent of all children in care, more than double their proportion of the population (RNZ 2019). There is little to indicate that the current removal of Indigenous children from their families will not, one day, be also recognized as the policy disaster that it is, just like the forced assimilation programs of the past.

So, given the cross-nation pattern of policy approaches and policy failures, seemingly on repeat, can the long history of poor Indigenous policy outcomes be viewed as inevitable? Here we draw from Scott's (1998) thesis, *Seeing like a State*, to conceptualize the terrain of Indigenous policy. This theory has had scholarly resonance in making sense of how state-preferred modes of organizing and managing Indigenous sub-populations are implicated in Indigenous policy failure (Andersen 2014; Walter and Andersen 2013). Scott's (1998) core argument is that four elements are needed, in combination, to create a social policy disaster of truly epic proportions. The first element is the deployment of a system of administrative ordering necessary for modern nation states to make a society legible. An example is a national census whose purpose is not only to enumerate but to describe a population across criteria deemed important for understanding that population, such as age, gender and employment status. Scott (1998) emphasizes that this is not a straightforward exercise. The state needs to undertake transformative simplifications whereby "exceptionally complex, illegible and local social practices" (1998: 2) are standardized to allow central recording and monitoring. The result is radically simplified understandings of social (we would add cultural) environments. Critically, for our arguments, the state's rationalizing and standardizing does not actually represent the reality of the society that is being depicted. Only the slice of that society that is of interest to the state is represented in the final product.

For Indigenous Peoples, the slice of our social and cultural realities represented in data collected about us is limited to those aspects of interest to the nation state. Transformed and recorded into state-defined terms and categories, the outcomes are the data which are the primary tool by which the nation state makes sense of its Indigenous population/s. These data, again in a commonality across CANZUS countries, play a much deeper role than being counts of Indigenous populations or neutral reflectors of Indigenous lives (Walter and Andersen 2013). Rather, these data drive a particular narrative of Indigenous Peoples, creating an underpinning framework of how Indigenous Peoples are recognized by the state (Andersen 2014). As argued later, and across many of the chapters of this book, the areas of interest of the national state in Indigenous Peoples do not, for the most part, align with the reality of Indigenous lives. Nor, in answer to our earlier question, do the narratives they construct serve Indigenous social and cultural interests or purposes.

The second element is what Scott (1998) calls a high-modernist ideology. This term translates to a self-confidence about scientific and technical progress associated with a presumed rational design for social order. In earlier times assimilationist policies were the prime example via their motivating presumption that Indigenous Peoples needed to be brought into the modern world. As a result, many Indigenous children were forcibly removed from their families, traditional lands and culture. But similar high-modernist ideology can be detected in the relatively uncritical embrace of Big Data technologies and privileging of Open Data policies required for these technologies now sweeping Western nations, including the CANZUS countries. It is also possible to identify the risks of policy failure in the translation of these technologies into social programs, again intrinsically linked to how the data are deployed. For example, tools such as predictive risk modeling (PRM) are beginning to be used in a wide variety of frontline services. Their use is largely motivated by a desire to reduce costs through targeting those most "at risk" (Keddell 2014). Yet there is growing evidence that racial biases find their way into algorithms. Cossins (2018) cites five examples from the United States, where the specific logics of artificial intelligence had resulted in prejudicial outcomes. Indigenous Peoples, overrepresented in datasets of disadvantage, are also likely to be overrepresented in those identified "at risk", and the consequential social intervention or formal surveillance. PRM does not even have to include an Indigenous identifier for Indigenous Peoples to be subject to disproportionate impacts of algorithm-informed decision-making (Kukutai and Walter in press). A study using PRM to predict child maltreatment in Aotearoa New Zealand excluded ethnicity. However, Māori children were still far more likely to be featured in the model outcomes because they, as all Indigenous children in CANZUS countries, are much more likely to live in poorer, heavily disadvantaged areas with relatively few services (Vaithianathan et al. 2013; Kukutai and Walter in press). A more recent example that links back to our earlier discussions of incarceration is the use of the Roc*Roi algorithm to assign risk scores of recidivism (Stats NZ 2018). The 30 personal variables used do not include ethnicity, but there are so many data points, which are strongly correlated with Māori ethnicity, that ethnicity is superfluous.

The third element identified by Scott (1998: 5) is an authoritarian state, willing and capable of using the full weight of its coercive power to bring these high-modernist designs into being. This addition of state power is what turns the bureaucratic rationalization of Indigenous populations (Indigenous data) into disciplining social policy. The plethora of deficit-framed Indigenous data informs the policy mind, to understand the Indigenous population as in need of remaking, via coercive means as necessary, into idealized, good Indigenous citizens (Moreton-Robinson 2009). While some might argue that the power of CANZUS countries is limited by democratic structures and citizens' rights, access to such rights is, and always has been, limited for Indigenous Peoples. Whether it be the violent breakup of the protests by Native American people at Standing Rock fearing the contamination of their water supply by oil from the North Dakota pipeline (Skalicky and Davies 2016) or the forced imposition on Aboriginal communities of "welfare quarantining" whereby recipients' payments are restricted to "state approved" purchases (Davey 2017), the use of coercion by state is woven into the practices of state/Indigenous interactions.

Scott's fourth element is a society that lacks the capacity to resist the machinations and policy imposition of the state. Again, a dramatic imbalance of power is the hallmark of the past and present relations between Indigenous Peoples and the non-Indigenous majority (Tuhiwai-Smith 1999). Indeed Scott (1998: 97) himself noted that Colonial regimes are particularly prone to social policy experimentation on Indigenous populations noting that "[A]n ideology of 'welfare colonialism' combined with the authoritarian power inherent in colonial rule have encouraged ambitious schemes to remake native societies".

Indigenous policy, fracasomania and data

The specific and limited slice of Indigenous life of interest to the state is heavily implicated in the how and why Indigenous policy continues to go dangerously awry. These data are the support system of the long history of failed policy schemes that attempt to "remake native societies". So deeply entrenched is this history that there is a generalized acceptance, by both policy makers and those subject to those policies, Indigenous Peoples, that Indigenous policy and policy failure are synonymous. Indigenous policy, across the CANZUS countries, is caught in a "complex of failure" or in the term coined by Hirschman (1963) using the Spanish translation, fracasomania. Indigenous policy is situated within a bureaucratic mindset which has made a comfortable adjustment to policy failure.

Hirschman (1963, 1975), drawing on his economic policy work in 1950s Colombia, was struck by a prevailing "categorical disappointment" of his fellow policy makers with previous endeavors. He theorized that this policy mindset, while dysfunctional in terms of policy outcomes, was also functional in that it allowed the "problem" to be addressed and readdressed continually. Policy failure might follow policy failure but policy makers took comfort in that at least action was being taken. Thus, the policy actors, usually from outside the community for which the policy is developed (in Hirschman's Colombia it was the World Bank), are driven by "a compulsive desire" to solve problems as rapidly as possible and tended to swing across policy measures. The assumed superiority of external expertise was unquestioned by either the outside policy makers or its Colombian recipients. To paraphrase Hirschman, such policies were prompted more by motivation than understanding, leading to imperiousness in their imposition. Imperiousness led to a failure to build the cumulative knowledge that would allow them to develop policies that truly understood the realities of the community to which they are being applied. Thus, despite a constancy of policy re-starts, the pervasive expectation of low performance led to little belief that any "new" policy approaches would actually succeed. Failure expectation was so ingrained that the prospect of further policy failure became easier for policy makers to manage than imagining, or preparing for, policy success.

Even a relatively simplistic analysis of the characteristics of the litany of Indigenous policy failure displays all four signs of Hirschman's (1963) complex of failure, fracasomania. First, Indigenous policy development was, and continues to be, largely devised and implemented by "outsiders" from the community of policy interest. It is these non-Indigenous outsiders, the most being from the dominant Euro-majority, who both diagnose the Indigenous problem and formulate the appropriate Indigenous-focused policy solutions. Hirschman's second sign of fracasomania, a failure to build cumulative knowledge on the policy topic, is linked to Indigenous policy's external genesis. An Australian example demonstrates both factors. As in other CANZUS countries, Aboriginal and Torres Strait Islander children record significantly lower school attendance rates than non-Indigenous children (82% to 93% in 2018). This is a long-standing issue. In 2014, a target to close the school attendance gap was added to the Government's signature Closing the Gap Indigenous policy framework (DPMC 2019). Policy implementation involved deploying a bevy of School Attendance Officers in Aboriginal communities across five states and territories. Known colloquially as "truancy officers" and referred to as such in the media (Stewart 2014), this terminology exposes the policy and public presumptions: that low school attendance is related to the poor individual choices of Indigenous children and families to skip school. Therefore, despite numerous reports indicating that low school attendance is multi-faceted, linked to diverse causes such as poorly performing teachers, poor relationships between schools and Indigenous families and a lack of services to address the many issues plaguing Indigenous children (Grindlay 2017), applying disciplinary policies to pressure on families and communities was the primary policy response.

A third sign of fracasomania is observed in the political response to policy failure, a rapid swing to new policy measures without evaluation of previous policy failure. Again, this element can be found in the school attendance policy implementation. Initially lauded as a success (Stewart 2014), such claims quickly died away as attendance rates for Aboriginal students did not improve in the following five years (2014–2018) (DPMC 2019). Responding to negative media reports, those with carriage for the policy pointed to an upcoming review of Indigenous policy. This renewal, they argued, would provide government agencies with a fresh opportunity to "redouble our efforts" to improve the lives of First Australians, including achieving better education outcomes (cited in Grindlay 2017).

Here also we observe the fourth sign of fracasomania; a broad-spectrum ennui as each successive failure of Indigenous policy is revealed. Over ten annual reports (2009–2018) to parliament of progress on Closing the Gap targets (which included improving school attendance rates), little or no surprise was expressed at the consistent lack of progress on the targets by the politicians making the report, by the media, or indeed by Aboriginal people living the results of the ongoing lack of improvement in life circumstances. Nor were there mea culpas from the responsible policy agencies. Rather, there was a ritual stating of the obvious, that the policy had failed, followed by the regular exhortation that we (politicians and policy makers) have to "do better", largely without any real expectation, by anybody, that the next round of Indigenous policy will actually do better. Within this performance there is an unstated, but largely accepted, premise that Indigenous policy problems are unsolvable because Indigenous Peoples are too problematic; an assumption supported by the existing Indigenous data of disadvantage. Ergo, no blame for policy failure can be apportioned to policy makers. Failure is normalized and continued failure is both expected and expected to be without repercussions (for policy makers).

Seeing Indigenous People like a state: emphasizing/disguising our difference

Public policy is the core business of the state. As such, policy making needs to be understood as much more than a strategic objective and recognized as long-established bureaucratic endeavor both served and shaped by an interlocking infrastructure (Andersen 2014, Walter and Andersen 2013). How the state "sees" its Indigenous population/s, in turn, serves and shapes the policy infrastructure with Indigenous data, the lens by which Indigenous Peoples are made visible. These data define who and what Indigenous Peoples are and who and what we are not. Indigenous data delineate what is seen and as importantly, what is not seen. Thus, both the overabundance of data depicting Indigenous difference and disadvantage, and the absence of Indigenous data that is not related to development measures are problematic. As per Scott, data's definitional role is shaped by its representation of Indigenous subjective realities, simplified and rationalized to reflect the interests of the state.

The interests of the state in relation to its Indigenous populations are, and always have been, deeply political. The interlocking infrastructure serving these interests are reflected in the Indigenous data/policy nexus. This nexus operates whereby data simultaneously emphasize and disguise Indigenous difference, as required. We argue that this variable positioning serves the purpose of perpetuating and buttressing the state's dominant national narratives. This is not to claim that nation state Indigenous data practice is always or even primarily deliberately nefarious in intent. The belief in the need for policies that "advance" Indigenous Peoples, as per Scott's high-modernist ideology, is often as genuine as it is mistaken. The policy environment operates in a complex of failure, resigned but dutiful in the efforts to "help" the sad plight of the Indigene. But it has lived reality consequences for Indigenous Peoples.

In CANZUS countries, emphasizing Indigenous difference from majority populations locates Indigenous Peoples within the national narrative as a deficit and problematic sub-population. This positioning has several roles. Most critically it acts as a foil to the historical foundations of the nation state; Indigenous dispossession and oppression. As King (2012) states, referring to Native American Peoples, Indigenous Peoples are deeply inconvenient, casting a pall over the nation state's legitimacy. Our continued existence is an existential threat to deeply held illusions that the lands from whom the non-Indigenous majority draw their wealth and identity are not the same lands taken and still kept by force from their Indigenous owners. Thus, situating the Indigene as "in need" repositions the state, not as the direct descendent of colonialism, and the inheritor of its spoils, but as the beneficent helper of those who cannot, despite the best efforts of the state, help themselves. A secondary benefit is that addressing Indigenous need is hegemonically positioned as what Indigenous nations and tribes must prioritize, rather than rights or political issues.

In this narrative, it is necessary for Indigenous Peoples, as a population, to be easily observable as pejoratively different from the Euro-majority. The "in need" aspect of discourse is served by a data infrastructure constructed around developmentally derived categories. The data outcome is what Walter (2016, 2018) describes as 5D data, a set of items related almost exclusively to measuring Indigenous difference, disparity, disadvantage, dysfunction and deprivation. Evidence to support this assertion is easily found via a Google search for statistics relating to Indigenous Peoples in any CANZUS country: Native American, Aboriginal and Torres Strait Islander, Māori, Native Hawaiian, First Nations or Alaska Native. No matter the peoples named, the result is the same; a list of 5D items such as poor health, high mortality, low educational outcomes, low school attendance and high incarceration. The portrayal is completed by simplistic presentations where the deficient Indigenous population is compared, in frequency tables or bar charts, to the normed non-Indigenous majority (Walter 2005, 2018; Kukutai and Walter 2016). Nationally, aggregate data reinforce the whole population story, discursively locating the demonstrated deficit as a population trait.

Seeing like a First Nation: Indigenous Data Sovereignty and data for governance

How do we halt the cycle of ongoing policy disasters fueled by how the state sees Indigenous Peoples in the data? How do we get the state and its policy infrastructure to see us differently? The key, as detailed later in this chapter and throughout this book, is Indigenous Data Sovereignty. Indigenous Data Sovereignty is operationalized via Indigenous data governance, which harnesses Indigenous decision-making across data lifecycles and ecosystems to assert Indigenous rights and interests (Smith 2016; Walter and Suina 2018). A central right is governance of the data generated by state infrastructure; changing the narrative of who we are to halt the endless cycle of fracasomania-driven policy. Such change at the state level will never come about through goodwill or good intentions. The national narratives of CANZUS countries have too much invested in keeping Indigenous Peoples visible only through the narrow lens of deficit data. To see us on our terms is not only not of interest to the state, it is important for the state to not be able to see us in other ways. To do so would allow other explanations of 5D data to come to the fore; those that include overt and covert systemic discrimination, intergenerational trauma and ongoing dispossession. To do so would make visible the primary attribute that Indigenous Peoples in CANZUS countries, internationally and intra-nationally, share: Anglo colonization.

Indigenous Peoples require not just governance of existing data, but access and control of data for governance (Smith 2016). Emphasizing our 5D data difference disguises our difference in areas unrelated to state-determined development goals. Indigenous populations in CANZUS countries are made up of multiple First Nations and the terms used to describe us; Aboriginal, Torres Strait Islander, Indian, Māori, Native Hawaiian, or even Indigenous, are not what we call ourselves. Rather, these terms were coined as a way of categorizing us in terms "seeable" by the colonizing state. Amalgamating us into a single amorphous sub-population renders invisible our substantial and meaningful distinctiveness across country, traditional and contemporary culture and knowledges, ways of life, urbanity and the varying impact of colonization and dispossession on our peoples, now and then.

For Indigenous Peoples, this currently unseen and mostly non-existent data reflecting our lived realities and our innate differences is a critical resource (Lovett 2016). First Nations, tribes, Iwi or community groups require what is currently excluded; disaggregated, contextualized data that represent Indigenous lifeworlds and Indigenous priorities (Walter and Andersen 2013; Walter 2016). The nation state is not delivering, so we must create or demand the data we need. Indigenous Peoples have always engaged with data and knowledge, holding and using such information to care for and support collective rights and interests. Also, like other nation states, First Nations governments and leadership structures need data to carry out the multitude of tasks that comprise governance (Cornell et al. 2004). Key among these tasks is making decisions about one's citizens, communities, and resources; in essence, devising and enacting policy. Indigenous governments, in whatever format, also need ways to honor, protect and control their data both internally and externally via Indigenous data governance. Rebuilding governance institutions increases Indigenous nation's capability to govern their own data thereby providing stronger evidence-based decision-making. Through this lens, Indigenous data governance depicts a reciprocal relationship between data for governance and governance of data (Carroll et al. 2019).

At the core of Indigenous data governance is Indigenous leadership. Indigenous-led and controlled decision-making ensures that Indigenous values, priorities, cultures and ways of knowing cohere in Indigenous data, making such data relevant, contextualized and aligned with the aspirations of Indigenous Peoples (Walter and Suina 2018; Rainie et al. 2019). Alongside Indigenous leadership, two key facets are required, in concert, to enact Indigenous data governance. The first is a matter of quality, relevance and access. The essential question here is: can First Nations obtain the data they need for governance? The second is a matter of ownership and control. Here, the essential question is can First Nations manage, protect and use that data? First Nations sovereignty sits at the center of this relationship between data for governance and governance of data (Carroll et al. 2019).

In colonial settler states where power dynamics are heavily stacked against Indigenous Peoples and are often a direct threat to sovereignty, how does Indigenous data governance begin to unwind the deep-seated policy failures? What are the challenges for Indigenous Data Sovereignty? Given the stark power asymmetries between nation states, researchers, other mainstream institutions and Indigenous Peoples, how do we prevent Indigenous Data Sovereignty from being co-opted and selectively appropriated into "policy" that may have unintended consequences?

The ongoing work of Indigenous Data Sovereignty

Enacting Indigenous Data Sovereignty requires interaction among Indigenous data, data governance and Native nation rebuilding (Rainie et al. 2017a). It reflects Indigenous Peoples' collective rights to self-determination and to govern data about our peoples, lands, resources and knowledges as expressed in the United Nations Declaration on the Rights of Indigenous Peoples (UNDRIP), a non-binding human rights instrument (Taylor and Kukutai 2015). As the data revolution has exponentially grown, the Indigenous Data Sovereignty movement has emerged as an Indigenous-led advocacy, education and research network of networks. Our shared purpose is to address global concerns, often at the nation state level, about protecting Indigenous data from misuse, ensuring Indigenous Peoples are the primary beneficiaries of their data and leveraging Indigenous data toward Indigenous aspirations. At its core, the Indigenous Data Sovereignty movement seeks to transform the data landscape to the benefit of Indigenous Peoples (Lovett et al. 2019).

Discussions on the link between Indigenous data and national and international policy have occurred at the United Nations Permanent Forum on Indigenous Issues. Indigenous participants at the forum have consistently addressed the need to develop more relevant statistical frameworks that are operationalized through data processes that prioritize Indigenous participation and leadership (Davis 2016). While data and data justice agendas of Indigenous Peoples vary across cultures and geographies, the demand for data that meet Indigenous aspirations and needs remain consistent. These universal Indigenous data requirements comprise disaggregated data; data that are relevant to Indigenous Peoples' ways of knowing and life ways; data that inform Indigenous nation rebuilding and data that disrupt the deficit narrative pervasive across policy spheres (Carroll et al. 2019; Rainie et al. 2017b; Walter 2018). At the heart of this policy is the problematic large-scale Indigenous exclusion from the Indigenous data terrain, again cross-nationally. And despite many years of Indigenous complaints of the lack of relevance of these data for Indigenous Peoples, there remains significant resistance to changing Indigenous data (and subsequent policy) practices (Kukutai and Walter 2015).

The OCAP® (ownership, control, access, possession) principles from Canada were an early response to the problematic data/policy nexus. Developed by First Nations to provide a new framework for data governance and statistical practices for health data, OCAP® asserts Indigenous Peoples and communities' right to control of their data to their benefit and to dismantle external deficit narratives. Housed at the First Nations Information Governance Center in Canada, OCAP® has been at the forefront of advocating and advancing the rights of Indigenous Peoples in relation to their data for almost a quarter century (FNIGC 2016). To prevent misuse and co-optation, the acronym was trademarked. Using the principles found in OCAP®, national bodies, educational institutions and others have altered their data practices to empower First Nations' control of their data (Walker et al. 2017).

By 2017, Indigenous Peoples in three Anglo-colonized societies had created Indigenous Data Sovereignty networks to advance Indigenous data rights and interests, with similar efforts underway across the globe (Lovett et al. 2019; Rainie et al. 2019; Kukutai and Taylor 2016; FNIGC 2018; Nickerson 2017). The Te Mana Raraunga Māori Data Sovereignty Network (temanararaunga.Māori.nz) formed in 2015 in Aotearoa New Zealand. Te Mana Raraunga enables Māori Data Sovereignty and advances Māori aspirations for collective and individual well-being by asserting Māori rights and interests in relation to data; ensuring data for and about Māori can be safeguarded and protected; requiring the quality and integrity of Māori data and its collection; advocating for Māori involvement in the governance of data repositories; supporting the development of Māori data infrastructure and security systems; and supporting the development of sustainable Māori digital businesses and innovations (TMR 2016).

The United States Indigenous Data Sovereignty Network (USIDSN; usIndigenousdata.org) emerged in 2016 to ensure that data for and about Indigenous Peoples and nations in the United States are used to the benefit of Indigenous Peoples toward collective and individual well-being. The USIDSN provides research and policy advocacy to advance Indigenous Peoples and nations' rights and interests in their data (USIDSN 2019). Created in 2017, the Maiam nayri Wingara Aboriginal and Torres Strait Islander Data Sovereignty Collective in

Australia (maiamnayriwingara.org) seeks to change data practices in relation to Aboriginal and Torres Strait Islander Peoples. A 2018 summit of Aboriginal and Torres Strait Islander leaders determined that Indigenous Peoples in Australia had the right to exercise control of the Indigenous data ecosystem inclusive of data creation, development, stewardship, analysis, dissemination and infrastructure to ensure that such data are contextual and disaggregated; relevant and empowering of sustainable self-determination and effective self-governance; accountable to Indigenous Peoples; and protective of Indigenous individual and collective interests (Indigenous Data Sovereignty Summit Communique 2018; Walter et al. 2018).

In 2017, founders of the three Indigenous Data Sovereignty networks and a collaborator working with Sami data sovereignty formed the International Indigenous Data Sovereignty Interest Group at the Research Data Alliance (RDA Group; rd-alliance.org). Participation with the RDA group has expanded activities and advocacy beyond North America and Australasia to include Indigenous Peoples and priorities from regions such as Southeast Asia, South America and Africa; engaged mainstream data actors; convened leading Indigenous data scholars in person for strategy, advocacy and policy advancement; and formalized a global movement (Carroll et al. 2019). The most impactful output of the RDA Group is the CARE Principles for Indigenous Data Governance (collective benefit, authority to control, responsibility, ethics) (RDA IG 2019). Reflecting the crucial role of data in advancing Indigenous innovation and self-determination, the CARE Principles are meant to affect change within external data stakeholders and the secondary use of data. The CARE Principles expand on mainstream principles, e.g., FAIR (findable, accessible, interoperable, reusable) concerned with data attributes (Wilkinson et al. 2016) to bring people and purpose into focus for data policies and practices. The CARE Principles enhance Indigenous Peoples' rights by providing direction to non-Indigenous data actors on relationships with Indigenous Peoples for the stewardship of Indigenous data. Operationalizing the CARE Principles requires policy and practice actions. Currently, efforts are underway to identify what implementing the CARE Principles might look like for both policies and mechanisms with a number of entities and across data environments, including the Research Data Alliance, the Open Data Charter and the Smithsonian Institution (Carroll et al. forthcoming).

In 2019, 18 Indigenous Data Sovereignty leaders from seven nation states held an international workshop in the Basque Country of Spain. The primary purpose was to further joint global work drawing the links for Indigenous Data Sovereignty to its foundations in international law and the United Nations Declaration of the Rights of Indigenous People in particular. The Oñati Indigenous Data Sovereignty Communique (GIDA 2019) detailed three key findings. These were that:

1. UNDRIP provides a necessary but insufficient foundation for the realization of Indigenous Peoples rights and interests in relation to data and that Indigenous Peoples also require Indigenous-designed legal and regulatory approaches to data founded on Indigenous Data Sovereignty principles

2. while national networks are best placed to respond to and progress data sovereignty for their peoples and communities, a global alliance is needed to advocate for and advance a shared vision for Indigenous Data Sovereignty
3. the international focus on the protection of personal data and privacy rights is inadequate for Indigenous Peoples. There is an urgent need for the development and implementation of collective Indigenous privacy laws, regulations and standards

The major outcome from the Oñati Workshop was the formation of the Global Indigenous Data Alliance (GIDA). GIDA and the GIDA website (GDA-global.org) were launched in September 2019 concurrently with the release of the CARE Principles.

The policy implications of Indigenous Data Sovereignty

Policy and Indigenous Data Sovereignty have multiple points and levels of intersection. Other chapters in this book discuss these across a diverse range of policy terrain including the legal instruments of the nation state, internal tribal or First Nations policies and laws, intra-nation state and intra-First-Nation organizational policy development and enactment and inter-institutional policy realms. Here, we restrict our comments to the implications of Indigenous Data Sovereignty on the most direct point of the data/policy intersection, that between the data collected by the nation state on the sub-population of policy interest, in this case, Indigenous Peoples. Most of these data are the product, or sometimes the by-product of administrative data collection, conducted and controlled by government and institutional entities.

The central role played by data is manifest at all key points of the policy life course. The conception of the policy problem, the determinations of the causes and parameters of the policy problem, the strategies deemed pertinent or possible by policy decision makers, the policy development framework, its implementation, deployment and monitoring, and in the case of Indigenous policy as we have seen, its frequent consequent abandonment, all pivot in one way or another, around data. As demonstrated in this chapter, the population of interest, Indigenous Peoples, are "made sense of" by the nation state's policy generation center, dramatically impacting what data are sought and used and the epistemic value given to different data sources, again at every stage of the policy life course.

The implications of Indigenous Data Sovereignty on nation state Indigenous-related policy are substantial. Indigenous Data Sovereignty inverts the standard Indigenous data/policy nexus. The assertion of the rights of Indigenous Peoples to data about themselves, their people, lands, resources, traditions and cultures challenges and in many cases refutes current Indigenous data processes at every point of the policy life course. The result is ontologically disruptive of the Indigenous data landscape. Inverting the central role of data dramatically changes the way data and the people those data represent are understood in the policy realm. The central policy/data question becomes, not what data do the nation state need to deal with the multiple problems of its remnant Indigenous populations, but what data are needed to meet the needs, priorities and aspirations of Indigenous Peoples?

This reframing of the underpinning policy assumptions completely alters the status quo of the Indigenous data environment. It immediately leads to other questions, such as whom should determine what it is important to know about Indigenous Peoples? Who should determine what data need to be gathered, how, where and at what levels should those data be gathered? Who should control those data once gathered and who should be able to access those data and for what purposes? Or what data is regarded as evidence in determining policy priorities or in evaluation of policy outcomes? And the list goes on. What is required is essentially a paradigm shift; a complete resetting of the Indigenous data/policy relationship, not a tinkering around the edges or small concessions to Indigenous data demands.

The key to achieving a new Indigenous data/policy relationship is Indigenous data governance. We require governance of data *and* data for governance and both governance directions are premised on Indigenous data leadership. In the governance of data arena, we need to be able to refute the current 5D data of disregard that dominates the nation state's Indigenous data narrative. In their place, we need the data to be able to tell our own stories of who we are as Peoples, at multiple levels of disaggregation and how we want to be known, to both the nation state and to ourselves. In the data for governance field, we need the data for nation rebuilding, to determine our own policy and program needs and to evaluate their efficacy. We need to ensure data indicators measure what is important and meaningful for the Indigenous People to whom those data relate. To achieve these aims, Indigenous Peoples need to be able to develop our own technical and human resource data capacities, policies and practices.

Conclusion

CANZUS countries share a history of Anglo colonization and a deep historic and contemporaneous failure of Indigenous-related policy. The social policy framework derived from current Indigenous data infrastructure in these nation states cannot and does not provide effective Indigenous policy outcomes. Nor does it provide the data that Indigenous Peoples need to develop and implement the policy and governance necessary for our nation rebuilding aspirations. As such, regardless of the eloquence or vehemence of state-based commitments to Indigenous well-being, the data/policy nexus mechanism continues nation states' purpose to do what they have always done: demonstrate Indigenous unfitness as a rationale for the denial of Indigenous rights. As shown throughout this and subsequent chapters, the social policy based around these numbers, more often than not, serve to reinforce the status quo of Indigenous improvisation and marginalization.

The denial of Indigenous rights extends to the denial of Indigenous data rights. The rapid pace of the global data revolution, epitomized through Big Data and the state and policy enthusiasm for Open Data, operate to further distance lived social and cultural realities from their database embodiment. With Big Data, understanding that dominant norms and social understandings, not statistical methods, determine social data meanings is even further concealed. Linking multiple 5D data sets (health, schooling, justice system, welfare, etc.) and/or mining other data will provide a bigger ball of data, but not necessarily a more informative one. No matter how sophisticated the linking or the analytical techniques used, if only deficit-related items (i.e., educational comparisons) are included the obtaining "results" outside of the tired existing trope Indigenous statistics is dim (Walter 2018). Open Data, without specific Indigenous data protocols, just expands the number of Indigenous statistical analyzes that are conceived and executed from non-Indigenous worldviews. As shown in this and subsequent chapters, the Indigenous data status quo and the policy complex of failure that it supports is being vigorously challenged by the growing and increasingly global Indigenous Data Sovereignty movement.

References

Andersen, C. (2014) *Métis: Race, Recognition, and the Struggle for Indigenous Peoplehood.* Vancouver: University of British Columbia Press.

Carroll, S.R., Rodriguez-Lonebear, D. and Martinez, A. (2019) Indigenous data governance: strategies from United States native nations. *Data Science Journal,* 18(1), 31. doi:10.5334/dsj-2019-031.

Chartrand, V. (2018) Broken system: why is a quarter of Canada's prison population indigenous? *The Conversation,* February 19. https://theconversation.com/broken-system-why-is-a-quarter-of-canadas-prison-population-Indigenous-91562 <accessed December 20, 2019>.

Colony of Victoria. (1859) *Select Committee Enquiry into the Present Condition of the Aborigines of this Colony and the Best Means of Alleviating Their Absolute Wants.* Select Committee of the Legislative Council. http://www.aiatsis.gov.au/_files/archive/removeprotect/92768.pdf <accessed February 2, 2014>.

Commonwealth of Australia. (1997) *Bringing Them Home Report of the National Inquiry into the Separation of Aboriginal and Torres Strait Islander Children from Their Families.* Human Rights and Equal Opportunity Commission. https://www.humanrights.gov.au/sites/default/files/content/pdf/social_justice/bringing_them_home_report.pdf.

Cornell, S., Curtis, C. and Jorgensen, M. (2004) *The Concept of Governance and its Implications for First Nations,* February 2004. https://hpaied.org/sites/default/files/publications/The%20Concept%20of%20Governance%20and%20its%.

Cossins, D. (2018) Discriminating algorithms: 5 times AI showed prejudice. *New Scientist.* https://www.newscientist.com/article/2166207-discriminating-algorithms-5-times-ai-showed-prejudice/.

Davey, M. (2017) *Cashless Welfare Card Treats Aboriginal People 'as Third-Class Citizens'.* https://www.theguardian.com/australia-news/2017/jan/10/cashless-welfare-card-treats-aboriginal-people-third-class-citizens.

Davis, M. (2016) Data and the United Nations declarations on the rights of indigenous peoples. In T. Kukutai and J. Taylor (eds.), *Indigenous Data Sovereignty: Towards an Agenda,* 25–38. CAEPR Research Monograph, 2016/34. Canberra: ANU Press.

Department of Corrections. (2019) *Prison Facts and Statistics—March 2018.* https://www.corrections.govt.nz/resources/research_and_statistics/quarterly_prison_statistics/prison_stats_march_2018.html <accessed December 20, 2019>.

Dickie, M. (2019) Rising rate of Aboriginal children in out-of-home care. *National Indigenous Times*. https://nit.com.au/rising-rate-of-aboriginal-children-in-out-of-home-care/.

DPMC (Department of Prime Minister and Cabinet). (2019) *Closing the Gap Report 2019*, Canberra.

FNIGC. (2016) Pathways to first nations data and information sovereignty. In T. Kukutai and J. Taylor (eds.), *Indigenous Data Sovereignty: Towards an Agenda*, 139–156. CAEPR Research Monograph, 2016/34. Canberra: ANU Press.

Fostering Together. (2019) *The Crisis Facing Native American Youth*. https://fosteringtogether.org/foster-care/greatest-need/native-american/.

GIDA (Global Indigenous Data Alliance). (September 2019) *Onati Indigenous Data Sovereignty (ID-SOV) Communique*. GIDA-global.org.

GIDA (Global Indigenous Data Alliance). (2019) *Who We Are*. https://www.gida-global.org/whoweare.

Government of Canada. (2016) *Report of the Royal Commission on Aboriginal Peoples*. https://www.bac-lac.gc.ca/eng/discover/aboriginal-heritage/royal-commission-aboriginal-peoples/Pages/final-report.aspx <accessed December 20, 2019>.

Government of Canada. (2019) *Indigenous Services Canada*. https://www.canada.ca/en/Indigenous-services-canada.html <accessed December 20, 2019>.

Grindlay, D. (2017) Indigenous and rural school attendance getting worse despite investment new report shows. *ABC News*, December 6, 2017. https://www.abc.net.au/news/2017-12-06/Indigenous-school-attendance-going-backwards/9230346.

Hirschman, A.O. (1963) *Journeys Towards Progress: Studies of Economic Policy Making in Latin American*. New York, NY: Twentieth Century Fund.

Hirschman, A.O. (1975) Policymaking and policy analysis in Latin America—a return journey. *Policy Sciences*, 6(4), 385–402.

Indigenous Data Sovereignty Summit Communique. (June 20th, 2018) *Aboriginal and Torres Strait Islander, Canberra, ACT, Maiam nayri Wingara*. Canberra: Data Sovereignty Collective and Australian Institute for Indigenous Governance. https://static1.squarespace.com/static/5b3043afb40b9d20411f3512/t/5b6c0f9a0e2e7.

Keddell, E. (2014) The ethics of predictive risk modelling in the Aotearoa/New Zealand child welfare context: child abuse prevention or neo-liberal tool? *Critical Social Policy*, 35(1), 69–88.

King, T. (2012) *The Inconvenient Indian: A Curious Account of the Native People of North America*. Toronto: DoubleDay Canada.

Kukutai, K. and Walter, M. (2015) Indigenising statistics: meeting in the recognition space. *Statistical Journal of the IAOS*, 31(2), 317–326.

Kukutai, T. and Taylor, J. (2016) Data sovereignty for indigenous peoples: current practice and future needs. In T. Kukutai and J. Taylor (eds.), *Indigenous Data Sovereignty: Towards an Agenda*, 1–24. CAEPR Research Monograph, 2016/34. Canberra: ANU Press.

Kukutai, T. and Walter, M. (in press) Indigenous data sovereignty: implications for data journalism. In J. Gray and L. Bounegru (eds.), *The Data Journalism Handbook*, 2nd Edition. O'Reilly Media, Inc.

Lovett, R. (2016) Aboriginal and torres strait islander community wellbeing: identified needs for statistical capacity. In T. Kukutai and J. Taylor (eds.), *Indigenous Data Sovereignty: Towards an Agenda*, 213–232. C1AEPR Research Monograph, 2016/34. Canberra: ANU Press.

Lovett, R., Lee, V., Kukutai, T., Rainie, S.C. and Walker, J. (2019) Good data practices for indigenous data sovereignty. In A. Daly, K. Devitt and M. Mann (eds.), *Good Data*. Amsterdam: Institute of Network Cultures Inc. ISBN:978-94-92302-27-4.

Maiam nayri Wingara. (2017) *Maiam nayri Wingara, Aboriginal and Torres Strait Islander Data Sovereignty Collective: About Us.* https://www.maiamnayriwingara.org/about-us 25e9cabf4a6/1533808545167/Communique%2B-%2BIndigenous%2BData%2BSovereignty%2BSummit.pdf.

Meyer, W.H. (2012) Indigenous rights, global governance, and state sovereignty. *Human Rights Review*, 13(3), 327–347.

Moreton-Robinson, A. (2009) Imagining the good indigenous citizen: race war and the pathology of patriarchal white sovereignty. *Cultural Studies Review*, 2, 61–79.

National Indigenous Australians Agency. (2019) *Closing the Gap.* https://www.niaa.gov.au/Indigenous-affairs/closing-gap <accessed December 19, 2019>.

NARF (Native American Rights Fund). (2019) *Meriam Report: The Problem of Indian Administration (1928).* https://narf.org/nill/resources/meriam.html.

Native America: A History. (2018) *Incarceration Rates for Native Americans.* http://michaelleroyoberg.com/current-events/incarceration-rates-for-native-americans/ <accessed December 20, 2019>.

NCTR (National Centre for Truth and Reconciliation). (2015) *Truth and Reconciliation Commission of Canada: Calls to Action.* http://nctr.ca/assets/reports/Calls_to_Action_English2.pdf.

New Zealand Government. (2019) *Te Puni Kōkiri Ministry of Māori Development.* https://www.govt.nz/organizations/te-puni-kokiri/ <accessed December 20, 2019>.

Nickerson, M. (2017) *First Nation's Data Governance: Measuring the Nation-to-Nation Relationship Discussion* https://static1.squarespace.com/static/558c624de4b0574c94d62a61/t/5ade9674575d1fb25a1c873b/1524536949054/NATION-TO-NATION_FN_DATA_GOVERNANCE_-_FINAL_-_EN.DOCX.

Price, J.N. (2019) *Real Solutions for Indigenous Problems.* Centre for Independent Studies. https://www.cis.org.au/commentary/articles/real-solutions-for-Indigenous-problems/.

Rainie, S.C., Rodriguez-Lonebear, D. and Martinez, A. (2017a) *Policy Brief: Data Governance for Native Nation Rebuilding (Version 2).* http://nni.arizona.edu/application/files/8415/0007/5708/Policy_Brief_Data_Governance_for_Native_Nation_Rebuilding_Version_2.pdf.

Rainie, S.C., Schultz, J.L., Briggs, E., Riggs, P. and Palmanteer-Holder, N.L. (2017b) Data as strategic resource: self-determination and the data challenge for United States indigenous nations. *International Indigenous Policy Journal*, 8(2). doi:10.18584/iipj.2017.8.2.1.

Rainie, S.C., Kukutai, T., Walter, M., Figueroa-Rodriguez, O.L., Walker, J. and Axelsson, P. (2019) Issues in open data: indigenous data sovereignty. In T. Davies, S. Walker, M. Rubinstein and F. Perini (eds.), *The State of Open Data: Histories and Horizons*, 300–319. Cape Town and Ottawa: African Minds and International Development Research Centre.

Research Data Alliance International Indigenous Data Sovereignty Interest Group. (September 2019) CARE principles for Indigenous data governance. *The Global Indigenous Data Alliance*. GIDA-global.org.

RNZ. (2019) *Young Māori Over-Represented in State Care and Detention.* https://www.rnz.co.nz/news/te-manu-korihi/386318/young-Māori-over-represented-in-state-care-and-detention.

Scott, J.C. (1998) *Seeing Like a State: How Certain Schemes to Improve the Human Condition Have Failed.* New Haven, CT: Yale University Press.

SCRGSP (Steering Committee for the Review of Government Service Provision). (2016) *Overcoming Indigenous Disadvantage: Key Indicators 2016.* Canberra: Productivity Commission.

Skalicky, S. and Davey, M. (2016) *Tension Between Police and Standing Rock Protesters Reaches Boiling Point.* https://www.nytimes.com/2016/10/29/us/dakota-access-pipeline-protest.html.

Smith, D.E. (2016) Governing data and data for governance: the everyday practice of indigenous sovereignty. In T. Kukutai and J. Taylor (eds.), *Indigenous Data Sovereignty: Towards an Agenda,* 117–138. CAEPR Research Monograph, 2016/34. Canberra: ANU Press.

Snipp, M. (2016) What does data sovereignty imply: what does it look like? In T. Kukutai and J. Taylor (eds.), *Indigenous Data Sovereignty: Towards an Agenda,* 39–56. CAEPR Research Monograph, 2016/34. Canberra: ANU Press.

Stats NZ. (2018) *Algorithm Assessment Report.* https://data.govt.nz/use-data/analyze-data/government-algorithm-transparency.

Stewart, A. (2014) Truancy officers boost attendance at remote indigenous community schools. *ABC On-Line,* February 27, 2014.

Taylor, J. and Hunter, B. (2001) Demographic challenges to the future of CDEP. In F. Morphy and W. Sanders (eds.), *The Indigenous Welfare Economy and the CDEP Scheme: Autonomy, Dependence, Self Determination and Mutual Obligation,* 95–107. Canberra: Australian National University.

Taylor, J. and Kukutai, T. (2015) Indigenous data sovereignty and indicators: reflections from Australia and Aotearoa New Zealand. *Paper Presented at the UNPFII Expert Group Meeting on The Way Forward: Indigenous Peoples and the 2030 Agenda for Sustainable Development,* United Nations HQ, New York, NY, October.

Te Mana Raraunga Māori Data Sovereignty Network. (2016) *Charter.* https://static1.squarespace.com/static/58e9b10f9de4bb8d1fb5ebbc/t/5913020d15cf7dde1df34482/1494417935052/Te+Mana+Raraunga+Charter+%28Final+%26+Approved%29.pdf.

Te Mana Raraunga Māori Data Sovereignty Network. (2018) *About Us.* te-mana-raraunga-m-ori-data-sovereignty-network/.

Tuhawai Smith, L. (1999) *Decolonzing Methodologies.* London: Zed Books.

US Department of the Interior, Indian Affairs. (2019) *About Us.* https://www.bia.gov/about-us <accessed December 20, 2019>.

US Indigenous Data Sovereignty Network. (2018) *About Us.* usIndigenousdata.arizona.edu.

Vaithianathan, R., Maloney, T., Putnam-Hornstein, E. and Jiang, N. (2013) Children in the public benefit system at risk of maltreatment. Identification via predictive modelling. *American Journal of Preventive Medicine,* 45I(3), 354–359.

Walker, J., Lovett, R., Kukutai, T., Jones, C. and Henry, D. (2017) Routinely collected indigenous health data: governance, ownership and the path to healing. *The Lancet,* 390, 2022–2023.

Walter, M. (2005) Using the power of the data in indigenous research. *Australian Aboriginal Studies,* 2, 27–33.

Walter, M. (2010) The Politics of the data: how the Australian statistical indigene is constructed. *International Journal of Critical Indigenous Studies,* 3(2), 45–56.

Walter, M. and Andersen, C. (2013) *Indigenous Statistics: A Quantitative Methodology.* New York, NY: Routledge.

Walter, M. (2016) Data politics and Indigenous representation in Australian statistics. In T. Kukutai and J. Taylor (eds.), *Indigenous Data Sovereignty: Towards an Agenda,* 79–98. CAEPR Research Monograph, 2016/34. Canberra: ANU Press.

Walter, M. (2018) The voice of indigenous data: beyond the markers of disadvantage. *First Things First, Griffith Review,* 2018(60), 256–263.

Walter, M., Lovett, R., Bodkin Andrews, G. and Lee, V. (2018). *Indigenous Data Sovereignty Briefing Paper 1. Miaim nayri Wingara*. Data Sovereignty Group and the Australian Indigenous Governance Institute.

Walter, M. and Suina, M. (2018) Indigenous data, indigenous methodologies and indigenous data sovereignty. *International Journal of Social Research Methodology*. doi:10.1080/13645579.2018.1531228. <Last date accessed August 28, 2018>.

Wilkinson, M., Dumontier, M., Aalbersberg, I. et al. (2016) The FAIR guiding principles for scientific data management and stewardship. *Scientific Data*, March 15, 2016. doi:10.1038/sdata.2016.18.

Zuberi, T. and Bonilla-Silva, E. (2008) Towards a definition of white logic and white methods. In W. Logical and W. Methods (eds.), *Racism and Methodology*, 3–30. Lanham: Rowman and Littlefield Publishers.

2 "Pushing the space"
Data sovereignty and self-determination in Aotearoa NZ

Tahu Kukutai and Donna Cormack

> Get out my face, we been pushing the space
> I don't want to play your game, running in my own race (ay)
>
> (JessB, 2018)[1]

Introduction

Since the publication of *Indigenous Data Sovereignty: Toward an Agenda* in 2016, Indigenous Data Sovereignty (IDS hereafter) activities have proliferated across the CANZUS states and beyond. National IDS networks have been established in Aotearoa New Zealand (Aotearoa NZ), Australia and the United States, with growing interest in the Pacific (Moana Research, 2019), Scandinavia (see Axelsson and Mienna, this book) and Mexico (Figueroa, this book). These sites of activism and advocacy build on the foundations laid by the pioneering First Nations Information Governance Center, widely regarded as the original IDS network (First Nations Information Governance Centre, 2016). There are now at least two international IDS networks, one affiliated with the influential Research Data Alliance (RDA IDS IG, n.d.), the other a network of networks known as the Global Indigenous Data Alliance (Global Indigenous Data Alliance, 2019). Collectively, the Indigenous scholars, practitioners and activists involved with these networks have advanced the increasing recognition of IDS as both an expression and an enabler of Indigenous rights, Indigenous well-being and self-determination. There is also a growing sense that IDS offers an alternative and potentially transformative vision of "good data" practices (Daly, Devitt & Mann, 2019), with possible benefits extending beyond Indigenous communities (Pendergrast, 2019).

To date, IDS networks have focused largely on self-organization, outreach and awareness. Most networks have published their own IDS charters, principles and/or guidelines (Global Indigenous Data Alliance, 2019; Maiam nayri Wingara, & Australian Indigenous Governance Institute 2018; Te Mana Raraunga, 2018a; Rainie et al., 2017), engaged in public advocacy and media commentary around specific IDS issues (Te Mana Raraunga, 2018b; Wezerek & Van Ripper, 2020) and actively socialized IDS concepts and principles within Indigenous communities and government agencies (see Sporle et al., this book). Less attention has been paid to the implementation of IDS through public policy, hence the timeliness of this book.

In this chapter, we examine the linkages between IDS, self-determination and policy, focusing on our own context of Aotearoa NZ. Specifically, we ask whether and how policy can realize the transformative potential of IDS to support Māori aspirations for self-determination. By policy we take a broad definition to include regulatory measures and laws, along with government agency actions and investment priorities. The focus on self-determination is important. All of the CANZUS IDS networks, as well as the First Nations Information Governance Centre, include self-determination provisions (Rainie et al., 2017; Te Mana Raraunga, 2018a). Notwithstanding the tremendous cross-national variation in political context, Indigenous Peoples generally agree that self-determination is an inherent right and desired outcome. Self-determination can be defined in various ways but typically requires that nation states recognize Indigenous Peoples' distinct forms of social organization, governance and decision making, and redistribute power so that Indigenous Peoples are the ones making decisions over matters that affect them (Toki, 2017; UN General Assembly, 2007).

Our central argument is that the fullness of IDS cannot be realized within the architecture of the colonial settler state. In Aotearoa NZ, as in the other CANZUS states, the approach to Indigenous policy has long been to contain and manage, rather than to enable genuine forms of Indigenous self-determination or autonomy. To give full effect to IDS—that is, for Indigenous Peoples to determine the means of collection, access, analysis, interpretation, management, dissemination and reuse of data from or pertaining to them (Walter & Suina, 2019)—requires a level of Indigenous power and autonomy *within* State systems that does not currently exist. So long as the constitutional position and policy raison d'etre of the State is to see itself as the sole source of sovereignty, and this is certainly the case in Aotearoa NZ, we see little prospect of this changing, despite the growing interest in IDS across government. Indeed, as we argue later in this chapter, data colonialism and "surveillance capitalism" (Zuboff, 2019) may well result in a deepening rather than redistribution of unequal power dynamics (Bigo, Isin & Ruppert, 2019).

To assert that IDS is unobtainable within State structures might seem unduly pessimistic given the aspirational framing of this book, but we offer two caveats. First, we believe that Indigenous data governance (IDGov) over government-held data in Aotearoa NZ can and should be an effective mechanism for implementing a limited form of IDS. Designed carefully, and supported by legislative powers, IDGov can protect against and mitigate some data harms, and increase the visibility of Māori rights and interests in data. However, there is also a very real risk that only the weakest forms of IDGov, such as voluntary frameworks and principles, will be implemented, and will serve as both the beginning and endpoint of the state's commitment to Māori Data Sovereignty (MDS). Second, we believe there is scope for policy to support Māori and iwi (tribal) nations and communities to develop and control our own data ecosystems (Gifford & Mikaere, 2019). We discuss what we see as the transformations needed to move from "data dependency" (Carroll, Rodriguez-Lonebear & Martinez, 2019) to data sovereignty, and the policy levers that might reduce barriers and generate opportunities for the development and enhancement of sustainable Indigenous-controlled data systems.

Data sovereignty, self-determination and tino rangatiratanga

The concept of self-determination is closely connected to the articulation of Indigenous Peoples' rights in the United Nations Declaration on the Rights of Indigenous Peoples (UNDRIP) and domestic treaties such as He Whakaputanga (1835 Declaration of Independence) and Te Tiriti o Waitangi[2] (1840 Treaty of Waitangi). A central tenet of Indigenous self-determination is that Indigenous Peoples have an inherent right to be in control of their destinies and to create their own political and legal organizations (Toki, 2017). Early global human rights instruments framed self-determination as, first and foremost, an individual right. The 1966 International Covenant on Civil and Political Rights, and International Convention on Economic Social and Cultural rights, for example, held that individuals should be able to "freely determine their political status and freely pursue their economic, social and cultural development". The right to freely determine political status and forms of development, including cultural development, is also reflected in Article 3 of the United Nations Declaration on the Rights of Indigenous Peoples (UNDRIP), but is framed primarily as a collective right. Articles 4, 5, 18, 19, 20 and 33 also contain provisions relevant to self-determination (Davis, 2016). Importantly, this also includes the right *not* to participate in state institutions (Art. 5).

Although self-determination is central to global human rights and Indigenous rights discourses, there are domestic nuances that IDS must speak to. In the context of Aotearoa NZ, Toki (2017) argues that tino rangatiratanga, a Māori concept that can be defined as "absolute chiefly authority", offers a stronger right for Māori than the "western paradigm" of self-determination. Whereas "self-determination derives from, and exists under, sovereignty as an international law norm", tino rangatiratanga exists independently of state sovereignty (p. 143). That is, tino rangatiratanga exists whether the state recognizes it or not. Māori have always maintained that sovereignty was never ceded in Te Tiriti and the independent Waitangi Tribunal confirmed this position in its landmark, but non-binding, 2014 report *Te Paparahi o te Raki* (Waitangi Tribunal, 2015). Tino rangatiratanga is closely aligned with another intrinsically Māori concept, mana motuhake (Matike Mai, 2016, pp. 33–34; also see Waitangi Tribunal, 2015). Jackson (2018a) argues that while sovereignty is not a Māori concept of power, mana is the "very Māori expression of the very human desire to be free and to make one's own decisions in one's land" (p. 6). Inherent in the notion of mana motuhake is the concept of mana whenua—to hold territorial rights associated with long-term occupation.

It is no accident that the Māori Data Sovereignty network centers the concept of mana in its name (Te Mana Raraunga means authority over data and data systems) and has prioritized Māori concepts in its founding charter and principles

(Te Mana Raraunga, 2016, 2018a). The rangatiratanga principle has three subprinciples relating to control, jurisdiction and self-determination. Control asserts the inherent right of Māori to exercise control over Māori data and Māori data ecosystems. Jurisdiction relates to decision making over the physical and virtual storage of data. Self-determination asserts Māori rights to data that are relevant and empower sustainable self-determination and effective self-governance. Thus, the principles express a reciprocal relationship between rangatiratanga and MDS, whereby MDS is both an expression of authority (control, jurisdiction), and a key enabler of collective autonomy in a much broader sense (self-determination).

Beyond Aotearoa NZ, there is increasing recognition that IDS is both a critical enabler of Indigenous self-determined development (for more on self-determined development, see Tauli-Corpuz et al., 2010) and a powerful tool for Indigenous resurgence and decolonization (Carroll, Rodriguez-Lonebear & Martinez, 2019). Legal scholar Chidi Oguamanam argues that IDS is "key to realizing the full and effective participation of Indigenous peoples in matters that affect them and the advancement of ... self-determined development" (2019, p. 11). The growing awareness of IDS reflects the increasing importance of data as a "core thematic of international development" and policy frameworks for engaging with Indigenous Peoples (p. 9). A similar point is made by Kukutai & Taylor (2016), who note that the functional implementation of UNDRIP rights are themselves reliant on data rights. Oguamanam goes further, arguing that data sovereignty is "a crucial and fairly new frontier of the struggle for self-determination and decolonization" (2019, p. 11). While some might question the framing of data as the new "frontier" (Prendergast, 2019), there is no denying that datafication and digitalization ushers in new opportunities and risks that IDS must confront, not the least of which data colonialism is (Kukutai & Cormack, 2019). It is to this we now turn.

Data colonialism

Data scholars and activists have theorized how contemporary data practices and relations represent a continuation of the processes and underlying belief systems of extraction, exploitation, accumulation and dispossession that have been visited on Indigenous populations through historical colonialism (Cloudry & Mejias, 2019; Kwet, 2019; Daly, Devitt & Mann, 2019; Sadowski, 2019). Imperialist, colonial logics are evident in the ongoing devaluation and suppression of Indigenous knowledge systems in contemporary data environments, in the imposition of technologies and infrastructure that maintain inequitable power relations (Kwet, 2019), and in the capitalist extractive logics that are embodied in many state data practices and relations (Sadowski, 2019).

Data is increasingly asserted as being an asset or resource (e.g., data.govt.nz), with claims that it is the world's most valuable resource. Though empirically founded, this framing of data is problematic insofar as it implicitly centers extractive logics (Prendergast, 2019). The narrative of digital economies and data as a resource to be harnessed shares common threads with neoliberal ideas of the "knowledge economy" (e.g. Smith & Smith, 2018). Sadowski (2019) contends that "framing of data as a natural resource that is everywhere and free for the taking reinforces regimes of data accumulation" (p. 2). Within capitalism, data are new commodities and new markets. However, the "same imperialist tactics are being replayed now, but updated for the digital age" (Sadowski, 2019, p. 3). For Māori, the mass production, collection, storage and use of data in Aotearoa NZ can be understood as a "replaying" of a familiar colonial experience, whereby "resources" are seen to be open for exploitation and extraction of profit, with little regard for Indigenous knowledge systems and ways of conceptualizing benefit. As Ricuarte notes, "Data centered economies foster extractive models of resource exploitation, the violation of human rights, cultural exclusion, and ecocide. Data extractivism assumes that everything is a data source" (2019, p. 352), a notion that is challenged by IDS.

Data colonialism also plays out through the surveillance practices that remain a feature of contemporary state data practices and systems for Indigenous Peoples (Daly, Devitt & Mann, 2019). In Aotearoa NZ, recent policy environments have bought heavily into the notion of evidence-based decision making, whereby claims are made for the central role of data in policy formulation and in driving social investment decisions (Stuart, 2019). The social investment approach that gained significant traction under the National Coalition Government (2008–2017) typified this way of thinking. Boston and Gill (2017) describe a social investment approach as increasingly depending on "integrated data, information sharing, risk profiling, actuarial analysis, outcomes-based contracting and joined up services" (p. 12). While some of the technologies and capabilities are new, such as the Integrated Data Infrastructure (see Sporle et al., this book), the conceptualization of Māori as watchable and in need of watching within contemporary data regimes is a continuation of coloniality, not a departure.

Māori policy: containment and "non-performativity"

Having surveyed the links between self-determination, tino rangatiratanga and IDS, and the risks of data colonialism, we now consider the broader context of Indigenous policy in Aotearoa NZ. While the motivating logics and desired outcomes of policies relating to Māori have shifted course over the last 170 years,[3] the one constant is the state's refusal to recognize or give effect to tino rangatiratanga. This provides an important context within which to assess current, and future, efforts to implement MDS policies.

From the mid 19th century until at least the 1970s, most aspects of Crown policy were explicitly directed at the assimilation of Māori into Pākehā society (Pākehā are White New Zealanders of largely British origins). In education, assimilation policy was tied to goals of "civilizing" and establishing mission schools, and later Native Schools under the Native Schools Act 1858 (Tomlins-Jahnke & Warren, 2011). One barometer of assimilation was the rate of interracial marriage. Thus, early–mid 20th-century census reports tracked the comparative rates of growth of the so-called Māori "half-caste" and "full blood" populations. In the post-World War II economic boom, assimilation policies gave way to integrationist policies that emphasized the incorporation of what Pool (1991) calls the "Māori reserve army of labour". Integral to this was the 1961 Hunn report which stimulated a major policy push to encourage Māori migration from rural to urban areas to take up work in the expanding manufacturing and services sectors. The late 1980s onward saw a stronger focus on health equity and closing socioeconomic gaps between Māori and non-Māori (Te Puni Kōkiri, 2000), coupled with policies to promote and protect Māori cultural institutions, including the Māori language te reo Māori. More recently, Crown policy has moved to have a broader "focus on families and children and attempts to introduce whole-of-government issues", including important developments in terms of a holistic family well-being "whānau ora" approach (Smith et al., 2019).

In her discussion of Māori involvement in foreign policy, Bargh identifies three key assumptions driving the Crown's approach that are germane to the MDS policy nexus. First, and most significant, is the taken-for-granted assumption that Māori ceded sovereignty in Te Tiriti. Second, that the Crown has the sole right to formulate foreign policy. Third, while there are many interest groups in a liberal democracy, Māori are simply "one interest group amongst many" (2012, p. 87). Relatedly, Tawhai and Gray-Sharp (2011) argue that the absence of strong Māori input or direction into the making of public policy maintains unequal power arrangements, even as it appears to be responsive to Māori concerns and priorities.

It is this appearance of doing something while doing nothing—either in the form of containment or non-performativity—that is most challenging for MDS. In containment, the policy approach is to limit the scope of Māori autonomy which has the effect of bringing Māori under the ambit of state control. A good example of this is the policy relating to kohanga reo or Māori language preschools. Kohanga reo emerged in the early 1908s, driven and funded by Māori mothers, grandmothers and their communities. By 1994, there were more than 800 of them. As genuine "flaxroots" initiatives, they were "expressions of mana Māori motuhake, education Māori controlled and operated" (Tomlins-Jahnke & Warren, 2011, p. 50). The first total immersion primary school (Kura Kaupapa Māori) was established in 1985. Initially, the Department of Education did not acknowledge Kura Kaupapa Māori and Māori parents funded and resourced them themselves until educational reforms in the late 1980s bought them, and kohanga reo, under state funding and accountabilities. Commenting on declining enrolments from the mid 1990s, a Waitangi Tribunal report argued that the kohanga reo movement had been "weakened more by the governmental failure to give it adequate oxygen and support than by any Māori rejection of their language" (2010, p. xi).

An alternative to the containment of Indigenous Peoples within policy domains is what Ahmed (2006, 2016) refers to as "non-performativity". Ahmed argues that the use of terms such as anti-racism, equity and diversity increasingly enable institutions to make visible and legible signs to the public that they are engaging in transformative practice, while doing very little. Her textual analysis shows how institutional commitment to action becomes the action, rather than the precursor for it (2006). A recent case in point is *He Korowai Oranga*, the Ministry of Health's Māori health strategy (Ministry of Health, 2014). Although an excellent strategy that had significant input from acknowledged Māori health experts, it has struggled to have its full potential impact realised. Poor quality health care and institutional racism are as much an issue for Māori as they ever were (see Waitangi Tribunal, 2019).

Although government agencies are showing an increasing interest in, and even appetite for, MDS, the specter of containment and "non-performativity" loom large. Take, for example, recent commitments by the National Statistics Office, Stats NZ, to uphold Te Tiriti, engage with Māori as a partner and co-design Māori-Crown co-governance of data across the whole of government (Gleisner, Downey & McNally, 2015; Stats NZ, 2019b, 2020). Outwardly, these responses are positive and enabling of MDS and self-determining aspirations. Yet, at the same time, the agency's Draft Algorithm Charter (Stats NZ, 2019a), which was under review at the time of writing, makes no mention of Te Tiriti, or even MDS. Rather, it merely seeks to "embed a Te Ao Māori perspective in algorithm development or procurement". Stats NZ's extensive use of alternative government data to plug missing data in the 2018 Census was undertaken with no Māori input into decision making, even though Māori and Pacific people were most affected by non-response (2018 Census External Data Quality Panel, 2019). Around the same time, the agency committed to trialing a Māori tikanga framework to guide decision making over who can access and analyze integrated Māori data, which includes all of the data sources used to fill census gaps (see Sporle et al., this book). This uneven approach means MDS applies in one context, but not in another. Māori authority is contained to decisions about who can access, analyze and disseminate findings from the integrated data, but decisions about whether Māori data should be integrated and made available at all, are higher-level prior decisions over which Māori appear to have no influence.

The Department of International Affairs (DIA), which houses the Government Chief Digital Officer (GCDO), has also made commitments to engaging Māori as Treaty partners and is promoting a national vision of "digital inclusion" as instrumental to the full expression of citizenship in a digital age (Department of Internal Affairs, 2019). At the same time, DIA is leading the government's digital strategy and proposing to offshore the storage of all government data, including Māori data, with no Māori data governance in place (O'Neill, 2019). This is a sharp departure from prior practice—until 2017 there were restrictions on government agencies offshoring identifiable health information (Ministry of Health, 2017). Furthermore, the presumption that digital inclusion is a mechanism for activating rights as citizens, is oddly blind to historical, and ongoing, instances of state surveillance of Māori and enduring Māori mistrust (Kukutai & Cormack, 2019). These examples illustrate the challenges of exercising mana motuhake when the state is making the consequential decisions and its power to "know" is potentially omnipotent. In such contexts, IDS is illusory and there is a real risk of being co-opted into our own surveillance.

The challenge for MDS advocates (and IDS more broadly) is finding the right balance between competing interests and priorities so that we keep steering a path toward the transformative vision that motivated the establishment of IDS in the first place (for a discussion on this tension in the context of IDGov, see Carroll, Rodriguez-Lonebear & Martinez, 2019). For some, that path might be premised on what Murphy (2008) calls a "relational" model of self-determination that emphasizes the need for shared decision making as well as self-government. This might be viewed as a pragmatic response when the "ideal of autonomy is constrained by the realities of interdependence" (p. 203). Applied to data, IDGov might serve as part of a broader strategy for advancing Indigenous self-determination that involves targeting a variety of complementary access points to data control. Ideally, the IDGov mechanisms for control would "recognize and promote sovereignty; lead with Indigenous core values; include dialogue comprised of multiple ways of knowing; utilize and support exiting tribal data governance protocols and procedures; engage and promote Indigenous scholarship; and conduct data science in service to communities" (Carroll, Rodriguez-Lonebear & Martinez, 2019, p. 12). For others, a preferred approach might be to focus on ways to realize IDS outside of state structures. In the Canadian First Nations context, Coulthard (2007) argues that the liberal politics of recognition risk "reproducing the very configurations of colonial power that Indigenous demands for recognition have historically sought to transcend" (p. 439). He argues for a turning away "from the assimilative lure of the statist politics of recognition … toward our own on-the-ground practices of freedom" (p. 456). Closer to home, but in a complementary vein, Jackson (2018b) argues:

> colonisation is an inherently illiberal as well as an unjust process, and to presume that some notion of Māori self-determination can be exercised within the systems it privileged is to follow the same strange and colonising thought that, contrary to all the evidence about the inalienability of mana, Iwi and Hapū nevertheless gladly surrendered it to the Crown (p. 106).

Our view is that turning our backs on state-controlled data systems could result in serious harm and deepening inequities, given the penetration of such systems into the daily lives of Māori families, and rapid developments in surveillance capacities, offshoring and the application of algorithmic decision making to Māori data. Advocating for the strongest form of Māori data governance (MDGov) within colonial state structures—that support aspirations for self-governance and autonomy with respect to Māori data—is both possible and necessary. But we are unconvinced that it will enable a substantive form of data sovereignty or mana motuhake in a broader sense. For the latter to occur requires what Coulthard might label a "radical alternative" to the colonial project, outside of settler state structures. There are ways that policy might facilitate the realization of MDS, both as an expression of mana motuhake, and as an enabler of self-determined development. We sketch out what we see as the core elements below.

From data dependency to data self-determination

To realize the substance, rather than the shadow, of IDS, Māori need to be able to freely determine the shape and form of our data ecosystems. The foundations of these digital data systems need to be built on our own tikanga (ethical principles, practices and processes for what is "tika" or right in a given context), mātauranga (knowledge systems and ways of knowing) and priorities. What might such a system look like? And what, if any, is the role of policy in enabling by Māori, for Māori data systems to come to fruition? Our intention here is not to prescribe a vision, but rather to identify key elements of what we think it might entail.

The emphasis on collective rights and reciprocal obligations is a common thread across all IDS networks and would form the fundamental building blocks of IDS ecosystems. Carroll, Rodriguez-Lonebear & Martinez (2019) describe this interconnectedness well:

> Indigenous data systems rely on shared responsibilities to ensure that Indigenous ways of knowing, being, and doing are transmitted from one generation to the next. Within this context, knowledge belongs to the collective and is fundamental to who Indigenous nations are as peoples
>
> (p. 3)

In settler state data systems, the collective is ever present but rarely acknowledged because of the narrow focus on individual data rights and protection. Taylor, Floridi & van der Sloot (2017) describe the evolving big data landscape as one where "risks relating to the use of big data may play out on the collective level, and where personal data is at one end of a long spectrum of targets that may need consideration and protection" (p. 10). Indigenous privacy interests are intertwined with concepts of community, sovereignty and self-determination. "In these communities, notions of property, ownership and privacy (Western in origin) are foreign to a normative and social system that emphasizes totality and interconnectedness" (Williams et al., 2011, p. 22). Despite the growing recognition that group privacy cannot be reduced to the aggregate privacies of its members, there are few examples, anywhere in the world, of collective data privacy approaches in law or other regulatory mechanisms. One exception is in Canada, where First Nations communities that have adopted the First Nations Information Governance Centre OCAP® principles have passed their own privacy laws (FNIGC, n.d.). Like other Indigenous Peoples, Māori have complex protocols around the protection and sharing of knowledge that safeguard information and maintain community cohesion. A tikanga-centered approach to creating collective data privacy frameworks, principles and protocols could protect group identities and collective privacy, build trust, reduce group harm in diverse social, cultural and environmental settings and resolve potential risks and tensions with individual data rights. In Aotearoa NZ, reviews of the Statistics Act and Privacy Act are in train but it is unlikely that Māori concepts of privacy will be recognized in either. While there is not yet a wider appreciation of the relevance and benefits of a collective Indigenous privacy approach, there is scope to develop frameworks and policies within Māori-controlled data environments such as tribal registers. These approaches would need to be acceptable to those from whom the data came and developed in conjunction with them. MDS principles used by other Indigenous communities, such as First Nations, provide a useful starting point, but would need to be tailored to meet local requirements and sensitivities. The development of community-focused privacy policies and approaches have potential outside of Indigenous communities. As O'Shea argues (2019):

> For privacy to be meaningful, it needs to be about winning back control over our own sense of self—demanding our rights collectively. It needs to drive a stake through the heart of these zombie digital doppelgangers. A better way to understand what we mean when we talk about privacy, then, is to see it as a right to self-determination.

How might policy enable MDS data systems built on tikanga, collectivism and interdependencies? The response, we believe, depends less on a particular policy, than a policy approach that creates an enabling environment for iwi and Māori-controlled data infrastructure. This in turn requires a level of investment in iwi and community-based systems and a willingness to relax the state's singular control over data "resources". The operational failures of the 2018 New Zealand Census—which resulted in poor quality iwi (tribal) data that could not be officially released—is a potent example of the risks of data dependency, and the need for innovative alternatives outside of state structures (2018 Census External Data Quality Panel, 2019; Kukutai & Cormack, 2019). One of the silver linings from Census 2018 was that it amplified questions about the fitness for purpose of the overall census model for meeting iwi data and information needs. For example, comparisons of census and iwi register data often reveal large differences in the size and age-sex composition of individual iwi. This is not surprising, given that census iwi affiliation is based on self-identification and iwi register affiliation is based on whakapapa or genealogical connection (Kukutai & Rarere, 2017; Mahuika, 2019). From a technical perspective, neither source is capturing the "true" population—there are omissions and biases in both. But what would complete enumeration look like? What is the "true" population? From a hapū or iwi worldview, it is all individuals descended from the eponymous ancestor of the hapū or iwi, regardless of whether or not they personally know or claim it. State data systems are neither capable, nor appropriate, for classifying, counting and tracking these collectives.

The as-yet unrealized potential is for a decentralized or distributed system that disperses data and power away from a central location or authority and puts Māori data in Māori hands. As Kwet has argued, "there are alternative technologies, models and ideologies for constructing a digital society aligned with human rights, democracy and socioeconomic justice, for which decentralised ownership and control of software, hardware, and the Internet are prerequisites" (2019, p. 4). In te Ao Māori, there are layers of collectives between the individual and the nation state—whānau (extended kin group), hapū (clan), iwi—that provide existing structures on which to map distributed networks. These human structures of interconnectedness have no parallels in the dominant group—in Aotearoa NZ, they are distinctively Māori.

This notion of a decentralized hapū and iwi data ecosystem shares some similarities with Cloudry & Meijas's (2019) proposal of data nationalization as a way for the global south to push back against data colonialism and surveillance capitalism. Nationalization of data involves storing data only on domestic servers and charging multinationals like Facebook for using citizens' data. While Cloudry & Mejas recognize that nationalization only offers a partial counter to data colonialism, as it still enables a form of data extraction to continue, the important point is that it shifts the locus of control back to those from whom the data derive.

Conclusion

IDS is both an extension of ongoing Indigenous struggles for sovereignty over land and for political autonomy, as well as being necessary to realize these rights and monitor progress toward them. Although we have considered the manifestations and implications in the specific context of Aotearoa NZ, this dual characterization of IDS transcends nation-state boundaries. Prevailing data practices and relations present many challenges for Indigenous Peoples. Some of these are new but many are familiar. This chapter has argued that contemporary data environments overwhelmingly reproduce imperial, colonial ideologies in how data is understood and valued. Proposed solutions, such as paying people for their data, do not disrupt extractive, neoliberal understandings of data but rather replicate them in Indigenous settings. Similarly, digital inclusion strategies are promoted as solutions to inequities within the digital economy, but risk co-opting Indigenous Peoples into oppressive structures that do not fundamentally change the underlying logics (Ricuarte, 2019).

Data colonialism is enacted through state policies (Ricaurte, 2019) in ways that undermine both IDS and tino rangatiratanga more broadly and perpetuate data harms for Indigenous Peoples. IDS can challenge the epistemic oppression built into data ecosystems, can trouble concepts of data, privacy and consent, and can resist harmful practices of surveillance, extraction and accumulation. However, without a fundamental disruption to the underpinning logics, it is likely that policy will revert to strategies of containment or will be "non-performative" in its "statements of commitment" (Ahmed, 2006, 2016) around MDS.

Self-determination and tino rangatiratanga requires us to imagine and re-member Māori data futures outside of the current dominant regimes. IDS can create spaces for this re-imagining of data, data practices and data relations, through engagement in what Browne calls "disruptive staring" (2015) at state policies and practices. Similarly, drawing on Tuck & Yang (2014), a politics of "refusal" that refuses colonial, neoliberal, extractive and accumulative data practices can create space for an alternative self-determined data future that is both a contribution to, and an enactment of, broader tino rangatiratanga. As we state in the introduction to this chapter, the fullness of IDS cannot be realized within the architecture of the colonial settler state. However, policy, both that developed at a local level as well as that within global instruments, may be able to support environments for the realization of IDS where those policies facilitate a divestment of state control and domination and involve a return of Indigenous lands and resources to Indigenous Peoples.

Notes

1 Used with the permission of JessB, an Aotearoa NZ-based hip hop artist. This track is from her album *Bloom* available on Spotify.
2 Te Tiriti o Waitangi/Treaty of Waitangi, signed by Māori chiefs and representatives of Queen Victoria is Aotearoa NZ's founding document, and has been called the Māori "'Magna Carta'".
3 The New Zealand Constitution Act 1852 set up the country's parliamentary system, based on the British model.

References

Ahmed, S. (2006). The nonperformativity of antiracism. *Meridians*, 7(1), 104–126.
Ahmed, S. (2016). How not to do things with words. *Wagadu: A Journal of Transnational Women's and Gender Studies*, 16, 1–8.
Bargh, M. (2012). Rights and sovereignty of indigenous peoples: implications for foreign policy. In J. Headley, A. Reitzig, & J. Burton (Eds.), *Public Participation in Foreign Policy*. London: Palgrave Macmillan.
Bigo, D., Isin, E., & Ruppert, E. (2019). *Data Politics: World, Subjects, Rights*. London: Routledge.
Boston, J., & Gill, D. (2017). Overview: Key issues and themes. In J. Boston, & D. Gill. (Eds.), *Social investment. A New Zealand policy experiment* (pp. 11–34). Wellington: Bridget Williams Books.
Browne, S. (2015). *Dark Matters: On the Surveillance of Blackness*. Duke University Press.
Carroll, S., Rodriguez-Lonebear, D., & Martinez, A. (2019). Indigenous data governance: strategies from United States native nations. *Data Science Journal*, 18(31), 1–15. doi:10.5334/dsj-2019-031.
2018 Census External Data Quality Panel. (2019). *Initial Report of the 2018 Census External Data Quality Panel*. Wellington: Stats NZ.
Couldry, N., & Mejias, U. (2019). Data colonialism: rethinking big data's relation to the contemporary subject. *Television & New Media*, 20(4), 336–349. doi:10.1177/1527476418796632.
Couldry, N., & Mejias, U. (2019). *The Costs of Connection: How Data is Colonizing Human Life and Appropriating It for Capitalism*. Palo Alto, CA: Stanford University Press.
Coulthard, G. (2007). Subjects of empire: indigenous peoples and the 'politics of recognition' in Canada. *Contemporary Political Theory*, 6, 437–460.
Daly, A., Devitt, K., & Mann, M. (Eds.). (2019). *Good Data*. Amsterdam: Institute of Network Cultures.
Davis, M. (2016). Data and the United Nations declaration on the rights of indigenous peoples. In T. Kukutai, & J. Taylor (Eds.), *Indigenous Data Sovereignty: Toward an Agenda* (pp. 25–38). Canberra: ANU e-Press.
Department of Internal Affairs. (2019). *Digital Inclusion Blueprint*. Wellington: Department of Internal Affairs. Retrieved from https://www.digital.govt.nz/digital-government/digital-transformation/digital-inclusion/digital-inclusion-blueprint/.
First Nations Information Governance Centre. (2016). Pathways to first nations' data and information sovereignty. In T. Kukutai, & J. Taylor (Eds.), *Indigenous Data Sovereignty: Toward an Agenda* (pp. 139–156). Canberra: ANU e-Press.

First Nations Information Governance Centre. (n.d.). *The First Nations Principles of OCAP®*. Retrieved from https://fnigc.ca/ocap.

Gifford, H., & Mikaere, K. (2019). Te kete tū ātea: towards reclaiming Rangitīkei iwi data sovereignty. *Journal of Indigenous Wellbeing: Te Mauri—Pimatisiwin*, 4(1), 6–14.

Gleisner, F., Downey, A., & McNally, J. (2015). *Enduring Census Information Requirements for and About Māori*. Retrieved from http://archive.stats.govt.nz/methods/research-papers/enduring-census-requirements-Māori/.

Global Indigenous Data Alliance. (2019). *GIDA—Who We Are*. Retrieved from https://www.gida-global.org/whoweare.

Jackson, M. (2018a). In the end "the hope of decolonization"". In E.A. McKinley, & L.T. Smith (Eds.), *Handbook of Indigenous Education*. Singapore: Springer.

Jackson, M. (2018b). Review of indigeneity: a politics of potential. *MAI Journal*, 7(1), 105–108.

JessB. (2018). *Pushing the Space. On Bloom [EP]*. Auckland: JessB.

Kukutai, T., & Cormack, D. (2019). Mana motuhake ā-raraunga: datafication and social science research in Aotearoa. *Kotuitui: New Zealand Journal of Social Sciences Online*, 14(2), 201–208.

Kukutai, T., & Rarere, M. (2017). Iwi sex ratios in the New Zealand population census: why are women so dominant? *New Zealand Population Review*, 43, 63–92.

Kukutai, T., & Taylor, J. (2016). *Indigenous Data Sovereignty: Toward an Agenda*. Canberra: ANU e-Press.

Kwet, M. (2019). Digital colonialism: US empire and the new imperialism in the global south. *Race & Class*, 60(4), 3–26.

Mahuika, N. (2019). A brief history of whakapapa: Māori approaches to genealogy. *Genealogy*, 3(2), 32. doi:10.3390/genealogy3020032.

Maiam nayri Wingara, & Australian Indigenous Governance Institute. (2018). *Key Principles*. Retrieved from https://www.maiamnayriwingara.org/key-principles.

Matike Mai. (2016). *He Whakaaro here Whakaumu mō Aotearoa. The Report of Matike Mai Aotearoa—The Independent Working Group on Constitutional Transformation*. Auckland: University of Auckland.

Ministry of Health. (2014). *The Guide to He Korowai Orange: Māori Health Strategy*. Wellington: Ministry of Health.

Ministry of Health. (2017). *Ministry Updates Cloud Computing Policy*. Retrieved from https://www.health.govt.nz/news-media/news-items/ministry-updates-cloud-computing-policy.

Moana Research. (2019). *Pacific Data Sovereignty. The 2019 Moana Research Seminar Series Report*. Auckland: Moana Research.

Murphy, M. (2008). Representing indigenous self-determination. *The University of Toronto Law Journal*, 58(2), 185–216.

Oguamanam, C. (2019). *Indigenous Data Sovereignty: Retooling Indigenous Resurgence for Development*. CIGI Papers No. 234. Ontario: Centre for International Governance Innovation.

O'Neill, R. (2019). *NZ Government Leaves Cloud Guidance Unchanged After Aussie Backdoor Law*. Retrieved from https://www.reseller.co.nz/article/657193/australian-backdoor-law-nz-government-leaves-cloud-guidance-unchanged/.

O'Shea, L. (2019). *Future Histories: What Ada Lovelace, Tom Paine and the Paris Commune can Teach us About Digital Technology*. Verso.

Pendergrast, K. (2019). The next big cheap. *Real Life*. Retrieved from https://reallifemag.com/the-next-big-cheap/.

Pool, I. (1991). *Te iwi Māori: A Population Past, Present and Future*. Auckland: Auckland University Press.
Rainie, S.C., Rodriguez-Lonebear, D., & Martinez, A. (2017). *Policy Brief: Indigenous Data Sovereignty in the United States*. Tucson, AZ: Native Nations Institute, University of Arizona.
Research Data Alliance International Indigenous Data Sovereignty Interest Group. (n.d.). Retrieved from https://www.rd-alliance.org/groups/international-indigenous-data-sovereignty-ig.
Ricuarte, P. (2019). Data epistemologies, the coloniality of power, and resistance. *Television and New Media*, 20(4), 350–365.
Sadowski, J. (2019). When data is capital: datafication, accumulation and extraction. *Big Data & Society*, 6(1). doi:10.1177/2053951718820549.
Smith, G.H., & Smith, L.T. (2018). Doing indigenous work: decolonizing and transforming the academy. In E. McKinley, & L. Smith (Eds.), *Handbook of Indigenous Education*. Singapore: Springer.
Smith, V., Moore, C., Cumming, J., & Bolton, A. (2019). Whānau ora: an indigenous policy success story. In J. Luetjens, M. Mintrom, & P 't.Hart (Eds.), *Successful Public Policy* (pp. 505–529). Canberra: ANU Press.
Stats NZ. (2019a). *Draft Algorithm Charter*. Retrieved from https://data.govt.nz/use-data/analyze-data/government-algorithm-transparency-and-accountability/draft-algorithm-charter/.
Stats NZ. (2019b). *Empowering Agencies to Use Data More Effectively*. Retrieved from stats.govt.nz/about-us/data-leadership#achieve.
Stats NZ. (2020). *Partnering with Māori*. Retrieved from https://www.data.govt.nz/about/government-chief-data-steward-gcds/videos/video-transcript-paul-clarke-partnering-with-m/.
Stuart, M. (2019). Potential liabilities: social investment policy as biopolitics in New Zealand—an examination of the National Coalition government's welfare policies. *Policy Futures in Education*, 17(3), 421–437.
Tauli-Corpuz, T., Enkiwe-Abayao, L., & De Chavez, R. (Eds.). (2010). *Towards an Alternative Development Paradigm: Indigenous People's Self-Determined Development*. Baguio City, Philippines: Tebtebba Foundation.
Tawhai, V., & Gray-Sharp, K. (2011). *Always Speaking: The Treaty of Waitangi and Public Policy*. Wellington: Huia Publishers.
Taylor, L., Floridi, L., & van der Sloot, B. (Eds.). (2017). *Group Privacy: New Challenges of Data Technologies*. Dordrecht: Springer.
Te Mana Raraunga. (2016). *Te Mana Raraunga—Māori Data Sovereignty Network Charter*. Retrieved from https://www.temanararaunga.Māori.nz/tutohinga.
Te Mana Raraunga. (2018a). *Principles of Māori Data Sovereignty*. Retrieved from https://www.temanararaunga.Māori.nz/.
Te Mana Raraunga. (2018b). *Te Mana Raraunga Statement on 2018 New Zealand Census of Population and Dwellings: A Call for Action on Māori Census Data*. Retrieved from https://www.temanararaunga.Māori.nz/nga-panui.
Te Puni Kokiri. (2000). *Progress Towards Closing Social and Economic Gaps Between … A Report to the Minister of Māori Affairs May 2000*. Wellington: Te Puni Kokiri.
Toki, V. (2017). Māori seeking self-determination or tino rangatiratanga? A note. *Journal of Māori and Indigenous*, 5, 134–144.
Tomlins-Jahnke, H., & Warren, K. (2011). Full, exclusive and undisturbed possession: Māori education and the Treaty. In V. Tawhai, & K. Gray-Sharp (Eds.), *Always*

Speaking: The Treaty of Waitangi and Public Policy (pp. 21–33). Wellington: Huia Publishers.

Tuck, E., & Yang, K.W. (2014). Unbecoming claims: pedagogies of refusal in qualitative research. *Qualitative Inquiry*, 20(6), 811–818. doi:10.1177/1077800414530265.

United Nations General Assembly. (2007). *United Nations Declaration on the Rights of Indigenous Peoples*.

Waitangi Tribunal. (2010). *Pre-Publication Waitangi Tribunal Report: Te Reo Māori* (Wai 262). Wellington: Waitangi Tribunal.

Waitangi Tribunal. (2015). *Whaia te Mana Motuhake/In Pursuit of Mana Motuhake: Report on the Māori Community Development Act Claim* (Wai 2417). Wellington: Waitangi Tribunal.

Waitangi Tribunal. (2019). *The Health Services and Outcomes Inquiry* (Wai 2575). Wellington: Waitangi Tribunal.

Walter, M., & Suina, M. (2019). Indigenous data, indigenous methodologies and indigenous data sovereignty. *International Journal of Social Research Methodology*, 22(3), 233–243.

Wezerek, X., & Van Ripper, D. (February 6, 2020). Changes to the census could make small towns disappear. *The New York Times*. Retrieved from https://www.nytimes.com/interactive/2020/02/06/opinion/census-algorithm-privacy.html.

Williams, J., Vis-Dunbar, M., & Weber, J. (2011). First nations privacy and modern health care delivery. *Indigenous Law Journal*, 10(1), 101–132.

Zuboff, S. (2019). *The age of surveillance capitalism*. London: Profile Books.

3 The intersection of Indigenous Data Sovereignty and Closing the Gap policy in Australia

Raymond Lovett, Roxanne Jones and Bobby Maher

Introduction

This chapter has three sections. The first describes the most significant change to Aboriginal and Torres Strait Islander legislation (and with it policy) in contemporary times—the 1967 Australian Constitution referendum—as the genesis to Aboriginal and Torres Strait Islander social policy change in Australia. We discuss the rationale at the time for the change to the Australian Constitution and highlight what the changes in Aboriginal policy arrangements brought about. The second outlines the development of Indigenous Data Sovereignty (IDS) in Australia and introduce the Closing the Gap policy (CTG) —the most recent major social policy development in Indigenous affairs of the last decade. The third and final section applies an assessment of the CTG in relation to IDS and Indigenous Data Governance (IDG). We conclude with guidance for the incorporation of IDS and IDG principles for future policy.

Section 1: Contemporary Aboriginal and Torres Strait Islander legislation and policy

Prior to 1967, states and territories retained all legislative and therefore policy responsibility for Aboriginal and Torres Strait Islander Peoples as the Commonwealth was legislatively excluded from law making for the population (United Kingdom House of Commons, 1900).

In the early 1960s, an increase in Aboriginal and Torres Strait Islander voices drew attention to the lack of Indigenous rights in policy making and the impact this was having on people's lives. In 1962, the Federal Council for Aboriginal Advancement (FCAA) lobbied for a referendum to amend section 51 (xxvi) of the Australian Constitution and repeal section 127 of the Constitution, giving the Commonwealth Government law making power in Aboriginal affairs. The rationale for the amendments was to have consistency and applicability of laws and regulations across all states and territories regarding Aboriginal people (National Museum of Australia, 1962). The advocacy for changes to the Constitution by Indigenous lobby groups convinced the Commonwealth to propose what was to become the successful 1967 referendum (House of Representatives, 1967).

The first change to the Australian Constitution, as a result of the referendum, was removal of wording from section 51 (xxvi) which read: The Parliament shall, subject to this Constitution, have power to make laws for the peace, order and good government of the Commonwealth with respect to:—(xxvi) The people of any race, other than the aboriginal race in any State, for whom it is deemed necessary to make special laws.(United Kingdom House of Commons, 1900, p. 19)

Section 51 (xxvi) was amended to: The Parliament shall, subject to this Constitution, have power to make laws for the peace, order and good government of the Commonwealth with respect to: - (xxvi) The people of any race in any State, for whom it is deemed necessary to make special laws. (United Kingdom House of Commons, 1900, p. 19)

The second change to the Australian Constitution was removal of section 127 completely. Section 127 stated: "In reckoning the numbers of the people of the Commonwealth, or of a State or other part of the Commonwealth, aboriginal natives shall not be counted" (United Kingdom House of Commons, 1900, p. 45).

There is evidence that indicates the removal of section 127 was justified on the basis that Aboriginal people could then be counted in the national official statistics—and this opened the way for data about Aboriginal people to inform policy (Gardiner-Garden, 1997). It is important to understand though, data had been collected on the number and distribution of Aboriginal people across the states long before 1967 as evidenced in Commonwealth census reports (Commonwealth of Australia, 1971).

What happened after the constitutional change?

The impact of the 1967 referendum increased Commonwealth government law making almost immediately. For example, less than one year after the changes to the Constitution, the *States Grants (Aboriginal Advancement) Act 1968* was passed by parliament (House of Representatives, 1967). Over the next decade the *States Grants (Aboriginal Advancement) Act* became the primary method of Commonwealth involvement in Aboriginal affairs through the provision of finance for the states initially for "Aboriginal advancement" in the form of finances for housing, health and education. The finance provided appears to be based on an amount calculated on Aboriginal populations within each of the States (House of Representatives, 1968). While Aboriginal population information was available prior to the referendum, increased efforts in the counting of Aboriginal people increased as one result of the changes (Commonwealth of Australia, 1973). The repeal of section 127 together with changes to section 51 has had a profound effect on the making of Indigenous social policy through increased data about Aboriginal people in Australia. The labeling in Indigenous social policy has, since the referendum, evolved from assimilation to self-determination, self-management, reconciliation, practical reconciliation and the present CTG. The governance structures of Indigenous affairs and policy in Australia have been punctuated by the setting up and dismantling of several different administrative and consultative mechanisms; at times, these changes have been communicated as needing to change because of "failure". The contested nature of the best approach to governance in this space has contributed to a lot of uncertainty about direction across crucial policy areas such as socio-economic independence and recognition of land and other rights. Despite this major shift in the language from an assimilationist agenda to the language of self-determination, there continues to be a limited ability for Indigenous Peoples in Australia to contribute to the policy agenda. One of the main barriers to taking the lead in the policy agenda is access to data for Aboriginal and Torres Strait Islander Peoples and communities to inform and therefore drive the policy agenda.

Aboriginal and Torres Strait Islander social policy, political philosophy and data representation

Social policy in Australia, including the CTG, and Indigenous policies before it, has been plagued by political philosophy tensions as evidenced in political statements and debates about Indigenous policy (*Financial Review*, 2018). The debates and approaches to policy frame Aboriginal people as passive policy recipients and often reinforce Indigenous Peoples as outsiders to the policy process. This is compounded when policies are reimagined over time with limited attention to the history of Indigenous Peoples' exclusion from the social and economic fabric of Australian society that was entrenched in past laws and policies. Data has been at the forefront of Indigenous policy re-engineering and these data are often interpreted through a political philosophy lens.

Policy in its simplest definition is a course or principle of action adopted or proposed by an organization, group or individual (Howlett & Cashore, 2014). While there are various definitions of social policy, the common elements encapsulate actions that improve the social well-being of society, including actions that improve well-being among those who experience inequity (McClelland, 2014). An action or proposed action relies on information or an evidence base to inform the decision about a course of action. Information used in deciding the policy course of action comes from the compilation of data to produce a view of the issue at hand and how policy levers can be used to make positive change. A policy or course of action is often also informed and implemented according to an underlying political philosophy or political process. It is the case that the policy (course of action) considers both a technical and political process in the design process (Howlett & Cashore, 2014).

In the political sense therefore, policy is the course of action or stance a political party or government is to pursue. Again, information is required to inform the course of action. But here, *political philosophy* plays a role in how policy is discussed, formulated and implemented. In Australia the overarching political philosophy is of a representative democracy. In a representative democracy, eligible people vote for candidates to carry out the business of governing on their behalf. It is the policies of parties that people vote for—in other words, it is the appeal of policies aligned with people's political philosophies that people vote for. The most common political philosophies include:

1. utilitarianism (takes a "morally" right action, based on the action that produces the greatest good)
2. egalitarianism (all persons have the same fundamental rights)
3. libertarianism (maximize political freedom and autonomy)

Underpinning philosophies are important in being able to recognize a course of action taken in social policy when made by governments.

The political philosophy and policy nexus

Political philosophy is crucial in policy processes as political philosophy reflects on how best to arrange the life of a society that includes political institutions and social practices (Miller, 1998). For example, the CTG aims to "Close the Gap in Indigenous disadvantage by improving outcomes between Indigenous and non-Indigenous Australians in the areas of life expectancy, health, education and employment" (COAG, 2008a). This policy is of equity of outcome (the opportunity to reach the same outcomes in life as non-Indigenous Australians is the stated policy objective). This policy objective has broad support within the general population with a majority of all Australians in the general community reporting governments must do more to address Indigenous disadvantage (Reconciliation Australia, 2019). However, there are underlying competing political philosophies as to how this should be achieved. Examples of this are seen in the Reconciliation barometer where two-thirds of responders report agreeing or being neutral on the topic of Aboriginal and Torres Strait Islander people being responsible for their own disadvantage (Reconciliation Australia, 2019).

There appear to be two prevailing political philosophies that dominate Indigenous social policy discussions and debate in Australia and are evidenced in many statements by political leaders—with statements providing clues to the underlying political philosophy. For example, recent statements by political leaders along the libertarian philosophy include: "if you have a go in this country, you get a go" (*Financial Review*, 2018) and are interpreted as—if you have the will and desire to achieve, you can achieve. Another example includes moralizing the right actions (utilitarianism): "get the kids to school, get the adults to work, and make communities safe" are promulgated as simple neutral statements of fact that will resolve inequality (Commonwealth of Australia, 2018). The predominance of liberalism and utilitarianism in Indigenous policy and particularly social policy continues despite the long and continuous calls by Indigenous Peoples locally and internationally for rights-based frameworks that are more aligned with an egalitarian framework (Human Rights and Equal Opportunity Commission, 2007; UN General Assembly, 2007). Both before and after the 1967 referendum, the political philosophy and Indigenous data nexus have been used to promulgate the trope of Indigenous people, families and communities as not having the will, capacity or desire to improve their situation. As a result, the State is required to step in and data (or a lack of data) has been used as the ultimate policy weapon, to justify extreme policy and legal intervention.

The Northern Territory Emergency Response intervention (NTER) is an example where decisions were placed in the hands of politicians, government officials and bureaucrats without consideration of the recommendations from the board of enquiry that conducted the review; this response was also made in the absence of data about child sexual abuse in Aboriginal communities, but with extensive data available about the life circumstances that contribute to violence including sexual violence across communities. The response was premised on the immediate need to ensure protection of children. The political philosophy guided the implementation of control measures within Aboriginal communities such as sending in the Army to conduct child welfare checks, quarantining welfare payments, banning alcohol sales and access to pornography in Aboriginal communities and to take control of Indigenous land tenure and access systems (leases and permits) (Maddison, 2008). To ensure the policy response could be enacted, suspension of the *Racial Discrimination Act 1975* was required, leaving Aboriginal communities and people feeling disempowered and excluded from any decision-making process. Further, the NTER policy response was inconsistent with the approach advised within the *Little Children Are Sacred* report (Anderson & Wild, 2007).

Section 2: Indigenous Data Sovereignty and Closing the Gap policy in Australia

The foundations of the IDS and IDG movement in Australia were and continue to be, fostered internationally. The embryonic phase of IDS organization in Australia was born at the initial meeting of a collective group of mostly Indigenous Peoples with concerns about Indigenous data that came together at an international event held in Canberra in 2015. The workshop resulted with a book being developed: *Indigenous Data Sovereignty–Towards an Agenda* (Kukutai & Taylor, 2016). Since the seminal publication on IDS, there is a growing group of people becoming involved in IDS in Australia primarily through the formation of the Maiam nayri Wingara (MnW) IDS collective and the Indigenous Data Network (IDN). Foundation workshops of MnW and IDN were held in 2017 and 2018. The formation of the IDN was prompted by a workshop at the University of Melbourne. This workshop discussed the concepts of IDS and IDG and also highlighted where IDS and IDG were already occurring. The forum also focused on the management of "legacy data sets" and "orphaned data"(Maiam nayri Wingara Indigenous Data Sovereignty Collective, 2018a).

In June 2018, the MnW collective co-hosted a summit with the Indigenous Governance Institute, with the objective to develop IDS principles for Australia. One of the key aims of the Indigenous Data Sovereignty Summit was to progress IDS and IDG through developing shared understandings and initiating an Australian set of IDG protocols and principles. A communique which outlines the IDS principles was developed (Maiam nayri Wingara Indigenous Data Sovereignty Collective, 2018b).

Both groups were set up for specific reasons—MnW to establish principles to guide Indigenous leadership and governance in the Indigenous data ecosystem (Maiam nayri Wingara Indigenous Data Sovereignty Collective, 2018b) and IDN to assist Indigenous communities in developing the technical capability and resources to enable them to manage their data for community advancement (Indigenous Data Network, 2019). Both groups share Indigenous community advancement at their core.

The Closing the Gap policy

The *2005 Social Justice Report* (Aboriginal and Torres Strait Islander Social Justice Commissioner, 2005) called for the Australian Government to commit to achieving health equality for Aboriginal and Torres Strait Islander Australians. In response to the *Social Justice Report*, the National Indigenous Health Equality Campaign commenced in 2006, now known as the Close the Gap campaign. The Close the Gap campaign launched by Oxfam was the "public face" of the National Indigenous Health Equality Campaign. The Close the Gap campaign is overseen by a steering committee that comprises over 40 national health organizations who are committed to addressing Aboriginal and Torres Strait Islander health equality. The National Indigenous Reform Agreement (NIRA), also known as Closing the Gap Strategy) is a Council of Australian Governments (COAG) agreement between the Commonwealth of Australia and the states and territories of Australia and was signed in 2007. The NIRA is based on "intergovernmental reforms to close the gap in Indigenous disadvantage"(COAG, 2008a).

COAG identified and endorsed six specific targets that they refer to as "The Building Blocks" to support the reforms aimed at Closing the Gap: early childhood; schooling; health; economic participation; healthy homes; safe communities; and governance and leadership. The core objectives of the NIRA are closing the life expectancy gap within a generation; halving the gap in mortality rates for Indigenous children under five within a decade; ensuring all Indigenous four-year-olds in remote communities have access to early childhood education within five years; halving the gap for Indigenous students in reading, writing and numeracy within a decade; halving the gap for Indigenous People aged 20–24 in Year 12 attainment or equivalent attainment rates by 2020; and halving the gap in employment outcomes between Indigenous and non-Indigenous Australians within a decade. In order to monitor and assess the progress toward achieving the core objectives of the NIRA , 27 performance indicators were developed "across seven domains of the Building Blocks for improving the gaps in disadvantage". The NIRA indicators were developed by COAG—an exclusive government body. The NIRA indicators are reported annually (Connors, 2011) through the Prime Minister's report to parliament, and often receive significant media coverage.

Section 3: Assessment of the Closing the Gap policy against Indigenous Data Sovereignty and governance principles

The CTG originates in the shift in legislative responsibility from states and territories to the Commonwealth as a product of the 1967 referendum. This change ushered in major reforms to Indigenous social policy making that are reflected in contemporary Australia. The intent of the amendment to the Constitution was primarily to ensure consistency of Indigenous legislation and therefore policy nationally. Prior to Commonwealth powers in Indigenous affairs, the states and territories had legislative responsibility for Indigenous affairs, including counting where people lived. The most contemporary policy reforms in Australia's Indigenous affairs have been driven by a need for data to simply understand who Aboriginal and Torres Strait Islander People are and where the populations are distributed. The 1967 referendum and the changes following largely amounted to a regular and consistent Aboriginal and Torres Strait Islander population count through the census (Taylor, 2009). Moving beyond simply counting and understanding who the Aboriginal and Torres Strait Islander population are, IDS and IDG in Australia seek to guide the data ecosystem to meet the needs of the population for which the data are about.

Importantly, there is increasing recognition that IDS principles in government policy require consideration, including a cohesive national strategy through a coordinated approach to Indigenous data (Commonwealth of Australia, 2019). To assess how the current policy approach to Indigenous affairs in Australia is occurring in light of IDS, we have undertaken an assessment of how "Closing the Gap" would fare in relation to the application of the principles. This serves two purposes—the first is to promote the principles including their practical application in the context of Indigenous policy at the national level and the second is to guide social policy makers in how the Indigenous Data Sovereignty principles can be used to make good social policy based in IDS principles.

MnW Principle 1: Indigenous Peoples have the right to exercise control of the data ecosystem including creation, development, stewardship, analysis, dissemination and infrastructure.

MnW Principle 4: Indigenous Peoples have the right to data structures that are accountable to Indigenous peoples.

Indigenous involvement in Australian Indigenous policy making and data has been largely relegated to representation on advisory groups for predetermined actions. This includes a range of structures concerning the CTG implementation and the data ecosystems supporting policy. While this offers an opportunity for Aboriginal and Torres Strait Islander Peoples to contribute to contextual viewpoints on policy and what data should be collected and statistical outputs, it is a far cry from IDS and is actually setting the agenda. Over the years, advisory groups, reference groups, advisory councils and even legislative functions have morphed or been disbanded all together. The data space has not been immune: for example, the National Advisory Group on Aboriginal and Torres Strait Islander Health Data Information and Data (NAGATSIHD), who provided advice to the Australian Health Ministers Advisory Council on the improvement of government health information about Aboriginal and Torres Strait Islander Peoples (Kukutai & Taylor, 2016) was disbanded in 2016. The development of agreements between Aboriginal and Torres Strait Islander Peoples and groups, the Commonwealth and state/territory governments concerning Indigenous health data governance principles and process are absent in Australia. There are few mechanisms for Aboriginal and Torres Strait Islander Peoples to lead or control data governance, other than at the local service or community level through organizations such as Aboriginal Community Controlled Health Organizations (ACCHOs).

In terms of accountability, the Australian National Audit Office asked if the Australian Government's contribution to CTG had been effectively monitored. The assessment states that "From 2008 to 2014 monitoring of the Australian Government's contribution towards Closing the Gap was only partially effective". Since 2015, monitoring has not been effective, as mechanisms for monitoring whole-of-government performance in Aboriginal and Torres Strait Islander affairs have ceased (The Auditor-General, 2019). The *Closing the Gap Prime Minister's Report* does not provide an objective assessment of contribution toward Closing the Gap.

Opportunities for IDG and IDS: most recently, the language in the CTG reports indicate the opportunity for greater control by Indigenous People: "priorities for the future involve creating more opportunities for shared decision-making, improving access to and collection of data to increase transparency" (Commonwealth of Australia, 2020, p. 9).

The opportunity for greater Indigenous control within the data ecosystems can come from lessons learned with other Indigenous populations. In Ontario, Canada, there is an agreement in place between the Ontario provincial government and the Chiefs of Ontario concerning data help by the State. A Data Governance Agreement serves to facilitate First Nations-engaged research and ensures that Indigenous Data Sovereignty principles are firmly established, including a grounding in the First Nation data principles of Ownership, Control, Access and Possession (OCAP®) (Schnarch, 2004). Through the agreement, any use of data held by the state that directly or indirectly identifies First Nations Peoples or communities is subject to First Nations governance processes. This ensures that all First Nations-specific analysis of state-held data is undertaken according to First Nations' collective priorities and applies Indigenous community-based research approaches.

In terms of data development, an important precedent was set at The United Nations Permanent Forum on Indigenous Issues (2006), with the United Nations Declaration on the Rights of Indigenous People declaration stating that: "Indigenous peoples will define their own understandings and visions of wellbeing from which indicators will be identified, and include the full participation of Indigenous peoples in the development of these indicators" (p. 15). Despite such declarations, in many countries (including Australia) policy development and application remains deeply rooted in improving Indigenous well-being, as it is perceived by the dominant (Western) non-Indigenous culture. This position is most clearly articulated in the framework underpinning the CTG suite of policies, where Indigenous outcomes are benchmarked against outcomes achieved by the non-Indigenous population

(Commonwealth of Australia, 2020). The use of a non-Indigenous perspective of well-being in the design and application of Indigenous policy is fundamentally flawed, as it does not account for Indigenous ways of life. What is needed is an appreciation of Indigenous well-being, as perceived by the Indigenous population itself. With a clearer understanding of Indigenous well-being and its determinants, more appropriate policy, and ultimately better outcomes, will be able to be achieved for this population—with the mantra of data by us, for us.

The unfortunate outcome of the current metrics and reporting of these metrics is one of blame and of a problem that requires fixing (Fogarty, Bulloch, McDonnell, & Davis, 2018; Walter, 2018) as one point of reference. There is hope, however. The most recent Commonwealth health policy at its core recognizes the importance of culture and how systemic racism impacts well-being (Commonwealth of Australia, 2015). While there is now recognition of these important constructs in social policy, metrics and who develops these is to be determined.

MnW Principle 2: Indigenous Peoples have the right to data that is contextual and disaggregated (available and accessible at individual, community and First Nations levels) and **MnW Principle 3**: Indigenous Peoples have the right to data that is relevant and empowers sustainable self-determination and effective self-governance.

The aim for Aboriginal and Torres Strait Islander populations to reach the same outcomes as the non-Indigenous population continues to ignore their cultural differences in aspirations and life values, and results in data that are focused on difference, disparity, disadvantage, dysfunction and deprivation (Walter, 2018). This is evident in the national CTG where the intent is to overcome disadvantage. The policy discussion (influenced by the statistical approach to reporting), however, often becomes politicized contributing to a narrative of failure and a waste of precious financial resources.

Much of the reporting of Indigenous data in Australia is at the national or jurisdictional level as it is for all Australians (Health & Welfare, 2018b, 2019). However, the Aboriginal and Torres Strait Islander populations have long called for appropriate disaggregation to inform their own development needs (Walter & Andersen, 2013) as well as access to or return of Indigenous data to communities for their use (Kukutai & Taylor, 2016). There has been recent positive movement on disaggregation and decision making about data with shared prioritizing of the policy and data agenda (Commonwealth of Australia, 2020). There has also been increasing attention on different conceptualizations and operationalizing data items of meaning to Indigenous communities through Indigenous-led research and data development (Jones et al., 2018).

We also sought to understand how these CTG performance indicators were developed and ask the following questions: do they reflect community priorities and were the targets developed in partnership with Aboriginal and Torres Strait Islander Peoples? Sullivan (2011) describes how the indicators of progress against the CTG targets were unclear and no explanation is given as to how the performance indicators were developed, or importantly, how these indicators reference the seven "Building Blocks" that underpin the CTG and agreement between the states and the Commonwealth. The focus of outcomes of the original policy reforms underlying the CTG included tackle smoking ("the single biggest killer of Indigenous people"); healthy transition to adulthood; making Indigenous health everyone's business; primary healthcare service that can deliver; and fixing the gaps and improving the patient journey. Aboriginal and Torres Strait Islander Peoples have not been included in the priority setting process and local community priorities are not built into the targets and indicators.

To implement IDS Principles 2 and 3, data development of concepts important to Aboriginal and Torres Strait Islander Peoples requires further development and the return of Indigenous data could be achieved with further expansion of data governance agreements.

MnW Principle 5: Indigenous Peoples have the right to data that is protective and respects our individual and collective interests.

The overarching statistical methods used in the reporting of Indigenous policy agendas including the CTG predominantly focus on disadvantage, relative rates (gap measurement) and comparing Indigenous with non-Indigenous populations, particularly around life expectancy and health outcomes (Altman, 2009; Jordan, Bulloch, & Buchanan, 2010).

Australian governments and policy makers rely heavily on data to shape and review policies and report on the progress of Indigenous outcomes. The approach to analysis of data often defaults to deficit framing. For example, the recent reductions observed within the last decade of a 10 percent decline in Indigenous smoking rates have instead been reported as a failure because there has also been a similar level of decline within the non-Indigenous population and therefore the decline within the Indigenous population relative to the non-Indigenous population has not changed (Health & Welfare, 2018a, 2018b). However, looking at the data within the Indigenous population (Lovett, Thurber, Wright, Maddox, & Banks, 2017) where between 2004–2005 and 2014–2015 there were significant reductions in smoking prevalence, with an estimated 35,000 fewer Aboriginal and Torres Strait Islander adults smoking daily (Lovett et al., 2017). While prevalence across Aboriginal and Torres Strait Islander Peoples remain high, there are fewer young adults taking up smoking which portrays positive gains across the population and a good news story for the nation (Lovett et al., 2017). Further, this piece of work reflects the importance of the national policy Tackling Indigenous Smoking program as an important contributor to reducing tobacco smoking. It also shows the relevance of analysis within a population to build sound policy. In contrast, the CTG continues to focus on comparisons between Indigenous and non-Indigenous Peoples rather than absolute change within the Aboriginal and Torres Strait Islander population which shows improvement through reduced prevalence of some health conditions and harmful health behaviors. There is a risk of perpetuating the myth that Aboriginal and Torres Strait Islander health and well-being is not improving which does harm (i.e., is not protective) (Harris, 2020).

This analysis also sought to understand how IDS was involved in the development phase of the CTG. The NIRA states: "To date, engagement with Aboriginal and Torres Strait Islander people on the development of the Closing the Gap agenda has been at a very broad level" (COAG, 2008a). There was an Indigenous engagement strategy written within the agreement; however, this is related to the implementation of programs, rather than the development of the reforms. There are also jurisdictional Indigenous advisory groups, representative bodies, sector-specific advisory groups and Indigenous organization–based advisory structures that support Closing the Gap (Thorpe, Arabena, Sullivan, Silburn, & Rowley, 2016).

The metric that the Closing the Gap strategy focuses on is flawed and contributes to the deficit discourse around Aboriginal and Torres Strait Islander health. The Closing the Gap strategy was based on the comparison of Aboriginal and Torres Strait Islander Peoples relative to non-Indigenous People. Accordingly, in order to "close the gap", Aboriginal and Torres Strait Islander health needs to improve faster than non-Indigenous health. The gap between Aboriginal and Torres Strait health and non-Indigenous health is relevant, though measurements of progress and improvement *within* the Aboriginal and Torres Strait Islander population is arguably more important. Changing the conversation from "not on track", to progress within the population can have positive effects on individuals and communities alike and is aligned with protecting Indigenous interests.

Opportunities for policy: enhancing Indigenous policy through IDS and IDG through a Commonwealth Indigenous data governance agreement

There have been a number of policy developments in Australia in recent times that have potential to foster the application of IDS and IDG. The appetite to reform the data landscape in Australia creates both opportunity and warning. For example, the Murray review in 2014 recommended the following: "Review the costs and benefits of increasing access to and improving the use of data, taking into account community concerns about appropriate privacy protections" (pp. xxiv). The review further highlighted that this recommendation warranted more in-depth discussion. This recommendation was tasked to the Productivity Commission and was the basis for the Productivity Commission's Inquiry into Data Availability and Use that sought to examine mechanisms to make better use of data holdings of the Government. The recommendations included major reforms to data access and use including through the creation of new legislation and systems to make data more available (Productivity Commission, 2017). While there was no consideration of IDS or IDG within the review (despite submissions being made on Indigenous Data Sovereignty), consultations concerning the development of the Data Sharing and Release Legislation has incorporated views from both the MnW and the IDN resulting in ensuring Indigenous Data Sovereignty and governance aspects being incorporated within the new legislation as the report highlighted:

> We heard the need to pay close attention to matters related to Indigenous data. We heard concerns relating to Indigenous access to Indigenous data and Indigenous data sovereignty. The National Indigenous Australians Agency is in the early stages of developing a more effective approach to Indigenous

data, including a possible whole-of-government Indigenous data strategy, and we are working together to get it right.

(Commonwealth of Australia, 2019, p. 7)

While the proposed legislative change is yet to occur, there is an opportunity to embed IDS or at a minimum IDG within this framework.

Our examination of the intersection of IDS and IDG in the CTG establishment and revision, highlights yet again an inability of the policy apparatus to engage in the discussion about what it is we are trying to improve and how we should measure and monitor Indigenous progress or achievement. We find that CTG, like other major Indigenous reform agendas, was born out of initial pressure from Indigenous groups and allies that forced governments into action.

Despite the initial CTG "targets" being focused on the population they were meant to be monitoring, implementation of data-monitoring processes without application of IDS and IDG have contributed to what is now understood by the polity and general public—that CTG is a policy failure. This result has occurred because Indigenous data frameworks are based on a comparative deficit-based analysis with the "normative" reference of non-Indigenous Australians as the optimal definition of what a "good life" is. Indigenous Peoples have stepped up once again to influence reforms both in the refresh of the CTG and in the major shift occurring in the broader data reform space to influence change more broadly.

Conclusion

The narrative of policies such as the CTG, continues to be directed by politicians of the day and their political agendas. Policy reform linking "statistical equality" implies that policy is driven by statistical comparisons between Aboriginal and Torres Strait Islander Peoples and the non-Indigenous population. The process of policy making, including data development for policy reform, therefore rarely includes Aboriginal and Torres Strait Islander perspectives, values and principles. Using comparable statistics to shape policies brings a focus on the deficit narrative. Government reports such as the *Prime Minister's Closing the Gap Report* and the *Overcoming Indigenous Disadvantage Report* continue to frame Aboriginal and Torres Strait Islander health and well-being through an ill-health lens of disadvantage and failure to reach statistical equality that omits an Indigenous worldview, aspirations or perspectives.

As a post-script, Indigenous affairs and policy in Australia are undergoing what is deemed in policy circles as a "refresh". The original 20-year Closing the Gap reporting cycle has made it apparent to all, including policy makers that Indigenous policy frameworks, as they are currently construed, and as demonstrated in this chapter, are not working. The use of data via the annual reporting against CTG targets is what has made what Aboriginal and Torres Strait communities and organizations have been saying for years, that current policy prescriptions were ineffective at best, undeniable. The other key message to governments and their policy makers, that Aboriginal and Torres Strait Islander communities and organizations themselves are best placed to shape and implement policy has also resonated.

In 2019, the Coalition of the Peaks, a representative body of around 50 Aboriginal and Torres Strait Islander community-controlled peak organizations entered a formal partnership with COAG, to share decision making on CTG. According to this agreement, over the next ten years CTG measures will be joint actions with the voices of Aboriginal and Torres Strait Islander Peoples central in all decision making (NACCHO, n.d.). After a year of Indigenous community consultation, this process will get underway in mid-2020. The question will be whether the new partnership on CTG will provide opportunities to embed Indigenous Data Sovereignty and governance processes that enhance control of data by Indigenous Peoples for the benefit of Indigenous Peoples and communities.

References

Aboriginal and Torres Strait Islander Social Justice Commissioner. (2005). *Social Justice Report 2005*. Retrieved from Sydney: https://goo.gl/HfhQY9.

Altman, J.C. (2009). *Beyond Closing the Gap: Valuing Diversity in Indigenous Australia* (Vol. 54). Citeseer.

Anderson, P., & Wild, R. (2007). *Ampe Akelyernemane Meke Mekarle ""Little Children are Sacred" Report of the Northern Territory Board of Inquiry into the Protection of Aboriginal Children from Sexual Abuse*. Darwin Retrieved from ISBN:978-0-9803874-1-4.

COAG. (2008a). *National Indigenous Reform Agreement (Closing the Gap)*. Retrieved from http://www.federalfinancialrelations.gov.au/content/npa/health/_archive/Indigenous-reform/national-agreement_sept_12.pdf.

Commonwealth of Australia. (1971). *Census of Population and Housing, 30 June 1966, Part 11. Race*. Canberra, Western Australia: William C. Brown, Governement Printer.

Commonwealth of Australia. (1973). *Characteristics of the Aboriginal and Torres Strait Islander Population*. Union Offset Co. Pty. Ltd.

Commonwealth of Australia. (2015). *National Aboriginal and Torres Strait Islander Health Plan 2013–2023* (978-1-74241-980-0). Retrieved from Canberra: https://www1.health.gov.au/internet/main/publishing.nsf/content/B92E980680486C3BCA257BF0001BAF01/$File/health-plan.pdf.

Commonwealth of Australia. (2018). *Parliamentary Debates: House of Representatives Official Hansard*. Canberra: Commonwealth of Australia.

Commonwealth of Australia. (2019). *Data Sharing and Release Legislative Reforms Discussion Paper*. Canberra: Commonwealth of Australia.

Commonwealth of Australia. (2020). *Closing the Gap Report 2020*. Canberra: Commonwealth of Australia.

Commonwealth of Australia Constitution Act [Australia]. (1900).

Connors, K. (2011). *Reporting Against the National Indigenous Reform Agreement: What Have We Learnt So Far?* Paper presented at the Indigenous Education: Pathways to Success. https://research.acer.edu.au/cgi/viewcontent.cgi?article=1119&context=research_conference.

Constitutional alteration (Aboriginals) Bill. (1967). *Second Reading Speech*, March 1, 1967.

Financial Review (Producer). (2018, 29/01/2020). *Transcript of New Prime Minister Scott Morrison's First Press Conference*. [Online Newspaper].

Fogarty, W., Bulloch, H., McDonnell, S., & Davis, M. (2018). *Deficit Discourse and Indigenous Health: How Narrative Framings of Aboriginal and Torres Strait Islander People Are Reproduced in Policy* (p. xii). Melbourne: The Lowitja Institute.

Gardiner-Garden, J. (1997). *The Origin of Commonwealth Involvement in Indigenous Affairs and the 1967 Referendum*. Canberra: Department of the Parliamentary Library. Retrieved from http://www.aph.gov.au/library/pubs/bp/1996-97/97bp11.htm.

Harris, R. (2020, February 12, 2020). Bid to close the gap on indigenous benchmarks has "failed". *Sydney Morning Herald*. Retrieved from https://www.smh.com.au/politics/federal/bid-to-close-the-gap-on-Indigenous-benchmarks-has-failed-20200211-p53zug.html.

Health, A. I. o., & Welfare. (2018a). *Australia's Health 2018*. Retrieved from Canberra: https://www.aihw.gov.au/reports/australias-health/australias-health-2018.

Health, A. I. o., & Welfare. (2018b). *Closing the Gap Targets: 2017 Analysis of Progress and Key Drivers of Change*. Retrieved from Canberra: https://www.aihw.gov.au/reports/Indigenous-australians/closing-the-gap-targets-2017-analysis-of-progress.

Health, A. I. o., & Welfare. (2019). *Australia's Welfare 2019: In Brief*. Retrieved from Canberra: https://www.aihw.gov.au/reports/australias-welfare/australias-welfare-2019-in-brief.

Howlett, M., & Cashore, B. (2014). Conceptualizing public policy. In I. Engeli, & C.R. Allison (Eds.), *Comparative Policy Studies: Research Methods Series*. London: Palgrave Macmillan.

Human Rights and Equal Opportunity Commission. (2007). *A Human Rights Based Approach is Vital to Address the Challenges in Indigenous Communities*. Press Release.

Indigenous Data Network. (2019). *The Indigenous Data Network: Position Paper*. Melbourne: Indigenous Data Network.

Jones, R., Thurber, K.A., Chapman, J., D'Este, C., Dunbar, T., Wenitong, M., ... & Lovett, R. (2018). Study protocol: our cultures count, the Mayi Kuwayu study, a national longitudinal study of aboriginal and Torres Strait Islander wellbeing. *BMJ Open*, 8(6), e023861. doi:10.1136/bmjopen-2018-023861.

Jordan, K., Bulloch, H., & Buchanan, G. (2010). Statistical equality and cultural difference in Indigenous wellbeing frameworks: a new expression of an enduring debate. *Australian Journal of Social Issues*, 45(3), 333–362.

Kukutai, T., & Taylor, J. (2016). *Indigenous Data Sovereignty: Toward an Agenda*. Canberra: ANU Press.

Lovett, R., Thurber, K., Wright, A., Maddox, R., & Banks, E. (2017). Deadly progress: changes in Australian Aboriginal and Torres Strait Islander adult daily smoking, 2004–2015. *Public Health Research & Practice*, 27(5), 2751742.

Maddison, S. (2008). Indigenous autonomy matters: what's wrong with the Australian government's "intervention" in Aboriginal communities. *Australian Journal of Human Rights*, 14(1), 41–61. doi:10.1080/1323238X.2008.11910845.

Maiam nayri Wingara Indigenous Data Sovereignty Collective. (2018a). *Data for Governance: Governance for Data*. Retrieved from Canberra: https://static1.squarespace.com/static/5b3043afb40b9d20411f3512/t/5b70e7742b6a28f3a0e14683/1534125946810/Indigenous+Data+Sovereignty+Summit+June+2018+Briefing+Paper.pdf.

Maiam nayri Wingara Indigenous Data Sovereignty Collective. (2018b). *Indigenous Data Sovereignty Communique*. Retrieved from Canberra: https://static1.squarespace.com/static/5b3043afb40b9d20411f3512/t/5b6c0f9a0e2e725e9cabf4a6/1533808545167/Communique%2B-%2BIndigenous%2BData%2BSovereignty%2BSummit.pdf.

McClelland, A. (2014). *Part 1: Introduction to Social Policy*. South Melbourne: Oxford University Press Australia.

Miller, D. (1998). *Political Philosophy*. Retrieved from https://www.rep.routledge.com/articles/overview/political-philosophy/v-1 doi:10.4324/9780415249126-S099-1.

NACCHO. (n.d.). *Coalition of the Peaks*. https://www.naccho.org.au/programmes/coalition-of-peaks/.

National Museum of Australia. (1962). *Collaborating for Indigenous Rights: National Petition Campaign, 1962–63*. Retrieved from http://Indigenousrights.net.au/subsection.asp?ssID=25.

Productivity Commission. (2017). *Data Availability and Use*. Canberra: Productivity Commission.

Reconciliation Australia. (2019). *Australian Reconciliation Barameter 2018*. Canberra: Reconciliation Australia.

Schnarch, B. (2004). Ownership, Control, Access, and Possession (OCAP) or self-determination applied to research: a critical analysis of contemporary first nations research and some options for first nations communities. *Journal of Aboriginal Health*, 1, 80–95.

States Grants (Aboriginal Advancement) Act. (1968).

Taylor, J. (2009). Indigenous demography and public policy in Australia: population or peoples? *Journal of Population Research*, 26(2), 115–130.

The Auditor-General. (2019). *Closing the Gap*. Canberra: Auditor-General Report.

Thorpe, A., Arabena, K., Sullivan, P., Silburn, K., & Rowley, K. (2016). *Engaging First Peoples: A Review of Government Engagement Methods for Developing Health Policy*. Retrieved from Melbourne: https://www.lowitja.org.au/content/Document/Lowitja-Publishing/Engaging-First-Peoples.pdf.

UN General Assembly. (2007). *United Nations Declaration on the Rights of Indigenous Peoples: Resolution/Adopted by the General Assembly* (Vol. A/RES/61/295). UN General Assembly.

Walter, M. (2018). The voice of indigenous data: beyond the markers of disadvantage. *Griffith Review*, 2018(60), 256.

Walter, M., & Andersen, C. (2013). *Indigenous Statistics A Quantitative Research Methodology*. New York, NY: Routledge.

4 Growing Pueblo data sovereignty

Michele Suina and Carnell T. Chosa

Introduction

Indigenous Data Sovereignty is a global phenomenon. Big data and the rapidly changing and increasingly powerful data technologies mean Indigenous Peoples world-wide experience many of the same data-related challenges. Yet Indigenous Data Sovereignty is, at its heart, a local phenomenon. A primary claim of Indigenous Data Sovereignty is of the data rights of the Indigenous data to whom the data pertain. Those Indigenous Peoples are most frequently not national populations but tribes, communities and individual Tribal Nations. This means that the advocacy work, data capacity building activity and enactment of Indigenous leadership in relation to Indigenous Data Sovereignty must also be at the local level. It is this local level enactment of Indigenous Data Sovereignty and Indigenous data governance that is the key focus of this chapter.

While relevant at all levels of Indigenous Data Sovereignty, at the local level, relationships and strategic partnerships are critical ingredients in the necessary mobilizing of Indigenous Nations and Peoples to transform the data landscape. It is relationships that provide the impetus and authority to shift the power back to Indigenous Nations to determine what data are necessary and what data are meaningful to inform Indigenous-led decision making in relation to policy. Efforts to advance Indigenous Data Sovereignty across all levels are growing in the United States. These include the drafting of the United States Indigenous Data Sovereignty Network, Indigenous Governance Principles at the University of California, Los Angeles "Policy Forum: The Governance of Indigenous Data" in May 2017. There is, however, still significant effort required to generate a greater awareness and understanding of the global Indigenous Data Sovereignty movement among tribes and tribal leadership. Before adopting Indigenous Data Sovereignty frameworks, tribal leaders need to be convinced of its potential to support local tribal efforts to control information and data about their people, lands, resources and all other aspects of their lives.

In this chapter, we will reflect on collaborative efforts between the Albuquerque Area Southwest Tribal Epidemiology Center (AASTEC) and the Santa Fe Indian School Leadership Institute (LI). This collaboration began in 2017 with the purpose of supporting local efforts to transform Indigenous health data as

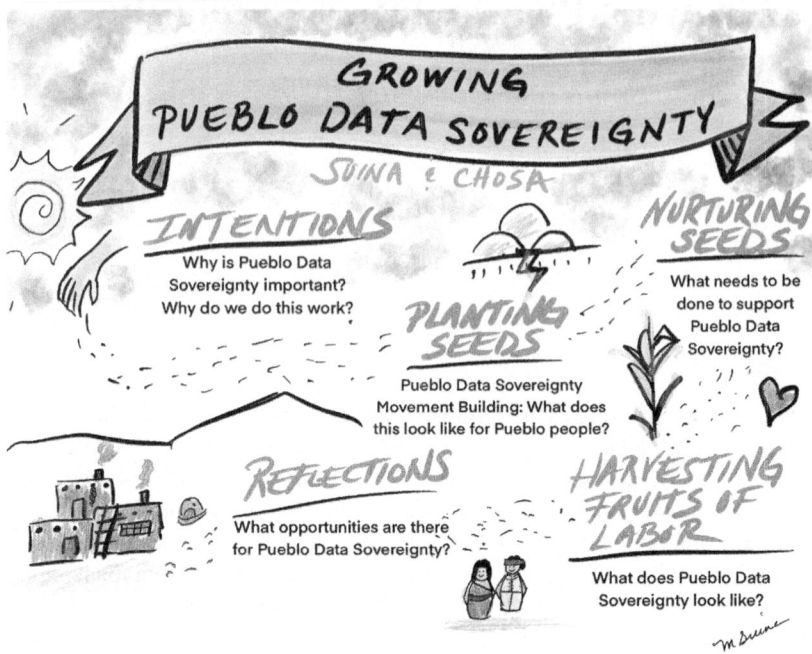

Figure 4.1 Growing Pueblo data sovereignty.

tribal-serving entities. We will also identify types of partnerships and community engagement necessary to move beyond awareness toward action and enactment of Indigenous Data Sovereignty. Finally, we will explore some lessons learned about how to grow Pueblo data sovereignty, to control data about Pueblo Peoples and Nations, by drawing from our positionality as Pueblo tribal members. These lessons have salience for other Indigenous Peoples in their Indigenous Data Sovereignty endeavors.

We have organized our chapter using a farming analogy, because farming and the values[1] associated with caring for our Mother Earth, her plant and animal life, and humanity around us are central to the vitality of Pueblo People. Data can also play a central role for our People when we define for ourselves what data is most meaningful and what data can best contribute to the greater good of our People. We divide our chapter into five sections that each address a key Pueblo data sovereignty enactment question and the formation and flow of these are depicted in our Pueblo data sovereignty graphic (Figure 4.1) These five sections are:

1. intentions—Why is Pueblo data sovereignty important? Why do we do this work?
2. planting seeds—Pueblo data sovereignty movement building: what does this look like for Pueblo People?

3. nurturing seeds—what needs to be done to support Pueblo data sovereignty?
4. harvesting fruits of labor—what does Pueblo data sovereignty look like?
5. reflections—what opportunities are there for Pueblo data sovereignty?

Intentions—Why is Pueblo data sovereignty important? Why do we do this work?

As Pueblo social justice practitioner-scholars, we were raised in our respective Pueblos (Cochiti and Jemez Pueblos, New Mexico, USA) connected to the *Pueblo way of life*[2] unique to our individual Pueblos. This background has shaped the work we both do today to advocate for Pueblo data sovereignty. Contribution and service to the community are also important Pueblo core values that guide our efforts to support Pueblo efforts to control data about us and how we conceptualize the purpose of Pueblo data (Chosa, 2017). From this perspective, data should contribute to the well-being and be in the service of the Nations and Peoples it is about. Data must not exploit, stigmatize or create a disconnection from what is most important to Pueblo Peoples by invalidating our knowledge systems. But perhaps most importantly, data must contribute to the preservation of Pueblo governance, self-determination and knowledge that has been entrusted to us by generations that have come before us.

"Aboriginal occupancy of the Southwest by the Pueblo people is estimated at about ten thousand years before Christ" (Sando, 1992). The 20 Pueblo Nations located within the southwestern United States in New Mexico and Texas therefore have a longstanding presence that long predates the Spanish, Mexican and American occupation of Pueblo ancestral homelands that began in the 1500s. Although there are similarities among Pueblo Nations, each has its own way of life. Each also has its own unique governmental systems and languages that are foundational to their inherent sovereignty given by the Creator (Dozier Enos, 2015). For example, the 19 New Mexico Pueblo tribes share five different languages with their own dialects, including, Tewa, Towa, Tiwa, Keres, and Zuni. Both Zuni Pueblo (Zuni) and Jemez Pueblo (Towa) speak their own language.

Similar to Indigenous Peoples around the world, the Pueblo world was violently disrupted by settler colonialism. Our Pueblo forefathers and foremothers fought to protect our way of life during the Pueblo Revolt of 1680 that ejected the Spanish out of Pueblo territory for 12 years to end Spanish tyranny. Pueblo Peoples remained in our ancestral homelands and were not relocated which allowed us to maintain our connection to this day to where our ancestors also inhabited. Despite colonial efforts to assimilate Pueblo Peoples into Euro-American society to leave our own ways behind, Pueblos remain strongly connected to our ancestral ways of being. This continuation of our strong Pueblo identity often is attributed to the strong stance our Pueblo ancestors took to expel the Spanish colonizers in order to protect all that was important to our existence—our way of life.

Our Pueblo Peoples have preserved our cultural knowledge, languages and way of life through oral transmission from one generation to the next. Each Pueblo still maintains their rich traditional calendar and ceremonial activities throughout the year that reaffirm our core values and cultural knowledge that our ancestors fought to keep (conversation with Regis Pecos). Community-wide participation in our ceremonial life has been critical for passing on our cultural knowledge to younger generations. For example, during our traditional Pueblo corn dances it is common to see our elder tribal members participating alongside our youngest tribal members that just have barely started school. Holding onto knowledge vital to maintaining who we are as Pueblo Peoples and Nations is critical for upholding Pueblo sovereignty. Therefore, respecting, nurturing and carrying forward our knowledge and way of life has been ingrained in us as Pueblo Peoples. Maintaining our Pueblo knowledge is a heightened priority due to external colonial threats to dismantle who we are as Indigenous Peoples. Despite governmental policies to assimilate us into mainstream US society and erase us, our people still hold onto who we are as Pueblo Peoples even though cultural and language loss across Pueblos is a reality.

In recent times information and data about us, such as health and education statistics, generated by external interests, has become another area that we are entrusted to protect and ensure will benefit our people. Indigenous Data Sovereignty has become an important tool to enable us, in this data space to preserve, fight for and win, and treasure all that is important to us now and in the future. Data sovereignty, as a movement, brought together the respective organizations of the authors, the AASTEC[3] and the Santa Fe Indian School Leadership Institute.[4] In 2017 we joined forces to support local tribal efforts in the Albuquerque area to gain control over their data by convening a Community Institute. Best described as a native policy convener think tank, the purpose of this institute was to learn how tribal serving organizations can best support tribal Indigenous Data Sovereignty efforts.

Participants at the 2017 Community Institute recognized that data sovereignty is a process that would initially involve strategic partnerships. Within this, tribal-serving organizations, such as AASTEC, would need to provide data-related support and technical assistance to tribal leaders and community members. The ultimate goal is tribes assuming ownership of their own data process including design, collection, analysis, reporting, storage and use of data. Establishment of tribal data policies defined by tribes and informed by local tribal data expertise were viewed as critical elements for tribes to achieve data sovereignty. Tribal-serving organizations, such as AASTEC and the Leadership Institute were tasked with playing a supportive role, helping to cultivate technical expertise by providing data-related workshops and training opportunities at the tribal level, as well as an advocacy role to influence change among external data systems (i.e., government, university, etc.) that capture tribal data. While the Community Institute provided AASTEC and the Leadership Institute with a roadmap for how best to support data sovereignty among the 27 tribes, Pueblos, Bands and Nations in the Albuquerque area, it also provided the opportunity for focused work with the Pueblos led by the Leadership Institute and initiating deeper thinking about how to apply Pueblo teachings to data sovereignty. These elements are described in the following sections of the chapter.

Planting seeds—Pueblo data sovereignty movement building: what does this look like for Pueblo people?

Looking at ways tribal communities already engage *within* is critical for understanding how to create a sustainable movement to achieve Pueblo data sovereignty. The work of co-author Chosa and the Leadership Institute of engaging Pueblo communities that draw from cultural-based philosophies provides rich examples of what movement building driven by Indigenous values looks like. The Leadership Institute creates and provides intentional opportunities where Native Peoples convene to develop solutions through program and policy recommendations from participants based on Pueblo cultural values.

Co-author Chosa (2016) has developed innovative community engagement opportunities for youth drawing from his own Pueblo's teachings and language to let young people know they belong to and are needed by their community. For example, in 2005 the Leadership Institute created an internship program to reconnect Pueblo youth with their tribal communities. The internship program, now called New Mexico Summer Youth Tribal Employment, ensured host sites provided opportunities for meaningful engagement between youth and their community to occur, making sure that internship placements aligned with both the students' college major and community-expressed needs. As a result, participating communities have retained their youth and the vital contributions youth make to their communities, strengthening the interrelationship between community and youth. This approach was inspired by Chosa's upbringing in Jemez Pueblo. This upbringing modeled participating and contributing to community as coming from having an unwavering sense of belonging to and love for community that is reciprocated by the community. Chosa refers to this interaction in his Towa language as "Attaching Your Heart" meaning when one makes themselves present to support or contribute to a family or community event. Oftentimes, this concept of Attaching Your Heart is also used as an invitation or a call to action to participate or engage in a larger initiative. Additionally, Chosa shares how the concept of belonging is critically tied to or is in relationship with the one who is attaching their heart. When one feels a sense of belonging, they are more likely to attach their heart, and vice versa; by attaching your heart, your level of belonging is strengthened.

Applying what Chosa terms as "homegrown models" based on local Pueblo philosophies and values such as Attaching Your Heart and belonging provides important frameworks for data sovereignty. First, they allow Pueblo Peoples to see themselves reflected back to themselves, leading to an increase in their engagement. The framework can also be reapplied to the very issues that necessitate engagement of Pueblo people. For example, because most Pueblo data is generated by outside entities or initiators with different values and ideas of who we are, the data does not really belong to us. We are not able to attach our heart to the data because it is not us nor does it reflect who we really are. Therefore, data about Pueblo Peoples may be viewed as irrelevant, invalid, unreliable and at worst be seen as harmful because it typically describes us in deficit terms (Walter

& Suina, 2018). Creating our own data for our own purposes and based on our own values, changes the way that data is viewed; they truly belong to us. Data that belongs to us would help us to attach our hearts and use the data to create meaningful programs and opportunities for our Peoples. Examining who initiates engagement and generates data is also critical for understanding where opportunities exist to encourage Pueblo participation in data creation and use.

For Pueblos, interdependence on one another has been critical for ensuring our existence. The interrelationship between the community and the individual plays a major role in maintaining interdependence to benefit the greater good. Similarly, interdependence among external tribal-serving entities is necessary to maximize our service to tribes and to provide relevant programming and resources to benefit the Peoples we serve. Partnering with the Leadership Institute in 2017 was an intentional strategy for AASTEC to elevate Indigenous Data Sovereignty among the tribes in our area. Based at the Santa Fe Indian School, a tribally controlled and operated school, the Leadership Institute is an important entity as it has served as a catalyst since 1997 to create discourse among tribes. The other central role of the Leadership Institute is to train community members and specifically youth on public policy issues in order to create systemic change starting within tribal communities. Because of their long track record utilizing Indigenous centered values and philosophies to engage people, the Leadership Institute is influential among tribal leaders, policy makers and tribal grassroots organizers.

Nurturing seeds—What needs to be done to support Pueblo data sovereignty?

In July 2018, the Leadership Institute convened the Pueblo Convocation[5] on Education that brought together nearly 700 Pueblo people to reimagine what education should look like for Pueblo students. This event was in response to the landmark court decision that found that the state of New Mexico violated the constitutional rights of Native American students to a sufficient education in the *Yazzie/Martinez lawsuit*.[6] During the Convocation, Pueblo Peoples put their hearts and minds together to begin to develop plans for a desired educational system for their children and youth to prepare for the 2019 state legislative session. Data sovereignty was included among the 13 breakout sessions. The outcome of these sessions was a set of recommendations that were presented to the 20 Pueblo governors for inclusion in a tribal resolution to guide efforts for reforming an inadequate education system.

The Convocation breakout session entitled "Data Sovereignty, Effective Uses of Data" discussed how data could be more effectively used by the Pueblos to make stronger arguments for change across the educational spectrum. Participants were asked during the breakout session what policies are needed so that tribes can control and influence data about them and for the data that does exist to be more effectively used. A determination of this discussion was that policies are needed that establish clear guidelines for Pueblo data. These include guidelines that identify: what types of data can be collected; how data should be collected; appropriate data sources; why data is being collected; and how data can be better used to benefit Pueblo Peoples. It was also determined that clear guidelines were needed to establish who can access data and who owns and controls Pueblo-related data. Although there was recognition that each Pueblo would need to establish their own review boards and advisory boards to determine their own research agendas/priorities, data policies and guidelines, there was also the idea expressed that Pueblos could band together and form an office of research if they desired to do so.

Participants in the data sovereignty breakout session also expressed the need for training and education on data for those in leadership positions. This training would equip Pueblo leaders to advocate for data sovereignty and how to use data and support the community at large to understand the importance of data and to gain a basic understanding of data terminology. Regarding practical matters, funding was recognized as a significant need. The following Pueblo data sovereignty protocol recommendations were made as a result of the session's rich dialog that occurred. These protocols were included in the Pueblo resolution:

1. Pueblos must recognize the important role of data collection. Data collection is now an important part of governance and ownership and application to assist and support communities.
2. Pueblos must develop strategies on how we can use data to advance our initiatives at multiple levels.
3. Pueblos must actively develop data sharing agreements.
4. Pueblos must consider developing internal and external policies so Pueblos can control and influence data about them.
5. Advocate to redefine "evidence-based" research and data collection in ways that enable Pueblos to define what evidence looks like and enables locally conducted research, enable data collection to be used as evidence to support initiatives, and enable programs that Pueblos know work for them.
6. Pueblo leadership must support and advocate for increasing base budgets for the existing tribal serving centers and institutes to continue these groundbreaking initiatives to expand their work and extend technical support to the Pueblo governments and Pueblo programs.

The actions that grew from the Pueblo Convocation on Education offered direction for continued Pueblo data sovereignty efforts. They also remind us that achieving data sovereignty will rely on multiple and ongoing endeavors involving many individuals (i.e., Pueblo leadership, community members at large, technical assistance providers, etc.), but the initiators of Indigenous Data Sovereignty must be our own Pueblo People.

Harvesting fruits of labor—What does Pueblo data sovereignty look like?

Understanding what sovereignty means to Pueblo Peoples, instead of external definitions, is critical for informing Pueblo data sovereignty efforts and in creating data governance mechanisms that align with traditional Pueblo governance that protect our way of life. Santa Clara Pueblo scholar, Anya Dozier Enos' (2015) education research outlines what inherent sovereignty means to Pueblo people. Drawing from interviews conducted with Pueblo people, Dozier Enos describes Pueblo inherent sovereignty as being *the core of life* or *the way of life* of Pueblo people, using the term *deep sovereignty* to describe this concept. Dozier Enos further explains that deep sovereignty is fundamentally different from political sovereignty because it is not restricted to the Western legal definitions that limit actual sovereignty of American Indian tribes in the United States. Pueblo data sovereignty plays an important role in maintaining inherent Pueblo sovereignty because the enactment of data sovereignty is through governance and decision making related to data matters about Pueblo people and nations.

Pueblos remain vigilant in the protection of our way of life. From the Spanish colonial period to save their native religion from the brutal Spaniards, our Peoples have kept Pueblo knowledge close at hand and away from the non-Pueblo world to protect our sacred way of life (Suina, 1992). Cochiti Pueblo scholar and tribal leader, Joseph H. Suina (co-author M. Suina's father) reflected on what this strategy looks like for many Pueblos in more recent times:

> Highly visible signs forbidding picture-taking, sketching and other forms of recording are posted on the outskirts as well as in the village center. Visitors' recording devices, such as cameras, can be impounded by tribal officials and violators are faced with a possible fine. Usually, the film is confiscated and a warning issued to the embarrassed offender. Occasionally a Pueblo village will be closed to the outside world for periods of two or three days to celebrate a private religious event. Not even the U.S. mail gets through. (p. 60)

Pueblos already have built-in mechanisms to protect their information from the outside world. Pueblos also have internal practices in place among their own people that limit access to certain types of information if a person is not yet ready for that information or if that information is not intended for that person (Suina & Smolkin, 1994). Examining already existing systems and practices is essential for developing Pueblo data governance mechanisms that better align with Pueblo knowledge practices that are connected to our own epistemological,[7] ontological[8] and axiological[9] frameworks. While there is value in current data governance mechanisms such as research codes, data sharing agreements, research review boards and other methods for tribes to control their data, there must also be a connection to our Pueblo value systems and knowledge worlds to mirror our own processes. Otherwise, we run the risk of invalidating our own knowledge by not applying it to protect our information and data.

Pueblo data sovereignty has become a more recent example of how Pueblos are challenging outside impositions of what is valid, important and truly represented by data and asserting their rights to determine what data is necessary for their own purposes. During the 2018 Pueblo Convocation, several rich examples of Pueblo Nations taking on a collection of data for their own purposes emerged.

For example, Pueblos are engaged in their own data collection for comprehensive community and land use planning efforts, understanding heritage language trends, and ensuring oversight of research by establishing research review mechanisms such as the establishment of an Institutional Review Board by one Pueblo. Pueblos are exercising their inherent rights as sovereign Nations to govern their data and information, as well as to create their own data.

Reflections—What opportunities are there for Pueblo data sovereignty?

In 2019, the Keres Children's Learning Center[10] held their Fourth Annual Language Symposium showcasing how Montessori education is being used to revitalize heritage languages. Tribal leader and keynote speaker Joseph H. Suina reflected upon Pueblo Peoples' ability to adapt outside ways to fit *them* by stating, "The genius of Pueblo people, we take something and make it fit us". Suina further explained that rather than Pueblo Peoples changing to fit the outside way or idea, Pueblo Peoples incorporate what is useful while still remaining who we are without losing what is important to the Pueblo world at the expense of what is being introduced such as the adoption of different teaching methods. For example, traditional holistic Pueblo pedagogy and the Montessori Method both focus on educating the whole child and have been woven together to support language immersion to revitalize language in one Pueblo. Likewise, Pueblo data could better serve Pueblo Peoples by being in alignment with our own values and realities instead of those that are important to government agencies, funders, universities and others that have staked a claim on information about us. Data can then become a better fit without Pueblos having to give up what is most important to them.

As Pueblo advocates for Pueblo data sovereignty, Suina's words resonate. The question becomes, how can the Indigenous Data Sovereignty movement fit the Pueblos so we can make it our own? Having a better understanding of this essential element of Pueblo data sovereignty is critical for supporting a movement for lasting change that aligns with what is most important for Pueblo Peoples. The work of Laguna Pueblo scholar and tribal leader Richard Luarkie (2017) examines the relationship between Pueblo Peoples and data and reminds us that "data and analytics are part of our culture and way of life and are not new to Pueblo people". Luarkie explains that Pueblo Peoples have in the past and to this day rely on the use of oral-based and visual data sets that have been guided by what Luarkie terms a "holistic world data-view" derived from our own Pueblo values and principles. Data collection, analysis, reporting and usage are something our people have already been doing prior to colonization. Being able to identify commonalities between Western-based data and existing Pueblo data and cultural practices that are built into our way of life is a way to make a connection with Pueblo Peoples regarding the relevance of data to who we are rather than data being disconnected from us. For example, epidemiological health data provides us with information that marks significant life events such as when a person is born and when a person leaves this world; data is collected that acknowledges these important events. In the Pueblo world these important events are recognized by the entire community. Quantitative data and Pueblo cultural practices both recognize the importance of these life events that must be noted. We need to identify where other areas align and examine ways to share information in a way that respects cultural values and teachings. This is an ongoing role of the tribal serving entities such as Albuquerque Area Southwest Tribal Epidemiology Center and the Santa Fe Indian School Leadership Institute.

Conclusion

Growing Pueblo data sovereignty will involve further exploration to understand how Pueblo Peoples view data through our own cultural lens and teachings to guide what data looks like and should look like for our people. Nurturing Pueblo data will take multiple engaged Pueblo community partnerships that recognize the role communities must play in order to be the bearers and ultimately the recipients of the data harvest. Engaged partners external to our communities can contribute to Pueblo data sovereignty by helping to cultivate technical data skills among Pueblo Peoples and to advocate for change among external data systems that collect our data. Sustainable production of Pueblo data by Pueblo Peoples will be a significant contribution that we can pass onto future generations. By doing this, we will protect all that our ancestors fought for throughout our history to ensure we are connected to our Pueblo way of life to maintain our inherent sovereignty gifted to us by the Creator.

Notes

1 Pueblo core values are love, respect, compassion, faith, understanding, spirituality and balance.
2 Pueblo way of life encompasses a connection to where our ancestors lived and where we still live today, the practice of Pueblo spirituality and ceremonies, use of heritage languages, maintenance of traditional governance systems and other ways of existence that connect today's Pueblo Peoples to our ancestors.
3 Albuquerque Area Southwest Tribal Epidemiology Center in Albuquerque, New Mexico, USA, was established in 2006 and is one of 12 Tribal Epidemiology Centers serving American Indians and Alaska Natives throughout the USA and serves tribal communities in New Mexico, southern Colorado and west Texas to provide high-quality health data, culturally congruent epidemiology/surveillance, capacity development, program evaluation and health promotion/disease prevention services.
4 The Leadership Institute (LI), based at the Santa Fe Indian School in Santa Fe, New Mexico, USA, was established in 1997 to create a space for discourse on a wide range of public policy and tribal community issues challenging the vitality and spirit of the 22 Tribal Nations in New Mexico.
5 The Pueblo Convocation is another Leadership Institute programmatic component that brings together a larger number of participants (between 500 to 800) to engage in an in-depth exploration of an issue area that may need formal multi tribal support.
6 The consolidated lawsuit, *Yazzie/Martinez* v. *State of New Mexico* challenged the state's failure to provide students—especially low-income, Native American, English

language learner (ELL), and students with disabilities—the programs and services necessary for them to learn and thrive, and challenged the state's failure to sufficiently fund these programs and services. On July 20, 2018, Judge Sarah Singleton ruled that all New Mexico students have a right to be college and career ready and that the state is failing to meet this obligation (http://nmpovertylaw.org/wp-content/uploads/2018/09/Graphic-Yazzie-Martinez-Decision.pdf).
7 Epistemology refers to the part of philosophy that deals with knowledge. (Oxford online dictionary)
8 Ontology refers to philosophy that deals with the nature of existence. (Oxford online dictionary)
9 Axiology refers to the study of the nature, types, and criteria of values and of value judgments, especially in ethics (Merriam-Webster online dictionary).
10 Keres Children's Learning Center KCLC is a Montessori early childhood education center that immerses Cochiti Pueblo children in their Keres language. The mission of KCLC is to reclaim our children's education and honor our heritage by using a comprehensive cultural and academic curriculum to assist families in nurturing Keres-speaking, holistically healthy, community minded and academically strong students (https://kclcmontessori.org/).

References

Chosa, C.T. (2016). New engagement programming with youth. *Journal of American Indian Education*, 55(3), 12–29.

Chosa, C.T. (2017). Attaching your heart: pueblo community engagement. In *Indigenous Innovations in Higher Education* (pp. 165–180). Brill Sense.

Enos, A.D. (2015). Deep sovereignty: a foundation for indigenous sustainability. In *Indigenous Innovation* (pp. 25–42). Brill Sense.

Luarkie, R. (2017). Rethinking data through pueblo interpretations. In *Indigenous Innovations in Higher Education* (pp. 123–141). Brill Sense.

Sando, J.S. (1992). *Pueblo Nations: Eight Centuries of Pueblo Indian History*. Clear Light Pub.

Suina, J.H. (1992). Pueblo secrecy: result of intrusions. *New Mexico Magazine*, 70(1), 60–63.

Suina, J.H., & Smolkin, L.B. (1994). From natal culture to school culture to dominant society culture. In *Cross-Cultural Roots of Minority Child Development* (pp. 115–130). Lawrence Erlbaum Associates, Inc.

Walter, M., & Suina, M. (2018). Indigenous data, indigenous methodologies and indigenous data sovereignty. *International Journal of Social Research Methodology*, 22, 1–11.

5 Indigenous data and policy in Aotearoa New Zealand

Andrew Sporle, Maui Hudson and Kiri West

Introduction

Māori Data Sovereignty has emerged as a critical policy issue as Aotearoa New Zealand develops world-leading linked administrative data resources. The development of the Integrated Data Infrastructure (IDI) (Statistics New Zealand 2017a) involved the application of existing official statistics legislation and policy to enable the creation of a government infrastructure to support the secondary use of data. This development was incremental, beginning as a technical exercise in data aggregation and linkage between government agencies (Statistics NZ 2003) before becoming a clear intention by the central government to use and share linked data as the source of information for its "social investment" expenditure (Foss and English 2015, Statistics New Zealand 2017b). The combined reach and potential of these new data resources extended their use to purposes beyond those for which they were originally collected (English 2016, Savage and Bycroft 2014) and the limitations of existing government policy created an impetus for discussions about the social and cultural license for data aggregation, linkage and use (New Zealand Data Futures Partnership 2016). Discussions were largely facilitated through government-led community engagement activities (Statistics New Zealand 2015), as well as direct advocacy by Māori organizations. This chapter describes the data system in Aotearoa New Zealand, the recent efforts to integrate Māori values, operationalize Māori Data Sovereignty and establish models for Māori data governance across agencies and New Zealand's official statistics system.

The data policy structure in Aotearoa New Zealand

Aotearoa New Zealand is part of the D7 network of the world's most advanced digital nations (digital.govt.nz 2018). The combination of its small population, a single national-level government (with no state governments), advanced digital infrastructure (Sapere and Covec 2015) as well as strong privacy and official statistics legislation enables substantial and timely national-level data policy change. Aotearoa New Zealand provides an intriguing context to explore the inclusion of Indigenous Data Sovereignty in policy as it has a sizable Indigenous population—16.5% in the 2018 Census (Stats NZ 2020a) with a shared language and a recent history of recognizing Indigenous Māori rights within legislation (e.g., *Treaty of Waitangi Act 1975*; *Māori Language Act 1987*; *Resource Management Act 1991*; *Māori Fisheries Act 2004*). There is also significant Indigenous research capacity, policy settings that support the integration of Indigenous knowledge into research activities (e.g., Health Research Council of New Zealand n.d.), and targeted approaches by national research policy agencies (e.g., Ministry of Research Science and Technology 2007).

Stats NZ Tatauranga Aotearoa (Stats NZ) is Aotearoa New Zealand's national statistics office and lead agency for government-held data, a role defined by its own legislation (*Statistics Act 1975*). Stats NZ is responsible for producing standard classifications and processes for data collection including supporting government agencies to build their capability and manage data as a valuable strategic asset. The Chief Executive of Stats NZ is also the Government Statistician and the Government Chief Data Steward, a role to provide "support and guidance so agencies can use data effectively, while maintaining the trust and confidence of New Zealanders" (digital.govt.nz 2020). This includes an explicit focus on data sharing as well as open data, as Aotearoa New Zealand is a signatory to the Open Data Charter (data.govt.nz. 2017). Under legislation, StatsNZ and the Government Statistician have roles that are relatively independent of the elected government, when compared with similar national statistics offices in the Organization for Economic Cooperation and Development (OECD) (s17 of the *Statistics Act 1975*).

The operation of the official data system in Aotearoa New Zealand is highly centralized compared with other OECD nations (OECD 2011) due to the combination of having a single, federal-level coordinated system and strong coordination between agencies leading data policy. Other agencies that have broad policy responsibilities around data include the Department of Internal Affairs, which hosts the Government Chief Digital Officer, who is the functional lead for digital services across government agencies, and the Social Wellbeing Agency (formerly the Social Investment Agency) whose role is to strengthen the use of data, analytics and insights in the social policy sector. The creation of Chief Data Steward and Chief Digital Officer roles as new cross-government functional leaders is intended to provide a coordinated, whole-of-government approach to data collection, storage and use (Stats NZ 2019a). The adoption of the Open Data Charter led to a cross-government program approach to making government data available for reuse which is reflected in the National Information and Communications Technology (ICT) strategy (ict.govt.nz. 2015) and the Strategy for a Digital Public Service (Government Chief Digital Officer 2018).

The Office of the Privacy Commissioner is an independent government agency that has a wide range of functions determined by the *Privacy Act 1993*, which applies to almost all individuals and organizations in Aotearoa New Zealand. Their work program includes data issues and they recently released, in conjunction with Stats NZ, the principles for safe and effective use of data and analytics (Privacy Commissioner and Stats NZ 2018). The Data Futures Partnership

(New Zealand Data Futures Partnership n.d.), an independent ministerial advisory group, produced Guidelines for Trusted Data Use after consultation with individuals, organizations and communities about their views on data sharing (Data Futures Partnership 2017). Alongside community engagement processes the regulatory and legal frameworks for the data systems in Aotearoa New Zealand are also evolving. Two key pieces of legislation, the *Privacy Act* and the *Statistics Act*, were put under review in 2017 with both bills in the midst of the parliamentary process in 2020.

Stats NZ hosts the IDI, a world-leading research database, which contains de-identified but linkable microdata about people and households comprised of over 60 datasets from a range of government agencies and non-government organizations, as well as Stats NZ surveys including the 2013 and 2018 Census. Other Government data sources can also be linked to the IDI including the Stats NZ Longitudinal Business Database and those at the Ministry of Health and Ministry of Education, which have unique identifiers for individuals using government-funded health and education services. These data resources have comprehensive coverage of all individuals and businesses in Aotearoa New Zealand and are being used for research purposes, subject to a range of access and publication controls.

A key discussion point for many people is that much of the data available within the IDI was not collected or consented to for research and data re-use is not being preceded by policy-level consideration of potential issues, including accounting for Indigenous values or concerns (Kukutai and Walter 2015). Data re-use constitutes secondary data use which has generally required the prior or follow-up consent or approval of individuals. Discussions about the value of data and the limits of secondary use are being conducted in Aotearoa New Zealand but often as a response to the development of the digital technologies that enabled more advanced ways to link datasets and generate valuable research and policy insights (Data Futures Partnership 2016; Tūhono 2017). The community engagement activities frame data as an important national strategic asset and aim to better understand where the "limits of public acceptance" or the "social license to use data" are in the absence of an explicit individual consent (Data Futures Partnership 2016).

As a concept, social license reflects a general understanding or social contract between citizens and the state, a process predicated on a relationship of trust and an expectation that the mandated body will act in the best interests of those affected by their decisions (Te Mana Raraunga 2017; Gulliver et al. 2018). This contrasts with the concept of cultural license, advocated by Te Mana Raraunga TMR as a necessary complement to social license, which focuses on the nature of the social contract that exists between Crown and iwi through their Treaty of Waitangi relationship.

Māori Data Sovereignty

While government agencies grappled with defining the limits of social license for data sharing, the concept of Māori Data Sovereignty was gaining traction amongst

Māori scholars as well as community-level practitioners. The publication of the seminal book, *Indigenous Data Sovereignty: Towards an Agenda*, cemented Māori Data Sovereignty as a key theoretical framework for concerns about data rights and interests, expectations of data governance and use, as well as Māori aspirations for control over Māori data (Kukutai and Taylor 2016; Hudson et al. 2018). Māori Data Sovereignty reflects a longstanding aspiration for rangatiratanga (sovereignty), a catch-cry that first found its expression in the fight for land but has since been used to advocate for Māori control over a variety of resources from fisheries to airwaves, from forests to intellectual property rights (Hudson et al. 2016).

The concept of Indigenous Data Sovereignty is a synthesis of discourses about cultural and intellectual property rights, Indigenous research ethics and Indigenous governance. While the language of Indigenous Data Sovereignty is new, it reflects core ideas first articulated in the Mataatua Declaration on Cultural and Intellectual Property Rights (Commission on Human Rights 1993) and expands them to assert rights over data generated by government agencies about Māori communities (Kukutai and Taylor 2016). Sovereignty implies the need for governance and the core themes of "data for governance" and "governance of data" are represented in the literature (Taylor and Kukutai 2015). In Aotearoa New Zealand, the governance relationship between the Crown (government) and Māori is shaped by the Treaty of Waitangi—especially where cultural identity and cultural resources are involved (Waitangi Tribunal 2011). Treaty-based responses such as the governance of resources (Harmsworth, Awatere and Robb 2016) and the health sector (Jansen 2016) include models of co-governance and collaboration, and successful models are informing approaches to how Aotearoa New Zealand approaches the governance of data resources.

Māori advocacy for Māori Data Sovereignty

The primary advocates for recognizing Māori rights and interests in data over the past four years have been Te Mana Raraunga Māori Data Sovereignty Network (TMR) and the Data Iwi Leaders Group. Te Mana Raraunga is a network of Māori researchers, data practitioners and community members who work toward developing a greater understanding and awareness of Māori Data Sovereignty and Māori data governance across communities and policy agencies (see https://www.temanararaunga.Māori.nz/whakapapa for more details). The group had its inaugural meeting in late 2015 following an international workshop in Australia (Kukutai and Taylor 2016) and subsequently developed a charter that has guided the organization structure and operation ever since (Te Mana Raraunga 2016). The group is run by a voluntary executive, has an open no-cost membership, creates public domain reference resources and operates a Māori data/ICT expertise database.

The Data Iwi Leaders' Group (ILG) is a subcommittee of the Iwi Chairs Forum, which is a platform for sharing knowledge and information amongst tribal authorities in Aotearoa New Zealand. The Data ILG consists of a number of tribal chairpersons, with support from a team of technical advisors (see https://iwichairs.Māori.nz), who recognize the importance of data to advancing their aspirations across a range of work streams including health, social, environmental and economic sectors. They were able to utilize their political mandate to engage directly with Government ministers in discussions about tribal expectations regarding access to data for governance and governance of data (Iwi Data Leaders Group 2019).

These two advocacy groups have worked in tandem utilizing the Mana-Mahi framework outlined in the Te Mana Raraunga Charter to delineate their respective responsibilities and support for each other's activities (Te Mana Raraunga 2016). The Mana component reflects the governance-level engagement of tribal leaders with Government ministers. The Mahi component relates to the operational relationships between government agencies and ILG technical advisors or Te Mana Rauranga advocates (Figure 5.1).

In the Mana space, the Iwi Leaders' Group engages in national policy development processes and quickly recognized the importance of data as underpinning the full spectrum of their advocacy and policy work. The Data Iwi Leaders Group has strongly advocated for Māori governance over Māori data (Iwi Data Leaders Group, ibid.), specifically seeking solutions to the 2018 Census which failed to produce iwi data of publishable quality. This resulted in the signing of a Mana Ōrite Relationship Agreement with Stats NZ, in which the parties have equal explanatory power but recognize their different approaches (Iwi Chairs Forum 2019). The aim of the agreement is to progress a Māori-Government joint work program including embedding a Te Ao Māori (Māori world view) lens into the way decisions are taken across the public sector data eco-system and to lead the process for "co-design" of Māori data governance across the government data eco-system. This includes work to address census data gaps and iwi data needs

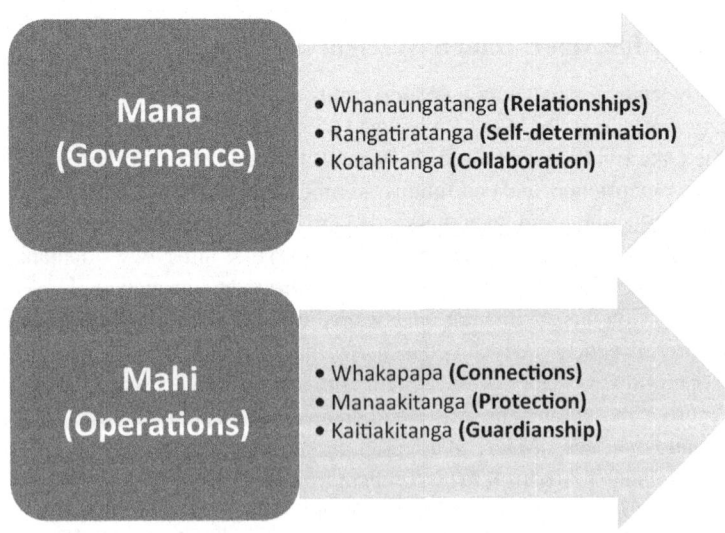

Figure 5.1 Mana-Mahi Framework (source: Te Mana Raraunga 2016)

over the next one to three years, and the development of a Treaty-based approach to data system governance (Stats NZ 2019b). An early part of the work program involved Stats NZ commissioning a report on the value of the Census to Māori (Bakker 2019). The Data Iwi Leaders Group are working with the Government Statistician in 2020 to co-design an approach to incorporate Te Ao Māori perspectives in processes, practices and data governance frameworks (Stats NZ 2019c).

Working in the "mahi" space, Te Mana Raraunga has been at the forefront of defining the parameters of Māori Data Sovereignty by publishing definitions for Māori data, Māori Data Sovereignty, Māori data governance, and Māori Data Sovereignty principles (Te Mana Raraunga 2018b). The Māori Data Sovereignty principles center Māori values and provide a conceptual framework for understanding Māori interests in the context of data. Formal TMR activities such as workshops or submissions are coordinated through the executive. Submissions have been made to the *Review of the 1975 Statistics Act* (Te Mana Raraunga 2018a), the *Law Commission Review on the Use of DNA* (Cormack 2019), the Draft Algorithm Charter (Te Mana Raraunga 2020), as well as public statements on social license (Te Mana Raraunga 2017) and the poor outcomes of the 2018 New Zealand Census of Population Dwellings for Māori (Te Mana Raraunga 2019). Individual members of the network also provide support to agencies and organizations on Māori Data Sovereignty and Māori data governance. TMR has hosted a number of events focused on Indigenous Data Sovereignty or Māori Data Sovereignty and presented to government agencies. This direct engagement with key government agencies has been influential in the positioning of Māori Data Sovereignty as an important component of the data policy discourse in Aotearoa New Zealand.

The breadth of capability and experience within the TMR membership provides a pool of expertise network members can draw upon to formulate well-informed responses to issues, including technical reports as supporting evidence. The presence of a significant academic contingent of TMR has lent itself well to the production of publications, which serve to articulate the key concerns for Māori communities (Kukutai and Taylor 2016; Rainie et al. 2019; Kukutai and Cormack 2019). In keeping with a commitment to maintaining relationships with community, the resulting documents and media links are posted on the TMR website to be publicly available as a reference resource.

Māori Data Sovereignty principles

The Te Mana Raraunga Charter states that "Māori data refers to data produced by Māori or that is about Māori and the environments we have relationships with". Data has been described by Iwi leaders as a "potential taonga, something precious that needs to be maintained, in relation to its utility" (Dr W. Edwards, TMR website). Data has been framed as a taonga, something precious or of value, in part because it evokes a cultural significance as well as the connection to rights arising from the Treaty of Waitangi. Article Two of the Treaty of Waitangi obliges the Government to actively protect taonga, consult with Māori in respect of taonga, give effect to the principle of partnership and recognize Māori rangatiratanga over taonga (Kahui

Legal 2016). The factors that relate to how communities might recognize the taonga nature of any dataset have been described by Hudson et al. (2018) as:

- provenance of the data: does the dataset come from a significant Māori source?
- opportunity for the data: could the dataset support Māori aspirations for their people or their whenua (land)?
- utility of the data: does the dataset have multiple uses?

This taonga-based approach is useful for determining which datasets might require the need for Māori governance and control over data as well as asserting a rights-based responsibility upon the government. However, TMR recognized the need to develop Māori Data Sovereignty principles to inform the recognition of Māori rights and interests in data, and the ethical use of data to enhance Māori well-being (Te Mana Raraunga 2018b). The principles emerged from a series of workshops and describe Māori concepts in the context of data.

- rangatiratanga/authority
- whakapapa/relationships
- whanaungatanga/obligations
- kotahitanga/collective benefit
- manaakitanga/reciprocity
- kaitiakitanga/guardianship

Once the principles had been developed, the impact and influence of the principles in the policy sector were evident almost immediately as they were referenced in a report on a Māori Data Futures workshop (Science for Technological Innovation NSC et al. 2018) and submissions to the new statistics legislation (Stats NZ 2019d).

Māori data audit tool

A regional consortia of health provider organizations developed a shared database to improve data quality and access by health care providers in the Auckland region. As one of the partners in the consortia is a Māori health provider and Indigenous Data Sovereignty advocate, a request was made to evaluate whether the data sharing agreement was consistent with the general tenets of Indigenous Data Sovereignty. As part of this evaluation, a Māori Data Audit Tool was developed to assess organizational readiness to address key values and issues identified within the Te Mana Raraunga Charter (Atatoa-Carr and Hudson 2017). The Māori Data Audit Tool focuses on the following areas:

- explicit recognition of Māori data
- collection of Māori ethnicity and iwi affiliation data
- recognition of the Treaty of Waitangi and Māori/iwi participation in governance, data sharing processes and dispute processes

- recognition of Māori rights and interests in relation to their own datasets and shared datasets
- data protection mechanisms and data use processes that support development rather than highlight deprivation
- alignment with Mana-Mahi principles of whanaungatanga, rangatiratanga, kotahitanga, whakapapa, manaakitanga and kaitiakitanga

The Māori Data Audit Tool is available on the TMR website and has been shared in a number of forums.

Agency responses to Māori Data Sovereignty

Awareness raising

The establishment of Te Mana Raraunga and the introduction of language around Māori Data Sovereignty created a clear relevance for Māori participation in data-related policy and provided a coherent Māori voice to raise concerns. Alongside the Data ILG, TMR has been a key source of information and advice for the implementation of Māori Data Sovereignty within the official statistics system.

As the Crown-mandated body charged with the collection of official statistics in New Zealand Stats NZ leads cross-agency responses to data governance as well as engaging Māori, including the Data ILG and Te Mana Raraunga, in these issues. Stats NZ has engaged in a number of Māori and Government events that have discussed the issue of Māori Data Sovereignty and Māori data governance (Table 5.1).

These awareness-raising activities have informed a number of practical initiatives and policy interventions within Stats NZ and across the broader government sector. The shift from developing awareness and understanding around Māori Data Sovereignty to building robust policies is a challenging one. However, a range of efforts have been made to address the issue of Māori participation in data governance and enhance institutional responsiveness. The following activities demonstrate specific initiatives Stats NZ has completed or are underway.

Table 5.1 Stats NZ engagement with Māori Data Sovereignty-focused events

2016–2018	Attendance at Te Mana Raraunga-led hui 2016–2018
August 2016	Māori and Social License hui
November 2017	Māori Data Governance workshop
December 2017	Supported Ngai Tahu Data Symposium
August 2018	Supported TMR-led Agency Approaches to Data Governance workshop
Oct 2018	Stats NZ Data Summit 2018—Jonathan Dewar (First Nations Indigenous Governance Center) & Tahu Kukutai (University of Waikato/TMR) were keynote speakers
June 2019	OECD international conference, Paris, Presentation on Indigenous Data Sovereignty (special topic)

- report on government agency engagement with Māori about statistical information needs (Stats NZ 2016)
- Pilot Partnership Program with six iwi members (2016–2017)
- Iwi and iwi-related classification standard review (by 33 new iwi members) (July, 2017)
- Te Ara Takatū 2018—census data for iwi and Māori (trial)
- Māori data governance co-design process, initiated in July 2018
- IDI Ngā Tikanga Paihere framework, piloted in 2019
- Tatauranga Umanga Māori/Māori Business Stats 2017–2018 (released in June, 2019)
- Indicators Aotearoa Ngā Tutohinga—selection of Te Ao Māori indicators, initiated in January 2019
- Census 2018—iwi Māori work plan to address gaps and deliver quality outputs for Māori
- Strengthening data capability with iwi and Māori (still in development)
- Te Kupenga Survey 2013 and 2018, General Social Survey (Te Reo attitudes module in 2016)

While Stats NZ has a formal governance responsibility for the entire Official Statistics System, each government department or agency is responsible for managing its own data in a manner consistent with legal requirements, government policy as well as the ethical and cultural expectations of the community. A number of other agencies have held workshops or sessions to improve their understanding of Māori Data Sovereignty including:

- Treasury Speaker Series (December 2016), Data and Development: Māori Interests in the Data Eco-System
- Te Puni Kōkiri (July 2017), Māori Data Sovereignty: Implications for policy
- Ministry of Education (August 2018), Māori Data Sovereignty: What does this mean for the Ministry of Education?
- Ministry of Health, engaged with Māori data consultant Kirikowhai Mikaere, and have developed a Māori Data Sovereignty and Governance Working Group in late 2019 to support the National Health Information Platform project
- Ministry of Social Development & Social Investment Agency (August 2018), Supported TMR led Agency Approaches to Data Governance
- Ministry of Business, Innovation, and Employment (September 2018), Māori Data Sovereignty and the National Research Information System
- Department of Internal Affairs (2018), Māori Digital Inclusion Strategy consultation
- Pharmac, (October 2018). Data and Health Inequity session
- Ministry of Social Development (November 2018) session on Data Sovereignty

Other agencies have engaged with Te Mana Raraunga to get advice or have people speak about Māori Data Sovereignty including the Department of Conservation,

Biosecurity NZ, and Te Arawhiti Department of Crown-Māori Relations. Explicit references to Māori Data Sovereignty have begun to emerge in consultancy reports to government agencies (Tiaho Ltd., Law Commission, McDonald-Sporle Ltd.), government documents (NEAC 2019) and correspondence (Stats NZ 2019b). Agencies are also starting to develop other tools and mechanisms which, while not explicitly addressing Māori Data Sovereignty, support the aim of greater Māori control over Māori data (e.g., Ministry of Education Te Mataaho a Iwi—Māori Dashboard (Ministry of Education 2019); Ministry of Social Development—Treaty Section in the PHRaE Framework (MSD 2018); Te Arawhiti Te Ao Māori Capability Framework for Public Service (Te Arawhiti 2019).

Examples of Institutional Responsiveness to Māori Data Sovereignty

The efforts of TMR advocates to address key conceptual challenges and develop practical guidance has led to the implementation of Māori Data Sovereignty in a number of policy settings. Innovations include service delivery changes, policy development or program development. Direct contact between TMR and the Government Statistician has proven to be an effective means to quickly address operational issues as well as engage with program development within Stats NZ. This relationship resulted in TMR being offered involvement in key decision-making processes such as the Statistics Legislation Review and the Iwi Classification Review. Direct access facilitated prompt dialog on highly contentious issues and was used to achieve a temporary moratorium on approvals for overseas-based researchers to access IDI data from outside the country.

Māori Data Sovereignty considerations have also become included in operational practice within some government institutions. The revised National Standards for Health and Disability Ethics reference the Māori Data Sovereignty Principles and the Te Mana o te Raraunga Model (National Ethics Advisory Committee 2019). Stats NZ used the Te Mana o te Raraunga model as the foundation for the development of the IDI Ngā Tikanga Paihere Framework, while the Ministry of Social Development has recently included Māori Data Sovereignty as a central element of their Whānau Wellbeing research program. Māori Data Sovereignty has also become embedded in research practice as researchers respond to changing expectations from communities, funding bodies and policy agencies (A Better Start 2018).

Te Mana o te Raraunga

The "Te Mana o te Raraunga Model" was developed to align Māori concepts with data rights and interests, and guide agencies in the appropriate use of Māori data (Hudson et al. 2018). Māori concepts relevant to the context of the secondary use of data were identified and each of the concepts has been associated with a characteristic relevant to data use which provides the foundation for an assessment question. The concepts cover three distinct types of questions, those relating to an assessment of the data itself (tapu, noa), those associated with the data use (tika,

Table 5.2 Assessment questions for Te Mana o te Raunga Model

Concept	Characteristic	Assessment question
Tapu	Level of sensitivity	"How sensitive is the data?"
Noa	Level of accessibility	"How accessible should this data be?"
Tika	Level of value	"How does the use of this data add value to the community?"
Pono	Level of trust	"Will the community support this use of the data?"
Mauri	Level of originality	"How unique is the data?"
Wairua	Nature of the application	"Is the data being used in the same spirit as its original use?"
Whakapapa	Level of relationship	"Does the user have an existing relationship with the data?"
Pūkenga	Level of expertise	"Does the user have the expertise and experience to use data in a culturally appropriate manner?"
Kaitiaki	Level of authority	"Will the data be protected from inappropriate use?"
Wānanga	Level of responsibility	"Does the institution have the necessary infrastructure to ensure the use of the data in a culturally appropriate and ethical manner?"

(Source: National Ethics Advisory Committee 2019)

pono, mauri, wairua), and those relevant to the data users (whakapapa, pūkenga, kaitiaki, wānanga) (Table 5.2).

Where the previously mentioned Māori Data Audit Tool was focused on the assessment of agency responsiveness to data needs, the Te Mana o te Raraunga Model assesses the data itself and generates a decision about the data and the level of governance that may be required (Hudson et al. 2018).

Ngā Tikanga Paihere

Ngā Tikanga Paihere is a framework which has been designed with the intention of building and sustaining a relationship of trust between the New Zealand public and Stats NZ (Stats NZ 2020a). The framework aligns the questions from the Te Mana o te Raraunga Model and is designed to work alongside the existing 5 Safes Data Access Framework (Stats NZ 2020b) to assess the cultural appropriateness of researcher requests to use Māori data within the IDI. Ngā Tikanga Paihere is intended to be used as part of the data access protocol for the integrated data infrastructure.

The assessment component of the framework works off of a points-based system and the score given to each application then informs the assessing committee's decision to either decline, approve or request additional material for applications to the IDI.

Table 5.3 Ngā Tikanga Paihere: Ma ngā tikanga e arahina—Be guided by good principles

Pūkenga (knowledge and expertise) Researchers can demonstrate an awareness of and intention to work with data in culturally appropriate ways.	**Have appropriate expertise, skills and relationships with communities**	Whakapapa (community relationships) Researchers have existing relationships with the communities the data comes from.
Pono (accountability and transparency) Level of accountability to communities of interest is explained and there is community support for the research.	**Maintain public confidence and trust to use data**	Tika (value for all) Research should be part of a body of work that contributes toward better outcomes for Māori and New Zealanders.
Wānanga (organizations) Institutions have established systems, policies and procedures to support culturally appropriate practices when working with data.	**Use good data standards and practices**	Kaitiaki (data stewardship and governance) Communities of interest are identified and involved in research decisions as early as possible.
Wairua (community good) Community objectives align with project research objectives and any potential harm to these groups is considered.	**Have clear purpose and action**	Mauri (data transformation and provenance) Researchers show how data transforms from its original collection purpose to support research objectives.
Noa (benefit and opportunity) Data is readily accessible and there is demonstrated awareness of the impact on communities of interest.	**Balance benefits and risks**	Tapu (sensitivity and risk) Sensitivities in the use of data are identified including privacy issues for whānau and identifiable groups.

Note: Text in Column 2 connect the items on each side (Columns 1 and 3).
(Source Stats NZ 2020b).

The integration of Māori values into data access processes supports the implementation of Māori data governance for specific activities. Ngā Tikanga Paihere has been piloted and is in the process of being formally published for use by Stats NZ within the IDI as well as other government agencies. The person primarily responsible for the development of the IDI Tikanga Framework within Stats NZ provided regular updates to Te Mana Raraunga as well as socializing its use with other agencies including the Social Investment Agency, Work Safe NZ, Treasury, Stats NZ, Otago University, Ministry of Social Development, Ministry of

Business, Innovation and Employment, Ministry of Primary Industries, Ministry of Justice, Archives NZ, Land Information NZ, Health Promotion Agency, Te Arawhiti, Accident Compensation Corporation, Ministry of Education, Ministry of Health, Te Puni Kōkiri, Office of the Privacy Commissioner, and the Māori Land Court.

Ministry of Social Development's Te Pou Tuatahi

In 2019, the Ministry of Social Development (MSD) launched Te Pae Tata, its new Māori Strategy and Action Plan, to "shift" the Ministry's approach to enable greater effectiveness in working with Māori. The purpose of Te Pae Tata is to embed a Māori world view into MSD to reflect their commitment as a Te Tiriti o Waitangi partner and prioritize the needs of whānau (MSD 2019). This revised strategy impacts upon both MSD's ongoing Whānau Wellbeing research program and the overall Data and Analytics Strategy. The Whānau Wellbeing research program is built around three strands, the first of which (Te Pou Tuatahi) focuses on the development of frameworks that guide the other two strands of evidence collection and application. Te Pou Tuatahi highlights the importance of understanding Māori Data Sovereignty and issues of privacy and ethics in responding to the different data needs and priorities of both Treaty partners (MSD 2019). This approach has led to a pilot project for the creation of community-defined and controlled local well-being and capability metrics. The intent is to create an alternative to the existing deprivation-based regional well-being measures and create information that is locally relevant, readily usable and strengths based. Community organizations will determine what to include in the metrics, with data from existing administrative data sources or collected themselves. Data will flow toward the community organization, who will steward data from multiple sources and control the creation of the well-being measures.

Māori Data Sovereignty in research policy and practice

One domain where Māori Data Sovereignty informed rapid change was the research sector. The Te Mana Raraunga executive includes leading Māori researchers and the Māori research workforce form a large component of meeting attendees and membership. Researchers began referencing Māori Data Sovereignty principles in research design and funding applications, resulting in the funding of research that included realizing Māori Data Sovereignty principles (Health Research Council 2018). The adoption of Māori Data Sovereignty in research practice aligned with the existing government research funding policy (Vision Mātauranga) to "unlock the innovation potential of Māori knowledge, resources and people" (Ministry of Research Science and Technology 2007, p. 2). At the time of writing, Te Rauika Māngai (the National Science Challenges cross-challenge Māori directors' group) have been lobbying for some time for an update to Māori research policy (Science for Technological Innovation NSC 2019), including a reference to Māori Data Sovereignty. However, Māori Data Sovereignty practice already features in work funded by several of the National Science Challenges, the Health Research Council and the Ministry of Business, Innovation and Employment as researchers include it in their research design. This development in research practice has spilled over into research within the policy agencies, with large agencies such as the MSD including Māori Data Sovereignty as a core part of their published research intentions (Shackleton et al. 2020).

Conclusion

Māori Data Sovereignty has become part of the standard policy discourse in Aotearoa New Zealand within five years of the first Aotearoa New Zealand-based meeting on the subject. Despite this high level of penetrance into the policy sector, the terminology and principles are only now starting to be included in official government policy documents. This exemplifies the slow-moving nature of the policy cycle as well as the long lead time for government-initiated policy work. That Māori Data Sovereignty is now appearing in policy documents at all is somewhat remarkable, as it articulates a position at odds with the open data intent of many high profile and well-funded government data policies and practices. This is probably the result of a combination of factors, including the general public disquiet about linked data, the statutory autonomy and policy reach of the Government Statistician role, and the coordinated approach of the Data Iwi Leader's Group and Te Mana Raraunga that delivered consistent messages to Government Ministers and Government agencies.

While there may be little official policy on Māori Data Sovereignty, the general awareness of Māori Data Sovereignty is now widespread to the extent that both the data workforce and Māori communities expect it to be addressed. This rapid spread is due in part to the activities of the Data ILG, TMR and their respective members as well as a number of high profile data issues in the last five years. The combination of public advocacy on policy issues and a large and broadly skilled membership enabled TMR to reach a large and diverse audience very quickly. The numerous presentations and the availability of published material provided readily usable resources with a consistent logic to those interested in moving from advocacy to incorporating Māori Data Sovereignty in their activities.

Māori Data Sovereignty is an idea that will prove to be a permanent part of the policy environment in Aotearoa New Zealand. Government policy is beginning to reflect the everyday acceptance of Māori Data Sovereignty principles within the broader data workforce and Māori communities. As data-relevant policies get revised or created, the policy debates now center on implementation of Māori Data Sovereignty rather than the acceptability of its foundational concepts. Despite these successes, engaging with the policy sector usually produces incremental and narrowly focused change. In Aotearoa New Zealand the policy void was filled by practice, as data practitioners advocated for and created Māori Data Sovereignty practice. Transforming practice within existing policies proved to be a quicker and more responsive way than policy change to begin to address emerging needs of a changing data environment. The combination of the consistency of the underlying principles across multiple domains of changed practice has resulted in emerging policies within specific domains of government beginning to reference data sovereignty. However, it is the prospect of partnership between the Crown and Māori at the level of governance over data that presents the promise of change that is systemic and enduring.

References

A Better Start. (2018). *A Better Start—E Tipu e Rea. Improving the Potential for all Young New Zealanders. Future Strategy 2019—2024*. Auckland: A Better Start. Retrieved from https://www.abetterstart.nz/key-publications/.

Atatoa-Carr, P., & Hudson, M. (2017). *Review of the Metro Auckland Data Sharing Agreement & Proposed Māori Data Governance Framework. Final Report for the Metro Auckland Data Stewardship Group*. National Institute of Demographic and Economic Analysis.

Bakker, C. (2019). *Value of the Census for Māori*. Wellington: Stats NZ. Retrieved from www.stats.govt.nz.

Commission on Human Rights Sub-Commission of Prevention of Discrimination and Protection of Minorities Working Group on Indigenous Populations. (1993). *Mataatua Declaration on Cultural and Intellectual Property Rights of Indigenous Peoples*. Retrieved from http://www.wipo.int/tk/en/databases/creative_heritage/Indigenous/link0002.html.

Cormack, D. (2019). *Submission on the Law Commission Review of the Law Governing the Use of DNA in Criminal Investigations in New Zealand on Behalf of Te Mana Raraunga (Māori Data Sovereignty Network)*. Retrieved from https://www.temanararaunga.Māori.nz/nga-panui.

Data Futures Partnership. (2017). *A Path to Social Licence Guidelines for Trusted Data Use*. Wellington: Data Futures Partnership. Retrieved from https://static1.squarespace.com/static/58e9b10f9de4bb8d1fb5ebbc/t/598d014fdb29d6ff0d50c317/1502413147674/A-Path-to-Social-Licence-Guidelines-for-Trusted-Data-Use-August-2017.pdf.

data.govt.nz. (2017). *Open Government Data Programme*. Retrieved from https://www.data.govt.nz/standards-and-guidance/open-data/open-data-nz/.

digital.govt.nz. (2018). *D7 Group of Digital Nations*. Retrieved from https://www.digital.govt.nz/digital-government/international-partnerships/d7-group-of-digital-nations/.

digital.govt.nz. (2020). *Government Chief Data Steward*. Retrieved from https://www.digital.govt.nz/digital-government/leadership-and-governance/government-chief-data-steward-gcds/. February 10, 2020.

English, B. (2016). *Budget Statement in Parliamentary Debates (HANSARD) FINAL DAILY Thursday*, May 26, 2016. Wellington: New Zealand House of Representatives. Retrieved from https://www.parliament.nz/resource/en-NZ/51HansD_20160526/e7d96b1e9402b66c15658f16bccf7fbc6b13ede8.

Foss, C., & English, B. (2015). *Govt Backs Data Forum's Recommendations*. Ministerial press release February 28, 2015. Wellington: New Zealand Government. Retrieved from https://www.beehive.govt.nz/release/govt-backs-data-forum%E2%80%99s-recommendations.

Government Chief Data Steward. (2018). *Data Strategy and Roadmap for New Zealand*. Wellington: Stats NZ. Retrieved from https://data.govt.nz/assets/Uploads/data-strategy-and-roadmap-dec-18.pdf.

Gulliver, P., Jonas, M., Fanslow, J., McIntosh, T., & Waayer, D. (2018). Surveys, social licence and the Integrated Data Infrastructure. *Aotearoa New Zealand Social Work*, 30(3), 57–71. doi:https://doi.org/10.11157/anzswj-vol30iss3id481.

Harmsworth, G., Awatere, S., & Robb, M. (2016). Indigenous Māori values and perspectives to inform freshwater management in Aotearoa-New Zealand. *Ecology and Society*, 21(4), 9. doi:10.5751/ES-08804-210409.

Health Research Council of New Zealand. (2018). *Te Hao Nui*. Retrieved from https://hrc.govt.nz/resources/research-repository/te-hao-nui.

Health Research Council of New Zealand. (n.d.). *Whāia te Ara Rangahau Hauora Māori Pathways for Māori Health Research*. Auckland: Health Research Council. Retrieved from https://hrc.govt.nz/resources/whaia-te-ara-rangahau-hauora-Māori-pathways-Māori-health-research.

Hudson, M., Farrar, D., & McLean, L. (2016). Tribal data sovereignty: Whakatohea rights and interests. In T. Kukutai, & J. Taylor (eds.), *Indigenous Data Sovereignty: Toward an Agenda*. Canberra: ANU Press.

Hudson, M., Anderson, T., Dewes, T.K., Temara, P., Whaanga, H., & Roa, T. (2018). He Matapihi ki te Mana Raraunga: conceptualising big data through a Māori lens. In H. Whaanga, T.T. Keegan, & M. Apperley (eds.), *He Whare Hangarau Māori—Language, Culture & Technology [E-book]* (pp. 62–71). Hamilton: Te Pua Wānanga ki te Ao, Te Whare Wānanga o Waikato.

ict.govt.nz. (2015). *Government ICT Strategy 2015*. Retrieved from https://www.ict.govt.nz/assets/ICT-Strategy/Government-ICT-Strategy-2015-A3.pdf.

Iwi Chairs Forum. (2019). *Data Iwi Leadership Group Mana Ōrite Agreement*. National Iwi Chairs Forum Quarterly Newsletter, December 2019. Retrieved from https://mailchi.mp/4629b9eff340/quarterly-newsletter-nicf?fbclid=IwAR2R14oafGXymIAri5vkFYJmVWvJSaylHG18S0orKkGaoPvjR1bJmhnOuQA.

Iwi Data Leaders Group. (2019). *Press Release: Data Iwi Leaders Group—Iwi Forging Closer Relationship with Stats NZ*. Retrieved from https://info.scoop.co.nz/Data_Iwi_Leaders_Group.

Jansen, R. (2016). Indigenous data sovereignty: a Māori health perspective. In T. Kukutai, & J. Taylor (eds.), *Indigenous Data Sovereignty: Towards an Agenda*. Canberra: ANU Press.

Kahui Legal. (2016). *Māori Data Sovereignty—Rights, Interests & Obligations Analysis*. Memorandum to the Independent Māori Statutory Board. Auckland: Independent Māori Statutory Board.

Kukutai, T., & Walter, M. (2015). Recognition and indigenizing official statistics: reflections from Aotearoa New Zealand and Australia. *Statistical Journal of the IAOS*, 31(2), 317–326. doi:10.3233/sji-150896.

Kukutai, T., & Taylor, J. (eds.). (2016). *Indigenous Data Sovereignty: Towards an Agenda*. Canberra: ANU Press.

Ministry of Education. (2019). *Te Mataaho-ā-Iwi Iwi Education Data Dashboard A Guide to Understanding the Dashboard*. Wellington: Ministry of Education. Retrieved from https://www.educationcounts.govt.nz/__data/assets/pdf_file/0009/195813/Iwi-Dashboard-User-Guide.pdf.

Ministry of Research Science and Technology. (2007). *Vision Mātauranga. Unlocking the Innovation Potential of Māori Knowledge, Resources and People*. Wellington: Ministry of Research Science and Technology. Retrieved from https://www.mbie.govt.nz/science-and-technology/science-and-innovation/agencies-policies-and-budget-initiatives/vision-matauranga-policy/.

Ministry of Social Development. (2018). *The Privacy, Human Rights and Ethics (PHRaE) Framework*. Wellington: Ministry of Social Development. Retrieved from https://www.msd.govt.nz/documents/about-msd-and-our-work/work-programmes/initiatives/phrae/phrae-on-a-page.pdf.

Ministry of Social Development. (2019). *Te Pae Tata: Draft Māori Strategy and Action Plan for Consultation*. Wellington: Ministry of Social Development. Retrieved from https://www.msd.govt.nz/about-msd-and-our-work/newsroom/2019/te-pae-tata-Māori-strategy-and-action-plan-consultation.html.

National Ethics Advisory Committee. (2019). *National Ethical Standards for Health and Disability Research and Quality Improvement*. Wellington: Ministry of Health. Retrieved from https://neac.health.govt.nz/publications-and-resources/neac-publications/national-ethical-standards-health-and-disability.

New Zealand Data Futures Partnership. (2016). *Exploring Social Licence: A Conversation with New Zealanders About Data Sharing and Use*. Retrieved from http://datafutures.co.nz/assets/Uploads/DFP-Engagement-doc-FINAL.pdf.

New Zealand Data Futures Partnership. (n.d.). *Data Futures Partnership: New Zealand's Data Future*. Retrieved from http://archive.stats.govt.nz/~/media/Statistics/about-us/corporate-publications/cabinet%20papers/nzdf-partnership-overview.pdf.

OECD. (2011). *Society at a Glance 2011: OECD Social Indicators*. Paris: OECD Publishing.

Privacy Commissioner and Chief Government Data Steward. (2018). *Principles for the Safe and Effective Use of Data and Analytics*. Wellington: Office of the Privacy Commissioner and Stats NZ. Retrieved from https://www.privacy.org.nz/assets/Uploads/Principles-for-the-safe-and-effective-use-of-data-and-analytics-guidance3.pdf.

Rainie, S.C., Kukutai, T., Walter, M., Figueroa-Rodriguez, O.L., Walker, J., & Axelsson, P. (2019). Issues in open data: indigenous data sovereignty. In T. Davies, S. Walker, M. Rubinstein, & F. Perini (eds.), *The State of Open Data: Histories and Horizons* (pp. 300–319). Cape Town and Ottawa: African Minds and International Development Research Centre.

Sapere & Covec. (2015). *Data Driven Innovation in New Zealand*. Report Commissioned by Innovation Partnership. Retrieved from https://innovationpartnership.co.nz/app/uploads/2017/04/Data-Driven-Innovation-in-New-Zealand-1-1.pdf.

Savage, T., & Bycroft, C. (2014). *Coverage Assessment in an Administrative Census: A Progress Report on Issues and Methods*. Retrieved from http://archive.stats.govt.nz/~/media/Statistics/surveys-and-methods/methods/research-papers/topss/coverage-assessment-administrative-census.pdf.

Science for Technological Innovation NSC, Data ILG, and Victoria University of Wellington. (2018). *Māori Data Futures—Hui Report*, May 9, 2018. Wellington, NZ: Science for Technological Innovation NSC.

Science for Technological Innovation NSC. (2019). *PM's Chief Science Advisor Says Hui with Māori Experts "Ka rawe!"*. Retrieved from https://www.sftichallenge.govt.nz/news-updates/pms-chief-science-advisor-says-hui-Māori-experts-ka-rawe.

Shackleton, N., D'Souza, S., Sporle, A., Milne, B., & Baker, K. (2020, forthcoming). *Te Pou Tuatahi: Whānau Wellbeing Research, Frameworks and Data Sources*. Wellington: Ministry of Social Development.

Statistics Act 1975. Available at http://www.legislation.govt.nz/act/public/1975/0001/latest/DLM430705.html.

Statistics NZ. (2013). *Feasibility Report: Linked Employer–Employee Data (LEED)*. Wellington: Statistics NZ. Retrieved from http://archive.stats.govt.nz/browse_for_stats/income-and-work/employment_and_unemployment/feasibility-report-leed.aspx.

Statistics New Zealand. (2015). *Crown–Māori Engagement and Statistical Information Needs*. Wellington: Stats NZ. Retrieved from www.stats.govt.nz.

Stats NZ. (2016). *Five Safes Internal Audit Programme*. Retrieved from https://www.stats.govt.nz/integrated-data/integrated-data-infrastructure#data-safe.

Statistics New Zealand. (2017a). *Integrated Data Infrastructure*. Retrieved from http://archive.stats.govt.nz/browse_for_stats/snapshots-of-nz/integrated-data-infrastructure.aspx.

Statistics New Zealand. (2017b). *Experimental Population Estimates from Linked Administrative Data: 2017 Release*. Retrieved from https://www.stats.govt.nz/experimental/experimental-population-estimates-from-linked-administrative-data.

Stats NZ. (2019a). *Fact Sheet. New Approach to Data Governance*. Wellington: Stats NZ. Retrieved from https://www.stats.govt.nz/about-us/data-leadership#governance.

Stats NZ. (2019b). *Aide Memoire to the Minister of Statistics: Stats NZ's Work with Māori on the 2018 Census for Minister Mahuta*. Wellington: Stats NZ. Retrieved from https://statsnz.contentdm.oclc.org/digital/collection/p20045coll25/search.

Stats NZ. (2019c). *Partnering to Increase Māori Participation*. Datability: Adding value to New Zealand's data. Issue 4, April 2019. Retrieved from https://us9.campaign-archive.com/home/?u=99cdc8c5f16e70b0211ff59d9&id=e02da6ed69.

Stats NZ. (2019d). *Towards New Data and Statistics Legislation: Summary of Submissions on 2018 Consultation*. Retrieved from https://www.stats.govt.nz/information-releases/2018-census-totals-by-topic-national-highlights-updated.

Stats NZ. (2020a). *2018 Census Totals by Topic—National Highlights (Updated)*. Retrieved from www.stats.govt.nz.

Stats NZ. (2020b). *Ngā Tikanga Paihere*. Retrieved from www.data.govt.nz.

Tahu Kukutai, T & Donna Cormack, D. (2019). Mana motuhake ā-raraunga: datafication and social science research in Aotearoa. *Kōtuitui: New Zealand Journal of Social Sciences Online*, 14:2, 201–208, doi: https://doi.org/10.1080/1177083X.2019.1648304.

Taylor, J., & Kukutai, T. (2015). *Report to the Academy of the Social Sciences in Australia on the Workshop Data Sovereignty for Indigenous Peoples: Current Practice and Future Needs* (9th–10th July 2015). Retrieved from https://socialsciences.org.au/publications/data-sovereignty-for-Indigenous-peoples-current-practice-and-future-needs/.

Te Arawhiti. (2019). *Māori Crown Relations Capability Framework for the Public Service*. Wellington: Te Arawhiti—Office for Māori Crown Relations. Retrieved from https://www.tearawhiti.govt.nz/assets/Tools-and-Resources/Māori-Crown-Relations-Capability-Framework-Guide-Bibliography.pdf.

Te Mana Raraunga. (2016). *Te Mana Raraunga Charter*. Retrieved from https://www.temanararaunga.Māori.nz/s/Te-Mana-Raraunga-Charter-Final-Approved.pdf.

Te Mana Raraunga. (2017). *Te Mana Raraunga Statement on Social Licence*. Retrieved from https://static1.squarespace.com/static/58e9b10f9de4bb8d1fb5ebbc/t/5924791cbf629a1367a65717/1495562526902/TMR+-+Statement+on+Social+and+Cultural+License.pdf.

Te Mana Raraunga. (2018a). *Submission on the Review of the 1975 Statistics Act*. Retrieved from https://static1.squarespace.com/static/58e9b10f9de4bb8d1fb5ebbc/t/5e79c36e04eae83ab4b83069/1585038192779/Submission+Oct+2018_+Te+Mana+Raraunga_Review+of+the+Statistics+Act.pdf.

Te Mana Raraunga. (2018b). *Principles of Māori Data Sovereignty*. Retrieved from https://www.temanararaunga.Māori.nz/nga-rauemi.

Te Mana Raraunga. (2019). *Te Mana Raraunga Statement on Independent Review of New Zealand's 2018 Census. Treaty-Based Data Governance and Partnership Crucial*.

Retrieved from https://static1.squarespace.com/static/58e9b10f9de4bb8d1fb5ebbc/t/5d547e42b346370001309d3f/1565818438747/Te+Mana+Raraunga+-+Statement+on+Independent+Review:for+release.pdf.

Te Mana Raraunga. (2020). *Submission on the Review of the Draft Algorithm Charter*. Retrieved from https://static1.squarespace.com/static/58e9b10f9de4bb8d1fb5ebbc/t/5e79c0fb3ccc1d093689c06d/1585037565865/TMR+Submission+on+the+Algorithm+charter+Feb+2020.pdf.

Tuhuno Trust. (2017). *Sharing Information for Wellbeing*. Hamilton. Tuhuno Trust. Retrieved from https://www.tuhono.net/.

Waitangi Tribunal. (2011). *Ko Aotearoa Tēnei: A Report into Claims Concerning New Zealand Law and Policy Affecting Māori Culture and Identity* (Vols. 1–2, Wai 262). Wellington, New Zealand: Government Printer.

6 Indigenous self-determination and data governance in the Canadian policy context

Robyn K. Rowe, Julie R. Bull and Jennifer D. Walker

Introduction

In 2015, Canada's 23rd federally elected Prime Minister, Justin Trudeau, took the nation's stage and vowed to make reconciliation with First Nations, Inuit, and Métis—the three distinct groups of Indigenous Peoples in Canada—a top priority (Galloway, 2015). The Trudeau Liberal government was not the first to address the well-being of Indigenous Peoples as a matter of national concern (Royal Commission on Aboriginal Peoples [RCAP], 1996). Rather, they came into power in Canada at a time when years of research had resulted in a range of recommendations and reports that laid not only the foundation but provided a structure for successful nation-to-nation rebuilding for Indigenous Peoples across the country (RCAP, 1996; TRC [Truth and Reconciliation], 2015). The map toward reconciliation was/is clearly marked and federal-level follow-through continues to be all that is needed. Trudeau's commitment included enacting the Truth and Reconciliation's *Call to Action* number 43 that calls on the federal, provincial, territorial and municipal governments "to fully adopt and implement the *United Nations Declaration on the Rights of Indigenous Peoples* [UNDRIP] as the framework for reconciliation" (TRC, 2015, p. 325; Galloway, 2015). More on the TRC will be shared within this chapter. This promise, in turn, reinforced a federal recognition that Indigenous Peoples' have the right to maintain, control, protect and develop Indigenous knowledge(s), information and institutions.

Since his election, Prime Minister Trudeau has repeatedly fortified his promises (Ketonen, 2019; Philpott, 2018); while onlookers across the country—Indigenous and non—wait patiently for a meaningful demonstration of this commitment. Unfortunately, despite the rhetoric in federal politics regarding nation-to-nation relationships and efforts to mobilize reconciliation, little has been done to actually implement the Calls to Action (TRC, 2015) or the UNDRIP (2016). In fact, many Indigenous land defenders and nation supporters are out of patience and are struggling to see Canada's commitment toward reconciliation come to fruition. The rights and jurisdiction of Hereditary Chiefs, who are part of pre-colonial Indigenous governance and leadership structures, are being actively undermined by corporations, with government support, resulting in ongoing threats to land water and traditional Indigenous territories (Unist'ot'en Camp, 2020; Indigenous Corporate Training Inc, 2016). Meanwhile, in other ways across the country, individuals, communities and organizations—Indigenous and allied—have been working toward creating the conditions, and building upon many previously formed foundations, in order to mobilize and support Indigenous sovereignty over Indigenous data, policies and programs.

A brief history of policy in Canada

For many thousands of years, prior to settler arrival, Indigenous Peoples were rich in culture, traditions and languages and lived on the lands that are now called Canada (TRC, 2015). With European arrival and settler expansion, policies were created that stripped First Nations, Inuit and Métis of this diversity while treaties were designed to cede and surrender Indigenous land to the Crown (TRC, 2015). In what has been described as *cultural genocide*, settler policies were aimed at assimilation and Indigenous elimination (TRC, 2015). These policies were designed to disempower Indigenous governments, undermine inherent Indigenous rights and lead to the surrendering of Indigenous traditional territories (TRC, 2015). This immense cultural disruption lasted for over a century and continues to have an impact on First Nations, Inuit, and Métis in Canada. This impact includes an increasingly widening gap in quality of health care experiences and higher rates of illness and disease (Smylie & Firestone, 2015; Harris et al., 2011).

The *Indian Act* (1985) was established in 1876 and is still a large part of the conversation for Indigenous Peoples around health equity and beyond because of its devastating and ongoing effects. The *Indian Act* "set the stage for a debilitating, systemic public policy that continues, in the modern-day, to powerfully shape patterns of Aboriginal health, social inequity and access to health care and other services" (Richmond & Cook, 2016, p. 4). In fact, despite the current political discourse toward reconciliation, the federal *Indian Act* continues to define who is and who is not Indian[1] under Canadian law (TRC, 2015; *Indian Act*, 1985).

The government of Canada has accepted its failure to support the health and well-being of First Nations, Inuit, and Métis and has even recognized its shame on the global stage at the UN General Assembly (Philpott, 2018). Canada has openly acknowledged that it has failed to respect Indigenous Peoples' inherent right to self-determination by subjecting First Nations, Inuit and Métis to "laws, policies, and practices based on domination and assimilation" (Philpott, 2018, p. 1650). Enactments of these laws led to child welfare policies, assimilation policies and enfranchisement[2] policies (*Gradual Civilization Act*, 1857). In fact, in 1920, the then Deputy Minister of Indian Affairs, Duncan Campbell Scott stated that "our object is to continue until there is not a single Indian in Canada that has not been absorbed into the body politic and there is no Indian question, and no Indian Department" (as cited in the Royal Commission on Aboriginal Peoples, 1996, p. 577). These ideas were (and in some ways still are) so ingrained in social and political thinking that enfranchisement was even referred to as a privilege within the *Indian Act* (RCAP, 1996). *An Act to Encourage the Gradual Civilization of the Indian Tribes in Canada of 1857*, more commonly known as the *Gradual Civilization Act* states (1857):

> It is desirable to encourage the progress of Civilization among the Indian Tribes in this Province, and the gradual removal of all legal distinctions between them and Her Majesty's other Canadian Subjects, and to facilitate the acquisition of property and of the rights accompanying it, by such Individual Members of the said Tribes as shall be found to desire such encouragement and to have deserved it. (1)

Acting on these policies led to the forced removal of First Nations, Inuit and Métis children from their homes and away from the cultural and linguistic influence of their families and communities (TRC, 2015). In fact, Canada has repeatedly highlighted that the effects of the residential and day school systems (where many First Nations, Inuit and Métis children were taken to be assimilated), its policies and the "historical denial of the rights of Indigenous peoples is directly linked to socioeconomic disparities, including poor health outcomes" (Philpott, 2018, p. 1650). Systemic policies continue to impact Indigenous lives while efforts to reconcile are further challenged by broken promises on the part of governments which reinforce Indigenous mistrust of the health care system (Vogal, 2015).

In order for policies and programs to offer effective solutions to the complex health and social realities that have resulted from ongoing colonization in Canada, quality information is key. Unfortunately, Indigenous health information is often produced and perpetuated by non-Indigenous Peoples for non-Indigenous health policy makers, which results in fragmentation and a continued need for Indigenous activism. For instance, under the provisions of the *Constitution Act, 1867* and the *Canada Health Act, 1984*, health care is a provincial responsibility in Canada. However, under the *Indian Health Policy, 1979* and the *Indian Act*, 1985, health care services for First Nations and Inuit are a federal responsibility (Government of Canada, 2019, 2014; *Canada Health Act, 1985*; *Constitution Act, 1867*). The result has been legislative confusion, intergovernmental disputes, and little-to-no accountability on the part of provincial and federal levels of government. A notable and high profile story highlighting the resulting unnecessary bureaucratic delays is the story of Jordan Anderson, a First Nations child whose family lived in a First Nations community who died waiting for care while federal and provincial governments disagreed about who would be responsible for paying for his health services (Government of Canada, 2020; Assembly of First Nations, 2018; MacDonald & Attaran, 2007). This resulted in the adoption of Jordan's Principle, which emphasizes the importance of prioritizing a child's health care needs at the first point of health care access, and the development of associated policies to put this principle into practice.

Regrettably, reporting on progress with respect to closing health and social gaps between Indigenous populations and other populations in Canada is often reduced to "checking the boxes" on Indigenous health disparities and fails to acknowledge the worldviews and priorities of Indigenous Peoples as autonomous individuals and self-determining collectives (Richmond & Cook, 2016). Despite the overemphasis on negative findings and persistent Indigenous health inequities, First Nations, Inuit and Métis are leading efforts to heal their people and communities through Indigenous-centered use of Indigenous data (Walker et al., 2017). For instance, in some provinces across the country, Indigenous health data is being governed by Indigenous Peoples. In Ontario, administrative health data about First Nations Peoples that is collected and held with the rest of the provinces' administrative health information is governed by First Nations through data governance agreements and internal policies put in place by the data custodian (Walker et al., 2017, 2018). More will be discussed on regionally specific Indigenous health data management throughout this chapter.

Chapter overview

In this chapter, we recognize the historical and ongoing impacts of colonialism (see, for example, TRC, 2015; National Inquiry into Missing and Murdered Indigenous Women and Girls [MMIWG], 2019; Young, 2015) and we take the position that, while colonialism is ongoing and the intergenerational trauma that has resulted from it are devastating, Indigenous Peoples have been and continue to be resilient Peoples who have worked tirelessly to preserve and advance self-determination. Indigenous groups in Canada have laid the foundations for research processes and policies that highlight Indigenous ownership and stewardship of Indigenous data. We highlight this as a critical time to prioritize how Indigenous leadership will translate those Indigenous data governance (ID-GOV) principles into Indigenous Data Sovereignty (ID-SOV) practice and effectively use data for governance. Indigenous groups recognize the importance of good information governance and the potential of information to guide improvements in policy that lead to better health and well-being outcomes for First Nations, Inuit and Métis across the country. In this chapter, we explore the current ID-SOV landscape in Canada and policies that impact ID-GOV and effective policy development. The timing of this work is critical and necessary as Indigenous Peoples in Canada continue to reclaim, regain and restore rights to self-determination, autonomy and self-government.

We begin this chapter in a time of post-contact; in a time already climatized to the *Constitution Act of 1867*; in a time when the *Indian Act* of 1876 and federal legislative authority over Indigenous Peoples already exists; in a time following the closure of the last of the residential schools (in 1996); and in a time when the federal government has publicly apologized (in 2008) and taken ownership for creating the discriminatory policies that led to these (and other) systems of oppression and assimilation (Indigenous and Northern Affairs Canada [INAC], 2010). We begin this chapter in a time when Canada has stated its support for the UNDRIP (INAC, 2017); a time when the Truth and Reconciliation Commission of Canada's Calls to Action have been federally acknowledged; and elementary, secondary and post-secondary schools across the country are formally recognizing the legacy of residential schools and students are learning about Canada's colonial history (Laanela, 2016). We begin this chapter in a time when, at

Indigenous self-determination and data governance 85

minimum, the perception of resilience, resurgence and rejuvenation is flourishing. Conversations around Indigenous sovereignty and governance are being heard in broadening public discourse and movements are happening in different ways across the country. We begin this chapter *today*.

Situating ourselves: research is relational

The rigid structure of Western institutions, research ethics boards (REBs) and research-funding mechanisms can be contradictory to what is needed for ethical research involving Indigenous Peoples. The systems are historically built on, and maintained by, colonial culture and influences, and often lack meaningful integration of Indigenous epistemologies and sciences. However, Indigenous individuals, researchers and organizations are seeing the benefits of using those systems to access Indigenous data and incorporating Indigenous knowledges into the use of those data (University of Manitoba, 2019; Tui'kn Partnership, 2015). In fact, the integration of Indigenous definitions of health and wellness within data ecosystems can enhance mainstream definitions of illness as more than just 'the absence of disease" by incorporating a whole health model that looks at the emotional, physical, mental and spiritual health of an individual (Castellano, 2015; King et al., 2009; Hart, 2002). Within this chapter, we draw on our combined experiences as Indigenous women and researchers to bring our shared knowledges together to articulate components of the current landscape in Canada regarding ID-SOV and its relationship to policy. Based on our shared and extensive backgrounds in Indigenous Data Sovereignty, health policy, ethics and research governance, we discuss the integration of Indigenous knowledges and the practical application of data sovereignty by First Nations, Inuit and Métis across Canada.

More than two decades of policy promising reconciliation

Reconciliation processes over the past two decades have pushed governments and the general Canadian public to acknowledge the impact of colonial assimilation policies (TRC, 2015). In this light, First Nations, Inuit and Métis and Canadian policy makers are grappling with how to navigate and improve Canada's complex Indigenous health policy landscape. Systemic policies rooted in the *Indian Act* are so embedded within health and social structures for Indigenous Peoples and communities that incremental improvements seem futile and widespread overhaul feels urgently needed. First Nations, Inuit and Métis have actively contributed to a number of federal, provincial and territorial efforts that have repeatedly made the promise of renewed and improved relationships between Indigenous Peoples and the Government of Canada (RCAP, 1996; TRC, 2015).

RCAP, TRC and MMIWG

In the wake of a land dispute that heightened tensions and made national headlines in the summer of 1990 between Mohawk (First Nation) protestors and the town of

Oka, Quebec in Canada, the Royal Commission on Aboriginal Peoples (RCAP) was established (RCAP, 1996; Goodleaf, 1995). In 1996, RCAP released a five-volume, 4000-page report with over 400 recommendations and set out a 20-year plan that aimed to *"renew* the original relationship and to restore the balance that it represented" between Indigenous people, the Government of Canada, and non-Indigenous people in Canada (RCAP, 1996, p. 39). The report documented and acknowledged Canada's efforts to assimilate and dominate First Nations, Inuit and Métis and laid the foundation for Canada's commitment to renewed relationships over the next 20 years. In fact, the Commission recommended "that the federal government establish a public inquiry to investigate the origin and effects of residential school policies and to recommend remedial action" (The Institute on Governance, 1997, p. 2).

Twelve years later, in 2008, the Truth and Reconciliation Commission of Canada was formed. This positive movement arose not as a result of the RCAP recommendations to the federal government, but rather as a result of a large class action lawsuit and civil litigation led by Indigenous Peoples who attended an Indian residential school (Bak et al., 2017; TRC, 2015).

The TRC came with a mandate to inform all people in Canada of the truth of the lived experiences of the children who survived the residential school system (TRC, 2015). It also aimed to provide an opportunity to guide and inspire healing for survivors, their families and future generations through truth telling; again, in an effort to reconcile relationships between Indigenous persons and the rest of Canada (TRC, 2015). The TRC's work also culminated in a final report that was released in 2015 that placed responsibility for injustices faced by First Nations, Inuit and Métis on the intentionally assimilationist, and discriminatory policies that formed the foundation of the colonial agenda and successive government policies.

According to often-cited and disparaging statistics on Indigenous Peoples in Canada, significant negative health gaps between Indigenous and non-Indigenous groups persist (AFN, 2017; TRC, 2015; King et al., 2009). Indigenous worldviews and traditional medicines continue to be alienated from mainstream health care (MacDonald & Steenbeek, 2015) and much of the data collected on or about Indigenous groups is done without input from Indigenous Peoples (Canadian Alliance for Healthy Hearts and Minds First Nations Cohort Research Team, 2019). Within the TRC (2015), Calls to Action number 18 and 19 specifically address the current state of Indigenous Peoples' health as a "direct result of previous Canadian government policies, including residential schools" (p. 160). The TRC advises government bodies to "recognize and implement the health-care rights of Aboriginal people as identified in international law and constitutional law, and under the Treaties" (p.160). Further, the Calls recognize the need to "establish measurable goals to identify and close the gaps in health outcomes ... in consultation with" Indigenous Peoples (TRC, 2015, p. 161). The TRC "mainstreamed" conversations about what Indigenous Peoples experienced for the more than 150 years that residential schools were operating across the country and laid out 94 Calls to Action as a new start on a path toward reconciliation in Canada.

The TRC (2015) called upon all federal, provincial, territorial and Indigenous governments, educational and religious institutions, and all persons in Canada to develop measures to improve the lives of Indigenous Peoples, including health, wellness, education, justice and cultural renewal. While federal-level policy has not officially been changed to reflect the TRC or the government's commitment to reconciliation, the wide-reaching effect of the TRC Calls to Action has resulted in improved policies at various organizational levels. For instance, the Canadian Public Health Association (CPHA)— which is an independent voice for the country on matters of health and that speaks up for individuals to all levels of government—has prioritized reconciliation by embedding the recommendations of the TRC into its policies (CPHA, 2019).

More recently, the *Final Report* of the National Inquiry into Missing and Murdered Indigenous Women and Girls was released (MMIWG, 2019). Intergenerational trauma, racism, abuse, ongoing economic and social challenges, and violence were prevalent themes discussed within the document. The *Final Report* also highlights how the current political system is failing to protect Indigenous Peoples. Calls for Justice highlight the ongoing need for cultural renewal and prioritizes appropriate information gathering and reporting on the number of MMIWG. This document affirms that persistent and deliberate human and Indigenous rights violations is the number one reason for the high rates of violence against women, girls and two-spirit, lesbian, gay, bisexual, transgender, queer, questioning, intersex, and asexual (2SLGBTQQIA+) people (MMIWG, 2019).

RCAP, TRC and MMIWG all reflect moments in recent Canadian history when the failure of colonial and subsequent government policies required the establishment of agendas designed to return sovereignty and governance to Indigenous Peoples. These are uplifting examples of Canada acknowledging the inherent rights of Indigenous Peoples; yet, in practice, the true implementation of these priorities and recommendations continues to be met by challenges, false hope and false promises. Each of the reports outline guiding principles grounded in First Nations, Inuit and Métis priorities. Examining each document provides a glimpse through time at social movements and evolving conversations which have led to discussions around data and sovereignty. Each document was a necessity of its time to help address health and wellness gaps for Indigenous Peoples and to offer guiding principles that advance national priorities. Yet today, we see an eerily similar case of tension between Indigenous land defenders, nation supports and the Government of Canada happening that echoes many of the same tensions that happened 30 years ago in Oka except this time protests are happening in support of Indigenous rights, across the country (Unist'ot'en Camp, 2020).

First Nations Principles of OCAP®

In the mid-1990s, structural and administrative challenges associated with the primary collection of Indigenous data were becoming clearer, resulting in an increasing dependence on the use of secondary data within research (Saku, 1999).

Meanwhile, ongoing amendments to the *Indian Act* were resulting in changes to who is and who is not considered a "status Indian" in the eyes of the government (*Indian Act*, 1985). Indigenous data gaps were being exacerbated by questions around identity and it was becoming increasingly challenging to gather accurate census data for individuals "on-reserve" (FNIGC, 2016). In an effort to address this gap, the federal government established the First Nations and Inuit Regional Health Survey (RHS) in order to specifically collect data from on-reserve populations (FNIGC, 2016). As a result, space was made within Canadian research environments that had the potential to reflect the socioeconomic aspirations, governance and jurisdiction of First Nations and Inuit in the country.

Recognizing data as a renewable and valuable resource with the potential to inflict policy change, the First Nations data governance movement began through the assertion of OCAP® principles, which outline the rights of First Nations to own, control, access and possess First Nations data (FNIGC, 2016, 2018). The First Nations Principles of OCAP® sparked a catalyst in the advancement of data sovereignty and governance for Indigenous groups across the country and beyond. These principles established clear expectations that have been essential to redirecting funding and efforts to ensure that First Nations have resources for data collection and storage at national and regional levels (FNIGC, 2016, 2018).

Learning and growing from OCAP®

Guided by OCAP® principles, in the year 2000, the Organization for the Advancement of Aboriginal Peoples Health which was later renamed the National Aboriginal Health Organization (NAHO) was established as an Indigenous-led and Indigenous-controlled not-for-profit organization with the mission of improving the physical, mental, emotional, social and spiritual health of Indigenous Peoples, families and communities (NAHO, 2017). NAHO recognized the complexities of Indigenous groups and established three centers: the First Nations Center, the Inuit Tuttarvingat and the Métis Center. In keeping with the priorities of Indigenous self-determination, NAHO worked to advance the individual and community needs of First Nations, Inuit and Métis through these three established centers.

Over time, the Inuit Qaujisarvingat (*kow-yee-sar-ving-at*) knowledge and research ethics priorities were transferred to the Inuit Tapiriit Kanatami (ITK), which prioritizes the advancement of Inuit self-determination at a national level in Canada (NAHO, 2017). ITK developed the National Inuit Strategy on Research (NISR) which lays the path toward improved policies, programs and services that address social, cultural, political and environmental priorities facing the Inuit. Specifically, the NISR makes recommendations to be addressed by political leaders that are working toward advancing reconciliation. These recommendations aim to advance Inuit governance in research, enhance the ethical conduct of research, align funding with Inuit research priorities, ensure Inuit access, ownership, and control over data and information and build capacity in Inuit Nunangat research (ITK, 2020, 2019).

Within NAHO, the Métis Center was a Métis-controlled national center that was dedicated to the improved health and wellness of all Métis in Canada (NAHO, 2017). Principles on ethical Métis research have been available for at least a decade that speak to reciprocity, relationships, respect, diversity, safety, inclusivity and appropriate outcomes (NAHO, 2017). In June of 2019, in what Prime Minister Justin Trudeau highlights as a "model of what reconciliation can be" (The Canadian Press, 2019a), self-governance agreements were signed between the federal government in Ottawa and the Métis nations of Alberta, Ontario and Saskatchewan (The Canadian Press, 2019b). Ideally, this historic step could mean that the Métis nations of these three provinces can improve policy and data environments, increase access to programs and services and ultimately improve Métis health and wellness.

NAHO was an internationally recognized producer of collaborative, community-led initiatives that included research and information on Indigenous individuals, families and communities. Core funding for NAHO's programming was provided by Health Canada until funding was cut in the 2012 federal budget which also led to the elimination of NAHO's centers (NAHO, 2017). While many of the programs from the NAHO centers were transferred to other established organizations, the elimination of NAHO and its centers is, unfortunately, another striking example of the federal government's failure to sustain meaningful commitments to reconciliation. It highlights the government's failures to honor Indigenous health priorities, to stand by their own apology for past government policies (INAC, 2010) and to follow through on their own commitments to improved relationship, reconciliation and improved health for Indigenous people (RCAP, 1996).

Impediments to the full implementation of OCAP®

Despite Canada's internationally recognized strengths in quality health care and public policy, challenges persist. Legislative obstacles continue to burden the operationalization of true data governance for First Nations, Inuit and Métis. This is demonstrated within the federal government's current relationship and imposed responsibility toward First Nations (*Indian Act*, 1985). Because of this relationship, "Canada collects and holds a significant amount of information on First Nations people" (FNIGC, 2014, p. 2). This information is regulated by the *Access to Information Act* (Government of Canada, 1985a), the *Privacy Act* (Government of Canada, 1985b) and the *Library and Archives of Canada Act* (2004). Gaps in these policies as they relate to First Nations governance and the full implementation of OCAP® principles lead to unfavorable conditions which limit First Nations' authority over information that is relevant to First Nations individuals and communities (see FNIGC, 2014). While these gaps have been pointed out specifically by the First Nations Information Governance Center as being impediments for the implementation of OCAP®, holes within privacy and information legislation that limit governance and autonomy impact *all* Indigenous lives and communities.

Regardless, Indigenous Peoples and organizations are partnering with scholars across the country to advance community engagement processes that lead to improved Indigenous data governance. The ripple effects of Indigenous Peoples asserting our inherent rights over our data has expanded beyond the First Nations' Principles of OCAP® within a space that has largely been dominated by settler worldviews. It has expanded to incorporate Indigenous-led and Indigenous-based research protocols, Indigenous jurisdictional control and a growing momentum toward best practices for how to conduct research using First Nations, Inuit and Métis data (Canadian Institutes of Health Research, Natural Sciences and Engineering Research Council of Canada, & Social Sciences and Humanities Research Council, 2018; FNIGC, 2016; TRC, 2015; RCAP, 1996). The First Nations Principles of OCAP® began by setting the standard for First Nations research and continues to guide how First Nations' data should be collected, used, stored and shared (FNIGC, 2016). Today, OCAP® continues to advance and has led to growing relationships between Indigenous groups and Indigenous researchers and allies who recognize the need for respectful and relevant research approaches that go beyond mainstream research approaches (see, for example, University of Manitoba, 2019; Pyper et al., 2018; Walker et al., 2018; Tui'kn Partnership, 2015).

Assessing Indigenous data quality in Canada

Following decades of work on Indigenous governance and gaining momentum in the wake of the Government of Canada's stated commitment to reconciliation and relationship building, First Nations, Inuit and Métis governance organizations are working toward strengthening Indigenous data governance, capacity and research innovation (see Walker et al., 2018; Smylie et al., 2018). Indigenous communities and organizations are reclaiming and asserting control over Indigenous data through the enactment of information governance at regional-specific levels. However, deficiencies in data quality, data relevance and data infrastructure continue to exist within First Nation, Inuit and Métis statistics (Smylie & Firestone, 2015).

Indigenous health information is often lacking consistent, inclusive and reliable information on Indigenous identity (Smylie & Firestone, 2015). This is largely because of the diversity of Indigenous groups within Canada and a lack of Indigenous identifiers within national health information.

While proxy Indigenous identification based on geographic location has been used in some research, this method is not as effective as having built-in Indigenous identifiers and geographic location is more effective for some Indigenous groups than others (Smylie & Firestone, 2015) While First Nations, Inuit and Métis make up the three distinct groups of Indigenous people in Canada, there are many sub-populations within these groups. Some groups are more likely to reside in different regions of the country, for example Inuit in northern regions and First Nations people on reserves designated by the *Indian Act*. In addition, different groups fall under varying degrees of federal, provincial and territorial jurisdiction (Smylie & Firestone, 2015). Federal, constitutional and treaty obligations add additional layers of complexity and potential fragmentation. An inability to link across multiple datasets that contain vital information about Indigenous identity, health services and determinants of health presents further challenges to the quality of Indigenous health data ecosystems (Smylie et al., 2018). These data deficits have led to prolonged challenges for Indigenous and non-Indigenous organizations, systems and services who are working to prioritize the health care needs of First Nations, Inuit and Métis. These points speak to Canada's long history of assimilatory practices and the "historic indifference to cultural specificity" (FNIGC, 2019, p. 56).

Governance in action

Currently, there is no cohesive or collective ID-SOV movement that includes all Indigenous groups in Canada. However, First Nations, Inuit and Métis peoples, communities and organizations across the country are working toward aligning ethical tensions and data sovereignty priorities with community, individual and collective worldviews. In an age of complex and rapidly changing digital ecosystems and big data, Indigenous Peoples are increasingly aware of the power of data as a resource that has far-reaching ethical, legal, medical and policy implications. More and more Indigenous groups are guiding data-driven advocacy and policy development. Indigenous and non-Indigenous Peoples are collectively recognizing and most-importantly, operationalizing Indigenous worldviews in order to promote the appropriate use and protection of First Nations, Inuit and Métis data.

In prioritizing data collection opportunities, Indigenous groups across Canada have advanced data stewardship and health data initiatives through technological advancements, unique partnerships and formalized data sharing agreements. First Nations, Inuit and Métis are each working at creating guidelines that offer best practices for how to conduct research using their nation-specific data. This is demonstrated by numerous efforts happening across the country. For instance, guided by the OCAP® principles, the Mustimuhw Community Electronic Medical Record (CEMR) (pronounced Moose-tee-muk) is a First Nations-owned health information system that is First Nations-designed and community based (Mustimuhw Information Solutions, n.d.). Currently, the Mustimuhw CEMR is being used by First Nations, health services and health authorities across the country in Alberta, British Columbia, Saskatchewan, Manitoba and Ontario (Mustimuhw Information Solutions, n.d.).

In Nova Scotia, the Tui'kn Partnership is a health collaborative that includes five First Nations communities on Cape Breton Island and is aimed at promoting joint planning that respects the mutual interests of the individuals, families and communities involved (Tui'kn Partnership, 2015). Further, understanding the value of data linkage in relation to improved health policy and positive health outcomes, the Unama'ki Client Registry through the Tui'kn Partnership has led to governance through data sharing agreements between the five involved First Nations, the Nova Scotia Department of Health and Wellness, and Health Canada. The Unama'ki Client Registry is the first community-owned, locally designed registry of its kind in Canada (Tui'kn Partnership, 2015). In Newfoundland and Labrador, Indigenous

Administrative Data Identifier Standard is setting and prioritizing administrative Indigenous health data quality standards for First Nations, Inuit and Métis in Newfoundland and Labrador (Department of Health and Community Services Newfoundland and Labrador Center for Health Information, 2017).

In Ontario, relationship building between ICES (a research institute that houses health-related data for Ontario), the Chiefs of Ontario (an advocacy and action body for the 133 federally recognized First Nations communities in Ontario), and other First Nations communities and organizations in Ontario has led to unique governance agreements and the linking of the Indian Register (includes status First Nations persons who are registered under the *Indian Act*) to the databases that house routinely collected provincial health administrative data (Pyper et al., 2018; Walker et al., 2017, 2018). This has led to research that has the capacity to uncover the status of health priorities that are unique to status First Nations Peoples living on and off reserve in Ontario, including diabetes (Slater et al., 2019; Walker et al., 2020, 2018), cancer (Chiefs of Ontario et al., 2017), opioid use (Eibl et al., 2017), aging (Walker et al., 2019) and mortality (Mamow Ahyamowen Partnership, 2019).

The First Nations Health and Social Secretariat of Manitoba (FNHSSM, 2019) prioritized health governance over health systems planning, policy development and health research. In 2019, a partnership between the Manitoba Center for Health Policy and FNHSSM resulted in the successful release of a report on the health of First Nations Peoples in Manitoba (University of Manitoba, 2019). This report is the result of formal research partnerships, information sharing agreements and First Nations health data linkage, "these agreements are historic in the formal recognition of First Nation data governance, in which First Nations exercise their inherent right to self-determination through oversight of their own data" (Katz et al., 2019, p. 3). In British Columbia, First Nations' Data Governance Initiative has established priorities around data and information governance that adhere to the need for timely access to accurate information (BCFNDGI, n.d.). The Alberta First Nations Information Governance Center (AFNIGC) upholds the principles of OCAP® and provides regular information, training, data collection, analysis and dissemination of that information through regularly released factsheets for and by Alberta First Nations (AFNIGC, 2015).

In the absence of a collective ID-SOV movement, these important local and regional movements continue to advance data governance and prioritize data sovereignty for First Nations, Inuit and Métis. Leaning on the best practices, policies, guidelines and priorities of other nations across the country can help to ensure that data can be used *by*, *for* and *with* Indigenous populations in ways that foster self-determination and well-being for First Nations, Inuit and Métis individuals, families and communities.

Indigenous Data Sovereignty in Canada today: a work in progress

Efforts Across the country highlight policy shifts that enable increased Indigenous control over Indigenous research and data through regional and local partnerships.

Indigenous and non-Indigenous individuals, communities and organizations are actively pursuing change and rising to the challenge of applying current ID-SOV and ID-GOV principles and priorities throughout their work. Many of these regional efforts rely on the strong foundation set by RCAP, the TRC and UNDRIP as guides and supports for the path forward. It is safe to say that Indigenous Data Sovereignty is a work in progress in Canada.

Many Indigenous scholars are feeling the landscape shift as precedent-setting priorities such as the Articles in the UNDRIP, the Calls to Action in the TRC, and the Calls for Justice in the MMIWG report are being recognized by federal, provincial, territorial and municipal-level governments. Yet, bold statements and government commitments to reconcile have not translated into the kind of national-level policy change and development that is needed to truly advance reconciliation. Data in the form of regularly collected administrative health care information have the capacity to create change by identifying health patterns, risks and trends and targeting specific programs that can help move populations to healing. Yet, despite this ongoing recognition, in the year 2020, many First Nations, Inuit and Métis communities lack access to "the minimum standards for the survival, dignity, and well-being" (UNDRIP, 2016) through appropriate health care, safe drinking water and equitable education.

Ultimately, a stronger commitment on the part of the federal government is needed to improve Indigenous health and the full implementation of ID-SOV principles in Canada. It is widely recognized that Indigenous priorities in urban, rural and remote First Nations, Inuit and Métis communities continue to be unaddressed (College of Family Physicians in Canada, the Indigenous Physicians Association of Canada, and the Society of Rural Physicians of Canada, 2019), even as we enter the year 2020, nearly two and a half decades after the recommendations of the RCAP. Yet, it is hard to forget that 30 years ago, conversations around information ownership, control and access of data for First Nations, Inuit and Métis were only just whispers. Today, these principles are widely recognized and increasingly understood. It is our hope that we will look back in 30 years at the road we have not yet traveled and see that Indigenous leaders are harnessing the power of data to inform their governance to impact nation-to-nation government policy. On the journey toward Indigenous Data Sovereignty and governance in Canada, it is empowering to see the ripple effects that small acts of sovereignty and governance are having across our nations and populations.

What is clear is that Indigenous-led initiatives are lighting the way forward for Indigenous Data Sovereignty and governance in Canada. Indigenous-led experience in developing Community EMRs such as Mustimuhw, and data linkage agreements such as the partnership between ICES and the Chiefs of Ontario, or the Unama'ki Client Registry generates new Indigenous knowledge that can be shared to help other Indigenous nations across Canada in their journeys to data sovereignty. Through measures that ensure autonomy and self-determination, the analysis of large datasets can lead to quality health care, can promote safe communities, and increase the cultural, educational and recreational resources available to First Nations, Inuit and Métis. Perhaps it is time to recognize that a new approach to policy development in Canada is needed. With the amount of research and information available today through the many initiatives that have been ongoing for over 20 years, it is no longer a conversation about complexity. Priorities and policy suggestions outlined within the RCAP, the UNDRIP, the TRC and the National Inquiry into MMIWG have acted as vessels of active resistance. Indigenous nations know that the path forward is complex and have already contributed to the plan for how to address this. It is time to force the production of policy where Indigenous Peoples are equal collaborators with the government throughout the policy production process. It is time for First Nations, Inuit and Métis communities to define what nation-to-nation rebuilding looks like. But most importantly, *today*, it is time for action.

Notes

1 Indian is a legal term that was imposed on First Nations, Inuit and Métis by the Government of Canada and continues to be used within legal documents today such as the *Indian Act*.
2 As part of an assimilatory practice, the *Gradual Civilization Act* of 1857 was designed as a way for status Indians (under the *Indian Act*) to enfranchise themselves by surrendering their legal and ancestral identities (Crey, 2009).

References

Alberta First Nations Information Governance Centre. (2015). *Welcome to the Alberta First Nations Information Governance Centre*. http://www.afnigc.ca/main/index.php?id=home.

Assembly of First Nations. (February, 2017). *The First Nations Health Transformation Agenda*. https://www.afn.ca/uploads/files/fnhta_final.pdf.

Assembly of First Nations. (2018). *Accessing Jordan's Principle: A Resource for First Nations Parents, Caregivers, Families and Communities*. https://www.afn.ca/uploads/Social_Development/Jordan%27s%20Principle%20Handbook%202019_en.pdf.

Bak, G., Bradford, T., Loyer, J., & Walker, E. (2017). Four views on archival decolonization inspired by the TRC's calls to action. *Fonds d'Archives*, (1). doi:10.29173/fa3.

British Columbia First Nations' Data Governance Initiative. *A Comprehensive Approach to Governing, Measuring and Reporting on Investments in First Nations Well-Being*. https://www.bcfndgi.com/.

Canada Health Act, c. C-6. (R.S.C., 1985). https://laws-lois.justice.gc.ca/eng/acts/c-6/page-1.html.

Canada Health Act. 1984, c.6, s.1 Crombie, D. (1979). Statement on Indian Health Policy. Government of Canada, Ottawa. http://publications.gc.ca/site/eng/9.865662/publication.html.

Canadian Alliance for Healthy Hearts and Minds First Nations Cohort Research Team. (2019). "All About Us": Indigenous Data Analysis Workshop—capacity building in the Canadian Alliance for Healthy Hearts and Minds First Nations Cohort. *CJC Open*, 1(6), 282–288. doi:10.1016/j.cjco.2019.09.002.

Canadian Institutes of Health Research, Natural Sciences and Engineering Research Council of Canada, and Social Sciences and Humanities Research Council. (December 2018). *Tri-Council Policy Statement: Ethical Conduct for Research Involving Humans*. https://ethics.gc.ca/eng/policy-politique_tcps2-eptc2_2018.html.

Canadian Public Health Association. (October 2019). *Policy Statement: Indigenous Relations and Reconciliation.* https://www.cpha.ca/sites/default/files/uploads/about/reconciliation/Indigenous-reconciliation-policy-e.pdf.

Castellano, M.B. (2015). The spiritual dimension of holistic health: a reflection. In M. Greenwood, C. Reading, N.M. Lindsay, & S. Leeuw (Eds.), *Determinants of Indigenous Peoples' Health in Canada: Beyond the Social* (pp. 33–37). Canadian Scholars' Press.

Chiefs of Ontario, Cancer Care Ontario and Institute for Clinical Evaluative Sciences. (2017). *Cancer in First Nations People in Ontario: Incidence, Mortality, Survival and Prevalence.* Toronto: Chiefs of Ontario, Cancer Care Ontario and Institute for Clinical Evaluative Sciences.

Constitution Act, 30 & 31 Vict, c 3. (1867). https://www.canlii.org/en/ca/laws/stat/30---31-vict-c-3/97547/30---31-vict-c-3.html.

Crey, K. (2009). *Enfranchisement.* Indigenous Foundations. https://Indigenousfoundations.arts.ubc.ca/enfranchisement/.

Department of Health and Community Services Newfoundland and Labrador Centre for Health Information. (December, 2017). *Newfoundland and Labrador Indigenous Administrative Data Identifier Standard. National Inquiry into Missing and Murdered Indigenous Women and Girls.* https://www.mmiwg-ffada.ca/wp-content/uploads/2019/05/40-NL_Indigenous_Administrative_Data_Identifier_Standard_FINAL__2017-12-12.pdf.

Eibl, J., Fung, K., Giannakeas, V., Gomes, T., Henry, D., Martins, D., Pyper, E., Walker, J., Antone, T., Carr, L., deGonzague, B., Jones, C., King, E., Yurkiewich, A., Binguis, N., Corbiere, Y., Davis Hill, L., Desmoulin, J., Hill, P., Logan, M., Mandamin, N., Nicholas, S., & Williams, S. (2017). *Opioid Use among First Nations in Ontario.* http://www.chiefs-of-ontario.org/wp-content/uploads/2019/05/Opioid-Use-Among-First-Nations-in-Ontario-2017-10-05.pdf.

First Nations Health and Social Secretariat of Manitoba. (2019). *About Us.* https://www.fnhssm.com/about-us.

First Nations Information Governance Centre. (April 7th, 2014). Barriers and levers for the implementation of OCAP™. *The International Indigenous Policy Journal*, 5(2), 1–11. doi:10.18584/iipj.2014.5.2.3.

First Nations Information Governance Centre. (2016). Pathways to first nations' data and information sovereignty. In T. Kukutai, & J. Taylor (Eds.), *Indigenous Data Sovereignty: Toward an Agenda* (pp. 139–155). Australian National University Press.

First Nations Information Governance Centre. (2018). *The First Nations Principles of OCAP®.* https://fnigc.ca/ocap.

First Nations Information Governance Centre. (2019). First nations data sovereignty in Canada. *Statistical Journal of the IAOS*, 35(1), 47–69. doi:10.3233/SJI-180478.

Galloway, G. (2015). Trudeau vows to develop plan to put Canada on path to "true reconciliation". *The Globe and Mail Canada.* https://www.theglobeandmail.com/news/national/truth-and-reconciliation-head-calls-for-action-as-final-report-released/article27762924/.

Goodleaf, D.K. (1995). *Entering the War Zone: A Mohawk Perspective on Resisting Invasions.* Theytus Books Limited.

Government of Canada, c. A-1, s. 13. (R.S.C., 1985a). *Access to Information* Act. https://laws-lois.justice.gc.ca/eng/acts/a-1/.

Government of Canada, c. P-21, a. 3 "personal information" (m). (R.S.C., 1985b). *Privacy* Act. https://laws-lois.justice.gc.ca/ENG/ACTS/P-21/index.html.

Government of Canada. (2014). *Indian Health Policy 1979*. https://www.canada.ca/en/Indigenous-services-canada/corporate/first-nations-inuit-health-branch/indian-health-policy-1979.html.

Government of Canada. (2019). Canada's Health Care System. https://www.canada.ca/en/health-canada/services/health-care-system/reports-publications/health-care-system/canada.html.

Government of Canada. (2020). *Jordan's Principle*. https://www.canada.ca/en/Indigenous-services-canada/services/jordans-principle.html.

Gradual Civilization Act, CAP XXVI. (1857). http://www.caid.ca/GraCivAct1857.pdf.

Harris, S.B., Naqshbandi, M., Bhattacharyya, O., Hanley, A.J., Esler, J.G., Zinman, B., & Group, C.S. (2011). Major gaps in diabetes clinical care among Canada's first nations: results of the CIRCLE study. *Diabetes Research and Clinical Practice*, 92(2), 272–279. doi:10.1016/j.diabres.2011.02.006.

Hart, M. (2002). *Seeking Mino-Pimatisiwin: AN Aboriginal Approach to Helping*. Fernwood Books Limited.

Indian Act, c.I-5. S.1. (R.S.C., 1985). https://laws-lois.justice.gc.ca/eng/acts/i-5/.

Indigenous and Northern Affairs Canada. (2010). *Statement of Apology to Former Students of Indian Residential Schools*. https://www.aadncaandc.gc.ca/eng/1100100015644/1100100015649.

Indigenous and Northern Affairs Canada. (2017). *United Nations Declaration on the Rights of Indigenous Peoples*. https://www.aadncaandc.gc.ca/eng/1309374407406/1309374458958.

Indigenous Corporate Training Inc. (2016). *Hereditary Chief Definition and 5 FAQs*. https://www.ictinc.ca/blog/hereditary-chief-definition-and-5-faqs.

Inuit Tapiriit Kanatami. (2019). *National Inuit Strategy on Research Roundtable: Summary Report*. https://www.itk.ca/wpcontent/uploads/2019/11/ITK_NISR_Roundtable_11.pdf.

Inuit Tapiriit Kanatami. (2020). *Inuit Tapiriit Kanatami*. https://www.itk.ca/.

Katz, A., Kinew, K.A., Star, L., Taylor, C., Koseva, I., Lavoie, J., Burchill, C., Urquia, M.L., Basham, A., Rajotte, L., Ramayanam, V., Jarmasz, J., & Burchill, S. (Fall, 2019). *The Health Status of and Access to Healthcare by Registered First Nation Peoples in Manitoba*. Manitoba Centre for Health Policy. http://mchpappserv.cpe.umanitoba.ca/reference/FN_Report_web.pdf.

Ketonen, K. (2019). Trudeau commits to indigenous health care overhaul. *CBC News*. https://www.cbc.ca/news/canada/thunder-bay/trudeau-Indigenous-health-care-1.5297959.

King, M., Smith, A., & Gracey, M. (2009). Indigenous health part 2: the underlying causes of the health gap. *The Lancet*, 374(9683), 76–85. doi:10.1016/S0140-6736(09)60827-8.

Laanela, M. (September 30th, 2016). Orange shirt day: how Phyllis Webstad's 1st day at residential school inspired a movement. *CBC News*. https://www.cbc.ca/news/canada/british-columbia/orange-shirt-day-1.3785597.

Library and Archives of Canada Act, S.C. c. 11. (2004). https://lawslois.justice.gc.ca/eng/acts/L-7.7/.

MacDonald, N., & Attaran, A. (August 14th, 2007). Jordan's principle, governments' paralysis. *Canadian Medical Association Journal—CMAJ*, 177(4), 321. doi:10.1503/cmaj.070950.

MacDonald, C., & Steenbeek, A. (2015). The impact of colonization and western assimilation on health and wellbeing of Canadian aboriginal people. *International Journal of Regional and Local History*, 10(1), 32–46. doi:10.1179/2051453015Z.00000000023.

Mamow Ahyamowen Partnership. (2019). *Learning from our Ancestors: Mortality Experience of First Nations in Northern Ontario*. https://mamowahyamowen.ca/wp-content/uploads/2019/12/Mamow-Ahyamowen-Mortality-2019.pdf.

Mustimuhw Information Solutions. (n.d.). *Designed by and for First Nations*. http://www.mustimuhw.com/.

National Aboriginal Health Organization. (2017). *About NAHO*. https://wayback.archiveit.org/9444/20171213190657/http://www.naho.ca/about/.

National Inquiry into Missing and Murdered Indigenous Women and Girls. (2019). *Reclaiming Power and Place: The Final Report of the National Inquiry into Missing and Murdered Indigenous Women and Girls*, Volume 1a. https://www.mmiwg-ffada.ca/wp-content/uploads/2019/06/Final_Report_Vol_1a-1.pdf.

Philpott, J. (2018). Canada's efforts to ensure the health and wellbeing of indigenous peoples. *The Lancet*, 391(10131), 1650–1651. doi:10.1016/S0140-6736(18)30179-X.

Pyper, E., Henry, D., Yates, E.A., Mecredy, G., Ratnasingham, S., Slegers, B., & Walker, J.D. (2018). Walking the path together: indigenous health data at ICES. *Healthcare Quarterly*, 20(4), 6–9. doi:10.12927/hcq.2018.25431.

Richmond, C.A.M., & Cook, C. (2016). Creating conditions for Canadian aboriginal health equity: the promise of healthy public policy. *Public Health Reviews*, 37(2), 1–16. doi:10.1186/s40985-016-0016-5.

Royal Commission on Aboriginal Peoples. (1996). *Report of the Royal Commission on Aboriginal Peoples*. Library and Archives Canada. https://www.baclac.gc.ca/eng/discover/aboriginal-heritage/royal-commission-aboriginal-peoples/Pages/final-report.aspx.

Saku, J.C. (1999). Aboriginal census data in Canada: a research note. *The Canadian Journal of Native Studies*, 19(2), 365–379. http://www3.brandonu.ca/cjns/19.2/cjnsv19no2_pg365-379.pdf.

Slater, M., Green, M.E., Shah, B., Khan, S., Jones, C.R., Sutherland, R., Jacklin, K., & Walker, J.D. (2019). First nations people with diabetes in Ontario: methods for a longitudinal population-based cohort study. *CMAJ Open*, 7(4), E680–E688. doi:10.9778/cmajo.20190096.

Smylie, J., & Firestone, M. (2015). Back to the basics: identifying and addressing underlying challenges in achieving high quality and relevant health statistics for indigenous populations in Canada. *Statistical Journal of the IAOS*, 31(1), 67–87. doi:10.3233/SJI-150864.

Smylie, J., Firestone, M., Spiller, M.W., & Tungasuvvingat, I. (2018). Our health counts: population-based measures of urban Inuit health determinants, health status, and health care access. *Canadian Journal of Public Health*, 109(5–6), 662–670. doi:10.17269/s41997-018-0111-0.

The Canadian Press. (2019a). *Métis Nations Sign Historic Self-Governance Deal with Ottawa*. https://globalnews.ca/news/5438360/metis-self-governance-alberta-ontario-saskatchewan/.

The Canadian Press. (2019b). *Trudeau Says Relationship with Metis is "Model of What Reconciliation Can Be"*. https://globalnews.ca/news/5388102/trudeau-metis-nation-reconciliation/.

The Institute on Governance. (1997). *Summary of the Final Report of the Royal Commission on Aboriginal Peoples*. https://iog.ca/docs/1997_April_rcapsum.pdf.

Truth and Reconciliation Commission of Canada. (2015). *Honouring the Truth, Reconciling for the Future: Summary of the Final Report of the Truth and Reconciliation Commission of Canada*. http://www.trc.ca/assets/pdf/Honouring_the_Truth_Reconciling_for_the_Future_July_23_2015.pdf.

Tui'kn Partnership. (2015). *Tui'kn Partnership: Because Health Belongs to All of Us*. www.tuikn.ca.

Unist'ot'en Camp. (2020). *Wet'suwet'en Supporter Toolkit 2020*. http://unistoten.camp/supportertoolkit2020/.

United Nations. (2016). *United Nations Declaration on the Rights of Indigenous Peoples*. https://www.un.org/development/desa/Indigenouspeoples/declaration-on-the-rights-of-Indigenous-peoples.html.

University of Manitoba. (2019). *Manitoba Centre for Health Policy: First Nation People's Health in Manitoba*. Manitoba Centre for Health Policy. https://d5d8ad59-8391-48029f0af5f5d600d7e9.filesusr.com/ugd/38252a_e6cb8d7b16d64161976ce7bd4d49599e.pdf.

Vogal, L. (2015). Broken trust drives native health disparities. *Canadian Medical Association Journal*, 187(1), E9–E10. doi:10.1503/cmaj.109-4950.

Walker, J., Lovett, R., Kukutai, T., Jones, C., & Henry, D. (2017). Indigenous health data and the path to healing. *The Lancet*, 390(10107), 2022–2023. doi:10.1016/S0140-6736(17)32755-1.

Walker, J.D., Rowe, R., & Jones, C.R. (2018). Describing the process of ethical conduct of research in an ontario-wide first nations diabetes research project. *CMAJ*, 190(Suppl), S19–S20. doi:10.1503/cmaj.180479.

Walker, J.D., Andrew, M., Bronskill, S., Smylie, J., Warry, W., Henry, D., Loft, D., Jones, C., Sutherland, R., Blind, M., Slater, M., Pitawanakwat, K., Mecredy, G., & Jacklin, K. (2019). *Ontario First Nations Aging Study: Overview and Report*. Sudbury: Ontario First Nations Aging Study.

Walker, J.D., Slater, M., Jones, C.R., Shah, B.R., Frymire, E., Khan, S., Jacklin, K., & Green, M.E. (2020). Diabetes prevalence, incidence and mortality in first nations and other people in ontario, 1995–2014: a population-based study using linked administrative data. *CMAJ*, 192(6), E128–E135. doi:10.1503/cmaj.190836.

Young, B. (2015). "Killing the Indian in the child": death, cruelty, and subject-formation in the Canadian Indian residential school system. *Mosaic: A Journal for the Interdisciplinary Study of Literature*, 48(4), 63–76. https://www.jstor.org/stable/44030407?seq=1.

7 The challenge of Indigenous data in Sweden

Per Axelsson and Christina Storm Mienna

Introduction

The traditional land of the Indigenous Sami people—known as Sápmi/Sábme/Sábmie/Saepmie, depending on the Sami language—is situated in the northern parts of Norway, Sweden, Finland and Russia. The size of the Sami population is estimated at between 75,000 and 120,000, with the majority living in Norway (Young & Bjerregaard 2019; Bartlett et al. 2007; Axelsson & Sköld 2011). Systems for collecting Sami population data are today non-existent and as a result, the Sami are invisible in official statistics (Axelsson et al. 2016). Subsequently, the knowledge of the Sami health situation is limited (Storm Mienna & Axelsson 2019).This statistical erasure is consistent across all countries inhabited by the Sami people.

Based on the "Ethnicity Counts database (eCount)", Mullane Ronaki (2017) investigated Indigenous Peoples' recognition in censuses globally and determined that systems for identification ranged from fixed categories to self-identification and that less than half of all Indigenous Peoples are still not recognized by their nation states. The Nordic countries and Russia fall into the "less than half" category. In a widely cited study on Indigenous and Tribal Peoples' health, Anderson et al. (2016) reported that 15 of 22 countries reported health and social data on Indigenous Peoples in their national systems. Furthermore, it was obvious that the CANZUS states maintained the best possibilities to accumulate a variety of data on Indigenous Peoples based on the system of self-definitions in censuses. The report concluded that data was a general concern and that "National governments should develop targeted policies for Indigenous and tribal health that address issues of health service delivery and the development of high-quality Indigenous data systems". Hence, there is little data produced by the state that the Sami can use and have the opportunity to take ownership of. Indigenous data that do exist are mainly produced by researchers and guarded by Swedish ethical protocols that do not take Sami ownership or control into account (Drugge 2016). Questions around Indigenous data ownership and control have yet not been on the political agenda in Sweden.

In Sweden, the focus of this chapter, the absence of state-collected Sami population data means that the government cannot provide any comprehensive understanding of the health and well-being of its only Indigenous People. This circumstance has repeatedly been criticized by international agencies but also from political institutions within the Sami society (Madden et al. 2016). The Organization for Economic Co-operation and Development report *Linking the Indigenous Sami People with Regional and Rural Development in Sweden* (OECD 2019), acknowledges that statistics have sometimes been criticized for poorly capturing key elements of Indigenous Peoples' lives, worldviews and societies. However, the statistical invisibility of the Sami severely hampers policy making and ways of knowing if policies are effective and legal requirements are met. The OECD recommended that Sweden, among other things, should "synthesize current data sources and identify data limitations in its use and dissemination", "increase research funding for Sami data collection" and "develop ethical guidelines for research on Sami" (OECD 2019, 54–55).

However, things have recently progressed due to increased pressure from Sami society and non-governmental organizations that have called for a truth and reconciliation commission (Sametinget 2019); ethical guidelines for Sami research (Kvernmo et al. 2018); a consultation order for Sami issues (Regeringen 2019); and enhancing the Sami Parliament's role and possibilities to collect data (OECD 2019). Together with the implementation of a Nordic Sami Convention (Sametinget 2019) it may open up discussions on ownership and governance of data. Meanwhile, there is limited knowledge of what Sami society thinks of recent, but increasingly influential, global discussions on Indigenous Data Sovereignty. This chapter, the first study based on material from focus group discussions from the HALDI project, examines how Sami people perceive and reflect upon the importance of control and ownership of data generated in Sami research.

The Haldi project—data and method

Despite a lack of governmental data in the Nordic countries, there are successful examples of population-based research such as the SAMINOR study led and governed by the Centre for Sami Health Research at the Arctic University of Norway (UIT). The SAMINOR study includes ethnic self-identification (Brustad et al. 2014) and the study comprises both a questionnaire and a clinical study that has run in two waves in selected municipalities in traditional Sami areas of northern Norway. The SAMINOR study has so far resulted in 52 peer-reviewed articles, eight PhD theses and extensive reports to participating municipalities describing the current health status in Norwegian Sápmi (Lund et al. 2007; SAMINOR 2020).

In 2018, the Swedish government funded a focus group study to prepare for a population-based research project called "HALDI—health and living conditions in Sápmi, Sweden". The HALDI project collaborates with the SAMINOR study and will be based on the international recommendation of ethnic self-identification (United Nations 2017, 203–206). The idea behind HALDI was initiated in 2015 and the following year the project obtained collective consent from the Sami Parliament in Sweden. The project is divided into different stages where the first stage involved focus group discussions (Marczak & Sewell 2006; Krueger & Casey 2014) in order to give Sami in Sweden room to broadly discuss issues relating to Sami health and what future health and well-being research is required. The results from the focus group discussions will be used in the second stage of the HALDI project and provide input to the questionnaire and the clinical examinations. The focus group project was approved by the Regional Ethical Review Board of Umeå, Sweden (Dnr 2017/408-31).

Sami perspectives on the ownership and governance of Sami health data

In 1977, the Swedish government recognized the Sami as an Indigenous People, in 1993, the Sami Parliament in Sweden was established and in 2011, the Sami people became recognized as a people in the Swedish constitution. These were unquestionably important achievements for the Sami people. At the same time, things went in the opposite direction concerning Indigenous data. A few years after the Swedish government had recognized the Sami as an Indigenous People in Sweden, the *Data Act* (1973:289, especially Prop 1981/82:189) established that the processing of data that reveals ethnicity or race was prohibited. Further research is needed, but when this regulation was introduced in 1982 there seemed to have been no arguments or discussions around expected shortcomings for the Sami people. The *Data Act* has been modified over time and currently sits under the General Data Protection Regulation (GDPR) within the European Union.

International governing instruments such as the United Nations Declaration of the Rights of Indigenous Peoples (UN General Assembly 2007) introduced in 2007 and eventually adopted by 148 countries have the potential to make states engage with Indigenous Peoples in meaningful ways to change the current state of affairs. For instance, Article 18 states that:

> Indigenous peoples have the right to participate in decision-making in matters which would affect their rights, through representatives chosen by themselves in accordance with their own procedures, as well as to maintain and develop their own Indigenous decision-making institution.

Moreover, the Sustainable Development Goals clearly states that more data is needed to be able to monitor the progress among Indigenous Peoples and ethnic groups (Balestra & Fleisher 2018). Despite this, few attempts have been made to improve data collection on issues relating to Indigenous or ethnic groups in Sweden as well as most of western Europe. There certainly are methodological and pragmatical issues that need to be solved to ensure ethnic data collection in western Europe (Simon 2017). Why is western Europe different? Simon (2017) summarized how in post–Second World War western Europe data on "race" and "ethnicity" was ignored because not only did it echo the countries' complex colonial histories, but it risked fragmenting the nation and undermining "social and political cohesion" and that "ethnic statistics reify and reinforce ascribed identities which are unstable and flexible" (Simon 2017, 2328).

Furthermore, the Nazi regime used demographic records to identify and locate ethnic groups, mainly Jews, for deportation to concentration camps (Luebke & Milton 1994). Adding to that, there was the science of racial biology that was strong, especially in Sweden in the first half of the 20th century. It is now common knowledge that demographic records collected by the state and the church were used in research to separate civilized "Nordic" races from the primitive "Indigenous Sami" races that was believed would soon die out (Axelsson 2010). This research was evidently done without any informed consent from the individuals affected by it and has remained an open wound, not only by the generation that lived through the Second World War and the era of racial biology but up until generations today (Heith 2015). Moreover, as late as 2013 it was discovered that Swedish police kept a secret register of Roma people (Axelsson 2015). The public reactions were of outrage and the Swedish state was convicted of ethnic discrimination in 2017 (Civil Right Defenders 2017). This made collection of ethnic statistics, an already sensitive topic, even more controversial and challenged the notion that the Swedish state could be trusted with the governance of any form of ethnic data. It is important to be aware of this historical backdrop to be able to understand the results from our focus group study.

A total of 11 focus group discussions were held in Sápmi, in northern Sweden during autumn 2018 and spring 2019. The focus group participants consisted of a diverse group of Sami individuals regarding gender, age and occupation. In total, 51 individuals participated in the group discussions. Two-thirds were women and the age spanned from 23 to 77 years of age. Before the focus group started every participant signed an informed consent form and the discussions were audio-recorded (ranging in duration between 28 and 117 minutes) and later transcribed verbatim. The discussions were mainly in Swedish and when Sami language was spoken, it was later translated and transcribed to Swedish. The transcriptions were analyzed according to content analysis described by Graneheim and Lundman (2004) and at a later stage reported back to each focus group for corrections and confirmation. The discussions focused on a variety of perspectives on health, well-being and health research, aiming to generate knowledge of issues relevant for the Sami people in Sweden and the upcoming health survey in particular. One section, or theme, was devoted to the issue of Indigenous data and governance of produced research data. The main question was who should own or govern the data produced in a future health research study with Sami participants' material.

The focus groups discussion that followed around this theme showed a diversity in opinions both between different groups but also between individuals in the same focus group. A pervading opinion in the groups was that data management about Sami people was of significant importance to building trust and acceptance in research. Regarding what governing body should be considered the owners of health research data, three suggestions emerged in the focus groups: the Sami Parliament, the healthcare authorities and the universities. Using quotes from the focus groups the following section illustrates some of the main arguments in each case. (See Swedish transcript in Appendix.)

The Sami Parliament

Even if there were individuals that expressed doubts that the Sami Parliament was the right authority to have the guardianship of research data, the majority thought that the Sami Parliament was the correct place for keeping and managing data, especially human biological materials.

> The Sami data should be under the auspices of the Sami Parliament.

The current obstacles with management of "ethnic data" also became evident.

> The Sami society should be owners, but we lack that sort of arrangement in Sweden, to make it possible.

Aware of the difficulties of Indigenous data, there were opinions that a Sami health institution should be established in Sweden. Some focus groups held the position that Sami committees or Sami organizations could also serve as potential guardians.

> You have to think that there is a need for a specific Sami health institution. This [institution] would have some kind of overall control of what happens and what it looks like, what needs to be done … . The most natural may be … or the most desirable would be that the Sami Parliament had some sort of overarching responsibility … as it now stands it might be difficult, though, to know how the Sami Parliament would be able to take care of it.

The healthcare authorities

Swedish healthcare authorities were mentioned by a few as possible owners of collected research data regarding health issues in Swedish Sápmi. However, it was considered important that data would be made easily accessible for future research and societal development.

> There must be some kind of an outcome. I mean, you do not do it just to get a paper that no one will have access to.

Some participants expressed distrust of the Swedish health system and perceived institutions to lack the required competence and understanding of Sami culture and living conditions.

> Regarding Sami health, the Regional health care authorities should have begun long ago. Because we are citizens too. And we, and the health care system, should welcome all citizens based on their situation and their needs. And today they don't. And that … it has been ignored. Due to ignorance, due to cowardice, due to prejudice, yes, whatever it is. Financial reasons.

The universities

For some of the participants, the ownership of Sami data was not an issue to be contested. They argued that, if they had given their consent to a study, the researchers could keep that data and use it whenever and however they saw fit, could manage Indigenous data and would see to it that laws and regulations were fulfilled.

> It feels safer if a university is responsible, I think it is safer.

Participants in these focus groups trusted that universities could manage data safely and securely.

Historical legacies

Another issue that originated from the discussions of data and data management had to do with previous data registers collected in the name of science or the state and sometimes both.

Several focus groups expressed a fear that the data risked being used in a wrong or damaging way for the Sami people, hence they were afraid of being identified as Sami in future data registers. Because of that, participants thought that the data should be owned and managed by Sami authorities.

> What we see today, how it has ... been used in the wrong way. I have thought of it, with measurements of skulls and everything, that it has made you ... you become a little afraid of how, ... how will it, as mum said, be used against us. Instead of making progress. Well, that's the fear I see. And that is why it is extremely important that ... all material is Sami owned.

There were a few examples of individuals that had no hesitation or fear that data collection such as medical records or data registers could be misused. A few individuals expressed that any research that could help inform society about Sami health outweighed the eventual risk of data being exposed. However, regardless of the question of ownership, focus group participants brought up the history of racial biology in Sweden as well as the persecution of Jews during the Second World War in connection with discussions about science and data registers.

> In the old days, when you researched something it became a register and you used it in some way. [...] And the same thing was the case, when the Sami Parliament was established, yes, now we will need to register as Sami. But ... I also wondered, what happens then? Then there will be a register of us Sami. And then "they" will take it. It will be like the Jews in Germany during the Nazi era. But that discussion has completely disappeared.

Some focus groups acknowledged the fear or research and registers but also highlighted and commented on the status quo that currently surrounds these questions.

> You are a little scared, and everyone, many Sami people are probably afraid to participate in surveys, because we have the legacy of race biology. We have Hitler and Jews. And many do not enroll in the Sami Parliament, older people, because they do not want to be registered. So we have something we deal with. But, but if we do not line up and participate in such things […] it will never be investigated.

Participants also expressed opinions that all research data should, as soon as it has been used, be destroyed or "reburied". This opinion was linked to an ongoing process of repatriation of Sami human remains in Sweden. In the 1950s an old Sami burial ground was excavated and 25 skulls were sent to the National History Museum in Stockholm for further research. These skulls were brought back to Sápmi and reburied in Liksjoe (Lycksele) in August 2019. (Radio Sweden 2019).

> And I mean, in the end you must have looked at it enough so that you have learned what to see. Then you need to return it in an honorable way. And in the meantime, I think I … then there should be strong ethical … guidelines for it. And one is that the Sami material, it must, yes, in some way be the protected by the Sami Parliament, or something like that.

The focus group participants were consistent in their explicit views that Sami research material and Sami research data should ideally be governed by Sami themselves and that researchers should seek permission to use it for research and the beneficence of the Sami people. At the same time, given the current circumstances and resources, it was obvious that participants expressed doubts if the Sami Parliament currently possessed the capacity to manage and govern health research data.

The results from the focus group discussions point to the Sami Parliament being considered the most credible authority to have the guardianship of research data regarding health issues linked to the Sami people. It was also evident that the participants thought that data should be owned and managed by Sami themselves, but recognized that no such system was currently in place to make that happen. If data would be managed by the Swedish healthcare system, people with competence in Sami culture and living conditions should be involved in the process and the decision making. Finally, it is obvious that the history and experiences of racial biology and Nazi Germany plays important roles in how science and data are perceived in Sápmi, in Sweden today.

Discussion

While the histories of the aftermath of the Second World War and racial biology linger and conceivably are reasons for the reluctance to do anything to meet the demands of Indigenous Peoples and ethnic groups that want and need accurate population statistics—the call for Indigenous Data Sovereignty has grown rapidly. Indigenous Data Sovereignty (IDS) has shifted the international conversation beyond data disaggregation, identification and access to consider issues of Indigenous Peoples' governance, ownership and control. The right of Indigenous Peoples to control data from and about their communities and lands—articulating both individual and collective rights to data access and to data privacy has been advocated by IDS networks worldwide (Kukutai & Taylor 2016; Raine et al. 2017; Rodrigues-Lonebear 2016) and also corresponds with the requests by the Sami people participating in the focus group discussions.

The focus group study carried out in late 2018 and early 2019 confirms that there is an existing fear among participants that science and research data involving Sami individuals, families and groups might be used for the wrong purposes, especially if data are stored in systems outside of Sami control. However, data management regarding humans has yet to be put on the political agenda of the Sami Parliament, but there are developments in a number of related areas. The Sami Parliament has established an ethical board, whose task is to develop advisory guidelines on issues relating to the return, storage and re-burial of Sami remnants in Sweden. Nevertheless, the ethical board has, at the time of writing, no responsibilities in research policy matters.

The Parliament has, by the Swedish state, been given the mandate to operate a system for managing regional statistical data—but only data that concerns the reindeer industry. The data concerns the number of reindeer owners, the size of herds, slaughter, the number of predators in reindeer herding areas and so on (Samediggi Rennäring 2017). There is still nothing in relation to official population statistics but there is a tendency of increasing focus on capacity building within the Parliament. In 2018, a committee responsible for health, the elderly and sports was established and in late November 2019, the Sami Parliament plenary adopted a health policy program. This program contained a call to the Swedish government to give the Sami Parliament the mandate to work with health issues (currently the Parliament lack that mandate) with accompanying increased funding. Nine areas were identified (not necessarily in this order): (1) language-and culture adapted health care, student health and care (2) public health work (3) research and center for Sami health research (4) accessible health care (5) influence (6) increased diversity and tolerance (7) national Sami health center (8) truth and reconciliation committee (9) implementation the UN Declaration on the Rights of Indigenous Peoples (Samediggi 2019). The Sami Parliament in Sweden has also responded to the Swedish government proposal for research policy where it was argued that the future Swedish research policy should target Sami research and establish research ethical guidelines for Sami research enabling comparative research in the four countries that include Sápmi (Samediggi 2019). Furthermore, *Sámiid Riikkasearvi* (*SSR*), a Sami organization in Sweden has developed and adopted a policy regarding research when collaborating with their organization (Sámiid Riikkasearvi 2019). All these actions can be seen as a conscious direction toward increased Sami self-determination in several questions regarding research, data management, health and ethics.

Although the Collective benefit Authority to control Responsibility Ethics (CARE) principles for Indigenous Data Governance (Global Indigenous Data

Alliance) within the IDS are devoted to data ecosystems, some of the principles fit well with the current discussion on research ethics in Sápmi. It is probably in this space where the discussion on IDS most likely will advance in Sweden and Scandinavia. A proposal of ethical guidelines for Sami health research and research on Sami human biological material have been put forward by a group of researchers together with the Sami Parliament in Norway. This document includes recommendations on carrying out research on/with Indigenous Sami (Kvernmo et al. 2018). Just as in the CARE principles, the proposal for ethical guidelines state that research should respect the values and reflect the diversity in the Sami culture and the Sami society, avoid stereotyping, benefit Indigenous communities, provide equal partnership and strengthen the Sami community at large.

> Relations between the Sámi communities and the researchers must be characterised by respect, reciprocity, equality, accountability, cultural assurance and Sámi self-determination in every research project, regardless of the project's objectives, design or method. These values are based on recognition and appreciation of the Sámi as a people and on respect for their integrity.
> (Kvernmo et al. 2018, 40)

However, the CARE principles have a stronger commitment to the authority to control, community use of data and capacity building than the proposed ethical guidelines. Particularly, the "authority to control" also resonated with the participants in the focus groups. However, they expressed doubts if the Sami Parliament currently possessed the capacity to manage and govern health research data. A main point with the Indigenous Data Sovereignty movement is to design and maintain relevant data for policy work in important areas of the society. If, for instance, the Sami Parliament would express a strong need for solid demographic data for planning their future, and also found ways to collect, store and manage this information, should not the state consider this? What is needed at the moment is a focus on IDS, reliable and increased funding and time for the Sami parliament to be able to build an active leadership regarding the governance of Indigenous data beyond reindeer husbandry.

Acknowledgment

We would like to thank all focus group participants across Sápmi, Sweden. Furthermore, we want to thank Eleonor Blind, Lena Maria Nilsson, Tobias Poggats and Petter Stoor for their help during the interviews. Thanks also to the researchers at the Várdduo—Centre for Sami research, Umeå University for commenting on the focus group guide. We also would like to express our thanks to the editors of the book and the reviewers for suggestion and comments to improve this chapter. This study was funded by the Swedish ministry of health and social affairs (dnr: S2018/03552/FS) and the Wallenberg Academy Fellowship (KAW 2012.0222 Axelsson).

References

Anderson, I., et al. (2016). "Indigenous and tribal peoples' health (The Lancet–Lowitja Institute Global Collaboration): a population study." *The Lancet*, 388(10040), 131–157.

Axelsson, P. (2010). "Abandoning 'the other'—statistical enumeration of Swedish Sami 1700s–1945 and beyond." *Berichte zur Wissenschaftsgeschichte*, 33, 263–279.

Axelsson, P., & Sköld, P. (2011, paperback 2013). *Indigenous Peoples and Demography. The Complex Relation between Identity and Statistics*. Oxford and New York, NY: Berghahn Books.

Axelsson, P. (2015). "Urfolkshälsa—utmanande och svårfångad." *Socialmedicinsk Tidskrift*, 92(6), 726–735.

Axelsson, P., Kukutai, T., & Kippen, R. (2016). "Indigenous wellbeing and colonization: editorial." *Journal of Northern Studies*, 10(2), 7–18.

Balestra, C., & Fleischer, L. (2018). *Diversity Statistics in the OECD: How do OECD Countries Collect Data on Ethnic, Racial and Indigenous Identity*, OECD Statistics Working Papers, No. 2018/09, OECD Publishing, Paris, France.

Bartlett, J.G., et al. (2007). "Identifying Indigenous peoples for health research in a global context: a review of perspectives and challenges." *International Journal of Circumpolar Health*, 66(4), 287–307.

Brustad, M., Hansen, K.L., Broderstad, A.R., Hansen, S., & Melhus, M. (2014). "A population-based study on health and living conditions in areas with mixed Sami and Norwegian settlements—the SAMINOR 2 questionnaire study." *International Journal of Circumpolar Health*, 2014, 73.

Civil Right Defenders. (2017). *Historic Court Ruling: Swedish State Guilty of Ethnic Registration*. https://crd.org/2017/04/28/historic-court-ruling-swedish-state-guilty-of-ethnic-registration/.

Drugge, A.-L. (2016). "How can we do it right?: ethical uncertainty in Swedish Sami research." *Journal of Academic Ethics*, 14, 263–279.

Global Indigenous Data Alliance. https://www.gida-global.org/care [accessed February 2, 2020].

Graneheim, U.H., & Lundman, B. (2004). "Qualitative content analysis in nursing research: concepts, procedures and measures to achieve trustworthiness." *Nurse Education Today*, 24, 105–112.

Hälsopolitiskt Handlings Program. https://www.sametinget.se/halsopolitik.

Heith, A. (2015). "Enacting colonised space: Katarina Pirak Sikku and Anders Sunna." *Nordisk Museologi*, (2), 69–83.

Hemställan om Sanningskommission Inlämnad. https://www.sametinget.se/129187.

Kotljarchuk, A. (2017). "World war II and the registration of Roma in Sweden: the role of experts and census-takers." *Holocaust and Genocide Studies*, 31(3), 457–479. https://www.muse.jhu.edu/article/682455.

Krueger, R.A., & Casey, M.A. (2014). *Focus Groups: A Practical Guide for Applied Research*. Sage Publications.

Kue Young, T., & Bjerregaard, P. (2019). "Towards estimating the indigenous population in circumpolar regions." *International Journal of Circumpolar Health*, 78, 1. doi:10.1080/22423982.2019.1653749.

Kukutai, T., & Taylor, J. (Eds.) (2016). *Indigenous Data Sovereignty: Toward an Agenda*. Canberra, Australia: Australian National University Press.

Kvernmo, S., et al. (2018). *Proposal for Ethical Guidelines for Sámi Health Research and Research on Sámi Human Biological Material*. Karasjok, Norway: Sámediggi.

Luebke, D., & Milton, S. (1994). "Locating the victim: an overview of census-taking, tabulation technology and persecution in Nazi Germany." *IEEE Annals of the History of Computing*, 16(3), 25. doi:10.1109/MAHC.1994.298418.
Lund, E., et al. (2007). "Population based study of health and living conditions in areas with both Sami and Norwegian populations—the saminor study." *International Journal of Circumpolar Health*, 66(2), 113–128. doi:10.3402/ijch.v66i2.18241.
Madden, R., Axelsson, P., Kukutai, T., Griffiths, K., Storm Mienna, C., Brown, N., Coleman, C., & Ring, I. (2016). "Statistics on indigenous peoples: international effort needed." *Statistical Journal of the IAOS*, 32(1), 37–41.
Marczak, M., & Sewell, M. (2006). *Using Focus Groups for Evaluation. Cyferbet Evaluation*. Tucson, AZ: The University of Arizona.
Mullane-Ronaki, M.-T.T.K.K. (2017). *Indigenising the National Census? A Global Study of the Enumeration of Indigenous Peoples, 1985–2014*. Thesis, Master of Social Sciences (MSocSc), University of Waikato, Hamilton, New Zealand. Retrieved from https://hdl.handle.net/10289/11175.
Nordic Saami Convention. https://www.sametinget.se/105173.
OECD. (2019). *Linking the Indigenous Sami People with Regional Development in Sweden*, OECD Rural Policy Reviews, OECD Publishing, Paris. doi:10.1787/9789264310544-en.
Proposition 1981/82:189 Om ändring i Datalagen m.m. webaccess: https://www.riksdage n.se/sv/dokument-lagar/dokument/proposition/om-andring-i-datalagen-1973289-mm _G503189/html.
Radio Sweden. (2019). *Largest Reburial in Swedish History as Sami Remains Laid to Rest (Broadcast 2019-08-09)*. https://sverigesradio.se/sida/artikel.aspx?programid=2054&a rtikel=7277599.
Rainie, S.C., Schultz, J.L., Briggs, E., Riggs, P., & Palmanteer-Holder, N.L. (2017). "Data as strategic resource: self-determination and the data challenge for united states native nation and tribes." *International Indigenous Policy Journal*, 8(2). doi:10.18584/ iipj.2017.8.2.1. http://ir.lib.uwo.ca/iipj/vol8/iss2/1.
Regeringen. (2019). *Remiss av Utkast till Lagrådsremiss En Konsultationsordning i Frågor som rör det Samiska Folket. Diarienummer: Ku2019/01308/RS*. https://www .regeringen.se/remisser/2019/07/remiss-av-utkast-till-lagradsremiss-en-konsultations ordning-i-fragor-som-ror-det-samiska-folket/ [accessed March 20, 2020].
Rennäring. https://www.sametinget.se/rennaring.
Rodriguez-Lonebear, D. (2016). "Building a data revolution in Indian country." In *Indigenous Data Sovereignty: Toward an Agenda*, edited by T. Kukutai, & J. Taylor. Canberra, Australia: Australian National University Press.
Sámediggi—The Sami Parliament in Sweden. Webpages [accessed February 2, 2020].
Sámiid Riikkasearvi. (2019). *Policy Regarding Research and Project Collaborations with Sámiid Riikkasearvi*. Sámiid Riikkasearvi.
SAMINOR Webpage Publications. https://uit.no/forskning/forskningsgrupper/sub?p_d ocument_id=425187&sub_id=617617 [accessed February 2, 2020].
Samisk Forskning i Svensk Forskningspolitik. https://www.sametinget.se/135662.
Simon, P. (2017). The failure of the importation of ethno-racial statistics in Europe: debates and controversies. *Ethnic and Racial Studies*. 40. 1–7. 10.1080. /01419870.2017.1344278.
Storm Mienna, C., & Axelsson, P. (2019). "Somatic health in the indigenous Sami population—a systematic review." *International Journal of Circumpolar Health*, 78(1), 1638195. doi:10.1080/22423982.2019.1638195.

Svensk Författningssamling. (1973). *Datalagen*, p. 289. https://www.riksdagen.se/sv/do kument-lagar/dokument/svensk-forfattningssamling/datalag-1973289_sfs-1973-289.

United Nations. (2017). *Principles and Recommendations for Population and Housing Censuses Revision 3*. New York, NY: Department of Economic and Social Affairs, p. 205.

UN General Assembly. (2007). *United Nations Declaration on the Rights of Indigenous Peoples: Resolution/Adopted by the General Assembly*, October 2, 2007, A/ RES/61/295. https://www.refworld.org/docid/471355a82.html [accessed February 2, 2020].

Appendix: quotations transcribed in Swedish from HALDI Focus Group

Det samiska materialet ska på något sätt stå under Sametingets beskydd.

Den samiska miljön är det som ska vara ägare, men vi har inte någon form av sådan i Sverige, som skulle vara möjlig att vara ägare av det.

Men man måste ju tänka sig att det behövs en särskild samisk hälsoinstitution. Som har någon slags övergripande koll på vad som händer och hur det ser ut, vad som behöver göras.... Det naturliga kanske är ... eller det mest önskvärda vore ju att Sametinget hade någon sorts paraplyansvar om det.... i det här läget kan det ju vara svårt och så, veta, hur Sametinget ska ta hand om, kunna ta hand om den, som det ser ut nu, då.

Fast det måste ju komma ut någonting. Alltså, och man gör ju inte det bara för att få ett papper som ingen ska ha tillgång till.

För att det här med samisk hälsa, det borde ju landstingen ha påbörjat för länge sen. För vi är ju medborgare vi också. Och vi, och vården ska ju möta folk utifrån deras situation och deras behov. Och i dag gör de inte det. Och det, man har som struntat i det. Av okunskap, av feghet, av fördomar, ja, allt vad det är. Kostnadsskäl.

Det känns tryggare att det är något universitet som ansvaret, jag tycker det känns tryggare.

Det vi ser idag, hur man har ... använt det på fel sätt. Jag har tänkt på det, med skallmätningar och allting , att det har gjort att man blir ... man blir lite rädd över hur, hur ... hur ska det, och lite grann som mamma sa, att använda det emot oss. I stället för att leda saken framåt. Det är väl den rädslan jag ser. Och därför är det oerhört viktigt att det är ... allt material är i samisk ägo.

Är det som gammalt, då ska man ta reda på och så blir det register och man använder det på något sätt. [---] Och samma sak var det ju, Sametinget inrättade, ja, nu ska vi registrera som samer. Men ... det var ju också som man undrade, vad händer då? Då blir det register på vem som är samer. Och sen tar de, det blir liksom med judarna i Tyskland under nazitiden. Men den diskussionen har ju helt försvunnit.

Man är ju lite rädd, och alla, många samer är nog rädda att delta i undersökningar, eftersom vi har det är arvet med rasbiologin. Vi har Hitler och judar. Och många skriver inte in sig i Sametinget, äldre, för att de vill inte stå registrerade.

Så vi har ju någonting vi lever under. Men, men om vi inte ställer upp och är med på sådana grejer, så blir det ju att det finns, det blir aldrig undersökt. Och jag menar, till slut måste man väl ha tittat så att man har lärt sig vad man ska se, va. Då ska man ju på ett hedersvärdigt sätt återbörda det. Och under tiden så tycker jag att jag ... då ska ju finnas en väldiga etiska ... riktlinjer för det. Och ett är ju att det samiska materialet, det ska ju, ja, stå under på något sätt Sametingets beskydd, eller någonting sådant där.

8 Data governance in the Basque Country

Victims and memories of violent conflicts[1]

Joxerramon Bengoetxea

Introduction

When there have been episodes of conflict and violence affecting the living together of peoples that identify themselves as distinct in a common territory, a key issue is how such conflict will be told and explained. Ownership over the conflict, and all the relevant data related to it, becomes crucial, and contentious. In the Spanish context, we can consider the ongoing political conflict in Catalonia and, to a lesser degree, in the Basque Country, as competing sovereignty claims. Whereas the Basque conflict (1968–2011) has been "infected" by terrorism and counterterrorism, the recent *Catalan process* (2014) has been peaceful, and generally perceived as such.

This contribution is about sovereignty and empowerment, not in the sense of secession, self-determination or autonomy, but over data. Data sovereignty or data governance is a broad theme concerning all "registered" and quantifiable knowledge regarding a people and the possibilities for such people to shape and own the data and the knowledge they originate or reflect. The data reflect a pre-configured type of knowledge that they represent; but data, once organized and "institutionalized" also generate knowledge, creating narratives about peoples, or their culture. This contribution tests and questions the very idea of autochthonous data sovereignty as regards data and narratives—constructed from such data—in the context of political violence in the Basque Country, more particularly victims and memory. Different actors with different agendas in the Basque political "conflict" relate to different data in order to construct or reflect competing narratives over collective memory and collective identity.

Two major differences of outlook can be identified: periodization of the "*conflicto*" (historical memory) and categorization of the victim/victimizer dynamics. Different moral conclusions are drawn from data-based narratives. They look into different historical moments of victimization or, when looking at the same period of violence and conflict, their categories of victims and victimizers are used in different ways, leading to different politics of memory. Periodization turns around the question how far back to go in the history of conflict: the Civil War, the dictatorship, the rise of ETA until the death of Franco, the transition and the *Amnesty Act*, the devolution of powers to the Basque Country and finally, the rise of Islamist Salafi terrorism.

The largest number of victims and human rights breaches took place in the years 1936–1945. Yet, this violent period of Spanish history is not present in the agenda on victims of terrorism. It is history: the agenda of the past. The "memory of the victims" in Spain normally refers, almost exclusively, to the victims of ETA violence. This is the present, recent or current agenda. Paradoxically, ETA's final ceasefire in 2011 seems to have had little impact on this agenda. The other conflicts, even the other victims in the ETA conflict are second-class victims, because they do not fit into the normative allocation of moral virtues and blame prevailing in the Spanish criminal justice system and political culture.

This is a classic use of data: to build a narrative that captures the supposed essence and experience of a group of people—victims—and defends their collective interests. In highlighting the contrast between the different political uses of "data" this chapter speaks to a key issue for data sovereignty, which suggests, among other things, the power to shape prevailing ideas of peoplehood, or victimhood, through data and narratives built around them.

Background to the Basque conflict

In the Basque Country, the "conflict" can be described politically as turning around the question of sovereignty, the struggle for self-government and recognition as a "people". The claims range from self-government to self-determination—a right to decide on political status—or to independence or secession. There are two major moments in the last hundred years of Spanish Basque conflict: one "historical", the other, "recent". The historical conflict was the result of the Franco dictatorship. The Basque Country (and Catalonia) achieved an autonomous status in Spain toward the end of the Second Spanish Republic (1936) but a *coup d'Etat* followed by Civil War and the Franco dictatorship brought an end to this freedom and left a record of thousands killed, summarily executed, disappeared or exiled. A recent report on mortal victims during the Civil War and the first years of the dictatorship (1936–1945) elaborated by the Basque Government, with the Chair of Human Rights of the University of the Basque Country and the Natural Sciences Institute, *Aranzadi*, has established that approximately 20,000 Basques were killed in that period, and 5887 of those deaths can be considered crimes against humanity. Most victims were in the Republican camp (but 955 were victims of Republican fire outside combat): 2252 died in prison, 1363 in bombings like the Gernika bombings that killed civilians, 895 were summarily executed and 1130 were extra-judicially executed. Repression in Franco's Spain was brutal and yet there was no experience of transitional justice of any sort in constitutional Spain until the *Act of Historical Memory* (2007). Some autonomous communities in Spain—Andalusia, Extremadura, Navarre—have adopted their own historical memory Acts and the Basque Country institutions are drafting a Bill on this issue (2019) following a popular legislative initiative.

The *recent* Basque conflict has been violent and created suffering and pain. When ETA was set up during the dictatorship (1958), memory of the Civil War and of the most violent repression of the Franco regime on political opponents

(1936–1945) was fresh. Ten years after its creation, ETA murdered its first intended victim, Melitón Manzanas,[2] head of the "social-political brigades" of the Spanish police in San Sebastian and former collaborator of the Gestapo. Because of his direct involvement in Human Rights violations and tortures he would count as victim and victimizer. This paradoxic *twist* raises the issue of moral and political ambiguity, which is difficult to reflect in the collection of data on victims.

The Basque Country, and Spain as a whole, have gone through a violent history over half a century. ETA murdered 837 persons. Thousands of persons were injured (3000), others were kidnapped, threatened, driven to pay ransom, so-called "revolutionary tax". Many of the victims were police or military but large numbers were civilians, Basque and Spanish. The fight against ETA by the Spanish State and Security Forces also produced victims of violence and human rights breaches (torture, paramilitary groups with ministerial involvement, shooting at demonstrators) and the criminal justice system has also produced much pain through official or lawful but over-punitive measures like large prison sentences, serving sentence in far-away prisons, abuse of preventive prison, confinement, not releasing seriously ill prisoners, amongst other measures. Dating that conflict is a contentious issue on its own: how far back do you go? Identifying the nature and ideology of the actors involved in the conflict is also a delicate task. As regards ETA, the best analysis to date is still Bullain's (2011). Transnational discourse and categories of "the fight against terrorism" have permeated the perception. The definition of the different elements or features of the conflict become very problematic: are there good and evil actors? Who defines the conflict? Who is a victim? How should prisoners be treated, and in what territory?

This contribution therefore intends to place these contentious issues in the broader discourse of Indigenousness (*indigeneité*) and data governance. Not all facets of the conflict can be analyzed here. We have selected the question of memory and data on victims to test the relevance and adequacy of the Indigenous Data Sovereignty discourse. Indigenous Peoples around the world have experienced violence and have a memory of violence and pain. Conflicts and struggles are an important part of their collective memory. Be it in the form of colonization, forced assimilation, deprivation of land and resources, neglect of cultural sites and traditions, and in more extreme forms of racial hatred, genocide, ethnocide. But are Basques a possible Indigenous case?

The Basques as an Indigenous People or as a minority

In order to know how to qualify the Basque People we would need to analyze the European system of governance, which shies away from the collective rights of Peoples, and rather focuses on the individual rights of the members of a national minority. The United Nations Declaration on the Rights of Indigenous Peoples (UNDRIP) does not define Indigenous People (IP); it gives a series of criteria of recognition, amongst which the subjective element is prominent. Indeed, self-identification of a people as an Indigenous People impregnates the UNDRIP.

The Basque People are established in several territories, the historical territories: three in the French Pays Basque, three in the Spanish Autonomous Community of the Basque Country, and the Spanish Foral Community of Navarre. There is also an important Basque diaspora, dispersed around the whole world, with some significant communities. The key subjective criterion of self-identification would need to enquire how the Basques in these territories see themselves: as an ethnic group, as a distinct original people, as a pristine people, as a demos, as a Nation, as a minority, as an Indigenous People, as Aboriginal, as First Peoples, First Nation or First Settlers, as part of the Spanish or French people, and so on. There are almost as many self-identifications as there are Basques.

The modern objective or substantive concept of Indigenous People points to the existence of an ethnic group, with a distinctive culture, that enjoys quasi-sovereign status and related rights like the right to self-determination, the right to land traditionally owned or occupied, the right to language. These rights are recognized in the UNDRIP. The IP would organize around autonomous and representative organizations that would account for a special "system" of governance. According to this substantive approach, there are no compelling reasons to rule out the Basques as an Indigenous People.

There is also a procedural approach to the concept of IP and it has much to do with the issue of prevalence: a minority people who were the first to settle in a certain territory but subsequently became a minority in the territory because of the prevalence of a different dominant people. This discourse can be found in many cases of IP, but not so clearly in the Basque Country, which is why "minority" is only a meaningful term if one considers Spain as a whole. If we follow this procedural approach, we relate back to the conflict on sovereignty. In spite of serious difficulties of definition and classification, we can provisionally hold that there are no sufficient grounds for considering Basques as Indigenous Peoples, mostly because they do not identify themselves as such. Similarly, Basques are not a minority within the Basque Country. Basques favor other collective identifications like ethnic group and nation. But there are equally no solid objections to deny that some Basques, individually, may consider themselves, or identify as Indigenous, and collectively, Basques make some cultural, political and legal claims they share with typical claims of IP, claims based on international law instruments.

Some typical issues of concern regarding the rights and claims of Indigenous Peoples following from UNDRIP are shared with national minorities as they follow from the European Framework Convention and from the Charter, but the UNDRIP goes considerably further in recognizing a rich panoply of rights. The typical claims made by IP and recognized in the Declaration are familiar for Basque ethnicity and politics. The rights and claims following from the UNDRIP have a collective dimension, that may occasionally need to be weighed and balanced with individual rights. Potential clashes can sometimes be the result of inter-sectorialities following from multiple identities that have traditionally suffered discrimination like being an Indigenous citizen speaking an Indigenous language, being a woman, and being homosexual. Rights recognized internationally need balancing in concrete situations and identities are often layered or patched together. Indigenous women can suffer additional violence and discrimination within their group, and homosexuality may not always be accepted, and overcoming the categories and exclusions is not easy for any of the actors concerned. This potential conflict raises the issue of intersectional or inter-sector identities but also that of individual rights of a collective nature, so typical of the European approach.

The Council of Europe has adopted important instruments using a different vocabulary. The most important ones are the Language Charter for Regional or Minority Languages and the Framework Convention for the Protection of National Minorities. The UNDRIP excludes Western Europe from the panoply of world regions where IP are present and this exclusion could mislead observers to conclude that Western Europe is free from the type of situations and normative claims made by IP as regards the procedural approach mentioned above. However, the Council of Europe has been dealing with similar concerns for decades. Issues like the protection and promotion of languages used by traditional minorities or the broader commitment to the protection of national minorities are the subject of two major instruments, i.e., the European Charter for Regional or Minority Languages (the Charter) and the Framework Convention for the Protection of National Minorities (the Framework Convention). Their relevance to the Basque Country is still under-explored and Basque politics have not really looked at the notion of national minorities, albeit the widespread identification of the Basque Country as a (minority) nation. The application of the national minority category to Spain by the Council of Europe monitoring mechanism has so far only looked at the Roma people. The category "minority" can be misleading and the existence of specific instruments—the European Charter of Local Self-Government and the Congress of Local and Regional Authorities—for the recognition of local and regional autonomy in Europe raises specific questions about labeling and identity. The political agenda in Spain has not really paid much attention to the rights of members of national minorities recognized by the State, probably because signatory states can adapt the framework convention's rights to their specific internal situations and therefore, non-observance has practically no legal or political consequence, unlike the human rights recognized in the European Convention.

Like the UNDRIP as regards IP, the Framework Convention does not contain a definition of "national minority" as there is no general definition agreed upon by all Council of Europe member states. Each party of the Framework Convention is therefore left with a margin of appreciation to assess which groups are to be covered by the Convention within their territory. A pragmatic approach was adopted, based on the recognition that at this stage, it is impossible to arrive at a definition capable of mustering general support of all Council of Europe member States. This decision must be made in good faith and in accordance with general principles of international law, including the principle of free self-identification, set out in Article 3 of the Framework Convention. But unlike the UNDRIP, this is an individual right: individuals may decide themselves whether they wish to be treated as belonging to a national minority or not. However, their decision must be based on objective criteria connected with their identity, such as their religion, language, traditions and cultural heritage.

Obtaining accurate statistics on the size of minority populations in European states is very difficult. Ethnic profiling in statistics is often prohibited. Many states do not disaggregate data on ethnic grounds for a variety of historical and political reasons and partly because states do not have reliable or up-to-date census figures. Religion can also be a taboo. Virtually all states in Europe have some population belonging to national minorities, but not all states recognize them. Sometimes this clashes with ideas of Republican equality (meaning citizen uniformity, as in France). Migrant communities, however, are not considered national minorities, within the scope of the European instruments.

Some of the key rights and obligations of the European instruments relate to the European Convention of Human Rights—freedom of expression and thought, of assembly-association, of information and others remind us of the UNDRIP— freedom to use the language in private and public, also in relation to administrative authorities where the request coming from areas inhabited by national minorities or in substantial numbers, "corresponds to a real need" (Art 10, 2nd paragraph), freedom to use their personal and place names and have them officially recognized (Article 11), education, including setting up their own schools in their language and of their language (Articles 12, 13 and 14). But the difficulty still lies in the identification of the subjects and right-holders. Identifying the subjects of the obligations is not problematic: States are the parties to the treaties. This sometimes leads to a difficult balance: national minorities exist, objectively, but they do not hold collective rights. Individuals can hold rights as members of national minorities. A tertium datur seems to emerge between the States and the individuals: national minorities. They have no rights and no obligations, but they are the source of individual rights and state obligations, as long as the state recognizes them.

Whatever the approach to the qualification of a people as Indigenous or minority—subjective, objective or procedural—data on the people concerned becomes a necessary tool. This requires examining the issue of data and sovereignty over data, even of data about sovereignty. Instead of data sovereignty we prefer to analyze it in terms of data governance.

Data governance of Indigenous and minority nations. The Basque data ecosystem

Can data be Indigenous, universal or local? There often is a perception of data as being neutral, just numbers, but this is misleading. Indigenous data refers to data information or knowledge, in whatever format or medium, about IP, or from IP, or that affects IP either collectively or individually, and ranges from language, to genetic data, environment or resources. These data can be *on/about* IP, data *for* IP (for them to access and make use of) and data *of/by* IP: knowing the data, owning the data, need to collect directly (Rainie et al. 2019). The scope of the Indigenous data ecosystem is vast and includes data generated or held by

Indigenous communities and organizations, governments, the public sector, international governmental organizations (IGOs), NGOs, research institutions and commercial entities. (Kukutai and Taylor 2016: 2).

The idea of "data sovereignty" can be seen as a derivative of the complex equation combining official and private mechanisms for "datafying" reality. The official records include statistics and the registry of personal data—such as identity, education degrees, health records and property—such as land and buildings, movables, shares, inheritance, trusts, intellectual property—and the private collection of information—such as consumer data, market data, products and goods data, banking and insurance data, commercial data—and all this information has increased exponentially in the digital age. Awareness of the existence of this immense but hardly visible digital dimension becomes crucial (Lovett et al. 2019).

Datafication is a descriptive concept, signaling some significant social and economic dynamics currently taking place. Everything about life, and death, that can be datafied will eventually be. But who, and for what purpose, is collecting and processing the data? Consequences depend on the type of data stored, the techniques used and on who decides about the knowledge and authority issues. Information on the many instances of collecting data is not always easy to obtain. Big data in the digital age and nation-state jurisdiction—data superhighways—over such data are going in different, sometimes opposite, directions (Cossins 2018). Transfer of data from one state to another often take place without the persons concerned knowing their data will be accessed by external governments. Indeed, statistics are linked to the science of state governance and administration. Indigenous Nations, and also minority Nations or national minorities are now asserting their own claims to data, registries and statistics, to all information concerning them, often disguised as "neutral" data. Knowledge infrastructures become necessary. These counter-hegemonic claims are rooted in their inherent rights to self-identification and self-determination as Peoples. Indigenous Data Sovereignty thus refers to the proper locus of authority over the governance of data about such Peoples, their territories and ways of life (Walter 2018).

But the claim to control data concerning people is also of direct concern to individuals, whatever their civil and citizen status, cultural and ethnic identity. The EU General Regulation on Data Protection that entered into force in 2018 is one of the most sophisticated normative developments over personal data collection, data use and the rights of individuals concerning their personal data. Empowering the individuals to understand the impact of data collection on their lives and welfare, to adopt the decisions concerning such data and regain control as citizens becomes of the essence. For IP there are additional and special concerns, as addressed in this book. In essence they involve a transition and awareness that moves from "my data" to "our data", creating citizen and people mindscapes, where relevant data are sorted out from data spam, secondary data are organized after all the necessary "cleaning" and relevant missing data are also identified. Repair and maintenance are important because they allow us to challenge linear thinking about big data. And the question of algorithms applied to the data follows next.

In the Kukutai and Taylor (2016) preface, Victoria Tauli-Corpuz UN Special Rapporteur on the Rights of Indigenous Peoples writes:

> The United Nations Permanent Forum on Indigenous Issues in its first and second sessions (2002, 2003) already recognised that a key challenge faced by national and international bodies is the lack of disaggregated data on Indigenous Peoples. The absence or lack of data that reflect where and how many Indigenous Peoples there are, and how they are faring in relation to the realization of their individual and collective rights is directly related to the weakness of governments and intergovernmental bodies in formulating and implementing Indigenous-sensitive decisions and programs.
>
> Indigenous Data Sovereignty thus refers to the inherent rights and interests IP have in relation to the creation, collection, access, analysis, interpretation, management, dissemination, re-use and control of data relating to IP, and to decide what, how and why such data are collected, accessed and used.
>
> (Kukutai and Taylor 2016: xi)

In a sense, it implies moving from data *about* to data *for* or *by* IP, but it is also, more ambitiously, a decolonizing methodology, a new epistemology capturing different world-views.[3]

Kukutai and Taylor frame their argument in terms of IPs' rights to self-determination (Article 3, UNDRIP), in relation to their political status and their economic, social and cultural development. But Indigenous Data Sovereignty is also about the resources and capabilities to collect and process data on your own people. This is the approach adopted by Snipp (2016: 40)

> That Indigenous people are typically poorer than the surrounding settler state has important implications for data sovereignty. This is because collecting data that can be turned into information and later organized into meaningful knowledge is a costly process. Censuses and surveys are very costly to conduct and even unobtrusive video surveillance must be processed to condense it and make it intelligible. This, too, often means that Indigenous communities must forgo having access to certain types of information about themselves or must rely on outsiders with the requisite resources to obtain this information. Of course, relying on outsiders typically involves significant compromises over the control of data and therefore data sovereignty."

Would it be conceivable, for instance, for an Indigenous People to have their own Internet domain *dot x* as in .nz or .uk or .eus for the Basque Country? Digital spaces are crucial new data ecosystems.

> While the Western idea of 'data sovereignty' can be seen as a product of the digital age and nation-state jurisdiction over such data, Indigenous nations are asserting their own claims to data sovereignty, which are rooted in their

inherent rights to self-determination as sovereign entities predating European settlers. Indigenous Data Sovereignty thus refers to the proper locus of authority over the management of data about Indigenous peoples, their territories and ways of life.

(Kukutai and Taylor 2016: 14)

Indigenous engagement in the setting of relevant indicators will be a key issue in the post-2015 UN development agenda built around the new Sustainable Development Goals (SDGs) (Kukutai and Taylor 2016: 5). Looking to the past but also to the future to consider how much of the past it is essential to preserve and project into the future, is essential in order to make sure that important values and legitimate interests are considered and reflected in the data governance.

Autonomous data governance in the Basque Country

Indigenous Data Sovereignty, as a field of study, could also be useful to describe and explain some interesting initiatives that are taking place in the Basque Country with a view to generating and preserving data and statistics for a territory that is not in line with the official demarcation. As explained in the introduction, the Basque Country is perceived as a cultural and "ethnic" community by many Basques, but there is no "official" administration, or common entity bringing together all seven Basque territories. It is therefore important to visualize the Basque People in their territorial complexity, and thus go beyond the official states—Spain and France—and European administrative regions—in order to take account of the complex territorial and identity dimensions of the Basque territories. Eustat is the statistical office of the Basque Autonomous Community and is restricted to data collection in the three territories of the Basque Autonomous Community. Its statistics are official. But there is an interesting, non-official and informal not-for-profit organization generating statistics and collecting data from different sources related to the economy, social relations and culture for the whole of the seven Basque territories. This is *Gaindegia*, the Basque observatory using Open Data, which can be accessed at www.gaindegia.eus and www.datuak.net.

Also, two centenary cultural societies, the Basque Society of Studies, *Eusko Ikaskuntza*, and the Academy for the Basque language, *Euskaltzaindia* collect data and generate autochtonous—local, original and autonomous—knowledge. One of their foundational visions was to collect and preserve relevant aspects of Basque culture through their ethnographic and folklore sections and the department on Basque dialects, before they faded away or evolved into modern technologies. This drive to collect data by ethnographer/anthropologists, linguists and archaeologists can be traced back to Larramendi, Peñaflorida and the Enlightenment, but was intensified by the influence of the romantics like von Humboldt and Lucien Bonaparte, and institutionalized by the founders of the two societies in 1918, namely Barandiaran, Aranzadi, Eguren, Azkue, and later by Caro Baroja and Mitxelena. Awareness of the need to collect and systematize data has a long and

Data governance in the Basque Country 121

solid history for the Basques, and action was soon taken to do so, until the dictatorship put an end to such endeavors which, nevertheless, continued in exile, and were resumed and intensified since the 1970s, after the death of the dictator. All these are issues and areas where data become necessary for self-identification and self-awareness as a People and can be seen as examples of Indigenous or minority nation data governance in the Basque Country. This chapter cannot describe the whole data ecosystem in the Basque Country, but will look specifically at one particular aspect, the recent initiatives set up during the last decade in order to deal with the data and narratives dealing with the violent political conflict of the last 50 years.

Data on memory and conflicting narratives: the Basque case

In this contribution, we are interested in the datafication and categorization or labeling that leads to the construction of data related to politically motivated violence in the Basque Country. There are data collection and algorithmic strategies related to the major interests in constructing a narrative about the conflict. The key questions raised at the beginning of this section gain full relevance: everything about life, and death, that can be datafied will eventually be. But who, and for what purpose, is collecting and processing what data? Consequences depend on the type of data stored, the techniques used and on who decides about the knowledge and authority issues. This takes us to the heart of our contribution.

Powers over all matters related to justice and the criminal justice system are reserved to the central State (in a federal system, this would be equivalent to the federation, or the national, federal, level). The Spanish parliament has thus adopted the key legislation concerning amnesty, victims, terrorism, the Criminal Code and Criminal Procedure, execution of penalties and the prosecution service, the penitentiary law and such matters. There is little, if any, scope left at the regional or federated level even if any of these powers are devolved. The only devolution in the criminal justice system so far has been the transfer of the management of prisons to the Catalan government. As regards victims of political violence, the topic of this contribution, Spain has adopted three major legislative instruments:

1. the *Amnesty Act of 1977*, clearing all possible crimes committed before that year including those committed by the State or its organs. This meant full impunity for state crimes. Victims of such crimes would be left unattended.
2. the *Act on Historical Memory 52/2007* of 26 December recognizes and expands rights and adopts measures in favor of those who suffered persecution or violence during the Civil War and the dictatorship.
3. the *Act 29/2011 on the Recognition and Comprehensive Protection of Victims of Terrorism* (amending and updating *Act 32/1999* of 8 October).

These laws make up a specific system for the protection of victims that defines the conflict as one of terrorism, clears possible state crime and recognizes, in practice, only one category of victim of terrorism. Periodization becomes crucial, since the Amnesty law was adopted one year before the Spanish Constitution, which seems to mark a full stop and new period. Anything that happened before the Constitution (1978) is historical. Whatever took place, under the aegis of the state, within the constitutional regime could not possibly be in breach of human rights and would not be ascribed to the State.

Jon Landa (2019: 208) considers the Spanish system for the protection of victims of violence as having two major traits: asymmetry and hierarchy. It is asymmetric because there are different standards of protection—attention, reparation, recognition, homage—depending on the victim/perpetrator relation. These different standards are conditional, not on the type of breach or crime, but rather on the actor or perpetrator. The type of human rights violation may be the same, but the nature of the victim changes. In my analysis, this is the other side of the so-called criminal law of the enemy (Jakobs), the memory of "our" victims, victimized by our enemy. Victims of ETA terrorism have maximum protection. Victims of other forms of terrorism especially those linked to paramilitary groups often find obstacles in their recognition as victims of terrorism, and thus reparation is also blocked. The European Court of Human Rights ruled on July 18, 2019, that this differentiation in the status of victim, and this corollary denial of reparation does not breach the right to the presumption of innocence recognized in the Convention (Article 6, 2).[4] Victims of the *Historical Memory Act* have a lower degree of reparation and recognition. Finally, victims of police abuses seeking recognition and reparation have sometimes seen the State questioning the perpetrations altogether, for cases occurring after 1978. This asymmetry and hierarchy of victims is built-in into the Spanish criminal justice system. It is supported by the major political parties in Spain.

The normative strategy adopted in the Basque Country (Basque Autonomous Community and Foral Community of Navarre) is within the framework of their limited powers, and always subject to the norms adopted by Spain. Therefore, the asymmetry and hierarchy of victims, depending on who was the perpetrator, still remains at large. The Basque Parliament adopted *Act 4/2008 of June* 19, 2008, on victims of terrorism and the Basque Government adopted the decree *107/2012 of June* 12 to repair victims of human rights abuses between 1978 and 1999. This was followed by *Act 12/2016 of July* 28 of the Basque Parliament, amended by *Act 5/2019 of April* 4, on recognition and reparation of those victims. The *Navarre Foral Act 16/2015 of April* 15 was enacted to recognize and repair victims of politically motivated acts of violence by groups of the extreme right or public servants. Both Acts, Basque and Navarrese, cover the final phase of the Franco dictatorship (1960–1978), in line with the *Spanish Act on Historical Memory*. This Act was declared unconstitutional by the Spanish Constitutional Court by a very thin majority alleging it invaded exclusive State powers to judicially declare that an individual was the victim of abuse by State servants. In a similar vein, the *Basque Act 12/2016 of July* 28, to recognize and repair victims of human rights abuses (1960–1978) was re-drafted in order to take into account that ruling, and the State announced it would not dispute the constitutionality of the

Act. However, MPs of political grouping Ciudadanos and Popular Party of Spain both lodged actions for constitutional review. Navarre adopted a law on historical memory and the Basque Autonomous Parliament was presented with a citizens' legislative initiative with a Bill on the subject.

Data and the "War" on numbers

Behind such legislative framing of victims (and perpetrators), there are different views as to what the Basque conflict, giving rise to political violence, is really about. This generates different explanations or theories about the conflict. The framing of the narrative about the conflict then shapes the categorization of the victims and perpetrators, and the preconceptions about the type of data that need to be collected. The data about the conflict diverge along two major axes: numbers and labeling of "victims" and time-periods. The debates around the numbers of victims and casualties depend on how the conflict is narrated, and on the labels that are used. The "war" on numbers relates to whether one includes victims of police abuse. This affects the categorization of the data on victims. The most accurate approximation to the numbers has been carried out by the Basque Government reports. The Basque Government produced a report on breaches of human rights in the years 1960–2013 based on research by Carmena, Landa, Mugica and Uriarte. It gives the following numbers: victims killed by ETA were 837; victims wounded by ETA are 2600; victims killed by State-related terrorism (paramilitaries) were 73; victims wounded by State-related terrorism were 426; victims killed by the action of State agents were 94 and victims wounded by the action of State agents are 746. This report does not include cases of torture. Another Basque Government research report, on torture and degrading treatment between the years 1960 and 2014, documented 4000 cases of alleged torture by State agents. It was carried out by IVAC, the Basque University Institute of Criminology and the team of Etxeberria, Martin and Pego and contains conclusions and recommendations. These numbers and reports are yet to be complemented by other types of victims: those 511 local counselors threatened by ETA (between 1999 and 2011) and needing bodyguards (Report by U Deusto Pedro Arrupe Institute of Human Rights, July 12, 2019), those extorted or subjected to preventive ransom money. The data are yet to be gathered in official reports.

Memorial data in the Basque conflict: two diverging sovereign views

There have been a number of memorial initiatives that are generating and keeping archives and media, legal and historical data as regards the different episodes or expressions of political violence that have taken place in the Basque Country. The ceasefire declared by ETA in 2011, the decommissioning of its arsenal in April 2017 and its final dissolution in May 2018 are triggering a "competition" on data and on figures concerning the victims of the conflict. The narratives constructed around such figures and phenomena tend to diverge. Historians are drawn into the debate, and institutions are financing research and memorial projects to construct versions of the truth about the past. This section analyzes, on the basis of their own webpages and legislation, the two main victim-recognition initiatives, one, the Centro Memorial de Víctimas del Terrorismo, incorporated by Spanish Parliament *Act 29/2011*; the other, Gogora Institute, incorporated by *Act 4/2014* of the Basque Parliament. The dynamics behind memory institutions, memorials and research projects launched and financed by the Spanish Government and those under the aegis of the Basque autonomous institutions all deal with the conflict in a certain way. But they frame it into different, not necessarily opposing, historical and normative narratives. These are not the only organizations dealing with memory of the violent conflict. There are several others, as mentioned below, and some of them have set up databases, repositories and listings.[5] Ownership over the discourse about the conflict is no monopoly of any of them, but the official organizations, like the two here analyzed, are particularly important in that they are the result of the will of the legislature, the political representatives of the whole of Spain and of the Basque Autonomous Community.

The Memorial Centre for the Victims of Terrorism

Act 29/2011 of the Spanish Parliament on the Recognition and Comprehensive Protection of Victims of Terrorism established the *Fundación Centro para la Memoria de las Víctimas del Terrorismo* (FCMVT) as a state public sector foundation, affiliated with the Ministry of the Interior, with a collegiate-like governing body that includes representatives of the government of Spain as well as those of the autonomous communities, the Cortes Generales [Spanish Parliament], the City Council of Vitoria-Gasteiz and the victims of terrorism. Victims of terrorism are grouped into different organizations, each of which elaborates its own data on victims. The purpose of the center is to preserve and disseminate the democratic and ethical values embodied by the victims of terrorism, building the collective memory of the victims and raising awareness among the population as a whole for the defense of freedom and human rights and against terrorism. Having declared that the victims of terrorism constitute "an ethical reference for our democratic system" and that they "symbolise the defence of freedom and the Rule of Law against the terrorist threat", the legislators established that

> "the public powers will contribute to the knowledge of the truth, attending to the real causes of the victims and contributing to an account of what happened that avoids moral or political equidistances, ambiguities or valuative (sic) neutrality, which reflects with absolute clarity the existence of victims and terrorists, of those who have suffered the damage and of those who have caused it, and which favors an outcome in which the victims feel supported and respected, without there being any justification for terrorism and terrorists".

These legal provisions establish the framework of principles under which the Memorial Center operates. They indicate a parti pris that gives victims of ETA

Data governance in the Basque Country 125

terrorism an enhanced or privileged moral and political predicament. This transpires in their historiography.

The Memorial Center has a documentation center specialized in terrorism and victims of terrorism with a four-fold function: (1) ensure the conservation of the collections; (2) create and maintain a national digital reference repository; (3) facilitate research; and (4) provide items for permanent and temporary exhibitions. It aims to gather all the collections (or digital copies) related to the civic movement, the pacifist movement, victim associations and foundations, law enforcement bodies, terrorist groups etc. The priority is to recover, centralize and digitize all those bibliographic, documentary, newspaper, photographic and audio-visual collections that today remain dispersed and, in some cases, in bad condition or even in danger of disappearing. It will create a Memory Bank, especially focused on the custody of testimonies of victims of terrorism, both those already made and those that will be made in the future, but also those of other key stakeholders, such as members of law enforcement bodies, judges, lawyers, journalists, intellectuals etc.

The same report adds that

> "a Memorial Centre brings together history and memories to reconstruct facts as accurately as possible and to extract the moral significance of the past for the present. As a result, in this Victims of Terrorism Memorial Centre, there will be an account of terrorism, the cause of victims, and the responsibilities of those who made it possible will be questioned in order to avoid it happening again.

The FCMVT is the first memorial center dedicated to the victims of terrorism in Europe and one of only a few in the world. It has been set up with one director (a journalist) and two sub-directors (historians), one media advisor and one lawyer, all male.

Gogora Institute for Remembrance, living together, and human rights

Gogora, (Memory or Bearing in Mind, in Basque) is an institutional forum where victims and society can share their remembrance of the past with a view to helping to build peaceful coexistence (living together). It was set up with the remit of coordinating public policies on remembrance in the Basque Country. Its job is to preserve and pass on the memory of the traumatic, violent and traumatic experiences of the past *hundred years*: the Civil War, the Franco dictatorship, the terrorism of ETA and unlawful counterterrorist attacks; memories of suffering unjustly caused and efforts to construct and defend democratic coexistence and a society based on human rights and peace, even in the most adverse circumstances.

Taking ethical responsibility for passing on democratic remembrance as its starting point, Gogora Institute seeks to establish *inclusive remembrance*, guaranteeing the engagement of the public. Only one limit is set on this dialog between memories: remembrance must *not be used to exclude events or seek equivalences* between them. Nor must it be used to justify any form of terrorism, violence or violation of human rights.

The prime function of Gogora is to coordinate public sector policy on remembrance. To that end, it coordinates the actions of the various institutions and social organizations that work in the field of remembrance and in promoting Human Rights, striving to achieve cooperation and collaboration between them, guaranteeing the broadest possible links with society.

Gogora Institute has four major functions:

1. commemoration: the organization of programs, publications, academic and cultural activities and events in general to keep alive the testimonies and memories of people and events significant for the formation of a free, democratic society.
2. conservation: the conserving of the heritage of democratic remembrance in the Basque Country in all its material forms. To that end, its activities shall include the establishment and maintenance of information archives and inventories of items and places linked to remembrance, be they objects, physical locations, social contexts or other elements that can serve for identification and social recognition.
3. research and investigation, including the reports on victims of the different acts of violence in the different periods covered. These reports are normally carried out by researchers from the Basque universities, with the additional involvement of the Basque Government or the provincial governments. Some of these reports have already been mentioned throughout this contribution.
4. education, participation and dissemination, integration and consultation of all affected.

The preface to *Act 4/2014* establishing the Institute makes direct reference to democratic memory as being related to freedom, equality and dignity of the person. Memory is seen as a right, not a duty. It fulfills the need for critical thinking about a traumatic past of Human Rights violations and the will to share such thoughts. In Gogora's webpage periodization is analyzed, in line with its own statutes. Briefly summarized, over the last hundred years, Basque Society has experienced *four traumas* of violence: the Civil War and the Franco dictatorship that make up historical memory, and ETA terror and unlawful counterterrorism that make up recent memory. These traumas have occurred in different historical periods: the Civil War and early dictatorship, the emergence of ETA violence in the second half of the dictatorship, the transition and democracy. The four traumatic episodes of violence, different as they are, have something important in common: they violated individual human rights generating direct victims, and also indirect victims and thus, they all inflicted an unfair suffering on Basque society. The memory and appraisal of the recent memory cannot be carried out without distinguishing the different periods and contexts: the last years of the dictatorship, the "transition" and the democratic period. In the worst circumstances,

Basques always aspired to live together in a democratic society based on freedom and peace and where human rights are observed.

Two different approaches

We have seen two different approaches to the memory of the victims of violent conflict: the Memorial Center closely follows the Spanish political system's view of the Basque conflict as reduced to ETA terrorism and its defeat by the democratic system and the Spanish security forces, and the Gogora Institute, which takes a larger view of the Basque conflict, going back 100 years and covering other forms of political violence; where ETA is the most important, but not the only, perpetrator of the recent memory period. The lexicon used in each of the memorials is notably different. Both are aiming to collect data and reconstruct facts as accurately as possible in order to preserve memory. The Memorial Center uses a securitarian semantic family—"terrorist threat", "terrorists", "terrorism", "the real causes of the victims", "victims of terrorism"—together with the language of morality—"ethical values embodied by the victims of terrorism", victims of terrorism as an "ethical reference for our democratic system", creating an "account that avoids moral or political equidistances, ambiguities" or "value neutrality", reflect with "absolute clarity who suffered the damage and who caused it". The Memorial Center clearly states the moral superiority of the victims of terrorism, making no attempt to explain the political motivations behind the acts of "terrorism". There is no historical periodization. Victims of terrorism have moral truth on their side and the role of the historian and the memorial is to clarify that truth.[6] This moral superiority of the victims of terrorism turns the unfairness and injustice of their victimhood into a higher "political" status, which leaves no scope for ambiguity, where victims can also be perpetrators, in different degrees, as pointed out in the introduction

By contrast, Gogora underlines and distinguishes historical periods and seeks an inclusive memory. It speaks of "democratic remembrance", "living together" (coexistence is the term sometimes used for the Spanish "convivencia" or the Basque "bizikidetza"), "democratic society", "Human Rights violations". The idea of inclusiveness and of consideration of all the variants of the violent conflict in the Basque Country is compatible with the moral rejection of all breaches of human rights. Remembrance must *not be used to exclude events or seek equivalences* between them. Nor must it be used to justify any form of terrorism, violence or violation of human rights. Victims and perpetrators are to be found in all sorts of camps and are not as neatly categorized into good and evil, and the ethical lessons or morale is to condemn all forms of violence. This approach is criticized by scholars involved with the Memorial Center.[7]

Conclusion: labeling and data

The different approaches of the victims and memory policies and their data governance have implications on the narratives of Basque conflict political violence. I find it impossible for any scholar in the Humanities and Social Sciences to take a *neutral* approach. My aspiration is impartiality and "equidistance", understood as equal rejection of all human rights abuses, whatever their source and their perpetrator. Equidistance should not mean that all actors in the conflict have committed the same amounts of harm, an area where data on victims becomes relevant, but all violations of human rights are blameworthy. Some violations are more serious than others. Yet difference in degree is not difference in nature; none can be excused, especially not on the grounds that the "other" has also committed a violation. A "terrorist" who is tortured or sent to distant prisons in isolation, becomes a victim. This victim status does not mitigate in any way the moral and legal blameworthiness of his crime. The moral superiority attached to victims lies in the fact that they never chose that status nor their suffering as victims, and their victimizers have the full moral blame because they chose to kill them or harm them.

ETA presented its victims as though they were casualties of a Basque "conflict", thus disguised their deliberate choice to harm each and every one of them. ETA hid behind the rhetoric of "armed conflict" with Spain in order to eschew ethical blameworthiness. Its victims were, instead, casualties of the struggle for freedom. The Franco dictatorship, after the Civil War, did the same toward the Republican "reds and separatists". But they were not casualties of war: they were killed, disappeared and persecuted for their ideas. The fight against ETA by constitutional Spain has similarly used the "rule of law" (*Estado de derecho*) as an excuse to hide from the moral harm caused by its decisions: to send ETA prisoners to far-away prisons, to block investigation of torture allegations, to deny the status of victims of terrorism to victims of paramilitary groups, to deny progress in grade to ETA prisoners, and other direct abuses.

Victims are always passive as victims, but sometimes victims are also perpetrators, and that is why turning the victim into an absolute category, implying a status of moral superiority is not morally credible. A "terrorist" and a "victim of terrorism" are not absolute categories, they are not permanent status or predicaments. A "former terrorist" and a "former torturer" can regain their dignity and aspire to live together, when they assume responsibility for the harm they created. This is the aspiration of an enlightened criminal justice system based on the dignity of the person. We need to become aware of the suffering we inflict, and sensitive to the suffering of all, including those we, wrongly, consider our "enemies". Data governance on memory of victims should take these considerations into account and reflect deeply on the labels used and the periods selected for the data. Furthermore, the interests and agendas of data collectors should be examined thoroughly as well. I hope to have contributed to making this point.

Notes

1 The research leading to this chapter has been done in the framework of Research Group GI UPV/EHU on Derechos Fundamentales y Unión Europea" IT1190-19the EU and Fundamental Rights (Unión Europea y Derechos Fundamentales) and also Research Program DER 2015-64599-P MINECO/FEDER UE "Factores postdelictivos y peligrosidad postdelictual"".

2   In 2001, the Spanish Government posthumously awarded him the golden medal on Civil Merit. ETA's first mortal and last victims, Civil Guard Pardines in 1968 and Gendarme Nerin in 2010 were both shot in police traffic checks.
3   Boaventura de Sousa Santos (2014).
4   The two cases (*Larrañaga Arando and Others* v. *Spain and Martinez Agirre and Others* v. *Spain*) concern the relatives of six victims killed by paramilitary groups. A 1983 Council of Europe Convention on Compensation of Victims of Violent Crimes allows withholding compensation if the victims had any relation with a violent organization. In my view, the case should have been brought under Protocol 1 of the Convention, in relation to Article 14.
5   Some organizations representing victims of ETA are AVT, FVT, or Covite. Some organizations from a Basque perspective are Argituz, Euskal Memoria, or Egiari Zor. Their websites contain interesting information.
6   Rivera (2018:13).
7   Rivera (2018) blames the Basque Government for carrying out memory without history, (17) and putting the different forms of violence at the same level (23).

References

Bullain, I. (2011). *Revolucionarismo Patriótico*. Tecnos, Madrid.
Cossins, D. (2018). Discriminating algorithms: 5 times AI showed prejudice. *New Scientist*. https://www.newscientist.com/article/2166207-discriminating-algorithms-5-times-ai-showed-prejudice/.
Landa, J. (2019). Biktimei buruzko politikak Euskadin: balantze labur bat eta etorkizuneko perspektibak. In J.M.L. Gorostiza and E.G. Carrera (eds.), *Euskadi Indarkeriaren Ondoren- Euskadi Después de la Violencia*, UPV/EHU Argitalpen Zerbitzua, Bilbao, 203–225.
Lovett, R., Lee, V., Kukutai, T., Rainie, S.C., and Walker, J. (2019). Good data practices for indigenous data sovereignty. In A. Daly, K. Devitt, and M. Mann (eds.), *Good Data*. Institute of Network Cultures, Inc., Amsterdam. ISBN:978-94-92302-27-4.
Kukutai, T., and Taylor, J. eds. (2016). In T. Kukutai and J. Taylor (eds.), *Indigenous Data Sovereignty: Toward an Agenda*. Australian National University Press.
Rainie, S.C., Kukutai, T., Walter, M., Figueroa-Rodriguez, O.L., Walker, J., and Axelsson, P. (2019). Issues in open data: indigenous data sovereignty. In T. Davies, S. Walker, M. Rubinstein, and F. Perini (eds.), *The State of Open Data: Histories and Horizons*. African Minds and International Development Research Centre, Cape Town and Ottawa, 300–319.
Rivera, A. (2018). El pasado como posibilidad. In A. Rivera (ed.), *Naturaleza Muerta. Usos del Pasado en Euskadi Después del Terrorismo*. Prensas de la Universidad de Zaragoza, Zaragoza.
Snipp, C.M. (2016). What does data sovereignty imply: what does it look like? In T. Kukutai and J. Taylor (eds.), *Indigenous Data Sovereignty: Toward an Agenda*. ANU Press.
de Sousa Santons, B., del Sur, E., and Barcelona, A. (2014). *Epistemologies of the South*. London: Routledge.
Walter, M. (2018). The voice of indigenous data: beyond the markers of disadvantage. *First Things First, Griffith Review*, 2018(60), 256–263.

9 Indigenous policy and Indigenous data in Mexico

Context, challenges and perspectives

Oscar Luis Figueroa Rodríguez

Introduction: Indigenous population in Mexico

The Political Constitution of the Mexican United States (Mexico) establishes under the 2nd article that:

> The Nation has a multicultural composition originally supported by its Indigenous people, which are those that descend from populations that inhabited the actual territory of the country at the beginning of colonization and that preserve their own social, economic, cultural and political institutions, or part of them.
>
> The consciousness of their Indigenous identity should be fundamental criteria to determine to whom Indigenous people ordinances are applied.
>
> Indigenous communities are those that form a social, economic and cultural unit, established in a territory and that recognize their own authorities in accordance with their uses and costumes.
>
> (Constitución Política de los Estados Unidos Mexicanos, 2019, p. 2)

This definition of indigeneity has been used as the basic reference in any matter regarding public policies toward Indigenous Peoples in Mexico. It is important to point out that the construction of this definition was made by the Constituent Congress in 1917; this Congress was integrated by 218 Congressmen (all men) of which only eight were Indigenous—3.66%— (Romero, 1978), which clearly indicates that there was not a sufficient number of Indigenous representatives participating in the construction of this definition, narrowing Indigenous communities' influence on their own definition.

It also—in general—aligns with the official definition of the United Nations (United Nations, 2007), The International Labor Organization (Indigenous and Tribal People Convention, n.d.) and the World Bank (Indigenous Peoples, 2019). Nevertheless, in practice its application (defining the exact number of Indigenous People in Mexico and developing a particular public policy for this population) has been a complicated task that has changed over time; in this sense, the concept of "Indigenous" is historical (Rubio, 2014) and thus has been historically defined according to the political and ideological context of Mexico's government at the time.

Since the development of the first national census in Mexico in 1895 until the last census in 2010, 13 censuses have been applied throughout the country. The federal government has attempted to quantify the number of inhabitants characterized as Indigenous in each census. Language has been the common criterion used to determine Indigeneity (population that speaks an Indigenous language) (Table 9.1). In the censuses of 1895 and 1921 the criterion of race was included, with the options of being Indigenous, mixed or White. In both cases the registration was done by asking the population what race they were; this could be considered as self-perception as Indigenous (Pla, 2011). In the 1921 census, almost 30% of the population considered themselves to be Indigenous (Rubio, 2014), even though only 15% of the population older than five spoke an Indigenous language. In the context presented at the beginning of the 20th century during which the idea of "modernization" was strongly embraced by Porfirio Diaz's government and the ones that followed, being perceived as an Indigenous country was not ideal; therefore, in the preceding censuses of that century the self-perception criterion was no longer included.

The 1930 census incorporated the concepts of monolingual and bilingual; this was a breakthrough for the federal government ability to quantify the proportions of population that spoke Spanish and any other Indigenous language. In the 1921 census, the option of speaking Spanish and another language (Indigenous or foreign) was acknowledged, since previously the instructions for completing the census form in the 1895 and 1900 censuses established that when a person spoke Spanish and an Indigenous language "preference will be given to record Spanish" as their language (INEGI, 2020). This indicated a preference toward not being Indigenous promoted by the state.

The ideological context during the first half of the 20th century supported by the ideas of scholars such as Manuel Gamio and Antonio Caso (both eminent non-Indigenous scholars in Mexico, the first an anthropologist and archaeologist and the second a philosopher) criticized the state's reliance on only language criteria for quantifying the Indigenous population. Gamio suggested the consideration of "race and culture and not just language" and Caso proposed the definition of Indigenous according to four elements: "physical features, culture, language and the sense of community" (Pla, 2011).

Thus, the 1940–1970 censuses incorporated cultural criteria presented as customs and habits to further identify who were Indigenous among the Mexican population. In the 1940 census a number of cultural differentiation criteria were included in the census: footwear—using regular shoes or *huaraches*[1] vs. being barefoot; food habits—eating wheat bread vs. *tortilla*[2]; clothing—material of the trousers or skirt; and if people slept in bed or cot vs. hammock or the floor in *petate*.[3] In the 1950 and 1960 censuses, footwear and food habits were considered and in the 1970 census only footwear was considered. As a result of the inclusion of these cultural elements, the number of inhabitants considered as Indigenous increased considerably (Pla, 2011; Rubio, 2014; Carrasco and Alcázar, 2009).

Table 9.1 Criteria to define "Indigenous population" in Mexico's census

Census year	Criteria	Items
1895	Language	Habitual language (Spanish or Indigenous language).
	Race	Race (pure Indigenous, Indigenous mixed with White or White).
1900	Language	Native language or spoken language (Spanish, French, English or an Indigenous language).
1910	Language	Native language or spoken language (Spanish, French, English or an Indigenous language).
1921	Language	Spanish or any other language spoken.
	Race	Race (Indigenous, mixed, White or any other).
1930	Language	Spanish or any other language spoken. The concepts of monolingual and bilingual were introduced.
1940	Language	Spanish or any other language spoken.
	Customs/habits	Customs or habitual (food habits—if people ate wheat bread; footwear—if they were barefoot, used *huaraches* or regular shoes; clothing—material of the trousers or skirts; and, if they slept in hammock, cot, bed or the floor).
1950	Language	Spanish or any other language spoken.
	Customs/habits	Customs or habitual (food habits and footwear).
1960	Language	Spanish or any other language spoken.
	Customs/habits	Customs or habitual (food habits and footwear).
1970	Language	Spanish or any other language spoken.
	Customs/habits	Customs or habitual (footwear).
1980	Language	Spanish or any other language spoken.
1990	Language	Indigenous language section (including if the person speaks an Indigenous language, which particular language and if Spanish is spoken too).
2000	Language	Indigenous language section (including if the person speaks an Indigenous language, which particular language and if Spanish is spoken too).
	Self-perception as Indigenous	Self-identification (question asking if people belonged to an Indigenous group).
2010	Language	The following questions were asked: if people spoke an Indigenous language, what particular language, if Spanish is also spoken, understanding of an Indigenous language and if according to any particular Indigenous group culture people consider themselves Indigenous.
	Self-perception as Indigenous	

Source: INEGI, Censos y Conteos de Población y Vivienda (https://www.inegi.org.mx/programas/ccpv/2020/default.html)

Once again this was inconvenient for the state. On one hand, accepting the fact that Mexico was an Indigenous country placed it further away from being a "modern" state. On the other hand, it presented the challenge of establishing a clear frontier between the Indigenous population and that known as "mestizo"[4] which constitutes a continuum (Knight, 2004) since several of the cultural features remained a part of the daily habits of the mestizo population. As a result, Mexico dropped the use of cultural criteria in following censuses to avoid further discussions that would lead to topics such as racism.

For the 1980 and 1990 censuses, only language criteria were used. Finally, the last two censuses included the self-perception criteria once again but presented in a different format. In 2000, a question asking if people belonged to an Indigenous group was included. In 2010, a whole section asked questions regarding if people spoke an Indigenous language, if they understood an Indigenous language even though they could not speak it, and if according to any particular Indigenous group culture they considered themselves as part of that culture. For the 2020 census, this section is expected to remain with the inclusion of an option for Afro-descendants too.

Indigeneity definition for public policy: INEGI, CONAPO and INPI

The institution in charge of the design, application, systematization and presentation of data obtained from the censuses is the National Institute of Geography, Statistics and Informatics (INEGI).[5] With the data obtained from INEGI, several other agencies develop analyzes and projections about social and economic variables—among others—for the population in general and by interest groups. It is important to mention that in the design and conduction of polls and censuses Indigenous participation has been limited if not null, particularly in the design, in terms of the approaches and interests on the data to be collected and its use.

According to the 2010 census (INEGI, 2010) of 112,336,538 inhabitants in the country, 6.5% over three years old spoke an Indigenous language and 21.5% considered themselves to be Indigenous (self-perception). Importantly, in the previous censuses, the age for considering if an individual spoke an Indigenous language was five; for the 2010 census that age was reduced to three, which is the age taken into account ever since. INEGI also performs a number of polls in relation to several topics, including a National Demographic Dynamic Poll (ENADID)[6] which was last conducted in 2018. This poll was based on projections developed from data gathered from a sample in order to observe trends. The ENADID included an "ethnicity index" composed of the variables (a) population over three years old that speak an Indigenous language and (b) population over three years old that consider themselves to be Indigenous (Figure 9.1). Out of a total population over three years old in Mexico of 119,713,142 inhabitants, 5.9% speak an Indigenous language; nevertheless, 33.7% consider themselves to be Indigenous regardless of not speaking an Indigenous language but considering a number of cultural elements commonly related to Indigenous communities and Indigenous lifestyle that people relate with (ENADID, 2018), including being part of an Indigenous household.

These results are interesting and require further analysis in order to better understand why the population that speak Indigenous languages is decreasing (from 6.3 to 5.9% in the 2006–2018 period) whilst the population that perceive themselves as Indigenous has increased (from 16.2 to 33.7% in the same period), taking into account the methodological nuances in both the census and the poll.

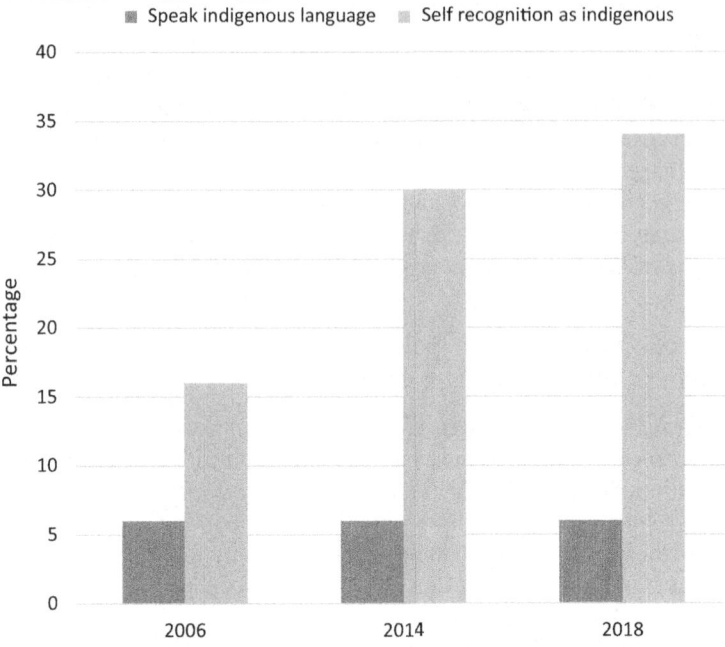

Figure 9.1 Ethnicity index in Mexico (ENADID 2006, 2014, 2018).

The National Population Council (CONAPO) is the organization in charge of demographic planning for the country in order to assure the equal participation of the Mexican population in programs for social and economic development (CONAPO, 2020). CONAPO estimates the Indigenous population in Mexico considering the following criteria: (a) population that speak an Indigenous language; (b) population that perceives themselves as part of an Indigenous group (self-perception) and (c) population that inhabit within a household with an Indigenous member (Indigenous language speaker or self-perceived as Indigenous) except in cases in which Indigenous individuals form part of the domestic service in the house, mainly in urban settings. CONAPO acknowledges the limitation of only considering language as the main criteria to define indigeneity and argue that:

> The figures of Indigenous language speakers represent a minimum dimension of the total number of Indigenous, since the penetration of Spanish in formal education, through bilingual schools, has led to the new generations not speaking the native language of their ancestors. Even after the mother tongue has been lost, many descendants of Indigenous language speakers maintain contact with their original communities and preserve several customs.
> (CONAPO, 2005, pp. 15–16)

The institution in charge of the matters related to the Indigenous and Afro-Mexican communities is the National Institute for the Indigenous Communities (INPI)[7]—formerly the National Commission for the Development of Indigenous Communities (CDI)—the purpose of which is to define, design, norm, establish, execute, coordinate, promote, monitor and evaluate policies, programs, projects, strategies and public actions to guarantee the exercise and implementation of Indigenous and Afro-Mexican communities' rights as well as their sustainable development and the strengthening of their culture and identity (INPI, 2020).

During the last administrations (2000–2018) in the country and before being converted into INPI by the current administration, the CDI established that the Indigenous population was all those inhabitants that were part of an Indigenous household in which the head of the house, its partner or any ascendant (mother, father, stepmother, stepfather, grandmother, grandfather, mother- or father-in-law) have declared to speak an Indigenous language (Rubio, 2014; CDI, 2014).

According to the Special Program for Indigenous People 2014–2018 of the CDI,[8] there were 15.7 million Indigenous inhabitants in Mexico, of which 6.6 million spoke an Indigenous language and 11.1 million were living within an Indigenous household. It acknowledged 68 different ethnic groups corresponding to 68 languages spoken across the country and it identified 25 Indigenous regions in 20 states and established that 624 of the 2,456 municipalities in the country were Indigenous (CDI, 2014).

The current administration (2018–2024), through the INPI, has presented the 2018–2024 National Program for Indigenous People, in which it establishes that in Mexico there are 68 Indigenous *pueblos* (ethnic groups) and the afro-Mexican people; 7.4 million of Indigenous language speakers (6.5% of the population); 12 million people inhabiting within Indigenous households (10.6% of the population); 25.7 million people self-perceived as Indigenous (21.5% of the population) and 64,172 localities with Indigenous population across the country´s territory (INPI, 2018).

Current state of Indigenous communities in Mexico

According to the National Evaluation Council (CONEVAL),[9] the Indigenous population in Mexico has presented an accentuated situation of poverty and vulnerability historically. In 2018, the percentage of the Indigenous population living under poverty conditions was 69.5% whereas the percentage of non-Indigenous population under similar conditions was 39%. Also, the highest percentage of Indigenous population under poverty conditions are located in those localities with the lowest number of inhabitants; so, 78.7% of the Indigenous population living in poverty live in localities of under 2,500 inhabitants (CONEVAL, 2019). This means that Indigenous communities are established mainly in rural areas throughout the country that present severe conditions of marginalization and vulnerability to their inhabitants. The country´s most marginalized municipalities happen to be mainly municipalities considered to be Indigenous or part of an Indigenous region located in rural areas (Figure 9.2).

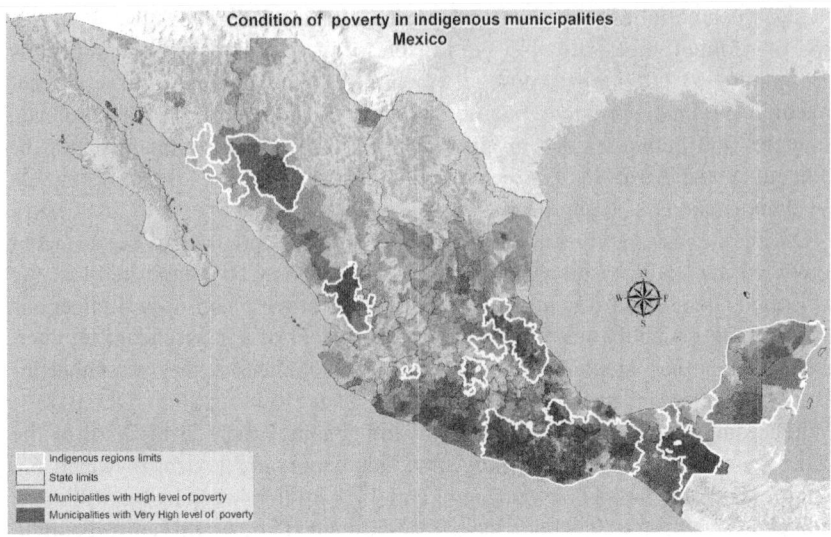

Figure 9.2 Map of Mexico Indigenous regions and marginality.

The *Poverty in the Indigenous population in Mexico 2008–2018* report (CONEVAL, 2019) noted that 50% of the Indigenous population live in rural localities whilst the rest of the population is mainly integrated by migrants and their families who migrate and get established in medium-sized and big cities because they are looking for better income opportunities. Some thrive and become part of the Indigenous population that are less poor and vulnerable, representing only 6.9% of the total Indigenous population. Nearly one in four Indigenous individuals live under extreme poverty conditions in comparison with one in 20 for non-Indigenous population.

Regarding deprivation of social services (Figure 9.3), lack of access to social security has the highest incidence among the Indigenous population, followed by the lack of access to basic housing services (running water, sewage and electric power), which once again is more extreme for Indigenous populations in rural areas where only one in five persons have access to basic housing services (CONEVAL, 2019). In general, according to this report, the Indigenous population has a higher percentage of its population in five of the six social deprivation categories in comparison with the non-Indigenous population, with only a lower figure in the access to health services. This is also noticeable when comparing figures corresponding to the years 2008 and 2018 for the Indigenous population (Figure 9.3) and is the only service in which the improvement is noticeable (health). This could be due to the health program developed by the last administration called the *seguro popular* (popular insurance) which had almost universal coverage in terms of the population registered. Nevertheless, being registered did not necessarily mean that, in the event of any medical condition or emergency,

Indigenous policy and data in Mexico 137

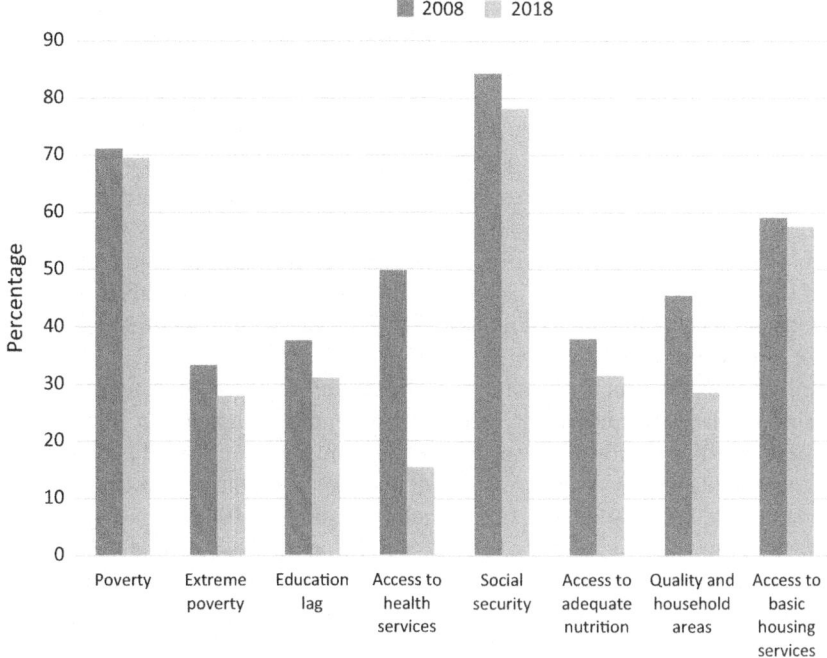

Figure 9.3 Social deprivation indicators 2008–2018 (CONEVAL).

facilities, treatment and medicines would be available in Indigenous contexts. An in-depth evaluation of the matter could help better document this subject area and aid understanding of why these problems are present.

Between 2008 and 2018, the Indigenous population under poverty conditions was reduced by 1.6 percentage points whilst during the same period for non-Indigenous population the reduction represented 2.2 percentage points. The Indigenous population members with reduced poverty conditions were mainly established in non-rural settlements. Finally, the report emphasized that poverty incidence has not been properly attended in terms of public policy for the Indigenous population since eight of every ten Indigenous Peoples members under 18 live under poverty conditions (CONEVAL, 2019).

The latest report of the United Nations (UN) special commissioner for Indigenous communities in Mexico establishes the following as the main areas of concern for Indigenous Peoples' rights: (a) land territories and natural resources; (b) development priorities, megaprojects, consultation and consent; (c) free determination and political participation; (d) violence, impunity and access to justice and (e) economic, cultural and social rights. The main recommendations presented in the report include, among others: (a) specialized attention for the recognition and protection of Indigenous communities' lands and territories; (b) any consultation about activities and measures that could affect Indigenous communities should be first done with Indigenous communities' members and adequate information about social, environmental and cultural impact should be provided, and no project should proceed without their free, prior and informed consent; (c) Indigenous self-government and autonomy systems should be promoted and strengthened; (d) collective and culturally appropriate protection measures in the defense of the rights of Indigenous communities and individuals at risk should be developed and the recognition of Indigenous justice systems should be reinforced; (e) efforts should be doubled to obtain specific information regarding health, education and other services and these services should be developed in consultation, coordination and collaboration with Indigenous communities in order to incorporate their proposals (Naciones Unidas, 2018).

A previous UN report carried out in 2003 established the following as priority affairs in relation to the human rights of Indigenous population in Mexico: (a) agrarian conflicts (land and resources); (b) political conflicts; (c) Indigenous communities in the justice system; (d) conflict in Chiapas; (e) the rights of Indigenous women, children and migrants; (f) education, language and culture and (g) constitutional reform and composition of Indigenous groups. The main findings pointed out in this report were (a) regardless of the efforts done by the Mexican state, the Indigenous population remain in a disadvantaged situation in relation to the rest of the population, being victims of discrimination and social exclusion; (b) there is a high and persistent level of conflicts around Indigenous communities commonly involving violence regarding agrarian, environmental and political issues; (c) the Indigenous population is vulnerable and victims of the judicial system from it suffer violations to their rights, physical integrity and even their lives with high degrees of impunity and corruption in the judicial system; (d) discrimination is manifest also in the distribution of wealth, goods and public services, the main victims within the Indigenous population being women and children (mainly female) as well as the migrant population and (e) in general, public policies regarding Indigenous population are limited and with a low budget, clearly pointing out that the Indigenous population is not a high priority for the Mexican state (Naciones Unidas, 2003).

It is evident that the problems remained the same during the 2003–2018 period. Public policies aimed to reduce the gap regarding the improvement of living conditions (health, education, economic security and housing services) as well as provide proper access to justice and conflict resolution (about land tenure, natural resources exploitation and all kind of projects) but they were neither appropriate nor relevant or sufficient judging merely by the fact that both commissioners point out the same issues as priorities to be attended to.

Indigenous Data Sovereignty in Mexico: toward an agenda

Clearly Indigenous communities in Mexico have been systematically excluded from development processes throughout the history of the country. Ever since the colonial period, Indigenous communities have been enslaved, marginalized and exploited through several mechanisms that ensured deprivation from their lands and resources including the violation of several of their human rights. There is not much available evidence in terms of evaluations about Indigenous-related public policy; except for some specific and monitoring reports from the National Evaluation Council mainly from Indigenous Rights and Infrastructure Programs, there are no impact evaluations with particular recommendations in order to improve general public policy for Indigenous communities.

The actual administration has established the following as priorities in the National Program for Indigenous People 2018–2024: (1) define and implement sustainable and intercultural integral development processes; (2) develop sustainable economic capacities; (3) development of social, communication, connectivity and broadcasting infrastructure; (4) constitutional and legal recognition of Indigenous rights in accordance with international treaties and jurisprudential criteria; (5) implementation of fundamental rights of Indigenous People as well as measures for the defense of land territories, natural resources and environment; (6) strengthen and reinvigorate language, values, knowledge and other elements that constitute Indigenous cultural and bio-cultural heritage; (7) develop affirmative actions and measures to secure the recognition, guarantee of and respect of Indigenous women's rights in their own contexts; (8) guarantee protection of and respect for Indigenous Peoples in a situation of vulnerability and victims of violence and discrimination rights and (9) right of participation, representation, consultation with and free prior and informed consent (INPI, 2018).

The previous Special Program for Indigenous Peoples (2014–2018) established the following priorities: (1) promote the recognition, rights and access to justice; (2) increase access to food, health and education; (3) provide services for infrastructure and housing with a sustainability approach; (4) improve the monetary and non-monetary income through the establishment of productive projects; (5) strengthen participative planning and government program coordination and (6) preserve and strengthen Indigenous Peoples culture recognizing its national heritage character. As can be observed, both programs establish access to rights, justice, participation, services and productive infrastructure as part of their priorities.

In all of these historic unsolved priorities and established proposals within the current development program, there is a common element: the use of data to generate information and knowledge and the particular way in which this information and knowledge is being integrated, used, controlled and exploited in a variety of contexts, industries, activities, processes and various stakeholders. In this sense, Indigenous Data Sovereignty (IDS) appears to be not only relevant but necessary toward creating fairer governance of Indigenous Peoples and their future prosperity.

Some of the main topics related to IDS that clearly present challenges and opportunities for Indigenous communities in the country are described in what follows (and displayed in Figure 9.4).

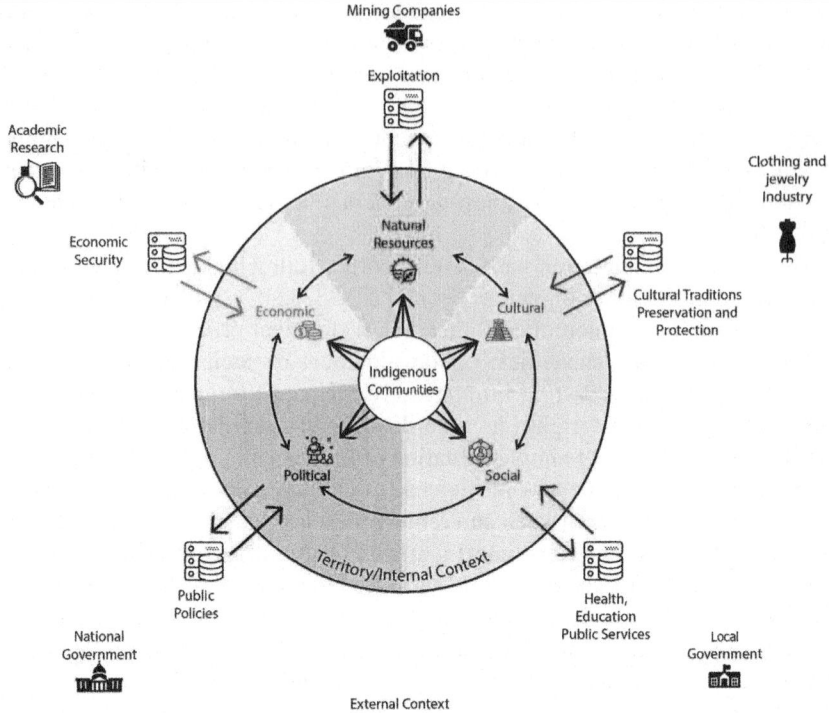

Figure 9.4 Indigenous data production and use.

Natural resources

Due to historic, economic, social and political reasons and being pursued or displaced, Indigenous Peoples have been scattered all over the country's territory into isolated regions with difficult access including a wide variety of ecosystems (e.g., desert, jungle, forest). Indigenous communities are landowners under a particular land tenure scheme in Mexico called *communal lands* with legal basis on the Agrarian Law, which establishes that "the community will determine the use of their lands, their division in different portions with diverse ends for the use of its goods" (Ley Agraria, 2019, p. 19). In general, Indigenous territories are related to a diverse variety of natural resources which include water, plants, wildlife, timber and minerals, to mention only some of the most relevant ones.

The exploitation and use of all of these resources correspond by law to Indigenous communities, with the exception of those regarded as strategic for national interest and well-being, which could be subject of expropriation by the state. In general, there is a lack of understanding around commercial value of most of these resources and the implication of the exploitation of them in terms of investments, infrastructure, health and environmental consequences. It has not been uncommon for historically external actors, such as academia, government officials and private stakeholders to conduct research to better understand and characterize natural resources within Indigenous territories sometimes without informing locals or even asking for permission.

One of the most controversial issues has been the development of extractive activities such as mining which have had a profound impact on Indigenous communities; concessions to explore and exploit mineral resources have accelerated in the past years supported by a number of legal reforms carried out in particular by the past two administrations (2006–2012 and 2012–2018 by Presidents Calderon and Peña, respectively). In this sense, it has been documented that:

> between 2000 and 2012, from the 28 million hectares identified as the hard core of Indigenous territories, around 2,173,141 hectares have been given under concession, mainly for metallic mining. This means that in the last 12 years Indigenous people have lost the jurisdiction of 7% of their territory only by mining concessions and frequently communities are not even informed.
> (Valladares, 2018, p. 3)

This is a clear example of how the lack of IDS has led to communities not being informed properly about their resources and the way they could be exploited with the environmental consequences of the exploitation techniques and methods including the use of heavy machinery and massive lixiviation processes mainly with sodium cyanide which is forbidden in several European countries (Boege, 2013).

Eckart Boege (2013) developed an analysis of Indigenous territories dispossession in Mexico and presents in his conclusions the following remarks: (1) some mining concessions include almost the totality of some small Indigenous communities such as *Kiliwas, Kikapoo, Cucapas, Pimas, Guarijios* and *Nahuas*; (2) the Indigenous communities most affected in terms of extension of the concessions are the *Rarámuris, Zapotecos, Chatinos, Mixtecos, Coras* and *Tepehuanes*; (3) mining companies buy or rent the land where they establish an exploitation, in case the local community refuses to sell or rent the state, supported by the mining law that allows them the right to expropriate the land in the benefit of public interest; (4) mining concessions for gold exploitation are dominant, this being the type of exploitation that uses cyanide in highly risky procedures for both human beings and the environment.

Cultural heritage

Several Indigenous cultural elements have also been subject to exploitation over the years. One of the most known cases involves the use of Indigenous patterns and techniques for clothing design purposes. In June 2019, the Mexican minister of culture accused Carolina Herrera[10] of using for their own benefit embroidery techniques and identity patterns from Indigenous communities for her 2020 collection. According to the minister of culture, some of the embroidery used by Carolina Herrera was taken from the Otomí community of Tenengo de Doria in the state of Hidalgo and others are typical of those from Tehuantepec, Oaxaca (Friedman, 2019). There is an evident resemblance and the designer even declared that the intention of using these patterns for her collection was as homage to Mexico; nevertheless, the fact remains that Indigenous communities are not informed about the use of their patterns and never receive any kind of royalties for the use of them.

It is important to point out that among the limitations that Indigenous communities face, there is a lack of general knowledge about legal considerations related to their cultural heritage, such as the registration of patents and intellectual property protection in order to obtain the rights to them, thus avoiding or being better equipped for litigating against plagiarisms such as this fashion industry example.

Social, economic and political needs and rights

The marginalization and exclusion that Indigenous communities have suffered put them in a very fragile position since the lack of opportunities is evident and the gap with the rest of the population in the country is considerable. As already presented, the social and economic conditions under which most Indigenous Peoples live limit the opportunities for them to develop and thrive.

The most evident areas reflected in some of the public policies implemented over the years are the social and economic topics. The need for basic services improvement is imperative and the creation of economic opportunities for Indigenous Peoples has been present in most of the efforts done by the Mexican government toward development.

Regarding rights, the former CDI in 2016 presented the amplified diagnosis for the Indigenous rights program in which it remarked that:

> the situation of the Mexican Indigenous population regarding the exercise of their collective and individual rights, is far from being fully reflected in national statistics and diagnosis, which makes it almost impossible to identify this population sector in front of the justice and quantitatively value the characteristics of the phenomenon. Nevertheless, important efforts to dimension the problem have been done, based on which elements have been found such as the lack of knowledge of their rights, limited capacities to enforce them, discrimination and insufficient economic resources to hire appropriate advice services and legal defense.
>
> (CDI, 2016, p. 8)

One of the most evident limitations for Indigenous Peoples when facing legal matters is the lack of financial resources to pay for lawyers. Even though the law requires the state to provide a lawyer free of charge, these professionals have work overloads and are not prepared to work with Indigenous Peoples in terms of understanding the language and culture of those to be defended.

Another situation relevant to Indigenous Peoples' rights is the presence of social conflicts which on occasions escalate into violent episodes. These conflicts are mainly over land property claims and because of the disrespect of political and religious diversity. Some of these conflicts result in those involved being forced to abandon their usual residency and become displaced peoples. Recently, some of these displacements have been forced due to the presence of drug cartels and the production of illegal plants such as poppy and marihuana.

Within Indigenous communities, women are among the most vulnerable. Domestic violence is not uncommon and adding to other variety of violence forms (economic, labor, psychological, etc.), these have become prioritized demands for Indigenous women along with sexual and reproductive rights. In some Indigenous communities, women are not allowed to participate in decision-making processes relevant for the entire community. Regarding access to rights, some government initiatives have been developed over the years including the project for Indigenous prisoner defense in the 1980s and the project seeking attention to the displacement of Indigenous Peoples in the 2000s.

The CDI, in 2016, established the limited capacity of Indigenous Peoples to exercise their rights as the main problematic situation regarding the rights of Indigenous Peoples. Rights are limited by discrimination specifically with respect to culture, the lack of support for rights promotion and cultural initiatives, lack of knowledge of rights, limited access to legal support, institutional weaknesses that cause the failure to guarantee the exercise of Indigenous rights and institutional designs oblivious to the needs of cultural diversity. The recommended actions in order to strengthen Indigenous capacities included improve access to justice, protection of cultural heritage and gender equity; also, the recommended actions for the exercise of Indigenous population rights included appropriate attention to legal matters, attention to displaced Indigenous population and access to specialized health services for Indigenous communities (CDI, 2016).

Once again there are no impact evaluations available to establish the effectiveness of the proposed actions regarding Indigenous rights during the past administration, but the fact that problems remain and are fully acknowledged by the current administration in its program can give us an idea of the persistence and complexity of them. IDS could help fill the gap regarding the lack of evaluations as an appropriate approach in the design and implementation of monitoring, evaluation and learning (MEL) local systems, controlled and used by Indigenous communities.

The OECD recommends four main areas to strengthen Indigenous economies:

1. improving Indigenous statistics and data governance
2. creating an enabling environment for Indigenous entrepreneurship and small business development at regional and local levels
3. improving the Indigenous land tenure system to facilitate opportunities for economic development
4. adapting policies and governance to implement a place-based approach to economic development that improves policy coherence and empowers Indigenous communities (OECD, 2019, p. 5)

The first of these points is basic in order to enable the successful development of the following ones, and it completely relies on IDS. The same report emphasizes that "the inclusion of Indigenous peoples in data governance will enable better data that incorporates their values and perspectives" (OECD, 2019, p. 9). The strategies suggested by this report include the inclusion of Indigenous representatives in national statistics agencies, adapting data collection to the needs of Indigenous Peoples, and providing tools for Indigenous communities to collect their own data (OECD, 2019). Nevertheless, these strategies will prove successful only to the extent that the necessary capabilities are developed among Indigenous actors, supported by appropriate technology and infrastructure availability.

Conclusion

Indigenous communities in Mexico need to be able to access, use, control and in general govern their data and information. In order to achieve data governance, public policy must be developed to remediate the three main data challenges for Indigenous Peoples: data collection, access and relevance. The first and the last are strongly related to the need to develop capacities within Indigenous communities to design and apply data collection methods and tools and also to develop skills to understand, interpret, analyze and even theorize from this data. As has been recognized internationally, Indigenous Peoples always were data stewards, collectors, analyzers and users (Kukutai and Taylor, 2016; Smith, 2016). Revitalizing these ways of knowing that have been suppressed by colonization as well as building new skills for data science and use are critical. However, the main challenge remains the condition of educational lethargy present among Indigenous children and youngsters (Figure 9.3) in addition to the necessity of better conditions for them to complete not only basic education but also to pursue higher degrees. There remains a critical need for IDS-related topics in the curricula of middle grades to create awareness among youth and to promote participation and consciousness regarding these issues.

The main limitation for accessing data is the general lack of infrastructure and technology in Indigenous communities. In general, Indigenous communities have limited access to modern technologies such as personal computers with an Internet connection. The federal government, foundations and WHO must facilitate access to technology for Indigenous communities in order to enhance access to data and improve decision-making processes on several levels including personal but also community and municipal. At a municipal[11] level, increased access to and relevance of data would enrich the participatory construction of municipal development plans required by law from each local administration thereby creating a scenario of better data for governance.

Finally, regarding IDS discussion in general from a global perspective, Latin American countries, particularly Mexico in this case, are only recently presenting the topic as part of the academic, public policy and general public discussion, unlike the CANZUS countries in which IDS has already obtained a certain level of dissemination reflected in the fact that IDS national networks have been established (for instance, the USIDSN and the Aotearoa Māori Data Sovereignty Network among others). A lot remains to be done and many challenges remain since a national agenda around IDS is only in the early stages of construction. This chapter presents the most evident of these challenges and there is still a long way toward achieving Indigenous emancipation.

Notes

1 *Huarache* is a popular style of handmade pre-Columbian footwear similar to a sandal.
2 *Tortilla* is a typical Mesoamerican thin flatbread made from corn.
3 *Petate* is a bedroll typical from Mesoamerica woven from fibers of palm.
4 The term *mestizo* was used by the Spanish Empire during the 16th century to refer to one of the castes that integrated the social stratification based on race hierarchies imposed in the American colonies which was the mix of White (European) and Indigenous (Amerindian) races.
5 www.inegi.org.mx.
6 https://www.inegi.org.mx/programas/enadid/2018/default.html.
7 The change from CDI to INPI responded primarily to political needs, since the Lopez administration has insisted in promoting a transformation in the country's public administration; thus the creation of new "Institutes". Nevertheless, the laws that create both CDI and INPI are quite similar, maintaining the general purpose of the agency.
8 This program used data obtained from the 2010 census.
9 CONEVAL uses data primarily from the censuses.
10 Carolina Herrera is a fashion designer founder of the Carolina Herrera fashion firm (www.carolinaherrera.com).
11 Municipalities are the basic political and administrative units in Mexico; the country as a federal republic is integrated by states and these states are divided into municipalities, which have their own local governments. Municipalities with more than 40% of their population regarded as Indigenous are also regarded as Indigenous municipalities.

References

Boege, E. (2013). El despojo de los indígenas de sus territorios en el siglo XXI. *Movimiento Mesoamericano Contra el Modelo Extractivo Minero*. Retrieved from https://movimientom4.org/2013/06/el-despojo-de-los-indigenas-de-sus-territorios-en-el-siglo-xxi/.

Carrasco, V.T. and Alcázar, C.T. (2009). *Los Pueblos Indígenas y los Censos en México y América Latina: la Cultura en la Definición de su Identidad*. Retrieved from https://archivos.juridicas.unam.mx/www/bjv/libros/6/2638/18.pdf.

CDI (Comisión Nacional para el Desarrollo de los Pueblos Indígenas). (2014). *Programa Especial de los Pueblos Indígenas 2014–2018*. Retrieved from https://www.gob.mx/cms/uploads/attachment/file/32305/cdi-programa-especial-pueblos-indigenas-2014-2018.pdf.

CDI (Comisión Nacional para el Desarrollo de los Pueblos Indígenas). (2016). *Diagnóstico Ampliado. Programa de Derechos Indígenas. Dirección de Derechos Indígenas 2016*. Retrieved from http://www.cdi.gob.mx/coneval/2015/cdi_prodei_diagnostico_ampliado_2016.pdf.

CONAPO (Consejo Nacional de Población). (2005). *Proyecciones de Indígenas de México y las Entidades Federativas 2000–2010*. Retrieved from http://www.conapo.gob.mx/work/models/CONAPO/indigenas_2010/Proyindigenas.pdf.

CONAPO (Consejo Nacional de Población). (2020). *Instituciones CONAPO*. https://datos.gob.mx/busca/organization/about/conapo.

CONEVAL (Consejo Nacional de Evaluación de la Política de Desarrollo Social). (2019). *La Pobreza en la Población Indígena de México 2008–2018*, August, 2019. Retrieved from https://www.coneval.org.mx/Medicion/MP/Documents/Pobreza_Poblacion_indigena_2008-2018.pdf.

Constitución Política de los Estados Unidos Mexicanos. (August 9, 2019). Retrieved from http://www.diputados.gob.mx/LeyesBiblio/pdf/1_090819.pdf.

ENADID (*Encuesta Nacional de la Dinámica Demográfica*). (2018). Retrieved from https://www.inegi.org.mx/programas/enadid/2018/default.html#Tabulados.

Friedman, V. (June 13, 2019). Carolina Herrera: ¿apropiación cultural u homenaje? *The New York Times*. Retrieved from https://www.nytimes.com/es/2019/06/13/espanol/cultura/carolina-herrera-disenos-mexicanos.html.

Indigenous and Tribal People Convention, 1989 (No. 169). (1989). Retrieved from https://www.ilo.org/dyn/normlex/en/f?p=NORMLEXPUB:12100:0::NO::P12100_ILO_CODE:C169.

Indigenous Peoples. (September 24, 2019). Retrieved from https://www.worldbank.org/en/topic/Indigenouspeoples.

INEGI. (2010). *Censo de Población y Vivienda 2010*. https://www.inegi.org.mx/programas/ccpv/2010/.

INEGI (Instituto Nacional de Estadística, Geografía e Informática). (2020). *Censos y Conteos de Población y Vivienda. Serie Histórica Censal e Intercensal*. https://www.inegi.org.mx/programas/ccpv/2020/default.html.

INPI (Instituto Nacional de los Pueblos Indígenas). (2018). *Programa Nacional de los Pueblos Indígenas 2018–2024*. Retrieved from https://www.gob.mx/cms/uploads/attachment/file/423227/Programa-Nacional-de-los-Pueblos-Indigenas-2018-2024.pdf.

INPI. (2020). *INPI ¿Qué hacemos?*. https://www.gob.mx/inpi/que-hacemos.

Knight, A. (2004). *Racismo, Revolución e Indigenismo: México 1910–1940. Volumen 1: Cuadernos de Estudios Sobre el Racismo*. México: Universidad Autónoma de Puebla.

Kukutai, T. and Taylor, J. (2016). Data sovereignty for indigenous peoples: current practice and future needs. In T. Kukutai and J. Taylor (eds.), *Indigenous Data Sovereignty: Towards an Agenda*, 1–24. CAEPR Research Monograph, 2016/34. Canberra: ANU Press.

Ley Agraria. (November 10, 2019). Retrieved from http://www.diputados.gob.mx/LeyesBiblio/pdf/13_250618.pdf.

Naciones Unidas. Asamblea General. (Junio 28, 2018). *Informe de la Relatora Especial de los Derechos de los Pueblos Indígenas Sobre su Visita a México*. Retrieved from https://www.hchr.org.mx/images/doc_pub/2018-mexico-a-hrc-39-17-add2-sp.pdf.

Naciones Unidas. Asamblea General. (Diciembre 23, 2003). *Informe del Relator Especial Sobre la Situación de los Derechos Humanos y las Libertades Fundamentales de los Indígenas, Sr. Rodolfo Stavenhagen*. Retrieved from http://www.hchr.org.mx/images/doc_pub/informerelatormexico.pdf.

OECD. (2019). *Linking Indigenous Communities with Regional Development, OECD Rural Policy Reviews*. Paris: OECD Publishing. doi:10.1787/3203c082-en.

Pla Brugat, D. (2011). Mas desindianización que mestizaje. Una relectura de los censos generales de población. *Dimensión Antropológica*, 18, 69–92. Retrieved from https://www.dimensionantropologica.inah.gob.mx/?p=7401.

Romero Flores, J. (1978). *Historia del Congreso Constituyente 1917–1917*. México: Editorial Gupy S.A. Retrieved from http://biblioteca.diputados.gob.mx/janium/bv/dp/hist_cong_const.pdf.

Rubio Badán, J.C. (2014). *Censos y Población Indígena en México. Algunas Reflexiones. Serie Estudios y Perspectivas*. México: CEPAL. ISSN:1680–8800. Retrieved from https://repositorio.cepal.org/bitstream/handle/11362/36858/S1420252_es.pdf?sequence=1&isAllowed=y.

Smith, D.E. (2016). Governing data and data for governance: the everyday practice of indigenous sovereignty. In T. Kukutai and J. Taylor (eds.), *Indigenous Data Sovereignty: Towards an Agenda*, 117–138. CAEPR Research Monograph, 2016/34. Canberra: ANU Press.

United Nations. (September 13, 2007). *United Nations Declarations of the Rights of Indigenous Peoples*. Retrieved from https://www.un.org/development/desa/Indigenouspeoples/wp-content/uploads/sites/19/2018/11/UNDRIP_E_web.pdf.

Valladares, de la C.L.R. (2018). El asedio a las autonomías indígenas por el modelo minero extractive en México. Iztapalapa. *Revista de Ciencias Sociales y Humanidades*, 85(39), 103–131, julio-diciembre de 2018. ISSN:2007-9176. Retrieved from http://www.scielo.org.mx/pdf/izta/v39n85/2007-9176-izta-39-85-103.pdf.

10 Indigenous Data Sovereignty
Quechan education data sovereignty

Jameson D. Lopez

Introduction

In the mainstream education literature in the United States, Indigenous youth and adult data tend to be ignored because of small sample sizes that make "statistically significant" inferences difficult to demonstrate (Shotton et al., 2013; Sumida Huaman et al., 2016; Walter & Anderson, 2013). One can witness the lack of Indigenous presence in mainstream data when looking at top-tier journals in higher education (*The Review of Higher Education, Journal of Higher Education, Research in Higher Education* and *Journal of College Student Development*) that include White, Black, Hispanic and Asian, but erase Indigenous students by categorizing them as "Other" (see Christensen & Harris, 2019; Creuseere et al., 2019; DesJardins et al., 2019; Radimer & Rowan-Kenyon, 2019). Additionally, the dominant societal understanding of Native Americans is constrained by the limitations found in data that reproduce bias narratives controlled by dominant cultures. For example, inconsistent data in the integrated postsecondary dataset in the United States reports institutional number of Indigenous students. The data are self-reported and often misrepresent the actual number of Indigenous students in the United States in postsecondary education.

Walter and Anderson (2013) state that statistical analyzes, "speak a 'truth' about the communities on which they shine their statistical light" (Walter & Anderson, 2013, p. 9). The dominant narratives often speak of high rates of suicide, diabetes, alcoholism and drug abuse to define Native American populations. In an education context, this results in stereotypes of Indigenous children that lead to at-risk resources as opposed to gifted education. To resist a deficit research approach that plagues Native populations (mostly from mostly non-Native researchers), Indigenous researchers advocate for Tribal Nations and researchers to gather our own data for data sovereignty.

Nonetheless, many Indigenous Peoples and Indigenous Nations still have confidence that quantitative research and methods can support Indigenous Peoples, as long as researchers on Indigenous environments understand how quantitative methods have historically harmed and overlooked our communities (Rodriguez-Lonebear, 2016; Shotton et al., 2013). In this chapter, I examine a case of Indigenous Data Sovereignty in practice, using the example of my tribal higher education department (Quechan). I first describe our efforts to establish data sovereignty, the solutions we found to create enough data to establish statistical power and to speak truth about our community. Additionally, Indigenous Data Sovereignty action is imperative to creating data that can help in the creation of policies that are reflective of the Indigenous communities they are intended to support. Next, I demonstrate how a quantitative methods frame through an Indigenous Data Sovereignty practice lens empowers our community education policies. Lastly, I describe the challenges that our community experienced going through the process of establishing more comprehensive data sovereignty.

Identifying available resources

In the following I start with a story as an analogy to the efforts I, along with other tribal members, put forward to help establish Indigenous Data Sovereignty practices in our tribe the Quechan Nation. Among the many first lessons I learned throughout my childhood, my mother taught me how to utilize what is available to accomplish a job. Although, I quickly learned it wasn't always possible. One of the first times I learned that what was available to me wasn't enough to accomplish a job was during a lunar eclipse. I remember attending school and the teacher giving us instructions about how to make eclipse glasses out of cereal boxes. It was interesting, as she cut holes so you could safely stare off at the sun while simultaneously protecting your eyes. It was brilliant in theory, but in reality, I knew it probably wasn't possible for me. About halfway through her presentation, I realized I couldn't build cereal box eclipse sunglasses at home, because our cereal came in bags. Even though we did have the occasional bran flakes that came with our commodity food, my family's access to boxed cereal was different than my White peers.

Have you ever had commodity food? For those of you who haven't, it's a part of a federal food distribution program for Natives in the United States. And if you really think about the history of commodity food, you realize that one of Native America's staples, Fry Bread, is an offspring of those government rations. I'm sure most of my Native sisters and brothers are also quite familiar with the golden brick: the glorified and highly anticipated commodity cheese. However, if you have ever survived on commodity food, you would know about another one of my favorites, commodity peanut butter. As my mother would grow tired of making school lunches in my later years of grade school, I became responsible for making my own lunches. I remember the first time I tried to make myself a peanut butter and jelly sandwich with commodity peanut butter. I attempted to smoothly spread the peanut butter when instantly the peanut butter crumbled the bread. Commodity peanut butter is like trying to put on your high school jeans after years of binging on frybread, honey and powdered sugar; everything just kind of crumbles and falls apart… including your self-esteem. I used to ask my Mom, "why can't we just get JIF (JIF is a brand of peanut butter)". My Mom hated when I complained, and rightfully so. She grew up often times without food, but my Mom was also patient with me. She showed me a little trick. She said,

"JD, go get the pancake syrup". I did, and she continued, "Put about a teaspoon of syrup and mix it together. Now try to spread the peanut butter on the bread". And boom! Wouldn't you know, I had made knockoff JIF. As I reflect now, Natives are the syrup to the stiff consistency of our society, because we can make the best of anything. I take the same approach to data.

Analogously, in the beginning stage of working with our tribe, I realized our Nation did not have the infrastructure that we often advocate for when trying to establish data sovereignty. We did not have servers, we did not have a dedicated space, we did not have a computer to house the data or even a dedicated external hard drive we could dedicate to housing our data. Similar to the eclipse sunglasses, we, as a higher education board, did not have access to the basic resources needed to accomplish a job. What was "normal" for researchers, even access to everyday resources is a challenge for Indigenous Peoples working to advocate for, and enact, Indigenous Data Sovereignty. I also realized that it was not necessarily a concern given the amount of challenges the community faced between our water rights, land rights, gaming compacts etc.

Even with these competing priorities, it is important to pursue Indigenous Data Sovereignty because it moves us into a more proactive space to support these urgent priorities. However, what was available to us was a few higher education board members who were dedicated volunteers that wanted to gather the data that they needed to make good decisions that would support an increase in the academic achievements of our tribal students. I sat in our meetings and we began to talk about data. We built policies around our data and with the support of the higher education board, we decided to use my PhD dissertation research project as one of our first attempts to establish our own educational data. The central research question I asked in my dissertation study was how do researchers operationalize the American Indian/Alaska Native (AI/AN) Millennium Falcon Persistence Model (see Lopez, 2018) in social scientific studies of AI/AN students? However, we wanted to build data that represented our community values and privileged our voices while being accepted by the outside world. We started to brainstorm questions or item development to measure constructs that reflected the values of our community. As Indigenous quantitative statistics prioritizes speaking truth about our community, we also follow the suggestions of Paris and Alim (2017) that posit educational outcomes must be measured according to the student cultural values. For example, in postsecondary literature students often claim the reason for going to college is to give back to their community. If giving back is an important motivation for going to college, maybe that should be the outcome variable because it is based on the students' cultural values.

Community values

Identifying and utilizing community values to decide which data to collect as a means of enacting and practicing data sovereignty can be quite difficult. Especially, given Tribal Nations do not always agree on what they value. Tribal citizens can identify differently, despite all identifying as Quechan. For example, in our tribal community some folks identify as being liberal while others identify as being conservative, some are two-spirit (how some Indigenous folks describe their sexual, gender and spiritual identity), some tribal members are mixed with other ethnicities and have citizenship with countries other than the United States like with Mexico. Some tribal members are Christian, some are traditional, some of the tribal members hunt and fish while others are vegans. The range of community values range so broadly that it can be difficult to measure educational outcomes or gather data that corresponds to our array of tribal values. Nonetheless, we tried to measure our community values, beginning this process by first attending our elder meetings.

With the support of a tribal council member, I was invited to sit at the table during elder meetings. As we passed around hot apple pies from McDonalds, I admired the smiles and laughter as the elders were speaking Quechan. Slowly they would ask me in English, which family I belonged to. I mentioned the names of my mother, father, uncles, aunts and grandparents until my elders felt satisfied. From that point, I sat in silence as I listened to their stories about what it meant to be Quechan, challenges in our community and hope for our people to work together in harmony caring for one another. The elders would gather to decide on issues around our ceremonies. In this particular meeting, some of the elders were questioning if it should be allowed to have cellphones in our Big House, where we held a portion of our overnight cremation ceremony. Some of our tribal kids were seen sitting in the wood pews watching YouTube and Netflix while their parents and grandparents paid their respect to the deceased through the night. It was eventually decided cellphones didn't have a place in the Big House, and if kids got tired, they could take a break outside. Talk of technology advanced conversations around how we would carry our ancient traditions in the modern world as Quechan People. One elder talked about our cremation ceremony origins, but more critical was the importance of remembering certain procedures through the ceremony based on the first cremation and remembering that what we do with our life will be mourned and celebrated. I learned, the cremation was central to our identity as Quechan, understanding the ceremony was important to our education but, more importantly, the ceremony allowed us to reflect on our life contributions to our community. The elders wanted our traditional knowledge to be passed on as they shared stories about how to mourn through our creation story. They talked about Rabbit pulling his ears off after the creator died and other rabbits throwing their ears into a fire during the creator's cremation. It was a sign that when someone passes away, we are losing a piece of us. Through these initial meetings and meeting with tribal officials, experts in Nation building and education, and various community members we realized that some of the first data to be collected in our community needed to reflect our Quechan identity. For example, adding variables from the Scale of Native Americans Giving Back (Lopez, 2020) such as I can speak my tribe's language; I have a close relationship with my tribal relatives; I participated in tribal ceremonies prior to attending college (e.g., cremation ceremony); I know my tribe's creation story. These questions would help researchers measure difficult constructs such as Indigenous identity. As part of our Indigenous Data Sovereignty enactment we would be creating important constructs to Quechan education. To begin that process, we went through the Institutional Review Board.

Institutional review board

The use of an Institutional Review Board (IRB) is an important process when working with Indigenous communities, and approval is dependent on healthy interpersonal relationships. Healthy interpersonal relationships mean relationships where you are not just going to someone when you need a favor, but rather building relationships through community events such as dinners, chicken scratch dances and other social events. The following is a description of the IRB process with the Quechan and Cocopah Nations. In November 2016, I requested to be on the Quechan Tribe's work session in December. I presented my research before the Quechan council and received verbal support from the council. However, due to unforeseen circumstances with the tribal election the following week, my request was tabled. After a few months of contact, and waiting, I was informed that I could request a letter of support from the higher education department. In February 2017, I requested and received a letter of support from the council; an essential element of community endorsement required before I could proceed.

Arizona State University's IRB examined my research proposal and approved this study to examine the postsecondary persistence model for Indigenous students. Participants were informed that there were no obligations to fill out the survey and that they could opt out of the study at any time. The information on the study was given on the online link before the survey, that also describes the purpose of this study and provides an option to see the results. Participants were given contact information to ask any questions about the study and given an opportunity to provide an email address if they wanted to see the outcomes of the study. The IRB was approved in March 2017. There was not a budget for this project, so most of what we were able to do came from a scholarship I received to help with participant recruitment and data collection. Again, this is a not uncommon challenge for those seeking to enact data collection using Indigenous Data Sovereignty practices.

Data collection

I collected data from Quechan students using the web-based instrument surveymonkey.com. Our Quechan higher education department was able to find addresses to do a small mail out to about 100 participants for a census sample, to whom I sent an introduction letter, a postcard with a link to the survey, a third follow-up using email and a final email requesting participation. We also utilized social media outlets ran by our tribal members and gave participants an option to provide their email address to enter a raffle for a chance to win one of four 50-dollar Amazon gift cards as incentives are important to participant recruitment (Dillman et al., 2014).

The research incorporates Indigenous quantitative methodologies through creating statistical data that privileges Quechan voices. For example, the variables developed for the study came from the community and uplifted Quechan voices in the research. Furthermore, our higher education department wanted to collect data that was relevant to our community as many federal data sources, such as the Beginning Postsecondary Students Longitudianl Study, use small samples and lack relevant variables that provide data that are inconsistent, irrelevant, poor quality, and produced/used within an environment of mistrust (Lopez & Marley, 2018; Rainie et al., 2017). Some of the variables we included were an attempt to measures constructs such as "giving back", and "cultural identity", that allow researchers to challenge dominant mainstream value systems, such as persistence and college GPA. Some of the giving back variables (Lopez, 2020) include I help organize community events (i.e., Indian Days, Pow Wows, Community dinners etc.); I notice positive change in the tribal members that I encourage; I pray for my tribal community; if possible, I always try to buy from tribal businesses. My suggestion to the higher education department was that eventually we could use giving back as an educational outcome of postsecondary education that is from a Quechan perspective as opposed to GPA, persistence or graduation rates.

The surveys were sent out and we collected responses from about 75 Quechan students, and it was the first data we collected from our tribe that would be housed by our tribe. I was able to run the analysis for the data and have data that was completely from our community collected and developed by Quechan tribal citizens. However, it was only the beginning to our plans for the higher education board. One other higher education board member and I continued to meet over the course of a year and further develop our tribal educational policies to include data collection and request funding for equipment to house the data. We met with our tribal higher education director, sat in our tribal council meetings and planned to petition our tribal council for financial support for equipment. However, the other board member fell ill and passed away. Our tradition doesn't allow us to mention their name, but she was a phenomenal woman with brilliant ideas. I feel what may be the biggest loss is she had ideas that no one else ever had. Additionally, she had a brave and dedicated spirit to make them happen. We mourned her and sent her into the afterlife with tribal rights through our cremation ceremony. However, the momentum after collecting our first round of data to establish comprehensive postsecondary education data for our tribe began to falter. Indigenous programs with limited access to resources that include human, social and monetary capital are often more vulnerable than other types of programs.

Lessons learned

There were several things I realized by attempting to establish data sovereignty with no financial support and just our will to do something to start. However, I personally took a lesson I learned in my early 20s while entering this work. Since I was a kid, I spent time all over The Rez during the summers. Some summers, I spent with my Nana, some summers, I spent with my uncles and aunts. And then some summers, I spent with my parents traveling to reservations across Turtle Island (North America). We always ate traditional foods, and as a child, I would sometimes refuse. I would occasionally push the food around with my fork to make it look like I ate, but I remember my Mom telling me, "Don't play with your food". It was a lesson that followed me in my adult years.

I spent one of my college summers in Nebraska for an internship. Quite honestly, I wasn't doing much with the internship, but it gave me a chance to chill with one of my bros. He was like a big brother and I think just about anybody who spent any amount of time with him has a story about his shenanigans. He always liked to be on the move, drive his war pony (personal car) around and keep busy. One day we were out and about, and we met an older woman. She was super kind and inevitably invited us to her grandson's 18th birthday. Keep in mind, we had just met her that day. My bro said, "Sure, we'll go". And before I knew it, evening struck, and we were talking with strangers outside a trailer house along the Missouri River. We ate, talked, played guitar and fished. It was a beautiful evening with some awesome Native People. We were swapping stories and toward the latter part of the night around the fire, a little German Shepherd puppy arrived. It was the cutest little dog. My bro saw the little puppy and started to pet him and wrestled the little dog with his hand. He was smiling and while keeping his eyes down fixated on the dog below, he asked, "is this puppy for the birthday boy?" The rummage of party noise waned and the empty sound of night and moonlight replaced the talking. No one answered my buddy. He was still smiling, but simultaneously looking around confused. Then his smiled turned into sole confusion.

I was also confused; did we do something? Both of our eyes wandered through the party, and eventually, the lady who extended the invitation walked in our direction. She motioned to us and we leaned in. She covered her mouth and in a slightly loud whisper said, "it's for the sacrifice". My bro who was still petting the puppy until the moment of her whisper immediately stopped and said, "oh". We were a little taken back, or at least I was. I never heard of that, just because we don't practice that in our tribe. When we left, I was still confused, but my buddy explained to me they were Sioux and it was part of their traditions. I told my bro, "You shouldn't play with your food".

I also realized that when in other people's communities, you shouldn't assume to know them just because they are Indigenous. Tribes are not monolithic and the policies that we do create need to be reflective on the Nations you are from. My first piece of advice is that we have to create policies that are relevant to our own community and owned by that community. It makes little-to-no sense to have the same policies as other Tribal Nations around data sovereignty practices, as tribes have different educational capacities, financial situations, geographic differences and traditions. So, what worked for us as Quechan may not work for larger tribes.

Accessibility and the ability to create relationships to move data initiatives was a key advantage to getting this work off the ground. However, the core underpinnings of Indigenous Data Sovereignty—Indigenous leadership and the data reflecting the needs, priorities, lifeworlds and aspirations of Indigenous Peoples remain. My second piece of advice is to not overthink creating Indigenous data sovereignty practices and the data that flow from these. Often, we wait for large amounts of funding or political support to establish our own data collection. At the end of the day a small group of people in our higher education board created a survey, sent it to people we had contact with and we were able to collect the best data that anyone in the world has seen about postsecondary education in the Quechan Nation. The data was from us and reflective of our community values.

Conclusion

In this chapter, I examined an Indigenous Data Sovereignty initiative among my tribal higher education department (Quechan). Our efforts to establish data sovereignty by using what was available allowed us to create enough data to establish statistical power, speak the truth about our community and demonstrate how quantitative methods through Indigenous Data Sovereignty empowers our community. There are three key takeaways from this experience and research. First, I believe what we can gather from this research is that we have to create policies that are relevant to communities and owned by that community. Too often, we rely on data that is not reflective of the communities in which policies are created from. Indigenous Data Sovereignty provides a framework and encourages tribes to gather their own data, no matter how humble the beginnings may be. Second, I described some of the challenges when collecting data representative of our community voices, maintaining momentum and creating data through our own processes that were best for an individual community. Although momentum is somewhat difficult to maintain in our communities because of limited amounts of capital, it is important to find the people who want to make change with you. A takeaway from this experience is that you can accomplish more when you are working with other members of the community as family as opposed to individuals. Third, one of the most rewarding parts of collecting our own tribal data was realizing we established the most comprehensive dataset on Quechan postsecondary education that the world has ever seen. No matter how humble or small our efforts may seem, realize that Indigenous Data Sovereignty in our communities allows us to own our history for our future generations of Indigenous Peoples.

References

Christensen, M. C., & Harris, R. J. (2019). Correlates of bystander readiness to help among a diverse college student population: An intersectional perspective. *Research in Higher Education*, 60(8), 1195–1226.

Creusere, M., Zhao, H., Bond Huie, S., & Troutman, D. R. (2019). Postsecondary education impact on intergenerational income mobility: Differences by completion status, gender, race/ethnicity, and type of major. *Journal of Higher Education*, 90(6), 915–939. https://doi-org.ezproxy1.library.arizona.edu/10.1080/00221546.2019.1565882.

DesJardins, S.L., Toutkoushian, R.K., Hossler, D., & Chen, J. (2019). Time may change me: Examining how aspirations for college evolve during high school. *The Review of Higher Education*, 43(1), 263–294. doi:10.1353/rhe.2019.0096.

Dillman, D.A., Smyth, J.D., & Christian, L.M. (2014). *Internet, Phone, Mail and Mixed-Mode Surveys: The Tailored Design Method.* Hoboken, NJ: John Wiley & Sons.

Lopez, J.D. (2018). Factors influencing American Indian and Alaska native postsecondary persistence: AI/AN millennium falcon persistence model. *Research in Higher Education,* 59(6), 792–811. doi:10.1007/s11162-017-9487-6.

Lopez, J. D. (2020). Examining construct validity on the scale of Native Americans giving back (SNAG). *Journal of Diversity in Higher Education.* 1–30. https://doi.org/10.1037/dhe0000181

Lopez, J.D., & Marley, S.C. (2018). Postsecondary research with American Indians and Alaskan natives: quantitative challenges and future directions. *Journal of American Indian Education,* 57(2), 5–34.

Paris, D., & Alim, H.S. (Eds.). (2017). *Culturally Sustaining Pedagogies: Teaching and Learning for Justice in a Changing World.* New York, NY: Teachers College Press.

Radimer, S., & Rowan-Kenyon, H. (2019). Undergraduate men's alcohol consumption: Masculine norms, ethnic identity, and social dominance orientation. *Journal of College Student Development,* 60(1), 1–16. doi:10.1353/csd.2019.0000.

Rainie, S.C., Schultz, J.L., Briggs, E., Riggs, P., & Palmanteer-Holder, N.L. (2017). Data as a strategic resource: self-determination, governance, and the data challenge for Indigenous nations in the United States. *The International Indigenous Policy Journal,* 8(2), 1–29.

Rodriguez-Lonebear, D. (2016). Building a data revolution in Indian country. In T. Kukutai, & J. Taylor (Eds.), *Indigenous Data Sovereignty* (pp. 253–272). Canberra, Australia: Australian National University Press.

Shotton, H.J., Lowe, S.C., & Waterman, S.J. (2013). *Beyond the Asterisk: Understanding Native Students in Higher Education.* Sterling, VA: Stylus Publishing.

Sumida Huaman, E., Martin, N., & Chosa, C. (2016). "Stay with your words": indigenous youth, local policy, and the work of language fortification. *Education Policy Analysis Archives/Archivos Analíticos de Políticas Educativas,* 24(52), 1–29.

Walter, M., & Andersen, C. (2013). *Indigenous Statistics: A Quantitative Research Methodology.* Walnut Creek, CA: Left Coast Press.

11 Indigenous Data Sovereignty and the role of universities

Tennille L. Marley

Introduction

American Indians and Alaska Natives (AIAN) and Indigenous Peoples (IP) throughout the world have long been subject to unethical research practices and abuse that continue today. In the United States, phrenology was practiced to establish White superiority and justify ongoing genocide (Thornton, 1987). In the 1860s, under the direction of the US Surgeon General, soldiers and army personnel were ordered to collect human remains and objects from battle sites, hospitals and burial grounds for research purposes. Not until 1990, with the *Native American Graves Protection and Repatriation Act* (NAGPRA) were AIAN Nations able to reestablish ownership and repatriate items, objects and human remains (Trope & Echo-Hawk, 1992). More recently, the Havasupai Nation settled with Arizona State University and the Arizona Board of Regents for improper research use of blood samples collected as part of a diabetes project. The issues associated with the Havasupai case included risks of harm, cultural harm, informed consent, stigmatization, identification, and control and ownership of data (Harmon, 2010).

Indigenous culture, intellectual property and knowledge continue to be abused, stolen, appropriated and exploited for various uses. Names and objects are used commercially and as sports mascots, such as the Cleveland Indians and Jeep Cherokee. So too do we see the appropriation of Indigenous data in the fashion world, such as headdresses and Indigenous-inspired textiles. In addition, data generated from research with and information about Indigenous Peoples are also at risk due to their availability online and in archives. These data and information that are used irresponsibly can threaten the cultural and political sovereignty of AIAN and other IP. Data that are stored in US government archives are especially at risk since they are part of the public domain and are available to the public for research and other purposes. For example, in 2015, Peter Nabokov, an anthropologist and professor at the University of California Los Angeles, edited and published *Origin Myths of the Acoma Pueblo* that included creation and migration songs and stories. Nabokov's book is a republication of an 1842 US government archived document (Hunt & Nabokov, 2015). The Acoma Nation have the sovereign right to own the contents of the book as intellectual property, the collective cultural expressions and traditional knowledge, but since the original book was held in government archives for over 75 years, it is considered part of the public domain and cannot be returned to them (Hurley, Kostelecky, & Aguilar, 2017).

Largely in response to previous and ongoing research abuses, many AIAN and other IP are now asserting their right to govern research in their communities. However, much research in Indigenous communities continues to be conducted by or with researchers at academic institutions. University institutional review boards (IRB) must increasingly contend with AIAN and IP asserting their rights to data. In this chapter, I discuss AIAN political and cultural sovereignty, Indigenous Data Sovereignty (IDS), AIAN research mechanisms, university IRBs and end with a discussion of what universities and researchers can do to respect AIAN and IP interests. As more IP assert data sovereignty, universities will have to grapple with Native Nations in order to conduct research in their communities.

Political sovereignty

In the United States, federally recognized AIAN nations hold a unique position as sovereign entities with a government-to-government relationship with the federal government. Recognition of this sovereignty can be traced back to the 1700s when European nations, and later the United States, entered into treaties with Tribal Nations (Wilkins & Stark, 2017). Because of this acknowledgment of their sovereignty, federally recognized American Indian Nations and Alaska Native corporations hold political statuses that are different than other racial/ethnic groups in the United States. In addition to being part of a racial/ethnic group, members of these federally recognized entities are also part of political group with special rights and benefits from the federal government (Wilkins & Stark, 2017).

AIAN and IP continue to fight to protect and assert their sovereignty with respect to governance, culture, research and other areas. In the past, non-Indigenous researchers have exploited AIAN and IP for their own benefit (Brayboy & Deyhle, 2000). As Lomawaima (2000) explains, "until quite recently ... researchers could set their own research agendas, devise their own questions, develop whatever methodology suited their agenda, and do as they pleased without having to consult with or defer to tribal polities" (p. 6). Consequently, more AIAN and IP are asserting their sovereignty with respect to research and securing rights and ownership of their knowledge, objects and cultural expressions that could be considered data by researchers.

Indigenous Data Sovereignty and qualitative data

Data ownership and data sharing are growing concerns among AIAN and other IP. No overarching legal structures exist in the United States to govern AIAN data ownership or sharing. As a result, AIAN data collected on AIAN lands are vulnerable to non-consensual use by other researchers for secondary analysis. Data sharing plans, including those governing qualitative datasets, are increasingly required by governmental and foundation research grants. The reuse of qualitative data is especially susceptible to causing harm for research participants and communities due to its sensitive nature (Heaton, 2004). These data can be difficult to anonymize or strip of sensitive information. In the context of secondary analysis, important indicators of meaning, such as metadata, are often missing thus making these data ripe for misinterpretation (Mills, 2017; Thomson et al., 2005). Other issues related to secondary use of qualitative data are ethical in nature, such as obtaining informed consent where future use of data is not known (Irwin, 2013).

Despite concerns regarding secondary analysis of qualitative data, interest in data sharing and archiving has increased among qualitative researchers (Elman, Kapiszewski, & Vinuela, 2010). Consequently, we are likely to see the increasing re-use of qualitative data concerning AIAN communities, which to date has largely only been the case with quantitative data. The long history of unethical research practices by Western researchers rings a warning bell that researchers much heed (Tsosie, 2007). I now turn to the Indigenous Data Sovereignty movement as an example of a critical framework that Native Nations and Indigenous communities can draw on to protect their data. Indigenous Data Sovereignty is: "[the] right of Indigenous Peoples to govern the collection, ownership, and application of data about Indigenous communities, peoples, lands, and resources" (Rainie et al., 2019). Article 31 of the United Nations Declaration on the Rights of Indigenous Peoples (2007), adopted by the United Nations General Assembly on September 13, 2007, and finally adopted by the United States in 2010, recognizes this inherent right. It states:

> Indigenous Peoples have the right to maintain, control, protect and develop their cultural heritage, traditional knowledge and traditional cultural expressions, as well as the manifestations of their sciences, technologies and cultures, including human and genetic resources, seeds, medicines, knowledge of the properties of fauna and flora, oral traditions, literatures, designs, sports and traditional games and visual and performing arts. They also have the right to maintain, control, protect and develop their intellectual property over such cultural heritage, traditional knowledge, and traditional cultural expressions.

Indigenous Data Sovereignty seeks not only to control, own and govern research and data, but also to protect sovereignty and culture that are often interlinked: "Qualitative" data, including cultural expressions, stories, interviews, oral histories, data from previous research.

Cultural sovereignty

Beyond the governance, collection and ownership of data, Indigenous Data Sovereignty also seeks to protect Indigenous cultural sovereignty. Indigenous sovereignty is threatened when cultural sovereignty is violated through exploitation, theft and misrepresentation of culture, especially through qualitative data, such as interviews held in government archives. As a result, it is important for AIAN nations to protect their cultural and political sovereignty by exercising

Indigenous Data Sovereignty. Coffey and Tsosie (2001) call for a vision of tribal sovereignty in which cultural sovereignty is fundamental. They define cultural sovereignty as,

> the effort of Indian nations and Indian people to exercise their *own norms and values* instructing their collective futures ... [it] is inherent in every sense of that word, and it is up to Indian people to define, assert, protect, and insist upon that right.
>
> (Coffey & Tsosie, 196)

Additionally, David Matheson, a Coeur d'Arlene leader, said, "[t]ribal sovereignty is more than a doctrine, it is our existence and our continued survival. ... Our culture is tied up in everything that we do" (Matheson, 2002, p. 18). Finally, W. Richard West, former director of the Museum of the American Indian states, "Political sovereignty and cultural sovereignty are linked inextricably, because the ultimate goal of political sovereignty is the protecting of a way of life" (as cited in Bordewich, 1997, pp. 171–172).

Ultimately, cultural sovereignty is essential for the survival of Indigenous Nations. Culture, including language, songs, oral histories/stories, dress, ceremonies, dances, etc., as well as land and community are at the core of Indigenous identity and way of life. As Deloria Jr (1979, p. 27) said:

> Sovereignty, in the final instance, can be said to consist more of continued cultural integrity than of political powers and to the degree that a tribal nation loses its sense of cultural identity, to that degree it suffers a loss of sovereignty

AIAN mechanisms for research

One of the ways in which AIAN nations exercise sovereignty is by creating and implementing laws and policies with respect to research taking place on their lands. AIAN nations have mechanisms to regulate research including the collection and use of data, data ownership, data archiving, control of intellectual property, Indigenous knowledge and cultural expressions. Some of the mechanisms include approval by Tribal Council, committee review, permits, legal contracts, research and ethics boards and other formal written policies (Macaulay et al., 1998; Nason, 1996). For example, Hopi and Navajo research guidelines extend back more than 20 years and express

> concerns about commercialization, alienation, and inappropriate dissemination of intellectual property and cultural patrimony ... [including] fair return, sharing of results, local availability of collected data in tribal archives, translation difficulties, challenges of consistency with federal agency regulations—that tribes are best suited to identify.
>
> (Lomawaima, 2000, p. 13)

Another example is with the *Inter-Apache Policy on Repatriation and the Protection of Apache Cultures* established in 1996 by the nine Apace Tribes. Driven by several acts including the *Native American Graves Protection and Repatriation Act of 1990* and other laws promoting the preservation of items, places, customs and beliefs, the policy was created to address "the abuse, destruction, and misappropriations [including unauthorized commercial use] of Apache culture, history, sacred places and objects, cultural property, religious freedom and cultural rights" (White Mountain Apache Tribe, 1996). "Cultural property in the policy are defined as images, text, music, songs, stories, symbols, beliefs, customs, ideas, and items linked to the history and culture of the Apache tribes in any media" (White Mountain Apache Tribe, 1996). The policy also objects to the "possession, public exhibition, scientific study, destructive analysis, or other inappropriate use of Apache cultural property (except as expressly permitted by the concerned tribe or when essential to a criminal investigation)" (Nason, 1996).

In the same year, at the American Indian Higher Education Consortium Native Research and Scholarship Symposium, scholars and tribal leaders emphasized a research agenda to help maintain sovereignty and nationhood. Intellectual property rights and the appropriation and exploitation of culture and knowledge, were topics of concern and they emphasized the need for more tribal regulation, monitoring and governance of research. A recommendation from the symposium included the creation of a "Council of Elders" at the tribal level to clarify which cultural practices should be protected and to limit "exploitation of our cultures by exposing our religions, social practices, languages, and cultural knowledge" (Bull, 1997).

Today, a growing number of AIAN nations are asserting and exercising sovereignty over research taking place on their lands and with their peoples by creating their own IRBs. Broadly defined, IRBs are administrative bodies that strive to protect the rights, welfare and privacy of human research subjects and have the authority to approve, disapprove, monitor and require modifications of all research that falls under its jurisdiction (45 CFR 46). Specifically, tribal IRBs assume responsibility for ensuring that research taking place on tribal lands is ethical and they oversee the research process (US Department of Health & Human Services, 2017). Their responsibilities include protecting the people, the nation, tribal communities and tribal resources.

The first AIAN nation IRB was the Navajo Nation Human Research Review Board (NNHRRB) established in 1996 and revised in 2002. It has the responsibility to "regulate, monitor, and control all research within the boundaries of the Navajo Nation" (Navajo Nation, 2005). The NNHRRB 12-phase process is as follows: (1) secure support via resolution with community partner; (2) secure letter of support(s) from tribal program(s) partner; (3) Human Research Review Board review of proposed research; (4) study presentation at an NNRRB meeting where study is approved, requires modification or disapproved; (5) implementation of study; (6) data analysis and presentation of findings at NNHRRB meeting; (7) work session with tribal partner and others to modify research report with unique partner interpretations; (8) submission of a comprehensive research report, including dissemination plan; (9) transfer of data to relevant partner; (10) submission of a complete, approved and publishable manuscript; (11) presentation of study results and implications to community and partners and (12) final data are given to the Navajo Nation Resource Center (Navajo Nation, n.d.). For research involving the collection of historic information, use of ethnographic methods to collect data, interviewed audio or video recordings, a permit must be secured by the Navajo Nation Historic Preservation Department. The department is charged with protecting, preserving and continuing Navajo cultural heritage and traditions to maintain the integrity of the Navajo Nation's traditions and cultures (Navajo Nation, 2019). The NNHRRN is just one example of an AIAN Nation exercising their political sovereignty over data and research, which falls under the definition of Indigenous Data Sovereignty (Carroll, Rodriguez-Lonebear, & Martinez, 2019).

The Indigenous Data Sovereignty movement is growing across the globe and the United States. An increasing number of AIAN and IP are moving toward Indigenous Data Sovereignty by enacting Indigenous data governance and other mechanisms. Indigenous data governance is determining "when, how and why our data ... are gathered, analyzed, accessed and used; and ensure that Indigenous data reflects ... [Indigenous] priorities, values, culture, lifeworlds and diversity" (Walter, 2018). The ways in which tribes are exercising Indigenous Data Sovereignty are by "developing principles of Indigenous Data Governance, research protocols, research review boards, data sharing agreements, and data repositories" (Carroll et al., 2019, p. 14).

University guidelines

Native Nations have long been subject to unethical research by researchers from academic institutions. One of the more recent and well-known research abuses occurred on the Havasupai Indian Reservation, located in Arizona. It is often referred to as the "Havasupai Blood Case". In 1990, as part of a study on diabetes, blood samples were taken from over 200 tribal members to identify genetic links with diabetes. The samples were widely shared and used to conduct studies of schizophrenia, inbreeding, evolution and migration that contradicted their stories and beliefs. In 2003, the Havasupai discovered that their blood samples were used outside the scope of what they believed they consented to and demanded the return of the samples. After six years of fighting, they settled with Arizona State University and the Arizona Board of Regents and as part of the settlement, the remaining samples were finally returned to them. Numerous research articles and dissertations were published using the samples and they were never recanted. This case is a demonstration of unethical research practices condoned by a university that has caused great harm to Indigenous Peoples (Harmon, 2010).

University IRBs are tasked with the responsibility of protecting the rights and welfare of human subjects involved in research as required by the "Common Rule" (45 CFR 56). The IRB reviews the proposed research and has the authority to approve, require modifications for approval and disapprove research according to the Common Rule. The foundation of the Common Rule is *the Belmont Report* that identifies basic ethical principles for biomedical and behavioral research with human subjects (National Commission for the Protection of Human Subjects of Biomedical and Behavioral Research, 1979). The principles of the Common Rule are respect for persons, beneficence and justice (US Department of Health & Human Services, n.d.). Respect for persons is practiced through informed consent; individuals are given the opportunity to choose to participate in a study or not. Potential participants are given information about the study, insuring that they understand the study and how it may affect them, and are informed that their participation is voluntary. Beneficence includes the assessment of risks and benefits; studies should be designed to maximize benefits while minimizing risks. And justice entails the selection of subjects, that procedures for the selection of subjects are fair and not exploitive (US Department of Health & Human Services, n.d.).

Given the history of research abuses Native Nations have undergone and the assertion of their sovereignty over research taking place on their lands, researchers and university IRBs have an obligation to understand research requirements (IRBs or other mechanisms) of Native Nations and how to manage the conditions and interests of their institutional IRBs and those of Native Nations. A growing number of universities are creating policies, procedures and guidelines to address tribal concerns, interests and requirements regarding research with Native Nations. Some, but not all, existing guidelines acknowledge tribal sovereignty, including following tribal laws and procedures for research. Some also recognize that the Common Rule does not provide adequate protections so additional IRB requirements are necessary. I provide three examples from the Oregon State University (OSU), the University of New Mexico (UNM) and the University of Montana (UM).

Oregon State University provides guidelines to help researchers conducting research with Native Nations. The guidelines state that in addition to the OSU IRB, proposed research may have to undergo additional reviews by Native Nations or tribally designated entities. In those cases, a letter of support or tribal resolution must be submitted to the OSU IRB as part of the review. After OSU IRB approval, the study documents can be sent out to other review boards if necessary. The guidelines also suggest researchers consider the following: (1) access to phone, email and/or transportation; (2) required resources from the tribe such as meeting space; (3) manuscript review prior to publication and (4) data ownership since OSU has a policy that requires study-related documents to be stored by the principal investigator in an accessible OSU-audit location for three years after the study ends (Oregon State University, 2016).

The UNM also provides guidelines for researchers with IP that acknowledges Native Nation sovereignty and the need for requirements beyond federal and university policies. The key principle is societal benefit wherein study results should be beneficial to the tribe and findings should be useful and accessible by providing information that offers potential solutions, including improved community well-being or positive policy impact. The policy encourages developing relationships with Native Nations that are sincere, enduring and based on trust to ensure that research is relevant and appropriate. Gaining permission and letters of support for a study is dependent on Native Nation procedures, whether it is a tribe or an outside entity. Some Native Nation procedures depend on obtaining university IRB approval prior to their review. Where that is the case, the researcher will have to amend their IRB according to tribal stipulations after the tribe approves their study. In terms of data ownership, the policy recognizes the right of Native Nations to own and control data collected in their communities, and researchers must comply (University of New Mexico, n.d.).

In addition, UM also provides comprehensive guidelines titled, "Collaborating with Indigenous People". The guidelines acknowledge tribal sovereignty and the rights of Native Nations to establish their own rules, policies and procedures for research on their lands. It also recognizes the rights tribes have over shared information such as cultural knowledge and traditions. Further, it details the right to stop research, control how any information will be used and that the information collected may become property of the Native Nation. In terms of approvals and agreements, Native Nations have the right to enter into agreements where the tribe assumes IRB. In addition, at a minimum, a project director or principal investigator shall work with and comply with IP requirements including collaboration, ownership and protection of information, and permission to disseminate research findings. The guidelines also state that a memorandum of understandings may be necessary in addition to UM or tribal IRB review. Some of the components may include collaboration, how the research will benefit the community, and ownership of data, as just a few examples.

Finally, the UM policy provides guiding principles for researchers with descriptions and vignettes. The principles include (1) Native centered; (2) respect; (3) self-reflection and cultural humility; (4) authentic relationships; (5) honor community time frames; (6) build on strengths; (7) co-learning and ownership; (8) continual dialog; (9) transparency and accountability; (10) integrity and (11) community relevance (University of Montana, n.d.).

The university IRB examples above demonstrate the varying degrees to which university research guidelines affirm Indigenous political, cultural and data sovereignty. While the OSU guidelines fall short in supporting Native Nation sovereignty, UNM and UM provide much more support with regard to cultural, political and data sovereignty. Although the OSU IRB require Native Nation approval as part of the research review process, it stipulates that the principal investigator, and not the tribe, store the data and study materials. The UNM and UM policies emphasize the obligation of the principal investigator to follow rules, regulations, policies and procedures of Native Nations. They acknowledge that Native Nations have their own rules, policies and procedures for research that include ownership, materials, information, samples and review for outside dissemination, sensitivity to traditions, knowledge and culture, that researchers must follow. Both the UNM and UM guidelines support the right to limit or restrict various types of information. Finally, the UNM and UM explicitly emphasize community benefit and collaboration. The UM and UNM demonstrate that university IRBs can support, respect and acknowledge tribal culture, political and data sovereignty.

Discussion and conclusion

American Indians, Alaska Natives and other IP have the inherent rights to govern research on their lands and through mechanisms of their choosing. In instances where there are limited or no research mechanisms in place, universities have an obligation to adopt guidelines that are respectful and mindful of tribal political, cultural and data sovereignty. Despite some procedures in place, issues exist that are not addressed and are outside the control of both tribal and university IRBs, namely archived, shared and open data. The use of these data (Indigenous intellectual property, knowledge, songs, oral histories/stories, ceremonies, dances, texts, images, names and objects) are especially at risk of exploitation, abuse, appropriation, theft and misrepresentation.

Universities and researchers have an obligation to acknowledge and respect tribal and cultural sovereignty, in part because of their long history of research abuses at the hand of researchers and because they can adopt and implement additional research guidelines beyond the Common Rule. University IRB guidelines can be broadened to include, at a minimum, acknowledging and respecting tribal sovereignty. They can further be expanded to adopt rules in alignment with Indigenous Data Sovereignty, including expanding respect for persons, beneficence and justice to include Indigenous communities (Research Ethics Training for Health in Indigenous Communities, University of Washington, 2018). The UM and UNM serve as models that university IRBs could adopt.

University IRBs could require additional training with respect to AIAN communities such as the Research Ethics Training for Health in Indigenous Communities (Ethics training toolkit) curriculum (University of Washington, n.d.). The AIAN-specific curriculum covers the following: (1) research with AIAN communities; (2) the history of ethical regulations; (3) what is human subjects research?; (4) institutional review board (IRB); (5) risks and benefits from research; (6) ensuring confidentiality and managing risk; (7) informed consent; (8) vulnerability; (9) children in research; and (10) unanticipated problems and reporting requirements in research. (Pearson et al., 2019). There are also a number of resources available to researchers regarding research with AIAN communities such as *Guiding Principles for Engaging in Research with Native American Communities* that was developed at the University of New Mexico and *Walk Softly, and Listen Carefully*, by the National Council of American Indians Policy Research Center and Montana State University Center for Native Health Partnerships (University of New Mexico, 2012; NCAI, 2012).

The exploitation, appropriation and misrepresentation of AIAN data have to end. As the Indigenous Data Sovereignty movement grows, universities and researchers will have to face IP and Native Nation political, cultural and data and research rights. Universities and researchers need to take it upon themselves to respect those rights to help ensure the survival of AIAN as distinctive, sovereign societies.

References

Bordewich, F.M. (1997). *Killing the White Man's Indian: Reinventing Native Americans at the End of the Twentieth Century*. New York, NY: Anchor Books.

Brayboy, B.M., & Deyhle, D. (2000). Insider-outsider: researchers in American Indian communities. *Theory into Practice*, 39(3 SRC—GoogleScholar), 163–169.

Bull, C.C. (1997). A native conversation about research and scholarship. *Tribal College*, 9(1), 17.

Carroll, S.R., Rodriguez-Lonebear, D., & Martinez, A. (2019). Indigenous data governance: strategies from united states native nations. *Data Science Journal*, 18(1), 31.

Coffey, W., & Tsosie, R. (2001). Rethinking the tribal sovereignty doctrine: cultural sovereignty and the collective future of Indian nations. *Stanford Law and Policy Review*, 12, 191.

Deloria Jr, V. (1979). Self-determination and the concept of sovereignty. In *Economic Development in American Indian Reservations* (pp. 22–28). Albuquerque: University of New Mexico Native American Studies Center.

Elman, C., Kapiszewski, D., & Vinuela, L. (2010). Qualitative data archiving: rewards and challenges. *PS: Political Science & Politics*, 43(1), 23–27.

Harmon, A. (April 21, 2010). Indian tribe wins fight to limit research of its DNA. *New York Times*. Retrieved from https://www.nytimes.com/2010/04/22/us/22dna.html.

Heaton, J. (2004). *Reworking Qualitative Data*. Sage.

Hunt, E.P., & Nabokov, P. (eds.). (2015). *The Origin Myth of Acoma Pueblo*. New York, NY: Penguin Classics.

Hurley, D.A., Kostelecky, S.R., & Aguilar, P. (2017). Whose knowledge? Representing indigenous realities in library and archival collections. *Collection Management*, 42(3–4), 124–129. doi:10.1080/01462679.2017.1392805.

Irwin, S. (2013). Qualitative secondary data analysis: ethics, epistemology and context. *Progress in Development Studies*, 13(4), 295–306.

Lomawaima, K.T. (2000). Tribal sovereigns: reframing research in American Indian education. *Harvard Educational Review*, 70(1 SRC—GoogleScholar), 1–23.

Macaulay, A.C., Delormier, T., McComber, A.M., Cross, E.J., Potvin, L.P., Paradis, G., Kirby, R.L., Saad-Haddad, C., & Desrosiers, S. (1998). Participatory research with native community of Kahnawake creates innovative code of research ethics. *Canadian Journal of Public Health*, 89, 105–108.

Matheson, D. (2002). Tribal Sovereignty: preserving our way of life. *Arizona State Law Journal*, 34, 15.

Mills, K.A. (2017). What are the threats and potentials of big data for qualitative research? *Qualitative Research*. doi:10.1177/1468794117743465.

Nason, J.D. (1996). Tribal models for controlling research. *Tribal College*, 7(2 SRC—GoogleScholar), 17.

National Commission for the Protection of Human Subjects of Biomedical and Behavioral Research. (1979).*The Belmont report: Ethical principles and guidelines for the protection of human subjects of research*. Retrieved from https://www.hhs.gov/ohrp/regulations-and-policy/belmont-report/read-the-belmont-report/index.html.

Navajo Nation. (2005). *About NHHRRB*. Navajo Nation Human Research Review Board, Navajo Nation Division of Health. Retrieved from http://www.nnhrrb.navajo-nsn.gov/aboutNNHRRB.html.

Navajo Nation. (2019). *Cultural Resources Compliance Section*. Navajo Nation Heritage and Historic Preservation Department. Retrieved from https://www.hpd.navajo-nsn.gov/.

Navajo Nation. (n.d.). *Navajo Nation Human Subjects Review Board Procedural Guidelines for Principal Investigators*. Navajo Nation Human Research Review Board, Navajo Nation Division of Health. Retrieved from http://www.nnhrrb.navajo-nsn.gov/pdf/Procedural%20Guidelines%20for%20PI.pdf.

NCAI Policy Research Center and MSU Center for Native Health Partnerships. (2012). *"Walk Softly and Listen Carefully": Building Research Relationships with Tribal Communities*. Washington, DC and Bozeman, MT: Authors.

Oregon State University. (2016). *Tribal Populations*. Office of Research Integrity. Human Research Protection and Institutional Review Board. Retrieved from https://research.oregonstate.edu/irb/policies-and-guidance-investigators/guidance/tribal-populations.

Pearson, C.R., Parker, M., Zhou, C., Donald, C., & Fisher, C.B. (2019). A culturally tailored research ethics training curriculum for American Indian and Alaska native communities: a randomized comparison trial. *Critical Public Health*, 29(1), 27–39.

Raine, S.C., Kukutai, T., Walter, M., Figueroa-Rodrigues, O.L., Walker, J. et al. (2019). Indigenous data sovereignty. In T. Davies, S. Walker, M. Rubinstein, & F. Perini (eds.), *State of Open Data: Histories and Horizons* (pp. 300–319). Cape Town: African Minds. doi:10.5281/zenodo.2677801.

Thomson, D., Bzdel, L., Golden-Biddle, K., Reay, T., & Estabrooks, C.A. (2005). *Central Questions of Anonymization: A Case Study of Secondary Use of Qualitative Data*. Paper presented at the Forum Qualitative Sozialforschung/Forum: Qualitative Social Research.

Thornton, R. (1987). *American Indian Holocaust and Survival: A Population History Since 1492 (The Civilization of the American Indian Series, Vol. 186)*. Norman: University of Oklahoma Press.

Trope, J.F., & Echo-Hawk, W.R. (1992). Native American graves protection and repatriation act: background and legislative history, The *Arizona State Law Journal*, 24, 35.

Tsosie, R. (2007). Acknowledging the past to heal the future: the role of reparations for native nations. In *Reparations Interdisciplinary Inquiries* (pp. 43–68). Oxford University Press.

United Nations Declaration on the Rights of Indigenous People. (2007). Retrieved from https://www.un.org/esa/socdev/unpfii/documents/DRIPS_en.pdf.

University of Montana. (n.d.). *Collaborating with Indigenous People. Research and Creative Scholarship*. Retrieved from http://www.umt.edu/research/compliance/IRB/Indigenous.php.

University of New Mexico. (2012). *Guiding Principles for Engaging in Research with Native Communities*. Retrieved from https://hsc.unm.edu/vision2020/common/docs/Guiding_Principles_Research_Native_Communities2012.pdf.

University of New Mexico. (n.d.). *Guidance on Research with American Indian Communities*. Office of the Institutional Review Board. Retrieved from https://irb.unm.edu/sites/default/files/Guidance%20on%20Research%20with%20AI%20Communities.pdf.

University of Washington. (2018). *rETHICS—Research Ethics Training for Health in Indigenous Communities*. Express Licensing Program. Retrieved from https://els.com

otion.uw.edu/express_license_technologies/rethics-research-ethics-training-for-health-in-Indigenous-communities.

U.S. Department of Health & Human Services. (2017). Part 46—*Protection of Human Subjects*. Office for Human Research Protections. Retrieved from https://www.hhs.gov/ohrp/regulations-and-policy/regulations/45-cfr-46/index.html.

U.S. Department of Health & Human Services. (n.d.). *45 CFR 46 FAQs*. Office for Human Research Protections. Retrieved from https://www.hhs.gov/ohrp/regulations-and-policy/guidance/faq/45-cfr-46/index.html.

Walter, M. (2018) The voice of Indigenous data, beyond the markers of disadvantage. *Griffith Review*, 60. Retrieved from https://griffithreview.com/articles/voice-Indigenous-data-beyond-disadvantage/.

White Mountain Apache Tribe. (1996). *Resolution of the White Mountain Apache Tribe of the Fort Apache Indian Reservation, Resolution* No. *10-96-238*. Retrieved from http://www.wmat.nsn.us/Legal_Scans/Resolutions/1996/10-96-238.%20Inter-Apache%20Policy.pdf.

Wilkins, D.E., & Stark, H.K. (2017). *American Indian Politics and the American Political System*. Rowman & Littlefield.

12 Narratives on Indigenous victimhood

Challenges of Indigenous Data Sovereignty in Colombia's transitional setting

Gustavo Rojas-Páez and Colleen Alena O'Brien

Introduction

The Indigenous communities of Colombia have borne the brunt of the country's violent history. Since colonial times, the Indigenous communities of Colombia have endured different forms of violence that have caused systematic dispossession of their lands, displacement and the loss of their cultural identity.

On November 12, 2019, the *Jurisdicción Especial para la Paz* "Special Jurisdiction for Peace" (JEP) produced a ruling (JEP 079/2019) that recognized the Awá, an Indigenous community in southern Colombia, as victims of Colombia's 50-year armed conflict (JEP, 2019). The JEP is a transitional justice (TJ) tribunal that resulted from the Havana Peace Accords signed between the Colombian government and the largest and oldest guerrilla group of Latin America, the *Fuerzas Armadas Revolucionarias de Colombia* "Revolutionary Armed Forces of Colombia" (FARC) in 2016. This ruling by the JEP has a symbolic meaning that illustrates how "historical injuries" (Castillejo-Cuéllar, 2013a) are interpreted through legal mechanisms that seek to address questions of structural injustice.

Ruling JEP 079/2019 is an important attempt to shed light on the complexity surrounding the territorial disputes that have marked Colombia's history, the way such disputes have affected the livelihood of the Indigenous communities and the interrelation and interdependence between the Indigenous peoples and the land. A salient element of the ruling is that it declares that nature has been a victim of Colombia's conflict and therefore rivers and other elements of the affected ecosystems have gained legal protection (JEP, 2019) a decision which takes into account Indigenous ontologies.

Although the JEP's decision replicates the spirit of Constitutional Court Order 004/2009, in which the Colombian Constitutional Court established that 32 Indigenous communities of the country are facing cultural and physical extermination, the JEP challenges legalistic and mainstream understandings of harm by incorporating Indigenous perspectives into the legal realm and questions anthropocentric foundations that have informed the nation state paradigm and its sovereignty. As a consequence, it is important to observe how the data on harm interrelate with the two legal decisions and the contribution to accountability processes of structural injuries endured by Indigenous communities. For instance, among the factors identified by Constitutional Court Order 004/2009 causing the disintegration, elimination and forced displacement of Indigenous communities in Colombia (Rodriguez et al., 2010), the court underscores that territorial dispossession has been caused by economic actors who, acting legally and illegally, have affected the livelihood of Indigenous communities dramatically. This draws attention to reparation policies and the accountability of economic actors involved in the Colombian conflict.

Against such a background, this chapter inquires into the legal representation of Indigenous communities in Colombia. In doing so, it reflects on the experience of an Indigenous community that—like the Awá people—has been considered to be a threatened community by Constitutional Court Order 004/2009: the Wayuu. It is of particular interest to us to inquire into the rationales that have recognized Indigenous victimhood and its meanings to counter the structural injustice that continues to mark Colombia's reality, despite the transitional discourse on peace purported by the Havana Accords.[1]

Based on the above-mentioned rulings (the JEP's Ruling 079 and Constitutional Court Order 004/2009), and the Victims Law of 2011, our analysis seeks to highlight the tension between the protection of Indigenous peoples and development discourse in contemporary Colombia. Addressing this tension is fundamental to understanding the way in which historical injuries are related to the expansion of the extractive economy in the Global South and highlighting the importance of Indigenous Data Sovereignty as a means of protecting endangered Indigenous peoples of Colombia, particularly with regard to their demands for territorial rights, food sovereignty and access to natural resources such as water.

Our analysis is concerned with the institutional ways in which Indigenous victims are defined through the lens of global dominant discourses related to conflict management such as transitional justice. Data sovereignty is contested in a transitional setting because states claim the right to control data in a very homogenous way, which replicates the idea of data "suzerainty" that characterized the colonial world (Pool, 2016). Suzerainty embodies the epistemic violence that endorsed colonial legal principles such as *terra nullius* which systematically denied the existence of Indigenous peoples and their epistemologies. Therefore, in this chapter, we argue that a meaningful policy on the historical redress of Indigenous peoples in Colombia's and other TJ settings of the Global South should include a broader discussion on development and Indigenous rights and their relationship with indigneous data. As Pool suggests, this policy should recognize that "before contact with imperial powers, Indigenous peoples had their own vibrant, meaningful bodies of data, over which they had DSov" (Pool, 2016, p57). Thus, this will prompt us to think about the temporalities informing the victimhood narratives surrounding TJ frameworks and their representation of Indigenous victims and structural injuries. By the same token, a broader understanding of Indigenous narratives would pose a challenge to the commodification of nature, which seems normalized in the global world and that justifies the creation of selective and exclusionary forms of control over access to resources such as water (Johnson et al., 2016).[2]

Structure

The chapter begins with conceptual frameworks and theoretical remarks and is then divided into three sections. In the first section, the historical representation of Indigenous peoples in Colombia is described. This section draws attention to the ways in which Indigenous communities have endured multiple forms of violence intensified by the racist discourses that marked the formation of the Colombian state and its policies regarding Indigenous communities. This section addresses the ways in which the foundational laws of the Colombian state reproduced violent elements of the colonial practices that characterized the conquest period.

The second section describes the TJ frameworks implemented in Colombia and analyzes the Indigenous victimhood narrative that informs them. Although our analysis draws on the ways in which Indigenous victims are defined by the legal frameworks, we suggest that this has an implication for the deployment of data related to the conflict and its memorialization.

The third section provides a historical account of the Wayuu community and its territorial organization since colonial times. The section also addresses the community's relationship with the TJ frameworks referred to in the previous section.

Our analysis suggests that despite their symbolic value, the TJ frameworks implemented over the past years have failed to address the structural injustice that has marked the unequal distribution of land in Colombia. In order to address this, we argue that the notion of Indigenous sovereignty as described in the United Nations Declaration on the Rights of Indigenous Peoples could play an important role in advancing accountability processes that elucidate the structural injuries endured by endangered Indigenous peoples of the country. Indigenous Data Sovereignty is crucial to understanding these injuries.

Conceptual frameworks and theoretical remarks

This chapter is rooted in the socio-legal approach to law. In particular, it uses elements of legal pluralism (Santos, 1995) to analyze how Indigenous sovereignty is understood in the context of global transitional justice. Our analysis is also informed by Global South scholarship and its critiques of development discourse. Specifically, we use the notion of coloniality (Quijano, 2000), which allows us to address the historical injustice faced by Indigenous peoples in contemporary Colombia. In combining these theoretical elements, the chapter attempts to problematize the ways data related to the historical injuries (Castillejo-Cuéllar, 2013b) experienced by Indigenous communities is treated within the legal and political arrangements that have informed Colombia's TJ processes over the past two decades. In this vein, the chapter follows Bengoetxea's contribution to this book, which shows that data related to victims in long-lasting periods of violence are contested. In our view, Bengoetxea's (2020) analysis is timely because it underscores the political uses of the data related to the victims of violent conflicts and their impact on the state's narratives about prolonged violence. In highlighting that the current politics of memory in Spain do not take into account the human rights violations that took place between 1936 and

1945—the period when most human rights violations occurred in Spain's recent history—Bengoetxea (2020) shows how the periodization of the violence of the past, in a transitional setting, gives rise to exclusionary practices that create hierarchies of victimhood. As will be seen, in the context of Colombia, Indigenous communities challenged the periodization of the conflict promoted by the state. From the perspective of Indigenous peoples, their territories have been affected since the conquest and therefore the historical injuries they have endured do not fit in the temporality of the violent past proposed by the state. This begs the question: is there a role for Indigenous sovereignty in a transitional setting? An affirmative answer to this question would necessarily imply a change in the way data related to historical injuries are stored by the state in a transitional setting. The politics of memory does not always account for historical redress and structural changes. Drawing on Bogoetxea's contribution, we argue that the sovereignty of the nation state in a political transition should coexist with the concept of Indigenous sovereignty. This means that interlegality (Santos, 1995), understood as the coexistence of multiple normative orders, should operate horizontally. Given that "ID sovereignty refers to the proper locus of authority over the management of data about Indigenous peoples their territories and ways of life" (Kukutai and Taylor, 2016), we cannot separate it from the right to self-determination of Indigenous peoples and their sovereignty (United Nations, 2007), which is under constant threat in Colombia, where ownership of the subsoil in Indigenous territories is claimed by the nation state—a form of legal deterritorialization (CCC Ruling 095/2018).[3] The data that emerge from long periods of violence are prone to reproduce dominant narratives about the conflict through the establishment of a nation state that controls data on the basis of sovereignty. Therefore, it is important to question the statistical portrayal of Indigenous victimhood and understand what it actually entails and who benefits from such representation (Walter, 2016). As Walter argues, a paradigm shift in the reductive and violent representation of Indigenous peoples within the nation state requires an epistemic and ontological disruption that values Indigenous narratives and knowledges (Walter, 2016)

As Bengoetxea (2020) maintains, dating a conflict is a contentious issue on its own. As a consequence, the criteria to define and use data can be politically instrumentalized by those who benefited from a specific periodization and narrative of the conflict, and therefore give way to a form of "victors' justice" in which historical justice cannot be considered; hence the relevance of the question: What is meant by Indigenous victims and whose suffering counts when it comes to defining victims in a TJ setting? Addressing this question is important for observing the global trajectories of victimhood narratives and their impact on the global discourse of TJ.

Section one: Historical representation of Indigenous peoples in Colombia

Independence from Spanish rule in 1819 did not bring about justice for the Indigenous peoples inhabiting present-day Colombia. Despite the formal changes in the laws of the new nation-state, the racist violence that justified the extermination of the Indigenous population of the Americas did not disappear. This is exemplified by several laws implemented during the 19th and 20th centuries. For instance, Law 89/1890 established that the Colombian constitution of 1886 would not apply to the Indigenous populations. The law described the Indigenous peoples as savages and deprived them of political or civil rights. Furthermore, the law granted Catholic missionaries the right to "civilize" Indigenous communities, which meant deterritorialization and the loss of Indigenous cultures. This can be seen at the very beginning of the law, which stated: "The republic's legislation will not operate among the savages who will be subjugated to civilization through missions" (authors' translation).

This law replicates the racist spirit that justified cultural genocides that took place throughout the 19th and 20th centuries in different places globally that endured colonialism such as the US and Australia. In the name of nation-building processes, Indigenous children around the world were taken from their communities and forced to learn the official language and religion (See Indian Act of Canada, Australia's apology to the Stolen Generation, legislation in Argentina on Indigenous communities.)

In Colombia, the extermination of Indigenous peoples went hand in hand with criminalization processes promoted by laws that, despite having been passed by the new independent nation state, mirrored the colonial violence of the conquest period. For instance, Law 40/1868 established prison sentences for Indigenous peoples who opposed the territorial expansion of the republic. According to Article 4 of the aforementioned law: "the executive power shall determine the imprisonment of the Indigenous tribes who attack the settlements or the agricultural establishments or that hinder commercial activities and the free movement through the roads and rivers of the republic" (authors' translation).

By the 1920's, direct violence against Indigenous populations was institutionally legitimized as a result of the implementation of large-scale economic projects. Oil and rubber exploitation caused the deterritorialization and subsequent disappearance of several Indigenous communities in the Amazon and the northern region of Santander. Historical sources such as Roger Casement's (1911) "Putumayo Rubber and Blood" have documented the enslavement and assassination of thousands of Indigenous peoples by the rubber industry in the Amazon. In a similar vein, based on archival research, scholars Velasquez and Castillo (2006) have documented the relationship between the imposition of the first economic enclaves of the oil industry and the extermination of Indigenous communities such as the Yariguies in Santander. In their analysis of a worker's testimony, these scholars show how direct violence was used against Indigenous communities that tried to defend their territorial rights:

> The supervisors were authorized by the TROCO's (Tropical Oil Company) managers and supported by the State public forces to capture the Indians who opposed the opening of trails that would facilitate the exploration and exploitation of oil, as a matter of fact, a good ransom was offered for the head of Pascual, the most feared [Indian] at that time.
> (Velasquez and Castillo, 2006)
> (authors' translation)

These legal representations of Indigenous peoples are indicative of how the promise of liberation that informed the discourse surrounding independence from Spanish rule was tarnished. This was because the laws of the new nation adapted the very colonial rationality that justified the conquest of the Americas. Simply put, the new nation's laws did not question the racist representation of Indigenous peoples imposed by colonial laws. This situation falls within what Peruvian intellectual Anibal Quijano termed coloniality (Quijano, 2000). As a result, the racial power structures of colonialism remained largely intact; hence, it is no surprise that most official languages and religions of the newly independent nations—in much of the world today—coincide with those imposed by the colonial rulers.

Another fundamental expression of coloniality concerns the ways in which the relationship with the land was regulated after colonial rule. According to colonial legal doctrines, the colonizers had the right to settle and control the land that they colonized because territories located beyond the borders of the empires were considered *terra nullius* (Horn, 2014). The implementation of this legal principle deterritorialized Indigenous peoples and did not recognize them as human beings. After independence from the Spanish rule, as we have previously mentioned, territorial rights were not recognized. In fact, even in the 20th century, institutions like *terraje* obliged Indigenous peoples to work in large portions of land called *haciendas*. The owner of the *haciendas* did not have to pay the Indigenous communities working on their disposed lands (Vasco, 2008).[4]

Although the enactment of the 1991 constitution recognized Indigenous sovereignty, the current situation of endangered Indigenous communities shows that coloniality persists and is normalized by the imposition of the large-scale extractive economy in the country, which significantly affects these communities. The extractive economy promotes the idea that land is a commodity and therefore should be exploited for economic purposes. Although this idea undermines the Indigenous worldviews that consider human beings as part of the land who cannot be separated from it, the extractive economy has become a globalized practice endorsed by development discourses. The question that springs to mind is: why is the human cost of the expansion of the extractive economy not challenged in countries whose Indigenous communities are facing extermination? Considering this question, scholar Julia Suarez-Krabbe argues that the impact of colonial practices on places like Colombia is made invisible because "the force of colonial discourse lies in how it succeeds in concealing how it establishes and naturalizes ontological and epistemological perspectives and political practices that work to protect its power" (Suárez-Krabbe, 2016).

Bearing this discussion in mind, in the second section of this chapter we will outline Colombia's TJ framework and its representation of the historical injuries endured by Indigenous communities. In doing so, we seek to present the complex interplay of Colombia's TJ setting; specifically we will refer to the Peace and Justice Law of 2005, the Victims Law of 2011 and the decrees that defined Indigenous victims in 2011. In these laws and decrees victims become data of the conflict. We relate these data on Indigenous victimhood to other legal mechanisms that have addressed Indigenous victimhood such as Constitutional Court Order CCC Order 004/2009 which defined endangered Indigenous communities. We are compelled to observe that one of the major challenges of the JEP would be the legal use and interpretation of these data.

Section two: A TJ framework in a context of inter-legality

Colombia's TJ framework comprises various laws and institutions that resemble different global discourses on reparations, human rights and victimhood. TJ discourse began in 2005, with the enactment of the Peace and Justice Law (Law 975/2005), which resulted from a political arrangement between the government at the time and one of the major actors of Colombia's conflict: the *Autodefensas Unidas de Colombia* "United Self-Defenders of Colombia"(AUC). The AUC were a right-wing paramilitary organisation that advanced violent securitization and anti-insurgency campaigns throughout the country; they committed massacres, extrajudicial killings and displacement. Similar to other actors in the conflict, such as the FARC, the paramilitaries fought for territorial control, impacting Indigenous communities through forced displacement, extrajudicial killings and massacres.

The handling of victims' right to truth has been one of the elements of the Peace and Justice Law that has been criticized at both local and international levels and the law is marked by contestation. Some victims groups have been critical of the truth delivery mechanisms established by the law (Castillejo-Cuéllar, 2013a) and others have rejected the state narrative surrounding the necessity of the law as an instrument to end paramilitary violence (Burnets, 2018). Regarding Indigenous sovereignty, the Peace and Justice Law did not have a component for Indigenous victims.

Social mobilization and also the state's requirement to meet human rights standards for foreign investment led to the enactment of the Victims Law in 2011 (Law 1448/2011). This law created a land restitution programme for victims of the conflict, which in some cases has allowed forcibly displaced people to return to their lands.[5] However, despite its symbolic meaning, the recognition of Indigenous sovereignty was not a priority for the policy makers supporting the Victims' Law, which was discussed in Congress without the presence of Indigenous communities (ONIC, 2012). Thus, after ONIC expressed discontent for not being invited to the congressional discussions in which the Victims Law was approved, which could have caused a constitutional challenge on the basis of Indigenous communities' right to prior consultation, the government decided to include an article that permitted the regulation of Indigenous victims through the enactment of a presidential decree (Decree-Law 4633/2011) (Aponte and Lopez, 2013). Unlike what happened with the creation of the Victims Law, representatives of Indigenous communities were consulted about Decree–Law 4633/2011. However, as Aponte and Lopez show, this consultation was implemented as a formal requisite and not as an instrument to guarantee the rights of Indigenous peoples and the recognition of legal pluralism (Aponte and Lopez, 2013).

The relationship between the Decree 4633/2011 and CCC Order 04/2009 referred to at the outset of the chapter is another problematic feature of the representation of Indigenous victims in Colombia's transitional setting. As we have previously mentioned, CCC Order 04/2009 declared the physical and cultural endangerment of Indigenous communities of the country. The order recommended the creation of 'safeguard plans' (*planes de salvaguarda*) for the protection of these peoples. In these plans, some Indigenous communities have denounced the systemic violation of their rights and have demanded the recognition of their territorial rights, which date back to the colonial period. In an attempt to bring closure to the conflict, Decree 4633 establishes that Indigenous peoples can be recognized as victims from 1985 onwards. This begs the question: are the Indigenous victims of CCC order 04/2009 different to those addressed by decree 4633/2011? And more importantly: can these communities construct a victimhood narrative that also respects their sovereignty and experiences? The interpretation or use of these data on Indigenous victimhood poses an important challenge for the JEP, which according to the Havana Accords will have jurisdiction for ten years.

By creating a specific temporality for the recognition of Indigenous victims, Colombia's TJ framework resembles what Rosemary Nagy has described as an isolationist approach to truth (Nagy, 2012). Nagy refers to this approach when analyzing the narrative that emerged from the South African Truth and Reconciliation Commission (SATRC). For Nagy and other scholars critical of the SATRC (Wilson, 2001), the truth produced by this commission was decontextualized and underestimated the systemic violence that characterized the apartheid regime. As a result, the state's responsibility in the systemic racism that informed the apartheid regime was erased and this did not allow for an adequate understanding of white settlement and its relationship with the structural injustice of apartheid. In this vein, Nagy argues that "the SATRC was vulnerable to claims that torture and killings were randomly committed by a few bad apples" (Nagy, 2012, p.350).

In the Colombian experience the temporality established by the decree on Indigenous victims entails the systemic denial of the historical injuries endured by Indigenous peoples from the colonial times until 1985. This means that historical injuries that have remained unaddressed during the country's republican history and that have a direct connection to the current predicament of Indigenous communities are not important for the Indigenous victimhood narrative informing the law (Lopez et al., 2019). Furthermore, the periodization established by the Indigenous decree has a second component that refers to the reparation measures related to violations of territorial rights. According to the decree: "restitution measures related to territorial affectations shall only proceed for events that occurred from January 1, 1991 onwards" (Decree 4633 2011). This means that major historical injuries caused by the deterritorialization of Indigenous peoples such as the Wayuu will not be considered in the transitional setting, nor will the genocides caused by the extraction of rubber in the Amazon nor the missions in Putumayo (Lopez et al., 2019), all of which happened prior to 1991.

Colombia's TJ framework, and its reductive treatment of Indigenous victims is illustrative of the ways in which data related to prolonged conflict benefit ahistorical understandings of suffering and justice. The framework also shows the global dynamics surrounding the legal knowledge production of the post-cold war period, which is characterized by a constant tension between understandings of Indigenous sovereignty and development.[6] Thus, although International law conventions such as ILO Convention No. 169 and the UN Declaration on the Rights of Indigenous Peoples protect Indigenous sovereignty, the moral force of these conventions is tarnished by the international investment law regime, which favors the interest of local business elites and transnational corporations. It is a situation of coloniality, through which Indigenous territories continue to be considered as *terra nullius*, in which natural resources are solely viewed as commodities. As a consequence inter-legality is instrumentalized discursively because it is operationalized through the nation state, which becomes the source of authority in a transitional setting, as in the case of the regulation of Indigenous peoples without taking into account their demands for historical justice. In this vein, Indigenous peoples of Colombia would benefit from a broad approach to truth (Nagy, 2012) that locates their historical injuries on a continuum of violence that has marked and continues to mark the very nature of the Colombian state. This broad approach seems to have influenced the JEP's recognition of nature as a victim of the conflict (JEP, 2019) as described in our introduction, but it remains to be seen if the ruling brings about social and political consciousness with regard to the harm caused not only by the war but also by the normalization of the extractive economy in the country. Similarly, the TJ discourse on enduring peace and non-repetition should engage with discussions about climate change and food security which have been advanced by Indigenous peoples of the country. At stake is the politics of data—in this case Indigenous victimhood narratives—and whether statistics related to prolonged conflict can counter the nation state dominant representation of Indigenous peoples which has historically benefited the status quo as Walter (2016) points out.

***

Thus far, we have described Colombia's TJ framework and its problematic representation of Indigenous victimhood. The remaining part of the chapter is concerned with the interpretation of the historical demands of the Wayuu within the legal arrangements that have regulated their Indigenous sovereignty. Specifically, we will analyze elements of the safeguard plan of the community and its relationship with the victimhood narrative of the TJ framework. At the end of this section, we will also refer to a recent effort of the community to counter the state's notion of development discourse: the autonomous consultation.

Safeguard plans emerged from CCC Order 004/2009. Through these plans, endangered Indigenous communities have the opportunity to share their experiences of violence and explain how displacement and other related crimes have affected their existence. In this vein, safeguard plans are a historical attempt to shed light on the violation of the collective rights of Indigenous communities. In the Wayuu safeguard plan (Asociacion de Autoridades Tradicionales de la Guajira 2014), the community advances demands for historical redress questioning the periodization of victimhood that has informed Victims Law (Law 1448/2011).

Section three: The Wayuu

The Wayuu are the largest Indigenous community of Colombia. They are mostly located in La Guajira, the northernmost department of Colombia and the border state of Zulia in neighboring Venezuela. In 2018, a national population survey established that the Wayuu population consists of 380,460 people (DANE, 2019), with the majority of them living in *rancherías*, collective systems of communitarian organization. *Rancherías* are characterized by having traditional orchards, irrigation systems and even graveyards. Similar to other border regions inhabited by Indigenous communities like Putumayo, La Guajira's territory has been historically treated as a marginal place. La Guajira is one of the poorest departments of the country, with 28% of the population living in extreme poverty.

Colonization has marked the historical formation of La Guajira. As a result of colonial violence, the Indigenous population of the Americas dropped significantly by the year 1600. This prompted the colonial powers to bring millions of slaves to the new world to continue with the extraction of minerals that characterized the colonial period. However, some of these slaves escaped to places far from the colonial metropolis and formed their own social systems. In La Guajira, their settlements were known as *rochelas*, and Afrodescendants, Wayuu and mestizo people lived there for many centuries after settling by the banks of the Ranchería River. *Rochelas* became essential for the irrigation systems used in *rancherías* by the Wayuu people and other ethnic groups of la Guajira (Ramírez et al., 2015).

Rancherías are fundamental to understanding the history of the Wayuu. As a communitarian system of territorial organization, the *rancherías* are an example of ancestral inter-legality and coexistence of different social orders, which dates back to colonial times. The historical injuries endured by the Wayuu community are related to the non-recognition of their territorial rights, as illustrated by the violent interventions such as the extractive project of the Cerrejon mine, and by the incursion of illegal and legal armed groups.

The Cerrejon mine

In the 1980's, the Colombian state granted licenses for the exploitation of coal in the Cerrejon mine, the largest open-cast mine in South America. Today, the extractive project produces 32 tons of coal per year which is exported worldwide yet the profitability of the mining project has not improved the living conditions of the Wayuu community. On the contrary, according to the community's narrative, the extraction of coal has dried their lands and affected the irrigation systems of their territories significantly. This situation has resulted from the mine's unnatural use of the Ranchería River, which has been deviated to supply the water required by the mine for the process of coal extraction. The Ranchería River was the only source of water in the mid and low Guajira, which are semi-desert regions (Molano, 2012). Data from a recent ruling by the Inter-American Commission of Human Rights (IACHR Resolution 60/2015) show that 4770 Wayuu children have died of malnutrition during the past decade, which is due in part to the lack of water because they cannot irrigate their crops. The community also maintains that inadequate access to drinking water has played an important role in this tragedy. In addition to water scarcity, the Wayuu people have also suffered from respiratory diseases caused by the polluted air that circulates in their territories and have suffered massive displacement, as discussed below.

This stark reality prompts us to reflect on the human costs of development projects promoted by the extractive economy in the Global South. Rather than bringing equality and better living conditions to La Guajira, the mining project has caused a humanitarian crisis in the department.

Bahia Portete massacre

In April 2004 a paramilitary unit cut off the heads of Wayuu midwives and tortured various other Wayuu women (Verdad Abierta, 2011). The paramilitaries were fighting for control of the port, which has historically been of great importance for the smuggling of goods, especially cocaine (Molano, 2012). The assassination of three Wayuu women and the forced disappearance of two others affected the social fabric of the community significantly. The Wayuu have a matrilineal hierarchy in which women represent authority within the community (ONIC). As a result of the paramilitary incursion which has been described as the *Bahía Portete Massacre*, 888 members of the Wayuu community were forcibly displaced mostly to places such as Uribia, Maicao in the Colombian side of La Guajira and Maracaibo in the Venezuelan side (Verdad Abierta 2011, CNMH, 2010). Later, a TJ tribunal created by the Peace and Justice Law revealed that the Bahia Portete massacre resulted from an alliance between paramilitary and state forces in La Guajira.[7]

This heinous event illustrates the persistence of the colonial treatment of Indigenous peoples and their territories throughout the existence of Colombia as a republic (1819–2019). As we mentioned in the introduction, in the colonial period, Indigenous peoples were dispossessed because their territories were considered *terra nullius*, that is, territories without trace of humanity and no property relations. Places located on the margins of the Colombian state such as La Guajira continue to embody the structural injury caused by the colonial principle of *terra nullius*. In these places, state sovereignty has only been exercized through militarization and extractive projects of natural resources. This is representative of the strategic relation of "inclusive exclusion", used by the Colombian state to control those places alien to the nationhood narrative (Uribe, 2017). The massacre was conducted by a paramilitary organization that was connected to state forces, thus allowing the state to continue its militarization of Wayuu territory while also claiming innocence and lack of knowledge because the campaign was conducted by an illegal armed group, not directly by Colombian soldiers.

The two above-mentioned events pose a challenge to the transitional justice frameworks implemented in the country. The challenge lies in the fact that the systemic harm endured by the Wayuu and other ancestral communities inhabiting La Guajira represents a form of structural violence that the legalistic character of TJ can hardly address. As a consequence, the Wayuu community became official victims of Colombia's conflict after the TJ tribunal ruling revealed that the Bahia Portete massacre resulted from an alliance between paramilitary and state forces in La Guajira. However, the notion of victim informing the TJ discourse constrains the legal investigation to the events related to the massacre. Accountability for the event will hardly address the systemic violation of the Wayuu's territorial rights, which would necessarily bring to the fore the role of the Cerrejon project. Overall, the difficulty resides in the differing interpretations of systemic suffering and the ways in which TJ discourse defines Indigenous victims in the country. Furthermore, the possibility of Indigenous sovereignty remains uncertain because in *terra nullius* places, different armed groups, including the state forces, continue to fight for territorial control (Lemaitre, 2015).

Wayuu safeguard plan

Although the conflict of the Wayuu community with the Cerrejon mine has been widely researched (Chomsky et al., 2007; Archila et al., 2015; Rojas-Páez, 2017; Avilés, 2019), it continues to exemplify the chronic impunity (Rojas-Páez, 2017) of the crimes of the powerful (Pearce, 1976). In fact, according to Avilés, between 2007 and 2017, the child mortality rate in Guajira exceeded "the deaths of Colombia's long running internal war during the same period" (Avilés 2019, p.1751). This situation illustrates the human cost of large scale extractive projects, through which the use of resources is decided by the interests of local and global investment elites rather than by the ancestral communities inhabiting the territories where resources are located. As Chomsky et al. (2007) show, deterritorialization of the Wayuu community is related to the beginning of the mining project, for which the construction of a railroad was necessary at the beginning of the 1980's. The communities were not consulted about the construction of the railroad because at that time ILO Convention 169 did not exist. In fact, when the convention was ratified by Law 21/1991, more than 1000 members of the community had already been displaced according to Wayuu anthropologist Weildler Guerra (2007). The construction of the railroad meant the destruction of sacred graveyards and the community was forced to excavate them and take the bones of their ancestors with them (Guerra, 2007). Nearly all the communities of La Guajira—15 out of 21—have been displaced since 1976 due to the expansion of the mine, with 700 Wayuu people resettled. How are these data related to the transitional setting and its narrative regarding victimhood of Indigenous victims?

In the community's safeguard plan, the Wayuu maintain that their territorial organisation differs from the reservation model established by Law 89/1890.

As mentioned earlier, this law was discriminatory because it characterized the Indigenous peoples as savages who should be civilized by missionaries. The law also established that the communities should be territorially organised into reservations (*resguardos*) in which Indigenous councils could be formed. Despite its racist grounds, these two elements of the law have been strategically used by the communities in their territorial disputes against landowners throughout the 20th century (Lemaitre, 2015; Vasco, 2008). For example, the lands of the reservations were difficult to sell because, according to the law, the "savages" inhabiting them lacked the capacity to exercise property rights.

Historically, the Wayuu have organized themselves through clans, which were not legally recognized for prior consultation. This resulted in the community's strategic adaptation to the reservation model, which is the only form of territorial organisation recognized by the state to use prior consultation. The safeguard plan shows that as a result of forced displacement many members of the community had to form settlements far from their territory, which has given way to a situation of deterriolization. Only the Wayuu who have organized through reservations and have been granted the respective legal recognition can be called victims according to the framework of the Victims Law. This shows how the attempt of TJ to establish a definition of Indigenous victims is arbitrary and divisive. As Nagy puts it, "drawing a line on the past denies continuities of violence and, in turn, colludes with understandings of reconciliation that seek to maintain the status quo" (Nagy, 2012, p. 360)

One major problem the community faces is caused by the Cerrejon mine, particularly the deviation of the Ranchería River for the construction of the Cercado dam. The community was not consulted with about this project. The dam provides the necessary water for mining and has dramatically restricted the community's access to the river. Colombia's Attorney General's words illustrate this situation "The Ranchería River in spite of being a good of public use, its water can be found in a dam to which the Wayuu would not have access" (Aviles 2019). Thus, the Wayuu's current situation challenges the restricted narrative surrounding the TJ discourse and calls for a broader understanding of structural injuries in which the human cost of development is scrutinized.

Autonomous consultation

Autonomous consultation is an internal decision-making practice, through which the Wayuu community expressed their dissent to the consultation process of the Cerrejon mine. This exercise of Indigenous sovereignty occurred within the initial phase of consultation about the Cerrejon project: the pre-consultation. The community was consulted about the deviation of 26 kilometers of the Ranchería River, which would provide the water for the extraction of coal. Initially the community's response to the representatives of both the government and the mining project was that they would consider the proposal and come up with an answer but they needed to dream about it first. In fact, their answer to the institutional actors of the consultation was: "Let us dream first. If the dream we have is a bad one, we will have to think about things more" (Guariyu, 2015, p 18).

Through the internal consultation the community realized that the extractive project would imply a resettlement of the community, which would mean that the community would have to live far from the Ranchería River. This was not an option for the community for several reasons. According to Wayuu cosmogony, the Ranchería River is the vein and heart of the community; therefore, the deviation of the river would mean the death of the entire community. Furthermore, their sacred medicinal plants grow along the river. In the end, the community asserted that they could not dream and thus were not able to give an answer. In their response they stated: "We cannot continue dreaming, because our dreams are not clear any longer ... with the arrival of the mine we have lost the capacity of dreaming...we should only dream again when mining leaves our territory" (Guariyu, 2015, p 23).

As mentioned above, the deviation of the Rancheria River occurred and this gave way to a complex situation for the community, with events that illustrate the genocidal and ecocidal sides of development. The internal consultation is not legally recognized by the Colombian state. However, if we understand Indigenous data (ID) sovereignty as the proper locus of authority over the Indigenous territories and ways of life as Kukutay and Tylor describe it (Kukutai and Taylor, 2016), it would be fundamental that justice bodies such as JEP do not lose sight of the epistemic and moral basis surrounding the justice demands made by the Wayuu and other Indigenous communities exercising their sovereignty.

Concluding thoughts

In this chapter, we have discussed the ways in which narratives related to Indigenous victimhood have emerged in Colombia's transitional setting. We have argued that the legal framework of the transitional setting does not account for structural injuries endured by Indigenous communities of the country. This is mainly due to the temporalities established by the legal frameworks that have informed Colombia's transitional setting. These temporalities fail to address the structural dynamics of the conflict which have a close relationship with the colonial representation of Indigenous peoples, which has not changed much in today's globalized world.

We have discussed how historical injuries are related to the expansion of the extractive economy in Colombia, drawing on the Wayuu experience as a case study, and have highlighted the importance of Indigenous Data Sovereignty as a means of protecting endangered Indigenous peoples of Colombia, particularly with regard to their demands for territorial rights and food sovereignty. Although the 1991 constitution recognized Indigenous sovereignty, the colonial narrative persists and is normalized by the imposition of the large scale extractive economy in the country, which significantly affects these endangered communities. As a result, inter-legality works in a complex interplay in which investors' interests prevail over progressive legal frameworks such as the UN Declaration on the Rights of Indigenous peoples and ILO Convention 169.

Due at least in part to the expansion of the extractive economy, the Wayuu people have lost their territorial rights, food sovereignty, and access to water.

Despite their symbolic value, the TJ frameworks implemented over the past years have failed to address the structural injustices in Colombia, including unequal distribution of land, and much of the forced displacement that occurred before 1985. By creating a specific temporality for the recognition of Indigenous victims, the state's responsibility in the systemic and structural injustice is erased and does not allow an adequate understanding of the complexities of the conflict or the violence that began in colonial times and that continue to affect Indigenous people today. If the state is really engaged with the promise of enduring peace informing the TJ discourse, it should not ignore the historical injuries endured by Indigenous peoples from the colonial times until 1985. Here lies a major challenge for the JEP but also for international justice bodies.

The notion of Indigenous Data Sovereignty could play an important role in advancing accountability processes that shed light on the structural injuries endured by endangered Indigenous peoples of the country. By taking into account the temporality as perceived by the Indigenous peoples themselves, as well as their narratives of resistance to extractive projects, we could reach a more accurate understanding of what they have suffered during the conflict. This could be fundamental to stopping the systemic violence against Indigenous communities in Colombia.

Notes

1 At the moment of writing this chapter, Indigenous peoples of Colombia have advanced a campaign against the recent assassinations of many of their members. According to the UN, 56 Indigenous persons have been killed in the Cauca region this year and 11 of those 56 people were human rights defenders. According to a report produced by ONIC, 135 Indigenous people have been assassinated since 2018. The name of the campaign is illustrative of this disturbing rate: STOP THE GENOCIDE.
2 Based on the literature of green criminology, Johnson et al. (2016) show that mainstream legal doctrines on property undermine the universal realization of the fundamental right to water because international legal arrangements protect corporate interest over human rights. The authors bring to the fore a fundamental problem of legal epistemology: corporations cannot be tried for human rights violations nor for ecocide.
3 Radical changes in the jurisprudence related to territorial rights and ownership of natural resources is one of the major challenges for Indigenous and *campesino* communities of Colombia. For instance CCC Ruling SU-095/2018 restrains the use of popular consultations related to extractive projects. In previous rulings the court endorsed the use of popular consultations as a mechanism of democratic participation (CCC Ruling T-445/2016).
4 *Terraje* was a feudal practice used by large landowners who occupied and disposed Indigenous territories from colonial times until 1970. The Indigenous communities were forced to work for free in their disposed territories. In exchange they could live in small portions of the large Haciendas. See Vasco 2008.
5 The law created a mechanism for the registration of victims Registro Único de Víctimas (RUV). Only 986,961 out of 8,816.30 victims registered have received reparations. This accounts for only 11% of the victims registered. See https://www.elheraldo.co/barranquilla/victimas-aun-falta-por-reparar-el-89-en-el-pais-dice-el-ruv-642068

6 This tension has been recently addressed by scholar M.L Böhm who analyzes eight Latin American cases in which human rights violations and environmental degradation are committed by transnational corporations. The cases documented by Böhm are illustrative of what she terms "the crime of maldevelopment", which is defined as the cause and result of interrelated forms of violence (structural, physical and cultural) endured by historically marginalized groups such as Indigenous communities. Although the outcomes of the cases seem to show that large victims groups seem irrelevant for the justice system, Böhm calls for a broader understanding of harm that revisits the human cost of the global deregulation of the economy. Böhm's suggestive work is a salient attempt to shed light on the invisibility of the communities affected by the crime of maldevelopment. In her words: "The impression that large victim groups are anonymous does not mean that they actually are. Every malnourished child has a name, every displaced indigenous person is an irreplaceable member of an ancestral group and each severely polluted lake is one fewer natural sources of water for a specific community" (Böhm, 2019 p. 2).

7 This uneasy link was common in places where extractive mining and energy activities took place. As a securitization strategy the government created mining and energy battalions. By 2014, there were already 21 batallions composed of 80.000 troops. See https://wri-irg.org/en/story/2014/colombia-militarisation-serving-extraction

References

Aponte, J., and López, L. (2013). El pluralismo jurídico indígena en la ley de víctimas. *Universitas Estudiantes*. Bogotá (Colombia) N° 10: 157–176, enero-diciembre 2013.

Archila, M., Arboleda, Z., Coronado, S., Cuenca, T., Garcia, M., and Guariyú, L. (2015). *"Hasta cuando soñemos" Extractivismo e interculturalidad en el sur de la Guajira*. CINEP.

Asociación de Autoridades Tradicionales de la Guajira Akalinjira Wa. 2014. *Plan de Salvaguarda Wayuu: Capítulo Riohacha*. Ministerio del Interior.

Aviles, W. (2019). The Wayuu tragedy: death, water and the imperatives of Global capitalism. *Third World Quarterly*, 40(09), 1750–1766. doi:10.1080/01436597.2019.1613638

Bengoetxea, J. (2020). *Data Governance in the Basque Country: Victims and Memories of Violent Conflicts* (in this book).

Böhm, M.L. (2019). *The Crime of Maldevelopment: Economic Deregulation and Violence in the Global South*. London: Routledge.

Bourgois, P. (2009). Recognizing invisible violence: a thirty year ethnographic perspective. In: B. Rylko-Bauer, L.M. Whiteford, and P. Farmer, eds., *Global Health in Times of Violence*. Santa Fe, NM: School for Advanced Research Press, pp. 17–40.

Burnets, G. (2018). *Chocolate, Politics and Peace-Building: An Ethnography of the Peace Community of San José de Apartadó*. Colombia: Palgrave Macmillan.

Casement, R. (1911). Putumayo caucho y sangre: Relación al Parlamento Inglés (1911) https://dspace.ups.edu.ec/handle/123456789/11516

Castillejo-Cuéllar, A. (2013a). Historical injuries, temporality and the law: Articulations of a violent past in two transitional scenarios. *Law and Critique*, 23(3), 47–66.

Castillejo-Cuéllar, A. (2013b). On the question of the historical injuries: Transitional Justice: Anthropology and the vicissitudes of listening. *Anthropology Today*, 29(1), 17–21.

Chomsky, A., Leach, G., and Striffler, S. (2007). *Bajo el manto del Carbón: Pueblos y Multinacionales en las minas del Cerrejón*. Colombia: Editorial, Pisando Callos.

CNMH. (2010). *La Masacre de Bahía Portete: Mujeres Wayuu en la mira*. Taurus.

DANE. (2019). Pueblo Wayuu: Resultados del Censo Nacional de Población y Vivienda 2018. Dirección Nacional de Estadística. Published on August 16, 2019. https://www.dane.gov.co/files/censo2018/informacion-tecnica/presentaciones-territorio/190816-CNPV-presentacion-Resultados-Guajira-Pueblo-Wayuu.pdf

Guariyu, L. (2015). Preámbulo. In: M. Archila, Z. Arboleda, S. Coronado, T. Cuenca, M. Garcia, and L. Guariyú, eds., *"Hasta cuando soñemos" Extractivismo e interculturalidad en el sur de la Guajira*. CINEP.

Guerra, W. (2007). Las comunidades indígenas de La Guajira ante el Proyecto carbonífero de El Cerrejón, 1991. In: A. Chomsky, G. Leach, S. Striffler, eds., *Bajo el manto del Carbón: Pueblos y Multinacionales en las minas del Cerrejón*. Colombia: Editorial, Pisando Callos, pp. 51–57.

Johnson, H., Nigel, S., and Reece, W. (2016). The commodification and exploitation of fresh water: property, human rights, and green criminology. *Institutional Journal of Law, Crime and Justice*, 44(2016), 146–162.

Horn, N. (2014). Eddie Maboo and Namibia. In: J.M. Barreto, ed., *Human Rights from a Third World Perspective*. Cambridge Scholars Publishing.

Kukutai, T., and Taylor, J. eds. (2016). Data Sovereignty for Indigenous Peoples: current practice and future needs. In: T. Kukutai, and J. Taylor, eds., *Indigenous Data Sovereignty: Toward an Agenda*. Australian National University Press.

ILO 169/1989. *Indigenous and Tribal Peoples*. International Labour Organization. https://www.ilo.org/global/topics/Indigenous-tribal/lang--en/index.htm

Lemaitre, J. (2015). *La Quintiada (1912–1925) La rebellion indígena liderada por Manuel Quintín Lame en el Cauca*. Bogotá: Universidad de los Andes.

Lemaitre, J. (2015). *Constitution or Barbarism? How to Rethink Law in Lawless Zones*. Constitution or barbarism? How to rethink law in lawless zones. In: C. Rodriguez, ed., *Law and Society in Latin America: A New Map*. Routledge.

Lopez, O., Rojas, T., Duarte, C., Boffey, G., and Betancourt, D. (2019). *Análisis de la Política Pública de Reparación a las Víctimas Pertenecientes a Comunidades Étnica y Culturalmente Diferenciadas*. Bogotá: Universidad Libre.

Molano- Bravo A. (2012). *La Guajira Despresada*. En El Espectador.

Nagy, R. (2012). Truth, reconciliation and settler denial: specifying the Canada–South Africa analogy. *Human Rights Review*, 13, 349–367. doi:10.1007/s12142-012-0224-4

Organización Nacional Indígena de Colombia, ONIC. https://www.onic.org.co/

Organización Nacional Indígena de Colombia, ONIC. (2012). Balance ONIC del Decreto Ley 4633/ 2011 y la Ley de Víctimas.

Pearce, F. (1976). *Crimes of the Powerful: Marxism, Crime, and Deviance*. London: Pluto Press.

Pool, I. (2016). Colonialism's and post-colonialism's fellow traveller: the collection, use and misuse of data on indigenous peoples. In: *Indigenous Data Sovereignty Toward and Agenda*. ANU Press.

Quijano, A. (2000). Coloniality of power, etnocentrism, and Latin America. *Nepantla, Views form the South*, 1(3), 533–580.

Ramírez, R., Naranjo, J., Múnera, L., Rodriguez, L., Granados, M., Usate, R., Arregocés, S., and Teherán, S. (2015). *Bárbaros Hoscos. Historia de la (des)Territorialización de los Negros de la Comunidad Roche*. CINEP.

Rodriguez, C., Orduz, N., Boada, S., Rubiano, S., and Arias F. (2010). *JUSTICIA GLOBAL 3. Pueblos indígenas y desplazamiento forzado. Evaluación del cumplimiento del Gobierno colombiano del auto 004 de la Corte Constitucional colombiana*. Universidad de los Andes.

Rojas-Páez, G. (2017). Understanding Environmental Harm and justice claims in the Global South: Crimes of the Powerful and People's Resistance. In: D. Rodríguez Goyes, H. Mol, A. Brisman, N. South, eds., *Environmental Crime in* Latin America. *Palgrave Studies in* Green *Criminology*. London: Palgrave Macmillan.

Santos, B. (1995). *Toward a New Common Sense: Law, Science and Politics in the Paradigmatic Transition.* London: Routledge.

Suarez-Krabbe, J. (2016). *Race, Rights and Rebels: Alternatives to Human Rights and Development from the Global South.* Lanham: Rowman and Littlefield.

Uribe, S. (2017). *Frontier Road: Power, History and the Everyday State in the Colombian Amazon.* Hoboken, NJ: Wiley.

Vasco, J.G. (2008). Quintin Lame Resistencia y Liberación. *Tabula Rasa*, 9, 371–383.

Velasquez, R., and Castillo, V. (2006). Resistencia de la etnia yariguies a las políticas de reducción y civilización en el siglo xix. *Historia y Sociedad*, 12, 285–317.

Verdad Abierta (2011). *La masacre de Bahía Portete*. Published April 19, 2011. https://verdadabierta.com/la-masacre-de-bahia-portete/

Wilson, R. (2001). *The Politics of Truth and Reconciliation in South Africa: Legitimizing the Post-Apartheid State.* Cambridge University Press.

Walter, M. (2016). Data politics and Indigenous representation in Australian statistics. In: T. Kukutai, J. Taylor, eds., *Indigenous Data Sovereignty Toward and Agenda.* ANU Press.

Rulings

Constitutional Court (11 de octubre de 2018) Sentencia CCC Ruling SU-095/2018, M.P. Cristina Pardo Schlesinger

Special Jurisdiction for Peace (JEP 079/2019). AUTO SRVBIT 079/ 2019 (Noviembre 12 de 2019)

Inter-American Commission on Human Rights, IACHR., Resolution 60/2015. December 11 of 2015

Regulations

Law 975 of 2005. por la cual se dictan disposiciones para la reincorporación de miembros de grupos armados organizados al margen de la ley, que contribuyan de manera efectiva a la consecución de la paz nacional y se dictan otras disposiciones para acuerdos humanitarios. July 25 of 2005. O.J. 45.980

United Nations. (2007). *United Nations Declaration on the Rights of Indigenous Peoples*

Decree 4633 de 2011. [Ministerio del Interior]. Por medio del cual se dictan medidas de asistencia, atención, reparación integral y de restitución de derechos territoriales a las víctimas pertenecientes a los pueblos y comunidades indígenas. Diciembre 09 del 2011. O.J. 48.278

Law 1448 of 2011. Por la cual se dictan medidas de atención, asistencia y reparación integral a las víctimas del conflicto armado interno y se dictan otras disposiciones. June 10 of 2011. O.J 48.096.

13 Kaupapa Māori-informed approaches to support data rights and self-determination[1]

Sarah-Jane Paine, Donna Cormack, Papaarangi Reid, Ricci Harris and Bridget Robson

Introduction

Although Indigenous Peoples have always had our own ways of conceptualizing health and well-being and our own systems for preventing illness and for healing, in many colonial nation states Indigenous health is primarily (re)presented through quantitative data and statistics, particularly in narratives of Indigenous health produced by colonial governments. As Walter & Andersen (2013: 8) note, these data not only (re)produce "knowledge" on Indigenous health, but "have also become the backbone for the creation and implementation of social policy for Indigenous peoples". Quantitative data are used to construct "truths" about Indigenous Peoples, including Māori, and analyzed to produce the "evidence" that is meant to inform health sector policies and interventions (Andersen & Kukutai 2016; Walter & Andersen 2013). Quantitative approaches have become relatively dominant in health research in Aotearoa. Within this broader umbrella of quantitative methodologies, the discipline of epidemiology has a powerful presence, often positioned as producing a higher or more reliable "evidence" relative to other methodologies. In this chapter, in line with Walter & Andersen (2013: 45), the term methodology refers to the beliefs about how research can produce knowledge, including what they term the "research standpoint" that involves the researcher's social position, and assumptions about epistemology, axiology and ontology, as well as the particular "theoretical frames" and methods that are used in research. Methods refers to the tools and procedures "for gathering and analyzing information" (Walter & Andersen 2013: 41).

The assumed superiority of quantitative methodologies in the health sciences in general, and epidemiology specifically, means that research approaches grounded in other ways of knowing are often represented as lesser. This positioning is resisted by Indigenous researchers and scholars (Andersen & Kukutai 2016), including Māori health researchers (Reid, Cormack & Paine 2019). Kaupapa Māori research approaches offer methodologies grounded in Māori values, knowledge systems and ontologies (Pihama 2010; Smith 2012a). Kaupapa Māori epidemiology challenges underlying assumptions of prevailing epidemiological methodologies and methods, proposing resistant and alternative ways to think about quantitative data, to formulate research questions, and to undertake research. In addition, Kaupapa

Māori epidemiology troubles the often-unquestioned assumption that quantitative methodologies, and in the health sciences, epidemiological approaches more particularly, provide the best "evidence" on which to base policies. This chapter presents and discusses examples of approaches developed in Aotearoa, including Mana Whakamārama (Equal Explanatory Power), and age-standardization to an Indigenous standard, and considers the role Kaupapa Māori epidemiology may have in re-visioning quantitative Māori health research methodologies and approaches. The chapter also explores how Kaupapa Māori quantitative approaches can support Māori data rights and Indigenous Data Sovereignty and contribute to broader goals of Indigenous self-determination. Indigenous Data Sovereignty is underpinned by "Indigenous collective rights to data about our peoples, territories, lifeways and natural resources" (Walter & Suina 2019) and is an expression of inherent Indigenous rights (Kukutai & Taylor 2016).

Knowledge, power and science

The (re)presenting of Indigenous Peoples and knowledges as inferior is fundamental to the work of colonialism, and particularly to Westernized imperial approaches to research and "science" (Smith 2012b; Whitt 2009). Rather than an unintended side-effect of colonization, the devaluing and destruction of Indigenous knowledge systems was an active and intentional part of the colonial project (Smith et al. 2016). As Māori ways of knowing were de-centered, Westernized imperialist approaches to knowledge and research were promoted as superior, more credible and more capable of producing "the truth".

Western colonial knowledge systems fixate on drawing boundaries between disciplines and organizing knowledge, and the methodologies related to the (re) production of knowledge, into hierarchies (Smith 2012a). In dominating research approaches in Aotearoa, quantitative and qualitative methodologies are generally positioned as separate, and sometimes in opposition, reflecting the tendency to dichotomization that characterizes "science" in Westernized academic settings. This separation between quantitative and qualitative approaches is in contrast with Indigenous approaches to knowledge that emphasize relationships and the interconnectedness and interdependence of all things, including systems of knowledge (Tsosie 2012). However, the quantitative/qualitative binary has become entrenched in many Westernized academic and research contexts. In addition, quantitative methodologies grounded in positivistic traditions, such as epidemiology, have become dominant in particular disciplines, including medical and health sciences.

When quantitative research is conducted from a positivist position, then it is limited in scope, privileging methods from Europe and ignoring Indigenous knowledges and methodologies. As Indigenous scholars state, positivism's assumption of a singular truth means that "Positivist research methods, therefore, promote epistemicide by oppressing varying worldviews" (Sandoval et al. 2016: 19). This epistemicidal logic is reflected in colonial narratives that discount Indigenous knowledge systems as being archaic and less sophisticated (Whitt

2009). For Māori, bodies of knowledge surrounding navigation, or the maramataka, for example, integrate diverse and multiple ways of knowing, including systems of counting and measurement (Smith et al. 2016). Coloniality, however, encourages us to stop seeing and imagining ourselves as producers of these kinds of knowledges, supporting the imperial research practices described by Linda Tuhiwai Smith within which Indigenous Peoples were positioned as objects and Indigenous knowledges, when acknowledged, were (re)produced as Western scientific discoveries (Smith 2012b), practices that continue today.

Quantitative research and epidemiology in racialized, colonial contexts

As noted above, quantitative research occupies a dominating position in health research and in producing knowledge about Māori health. Quantitative health research often draws on epidemiological methodologies and theories to produce and analyze data, to make claims both about the patterning of Māori health and about factors or circumstances that are thought to shape these patterns. Epidemiology has been defined in many ways, including as:

> the science and practice which describes and explains disease patterns in populations, and uses this knowledge to prevent and control disease and improve health … . The central paradigm of epidemiology is to seek differences and similarities ("compare and contrast") in the disease patterns of populations to gain new knowledge. (Bhopal 2016)

However, epidemiology has often been silent on the theoretical assumptions that shape much of the "science and practice" (Bhopal 2016) of the discipline (Krieger & Zierler 1996), failing to situate epidemiology within its broader historical, social and political context. Nancy Krieger has called for epidemiologists to both consider and be explicit about the theories that shape their methodologies and methods (Krieger 1994, 2011). Definitions of epidemiology as the study of the distribution and determinants of disease frequency and outcomes between populations, for example, often fail to acknowledge fundamental and critical questions of how we understand who counts as a population in the first place, nor how researchers are positioned in relation to the population they are "studying". How we conceptualize populations necessarily influences how we see data about populations and what we say about it. As Krieger (2012: 649) suggests "populations are first and foremost relational beings, not "things." They are active agents, not simply statistical aggregates characterized by distributions". In racialized contexts, concepts of a "population" cannot be understood outside of colonial racial classifications that ordered Indigenous Peoples into hierarchies, yet much epidemiological research fails to engage meaningfully with this context of population data.

The unsafety of epidemiology, as one branch of quantitative methodologies, for Māori and Indigenous Peoples becomes apparent when we trace the history of the discipline and contextualize it in terms of its relationship with the eugenics movement and White supremacist thought (Zuberi 2000). Epidemiology draws heavily on statistical practices that were developed to mark non-White people and communities as deficient and deployed to support imperial claims about the (in)humanity of people racialized as inferior (Zuberi 2000). Colonialism wielded quantitative methods and statistics, such as land surveyance, demography and cartography, to dismember Indigenous ways of knowing and our relationships with our lands and communities (Andersen & Kukutai 2016), whilst at the same time constructing new "truths" about Indigenous Peoples as un-knowing and unscientific (Smith 2012a; Whitt 2009). Statistics and quantitative research then, as other scholars have noted, forms a critical part of the architecture of Whiteness in colonial systems and structures, including in the production and analysis of data in research and policy settings.

While debates and contestations exist within the field of epidemiology (Wemrell et al. 2016), positivist quantitative research methodologies and methods, including epidemiology, generally rest on several powerful ontological and epistemological assumptions. Firstly, quantitative methodologies tend to embrace the idea of objectivity and a presumed separation of body and mind, reinforcing colonial logics that demarcate boundaries between land and people and contemporaneously between people and data. Objectivity, as a value in quantitative research, can be weaponized to create distance and hierarchy within and between populations, furthering the analytic focus on human difference rather than sameness and fostering the notion that we as peoples are separate from the data that we produce or examine. The value placed on notions of objectivity is in contrast to Indigenous relational ways of being and knowing (Blackstock 2009), and encourages researchers to act as if they, their data and their research practices, are unconnected from broader contexts and histories (Cram 1997), or from their underlying theoretical beliefs. However, as Bonilla-Silva and Zuberi state:

> Statistical analysis is connected to an underlying theory. Statistical results, themselves, do not prove anything beyond the numerical relationship between two or more lists of numbers or variables. The connection of these variables in the real world requires a causal theory ... it is irrelevant whether the [researcher] is aware of the theory.
>
> (2008: 9)

A second and closely related claim is that data produced through statistics represent a fixed and discoverable social reality, rather than one that is partial and contingent on the researchers, their worldviews and their methodologies (Walter & Suina 2019). This claim serves to divert attention away from the racist foundations of particular methodologies and use of quantitative data in the service of colonial logics (Walter & Andersen 2013), by presenting quantitative research about Māori as simply factual representations of situations whose causes lie in Indigenous minds, bodies and behavior. It reifies positivism's investment in the notion of a singular truth, sustaining disregard for multiple coexisting and interrelated knowledges (Whitt 2009).

A third claim is that quantitative data speak for themselves. This claim rests on both the assumption of objectivity that data are separate from us and on the claim to represent a pre-existing, rather than socially constructed, reality. However, as Bonilla-Silva and Zuberi note

> Data do not tell us a story. We use data to craft a story that comports with our understanding of the world. If we begin with a racially biased view of the world, then we will end with a racially biased view of what the data have to say.
>
> (2008: 7)

While many quantitative researchers assert that they report only on what the data say, the fundamental questions about what data are included, and how they are analyzed and interpreted, are determined by the researchers (Cram 1997). In our shared history where the role of the researcher has largely been held by non-Indigenous People, this claim also serves to block Indigenous Peoples from speaking back to problematic data as though our lived experiences are irrelevant in the face of objective, quantitative results.

Kaupapa Māori research and Kaupapa Māori epidemiology

Kaupapa Māori research approaches in the 1980s and 1990s developed as part of broader movements in education and elsewhere to resist the dominance of colonial institutions and structures and reassert Māori rights to self-determination (Bishop 1998; Smith 2012b). Kaupapa Māori takes for granted the legitimacy of Māori ways of being, doing and knowing, is concerned with collective well-being and benefit, and is grounded in commitments to self-determination and transformation (Bishop 1998; Smith 2012a). In relation to research, Bishop states that it "is predicated on the understanding that Māori means of accessing, defining, and protecting knowledge existed before European arrival in New Zealand" (1998: 201). Kaupapa Māori research approaches are explicitly concerned with undertaking research that will benefit Māori communities and center Māori realities (Pihama 2010; Smith 2012a, 2012b).

Within this broader context, the development of Kaupapa Māori quantitative approaches in health responded to key issues of the time. These included movements for recognition of sovereignty, te Tiriti o Waitangi, and land rights, such as the 1975 Land March, the (re)occupation of Takaparawha and the establishment of the Waitangi Tribunal, as well as the anti-racism protests of the 1981 Springbok tour, and Māori women's movements that challenged oppressive systems. Examples of quantitative Māori health research in the 1980s and 1990s also built on a long history of Māori communities documenting and commenting on Māori health. The foundational 1984 Rapuora Survey on the health of Māori women, was carried out by Te Rōpū Wāhine Māori Toko i te Ora Māori

Women's Welfare League, led by Erihapeti Murchie, and challenged then prevailing approaches to surveys by embedding Kaupapa Māori principles (Murchie 1984). The *Hauora* series of books on Māori health statistics, the first of which was published in 1980 by Professor Eru Pōmare, also utilized quantitative data to produce statistics documenting Māori health outcomes.

In 1996, Māori health researchers at the first Hui Whakapiripiri at Hongoeka Marae produced the *Hongoeka Declaration*, a statement that rearticulated Māori rights to control research about Māori health and laid out commitments including to developing and using Kaupapa Māori research approaches (Te Rōpū Rangahau Hauora a Eru Pōmare 1996). An example of a Māori-led health study undertaken in partnership with Māori communities was the "Mauri Mahi, Mauri Ora, Mauri Noho, Mauri Mate: the Health Effects of Unemployment and Redundancy" study (Keefe et al. 1999). The study incorporated epidemiological methods (a retrospective cohort study) and Kaupapa Māori research approaches to explore the health impacts of factory closures on Māori (Keefe et al. 1999) and embodied many of the processes and practices that characterize Kaupapa Māori epidemiology today, including whānau, consultation, whakapapa and reciprocity. Not surprisingly, the project was impactful, not only in terms of scholarship and knowledge production related to the effects of mass unemployment events for Indigenous communities but also in the way that the research enhanced the voices of those directly affected by neoliberal reforms of the 1980s and 1990s. For Māori health researchers attempting to create space for Kaupapa Māori epidemiology in the academy, the paper by Keefe and colleagues (1999) was foundational in the way it positioned Kaupapa Māori approaches to epidemiology as necessary for reducing the risks of scientific colonialism. As they wrote:

> Positioning ourselves as insiders is in direct contrast to approaches that insist that the self be submerged so that the social scientist is unbiased and objective (Collins 1991). Instead we make use of and trust our own "personal and cultural biographies as significant sources of knowledge" (Collins 1991). However, this does not mean that we are unable to carry out research ethically, systematically and "scientifically" (Smith 1995). (1999: 13)

Other studies have been undertaken since that time looking at various health issues, including, for example sleep problems (e.g., Paine et al. 2005, 2013), cardiovascular health (Pitama et al. 2011), cesarean sections (Harris et al. 2007), breast cancer (Curtis, Wright & Wall 2005) and dialysis (Huria et al. 2018). Within a broader international context, the development of Kaupapa Māori epidemiological studies aligns with parallel activities being undertaken by Indigenous scholars and researchers in relation to Indigenous health in Hawai'i, and in the nation states currently known as Australia, Canada and the United States (Prussing 2018).

Kaupapa Māori epidemiology in Aotearoa is part of wider activities to uphold Māori rights as tangata whenua in relation to data and research methodologies and methods. Four of these rights are discussed below as examples of how Kaupapa

Māori epidemiological research can work alongside and support Indigenous Data Sovereignty and broader rights to self-determination.

The right to monitor the Crown

> Māori have the right to monitor the Crown and to evaluate Crown action and inaction … . As tangata whenua, our duty includes ensuring the wellbeing of all people in our territories, Māori and tauiwi. This necessitates Māori monitoring health, including any disparities in health outcomes between Māori and non-Māori.
>
> (Reid & Robson 2007: 1)

Kaupapa Māori epidemiology is not simply a "Māori way" of analyzing, describing and explaining patterns and drivers of health or an "equity-lens" through which health data can be filtered. It is a theoretically driven approach to undertaking quantitative health research that utilizes epidemiology as a tool to monitor Crown "action and inaction". In Kaupapa Māori epidemiology, Māori hold the power to ask questions about and monitor the State's obligations under te Tiriti o Waitangi and in relation to the United Nations Declaration on the Rights of Indigenous Peoples (UNDRIP). Kaupapa Māori epidemiology speaks back to colonial interpretations of Māori health inequities as natural or due to innate problems with Māori communities or culture, and argues for the right to use data and statistics to shift the gaze toward the organization of society, and the role of the health system, including health policy, in creating and sustaining health inequities. Through prioritizing the examination of power relations between individuals, groups and populations within society, Kaupapa Māori-driven epidemiology allows for us to see the patterns of ill-health and disease as a consequence of colonization and the social and political relationships between Māori and the Crown (Keefe et al. 1999). It also encourages this same shift in the development of policy, away from policies that aim to act on Māori individuals or communities, to policies that seek to address the social and structural drivers of health.

The development of Kaupapa Māori epidemiology has not been smooth or without controversy. Indigenous memories of harmful quantitative health research have meant that some communities are hesitant to consider the potential for epidemiology, and other methodologies that are strongly linked to positivistic traditions, to be transformational (as was the original goal of Kaupapa Māori epidemiology), an understandable position in light of how quantitative methods are used to reinforce colonial projects (Smith 2012b). In particular, some of the early work was criticized for the use of a Māori/non-Māori analytical frame, which was viewed as an attempt to measure Māori experiences of health and health care relative to those of the Pākehā majority as though this was a standard we should aspire to (Reid, Robson & Jones 2000). To the contrary, the use of Māori/non-Māori analyzes acknowledged the fundamental nature of our relationship with the Crown affirmed in te Tiriti o Waitangi and our expectations of good governance and for equity. In Aotearoa, Māori have the right to expect at least the same level of health as non-Māori. Therefore, the documentation of inequities in health outcomes, health service utilization and quality of health care exposes the multiple ways in which non-Māori accrue benefit from a health system that they constructed, control and continue to shape. A Māori/non-Māori analysis of health also highlights the way that institutional racism operates within the health system to provide advantage to some groups relative to others.

The right to be counted

> Being counted is an acknowledgement of both existence and value. It means that one matters.
> (Te Rōpū Rangahau Hauora a Eru Pōmare 2000)

Epidemiology, as a study of population patterns, has a primary interest in being able to define a population—who is included or not and where the boundaries of belonging are. As noted earlier, epidemiology is fundamentally concerned with measuring (ill-)health within and between populations (Bhopal 2016). However, there are longstanding, and well-documented issues with the (mis)counting of Indigenous populations in relation to health data (e.g., Anderson et al. 2016), including for Māori (e.g., Cormack & Harris 2009). In addition to issues with the construction of colonial nation-state schema for classifying Indigenous Peoples (Cormack, Reid & Kukutai 2019), is the fact that many official systems fail to count Indigenous populations consistently or appropriately even by their own standards, flawed though those standards may be. Research in Aotearoa has documented significant under-enumeration of Māori in vital statistics historically, including in birth and death registrations (e.g., Cormack & Harris 2009; Te Rōpū Rangahau Hauora a Eru Pōmare 2000), as well as in the population census (Kukutai & Cormack 2018). Health data also continue to undercount Māori in many key datasets, including hospitalizations (Cormack & Harris 2009; Scott et al. 2018). Given that these datasets tend to be the basis of population numerators and denominators for analysis, implications for quantitative Māori health research are significant

Walter (2018) describes the "paradox" of Indigenous data, whereby there is "too much" of some types of data, and "too little" of other types. Similar to other Indigenous Peoples, data gaps for Māori continue to exist, where data relevant to understanding Māori health and well-being and developing appropriate policy responses, are not available or are incomplete, because data are not collected or are not disaggregated to allow for exploring patterns and outcomes for Māori separately. Policy developed in these contexts will continue to serve settler colonial interests. Part of the work undertaken in Kaupapa Māori epidemiology, then, is to advocate for the right of Māori to be counted in datasets of importance or relevance to us, or that may be important for understanding health for our communities, a shared goal of Indigenous Data Sovereignty. This has included, for example, work to both promote the appropriate collection and use of ethnicity data in key settings, as well as the development of statistical methods to adjust for the undercount of ethnicity in current datasets to provide for better estimates (Cormack & Harris 2009; Robson & Harris 2007).

The right to have a powerful voice

> Māori have the right to recognition as a people, not a minority group nor a subgroup whose needs are subsumed by those of the total population ... . These rights are pertinent to the design, analysis and reporting of surveys.
>
> (Te Rōpū Rangahau Hauora a Eru Pōmare 2002)

Epidemiological studies and national monitoring surveys that take a total population approach inevitably produce evidence that favors numerically dominant groups in society (Simmonds et al. 2008), creating stories (and policies) that highlight their profile of exposures or access to the social determinants of health whilst at the same time subsuming Indigenous experiences of the health system within those of the total population (Robson & Reid 2001). In Aotearoa, for example, it is not uncommon to hear claims of success when Māori make up 15% of a study sample, as though our rights to participate in health research are directly linked to our proportion of the total population. Policies and programs developed from this type of thinking and data are more likely to meet non-Indigenous needs, silencing the existence and extent of inequities and limiting potential for meaningful interventions as they will be unlikely to reflect the needs of those with the greatest risks (Robson & Reid 2001).

Mana Whakamārama, or equal explanatory power, was an early step toward bringing Māori voices to epidemiology, recognizing Māori statistical needs as having equal status with those of the total population (Te Rōpū Rangahau Hauora a Eru Pōmare 2002). Equal explanatory power foregrounds the importance of having sufficient statistical power to conduct analyzes for Māori to the same depth and breadth as non-Māori, allowing the estimation of population prevalences for Māori and non-Māori populations, whilst at the same time enabling comparisons to be made. Māori epidemiologists argued for the stratification of survey samples by ethnicity in order to explore factors contributing to differences in the prevalence of health outcomes and to enable the comparison of distributions and profiles of "risk factors" by ethnicity. Similarly, stratification by socioeconomic deprivation was also argued to be important not only for understanding the extent to which economic or non-economic consequences of colonization and racism underlie health inequities but also for creating knowledge for action (Krieger 2019).

The expansion of the principles of equal explanatory power from the original cross-sectional national surveys (Mihaere et al. 2009; Paine et al. 2005) to longitudinal cohort studies (Paine et al. 2013) and randomized controlled trials (Selak et al. 2013; Bramley et al. 2005) showcases the level of success that can be achieved when Mana Whakamārama is understood as more than just "tweaking" the way that epidemiologists and biostatisticians approach survey sample design but rather as space for Indigenous knowledges to support excellence and innovation in research design and data practices.

However, the stratification of samples by ethnicity in and of itself is not enough to mitigate the risks of harmful health research and the critical importance of equal *analytical* power, described as "the power of definition, explanation and meaning" (Te Rōpū Rangahau Hauora a Eru Pōmare 2002) appears to have been lost or ignored in the way Mana Whakamārama has been taken up in some spaces. Equal analytical power argues that the transformation of health outcomes requires Māori to be involved not only as participants but also as data gatherers, data analyzers, data interpreters and data governors. Although some non-Māori have adopted the principles of equal explanatory power into their study designs, the creation of safe relations between the researchers and participants (Fink et al. 2011) and interpretation of Māori health data as a reflection of our historical and contemporary realities (Reid, Cormack & Paine 2019) not only requires Indigenous leadership but also a critical scholarship at every step of the research process. Equally important is to challenge the framing of this valid methodological approach to enhance Māori representation in health research as "over-sampling", when the reality is that Western epidemiology has allowed non-Māori to be "over-sampled" and thus over-represented in health research for years (Te Rōpū Rangahau Hauora a Eru Pōmare 2002).

A further example of a Kaupapa Māori response to the right to be represented and heard in research is age-standardization to an Indigenous population. Age-standardization is an epidemiological technique used to compare overall morbidity or mortality rates between groups differing in terms of their age-structures. The choice of standard population is important because in the process of standardizing health data we are emphasizing those events that are more common in the age-groups represented by the standard population. Thus, an older standard population will put more weight on events such as cardiovascular disease (CVD) or cancer-related deaths, whereas a younger standard population will have greater weight on childhood events.

The choice of standard population matters for Indigenous health. If we choose to use an older standard population, such as the World Health Organization (WHO) standard, then the age-standardized rates produced will more closely reflect non-Indigenous rates and therefore give more weight to the non-Indigenous population experience. The development of an Indigenous standard population, as described by Simmonds and colleagues (2008), was a critique of the assumptions and practices that underpin age-standardization and showed how analytical choices can affect the magnitude of mortality rates, rate ratios and rate differences, the relative ranking of causes of death and the relative width of confidence intervals.

Mana Whakamārama and age-standardization to an Indigenous standard are expressions of self-determination in health research, initially demonstrating how Māori leadership in epidemiology could result in large numbers of Māori respondents in national surveys but also extending to the development of critical epidemiological techniques. Although they were developed to improve and enhance the monitoring of Māori health status and health inequities by the Government, the State continues to demonstrate its dedication to re-creating itself rather than the sovereignty goals that underpin Kaupapa Māori epidemiology.

For example, recent Ministry of Health reports suggest they have removed equal explanatory power from the design of the NZ Health Survey despite recognizing the importance of these principles for meeting their Treaty obligations (Ministry of Health 2019). Similarly, significant changes to the methodology used for the 2018 Population Census resulted in the lowest Māori response rate in modern times (Kukutai & Cormack 2018). Despite the availability of proven quantitative research approaches and Indigenous data expertise, it is clear that securing our tangata whenua interests in and rights to good data will require a re-visioning of the role of the State in collecting and analyzing Māori health data, aligning with principles of Māori Data Sovereignty (Te Mana Raraunga 2018).

The right to name racism and colonialism

The attentiveness to history and context of Kaupapa Māori research supports the right of Māori to name the systems and structures of racism and colonialism that create and maintain White privilege in society, thereby shaping Māori health experiences and outcomes over generations (Keefe et al. 1999). Māori have continued to question the utility of statistics about Māori health that are not contextualized:

> Analysis and commentary complement statistics to give a fuller portrayal of Māori health. Statistics alone may show differences in health status, but are of limited use unless there is informed interpretation to highlight causes of differences and to point to remedial action. This volume also draws attention to Māori ill-health being to a great extent as a result of socio-economic and socio-cultural factors which have their roots in colonialism, and the struggle to adapt to rapid change arising from post-World War Two urbanisation. Until the grievances arising from failure to honour the Treaty of Waitangi are resolved, Māori ill-health will remain a problem.
> (Murchi E, in Pomare et al. 1995: 14)

Kaupapa Māori epidemiology requires researchers to move from description to explanation and theorization of the processes that are implicated in health outcomes, a call that has been made by other scholars for a more critical epidemiology (e.g., Jones 2001; Krieger 2019). It supports challenges to epidemiology's tendency to regard categories of "race"/ethnicity as risk factors in themselves, rather than as markers of the riskiness of living in colonial, racialized societies (Cormack et al. 2019; Jones 2001; Te Rōpū Rangahau Hauora a Eru Pōmare 2002). As Kaupapa Māori health researchers have stated:

> The lack of vigorous exploration of the basis of Māori and non-Māori differences in health data is distancing, othering, and a breach of rights. It indicates a lack of serious intention to properly address disparities and prevents others from taking up that challenge as fully equipped as possible. It is also wasteful.
> (Te Rōpū Rangahau Hauora a Eru Pōmare 2002: 17)

Re-visioning Māori health research: epidemiology, Māori Data Sovereignty and self-determination

Kaupapa Māori epidemiological methods have pushed health researchers to think more critically about some of the previously taken-for-granted practices and conventions in epidemiology, including the definition, collection and use of ethnicity data, approaches to recruitment and sampling, statistical techniques such as age-standardization and stratification, and perhaps more fundamentally, the nature of relationships between "researchers" and the "researched", the positionality of the researchers and the theoretical underpinnings of epidemiology as a "science". Indigenous scholars Andersen & Kukutai state that the:

> defining characteristic of historical quantitative research involving Indigenous individuals and communities is that quantitative researchers engaged in virtually no collaboration with Indigenous peoples with respect to the categories used to organize the information they proposed to collect, the specific questions asked, the communities from which the information was drawn and the eventual interpretations derived from these efforts.
>
> (2016: 45)

In contrast, Kaupapa Māori epidemiology also offers potential for a more critical, contextualized and compassionate methodology, and a reconfiguration of data relations and data practices within quantitative research. Applying Kaupapa Māori principles and values to epidemiology requires not only a questioning and re-imagining of dominant epidemiological tools and methods, but an opening of the methodology itself. Kaupapa Māori epidemiology can push back against the dis-membering of Indigenous Peoples from data "about" us, by an attentiveness to history and context, but also through an expectation that Kaupapa Māori epidemiology is done "by us, for us", with Māori at the center. In this way, Kaupapa Māori epidemiology is in alignment with principles and goals of Indigenous Data Sovereignty, and is more likely to lead to policies that turn away from reductive, deficit models to support broader goals of Indigenous self-determination

However, the reach of Kaupapa Māori epidemiology into the Westernized institutions that fund and produce the majority of quantitative health research in Aotearoa is limited. Much quantitative health research remains tightly and narrowly focused on description—that is, pointing out where ethnic inequities exist between populations—with relatively few studies (or researchers) prepared to reveal and confront the ways in which power and privilege are linked to their existence. It is this research that often shapes the types of policy responses and interventions that are prioritized or championed. Maggie Walter's important observations about 5D data that focuses on Indigenous difference, disparity, disadvantage, dysfunction and deprivation (Walter 2018) remind us that Kaupapa Māori epidemiological techniques, in their own right, are not decolonizing. Knowing how to design studies to incorporate equal explanatory power for Māori, for example, or to age-standardize rates to an Indigenous standard are not sufficient to achieve Māori rights to health equity or self-determination. Transformation will require a laying bare of epidemiological thinking through deeper understanding of the ways the discipline has contributed to the disempowerment of Indigenous Peoples.

It remains important to think about the ways in which Kaupapa Māori epidemiology challenges the discourse of the "deficit Indigene" (Walter & Andersen 2013). In recent years, there has been a re-focusing on strengths-based analysis when reporting on Māori health as though studies that seek to uncover stories of resilience and flourishing, even when led by non-Māori researchers, are necessarily safer, more ethical, and therefore preferred. Indigenous refusal to be part of what Tuck (2009) describes as "damage-centered" research is both valid and important when we remember the ways in which quantitative research methodologies have been used to document and display stories of "pain" and "damage" (Tuck 2009) without any intention of using these data to re-create a vision of health that is grounded in rangatiratanga. However, we contend that the full expression of our sovereignty will not be achieved through resilience frameworks, as by definition they are concerned with identifying the factors and behaviors that enable individuals and communities to survive in the face of ongoing coloniality and structural violence. When we limit our vision for Indigenous health to a resilience-based analysis we risk buying into the colonial binary of "good" and "bad" Māori and invisibilizing the way in which interlocking systems of oppression operate to structure the lives of Indigenous People over generations. Smith and Smith assert that "It is important to have a nuanced, theorized, and accurate understanding of what has gone wrong in order to develop more effective transforming responses" (2018: 4). The balance is to achieve this understanding without producing the types of discourses of "pain" and "damage" Tuck (2009) refers to, while allowing for a centering of Indigenous futures and aspirations outside of resilience models of thinking.

In considering how epidemiology can support Indigenous Data Sovereignty and Māori self-determination, we cannot ignore the ways in which statistics and epidemiology contribute to the suppression of Indigenous ways of being and knowing and marginalization of our communities, and often shape much of the policy that has everyday impacts for Indigenous Peoples' lives. The rhetoric of epidemiological studies as aligned with social justice and human rights can hide the coloniality that remains embedded within much epidemiological practice. An interest in ethnic health inequities can feed into the colonial obsession with marking those that are different and then using this to assert control over the lives of those deemed as "others". To decolonize epidemiology we will need to "de-link" (Mignolo 2007) this quantitative research approach from its origins in eugenics and White supremacy, and from its links to capitalism and other co-constitutive systems of oppression, and create alternatives that foreground Indigenous epistemologies.

Conclusions

Within the current context of local and global movements of Indigenous Data Sovereignty, as Indigenous researchers and communities are considering how we can exercise greater control over Indigenous data, disrupt harmful data practices and (re)establish good data relations, it is timely to consider the role of Kaupapa Māori epidemiology and its relationship to policy-making. In Aotearoa, Kaupapa Māori epidemiology developed in response to the silencing of Māori priorities and expectations within research and the policy process. Kaupapa Māori epidemiology was a reclamation of power and an affirmation of Māori rights to produce knowledge that we knew was required for the development of good health policy, and for the purpose of achieving rangatiratanga for Māori. We acknowledge the troubled nature of State policy development and implementation in colonial contexts (Kukutai & Cormack, this book). However, health policy that is informed by Kaupapa Māori methodologies has greater potential to be transformational for Māori communities than the status quo.

While Kaupapa Māori epidemiology can provide counter-discourses that are contextualized and connected to broader goals of transformation and can provide tools to explore particular research questions, we recognize there is also the potential for our engagement with epidemiology to reify its problematic assumptions and its dominance in health research. Yet, Kaupapa Māori epidemiology can also be understood as an act of resistance, that speaks back to harmful quantitative methodologies, and to the dismissal of multiple ways of knowing and coming to knowledge. Kaupapa Māori epidemiology remains committed to the importance of visioning our Indigenous humanity in health research and seeks to re-humanize data and data practices, by reminding us of our interconnectedness with data and that data are shadows of us and represent people and all our relations. The goal of Kaupapa Māori epidemiology, in line with Indigenous Data Sovereignty, is to realize self-determination that will allow us to move away from the often necessary work of reacting and responding to try to minimize data and research harms for Indigenous people, to re-collect our histories as scientists, knowledge creators and policy-makers and to use these memories to undertake epidemiology for ourselves and for the purpose of supporting healthy, (re)established knowledge systems and research practices focused on Indigenous well-being and futures.

Note

1 We would like to acknowledge the conversations and collective theorising and action that has happened with past and current colleagues and friends at Te Rōpū Rangahau Hauora a Eru Pōmare that has influenced our thinking and writing in this chapter. Tēnei te mihi nui ki a koutou katoa.

References

Andersen, C., & Kukutai, T. (2016). Reclaiming the statistical "native": quantitative historical research beyond the pale. In C. Andersen, & J. O'Brien (eds.), *Sources and Methods in Indigenous Studies* (pp. 55–62). New York, NY: Routledge.

Anderson, I., Robson, B., Connolly, M., Al-Yaman, F., Bjertness, E., King, A., et al. (2016). Indigenous and tribal peoples' health (the Lancet-Lowitja Institute global Collaboration): a population study. *Lancet*, 388(10040), 131e57.

Bhopal, R. (2016). *Concepts of Epidemiology: Integrating the Ideas, Theories, Principles, and Methods of Epidemiology*. Oxford: Oxford University Press.

Bishop, R. (1998). Freeing ourselves from neo-colonial domination in research: a Māori approach to creating knowledge. *International Journal of Qualitative Studies in Education*, 11(2), 199–219.

Blackstock, C. (2009). First nations children count: enveloping quantitative research in an indigenous envelope. *First Peoples Child & Family Review*, 4(2), 135–143.

Bonilla-Silva, E., & Zuberi, T. (2008). Towards a definition of white logic and white methods. In T. Zuberi, & E. Bonilla-Silva (eds.), *White Logic, White Methods: Racism and Methodology* (pp. 3–27). Lanham, MD: Rowman & Littlefield Publishers.

Bramley, D., Riddell, T., Whittaker, R., Corbett, T., Lin, R.-B., Wills, M., et al. (2005). Smoking cessation using mobile phone text messaging is as effective in Māori as non-Māori. *New Zealand Medical Journal*, 118, U1494.

Collins, P.H. (1991). Learning from the outsider within. In M. Fonow, & J.A. Cook (eds.), *Beyond Methodology: Feminist Scholarship as Jived Research*. Bloomington, IN: Indiana University Press.

Cormack, D., & Harris, R. (2009). *Issues in Monitoring Māori Health and Ethnic Disparities: An Update*. Wellington: Te Rōpū Rangahau Hauora a Eru Pōmare.

Cormack, D., Reid, P., & Kukutai, T. (2019). Indigenous data and health: critical approaches to "race"/ethnicity and Indigenous data governance. *Public Health*, 172, 116–118.

Cram, F. (1997). Developing partnerships in research: Pākehā researchers and Māori research. *SITES*, 35, 44–63.

Curtis, E., Wright, C., & Wall, M. (2005). The epidemiology of breast cancer in Māori women in Aotearoa New Zealand: implications for screening and treatment. *New Zealand Medical Journal*, 118(1209), U1297.

Fink, J.W., Paine, S.-J., Gander, P.H., Harris, R.B., Purdie, G. (2011). Changing response rates from Māori and non-Māori in sleep health postal surveys. *New Zealand Medical Journal*, 124(1328), 52–63.

Harris, R., Robson, B., Curtis, E., Purdie, G., Cormack, D., & Reid, P. (2007). Māori and non-Māori differences in caesarean section rates: a national review. *New Zealand Medical Journal*, 120(1250), U2444.

Huria, T., Palmer, S., Beckert, L., Williman, J., & Pitama, S. (2018). Inequity in dialysis related practices and outcomes in Aotearoa/New Zealand: a Kaupapa Māori analysis. *International Journal for Equity in Health*, 17(1), 27.

Jones, C. (2001). Invited commentary: "race," racism, and the practice of epidemiology. *American Journal of Epidemiology*, 154(4), 299–304.

Keefe, V., Ormsby, C., Robson, B., Reid, P., Cram, F., & Purdie, G. (1999). Kaupapa Māori meets retrospective cohort. *He Pukenga Korero*, 5(1), 12–17.

Krieger, N. (1994). Epidemiology and the web of causation: has anyone seen the spider? *Social Science & Medicine*, 39, 887–903.

Krieger, N., & Zierler, S. (1996). What explains the public's health?: a call for epidemiologic theory. *Epidemiology*, 7(1), 107–109.

Krieger, N. (2011). *Epidemiology and the People's Health: Theory and Context*. New York, NY: Oxford University Press.

Krieger, N. (2012). Who and what is a "population"? Historical debates, current controversies, and implications for understanding "population health" and rectifying health inequities. *The Milbank Quarterly*, 90(4), 634–681.

Krieger, N. (2019). Measures of racism, sexism, heterosexism, and gender binarism for health equity research: from structural injustice to embodied harm—an ecosocial analysis. *Annual Review of Public Health*, 41(1), 37–62.

Kukutai, T., & Taylor, I. (2016). Data sovereignty for indigenous peoples: current practice and future needs. In I. Taylor, & T. Kukutai (eds.), *Indigenous Data Sovereignty: Toward an Agenda* (pp. 1–22). Canberra: ANU Press.

Kukutai, T., & Cormack, D. (2018). Census 2018 and implications for Māori. *New Zealand Population Review*, 44, 131–151.

Mignolo, W.D. (2007). Delinking: the rhetoric of modernity, the logic of coloniality and the grammar of de-coloniality. *Cultural Studies*, 21(2–3), 449–514.

Mihaere, K.M., Harris, R., Gander, P.H., Reid, P.M., Purdie, G., Robson, B., & Neill, A. (2009). Obstructive sleep apnea in New Zealand adults: prevalence and risk factors among Māori and non-Māori. *Sleep*, 32(7), 949–956.

Ministry of Health. (2019). *Methodology Report 2018/19: New Zealand Heath Survey*. Wellington: Ministry of Health.

Murchie, E. (1984). *Rapuora: Health and Māori Women*. Wellington: Māori Women's Welfare League.

Paine, S.-J., Gander, P.H., Harris, R.B., & Reid, P. (2005). Prevalence and consequences of insomnia in New Zealand: disparities between Māori and non-Māori. *Australian and New Zealand Journal of Public Health*, 29, 22–28.

Paine, S.-J., Priston, M., Signal, T.L., Sweeney, B., & Muller, D. (2013). Developing new approaches for the recruitment and retention of indigenous participants in longitudinal research: lessons from E Moe, Māmā: maternal sleep and health in Aotearoa/New Zealand. *MAI Journal*, 2(2), 121–132.

Pihama, L. (2010). Kaupapa Māori theory: transforming theory in Aotearoa. *He Pukenga Kōrero*, 9(2), 5–14.

Pitama, S., Wells, J.E., Faatoese, A., Tikao-Mason, K., Robertson, P., Huria, T., et al. (2011). A Kaupapa Māori approach to a community cohort study of heart disease in New Zealand. *ANZJPH*, 35(3), 249–255.

Pomare, E., Keefe-Ormsby, V., Ormsby, C., Pearce, N., Reid, M.J., Robson, B., & Watene-Haydon, N. (1995). *Hauora: Māori Standards of Health III: A Study of the Years 1970–1991*. Wellington: Te Rōpū Rangahau Hauora a Eru Pōmare.

Prussing, E. (2018). Critical epidemiology in action: research for and by indigenous peoples. *SSM—Population Health*, 6, 98–106.

Reid, P., Robson, B., & Jones, C.P. (2000). Disparities in health: common myths and uncommon truths. *Pacific Health Dialog*, 7(1), 38–47.

Reid, P., & Robson, B. (2007). Understanding health inequities. In B. Robson, & R. Harris (eds.), *Hauora: Māori Standards of Health IV. A Study of the Years 2000–2005* (pp. 3–10). Wellington: Te Rōpū Rangahau Hauora a Eru Pōmare.

Reid, P., Cormack, D., & Paine, S.J. (2019). Colonial histories, racism and health—the experience of Māori and Indigenous peoples. *Public Health*, 172, 119–124.

Robson, B., & Reid, M.P. (2001). *Ethnicity Matters: Māori Perspectives Paper for the Review of the Measurement of Ethnicity in Official Statistics*. Wellington, NZ: Stats NZ.

Robson, B., & Harris, R. (eds.). (2007). *Hauora: Māori Standards of Health IV. A Study of the Years 2000–2005*. Wellington: Te Rōpū Rangahau Hauora a Eru Pōmare.

Sandoval, C.D.M., Lagunas, R.M., Montelongo, L.T., & Díaz, M.J. (2016). Ancestral knowledge systems: a conceptual framework for decolonizing research in social science. *AlterNative: An International Journal of Indigenous Peoples*, 12(1), 18–31.

Scott, N., Clark, H., Kool, B., Ameratunga, S., Christey, G., & Cormack, D. (2018). Audit of ethnicity data in the Waikato Hospital Patient Management System and Trauma Registry: pilot of the Hospital Ethnicity Data Audit Toolkit. *New Zealand Medical Journal*, 131(1483), 21–29.

Selak, V., Crengle, S., Elley, C.R., Wadham, A., Harwood, M., Rafter, N., et al. (2013). Recruiting equal numbers of indigenous and non-indigenous participants to a "polypill" randomized trial. *International Journal for Equity in Health*, 12(44). doi:10.1186/1475-9276-12-44.
Simmonds, S., Robson, B., Cram, F., & Purdie, G. (2008). Kaupapa Māori epidemiology. *Australasian Epidemiologist*, 15(1), 2–6.
Smith, G. (2012a). Kaupapa Māori: the dangers of domestication. *New Zealand Journal of Educational Studies*, 47(2), 10–20.
Smith, L.T. (1995). Re-centering Kaupapa Maori research. Paper presented at *Te Matawhanui Conference*, Massey University. Massey University, New Zealand: Department of Māori Studies.
Smith, L.T. (2012b). *Decolonizing Methodologies: Research and Indigenous Peoples* (2nd edition). New York, NY: Zed Books.
Smith, L.T., Maxwell, T.K., Puke, H., & Temara, P. (2016). Indigenous knowledge, methodology and mayhem: what is the role of methodology in producing indigenous insights? A discussion from Mātauranga Māori. *Knowledge Cultures*, 4(3), 131–156.
Smith, G.H., & Smith, L.T. (2018). Doing indigenous work: decolonizing and transforming the academy. In E. McKinley, & L. Smith (eds.), *Handbook of Indigenous Education*. Singapore: Springer.
Te Mana Raraunga. (2018). *Principles of Māori Data Sovereignty*. Retrieved from https://www.temanararaunga.Māori.nz/.
Te Rōpū Rangahau Hauora a Eru Pōmare. (1996). *Hui Whakapiripiri: A Hui to Discuss Strategic Directions for Māori Health Research*. Wellington: Te Rōpū Rangahau Hauora a Eru Pōmare.
Te Rōpū Rangahau Hauora a Eru Pōmare. (2000). *Ethnicity Matters: Review of the Measurement of Ethnicity in Official Statistics. Māori Perspectives Paper for Consultation*. Wellington: Te Rōpū Rangahau Hauora a Eru Pōmare.
Te Rōpū Rangahau Hauora a Eru Pōmare. (2002). *Mana Whakamārama—Equal Explanatory Power: Māori and Non-Māori Sample Size in National Health Surveys*. Wellington: Public Health Intelligence, Ministry of Health.
Tsosie, R. (2012). Indigenous peoples and epistemic injustice: science, ethics, and human rights. *Washington Law Review*, 87, 1133.
Tuck, E. (2009). Suspending damage: a letter to communities. *Harvard Educational Review*, 79, 409–428.
Walter, M., & Andersen, C. (2013). *Indigenous Statistics: A Quantitative Research Methodology*. Left Coast Press.
Walter, M. (2018). The voice of Indigenous data: beyond the markers of disadvantage. *Griffith Review*, 60, 256.
Walter, M., & Suina, M. (2019). Indigenous data, indigenous methodologies and indigenous data sovereignty. *International Journal of Social Research Methodology*, 22(3), 233–243.
Wemrell, M., Merlo, J., Mulinari, S., & Hornborg, A.C. (2016). Contemporary epidemiology: a review of critical discussions within the discipline and a call for further dialogue with social theory. *Sociology Compass*, 10(2), 153–171.
Whitt, L. (2009). *Science, Colonialism, and Indigenous Peoples: The Cultural Politics of Law and Knowledge*. Cambridge: Cambridge University Press.
Zuberi, T. (2000). Deracializing social statistics: problems in the quantification of race. *The Annals of the American Academy of Political and Social Science*, 568(1), 172–185

14 The legal and policy dimensions of Indigenous Data Sovereignty (IDS)

Rebecca Tsosie

Introduction

The Indigenous Data Sovereignty movement asserts that Indigenous Peoples and Native Nations ought to control the collection and use of data by and about them, for their own purposes and in alignment with their collective right to self-determination.[1] This prescriptive statement tracks the language of national and international discussions about "data sovereignty", although those discussions generally concern the interactions of nation-states with each other, with individual persons and with private corporations. The concept of Indigenous Data Sovereignty redirects the broader discussion to recognize the autonomy of Indigenous Peoples and their distinctive interests in governing their data.

Indigenous Peoples were absent from the conceptual framing of data sovereignty under national and international law, which is a form of "epistemic injustice" (Tsosie 2012). Epistemic injustice relates to the knowledge practices of a society and results when a group is excluded from being able to create or communicate meaning (Fricker 2007). If a group is excluded from the act of creating meaning, this is a "hermeneutical" injustice. If a group is excluded from being able to communicate meaning, this is a "testimonial" form of injustice. To the extent that groups are excluded from the epistemic practices of society, they risk suffering harms that will not be redressed. Through their advocacy, the proponents of Indigenous Data Sovereignty have moved Indigenous Peoples into the discussion of "data sovereignty". This is important for two reasons. First, in any contested area where "resources" are accorded value, the tendency of settler nations is to apply the same frameworks of "property" or "governance" that it applies in other areas. Indigenous rights have been marginalized for centuries by colonial doctrines, such as the doctrine of discovery, that were applied at the date of European contact and perpetuated in each subsequent era.[2] Those doctrines "diminished" the quality of Native sovereignty and property in relation to the analogous rights of European nations. The colonial "foundation" for understanding Native rights continues to be deployed as a justification for *further* diminishment of Native rights, in this case to intangible informational resources.

Secondly, the advocacy of Indigenous Data Sovereignty proponents has opened the space to determine whether the concepts and terms used by nation-states can operate effectively to meet the interests and concerns of Indigenous Peoples. If the *same* terms are used, but the *meaning* differs for Indigenous Peoples, as compared to nation-states, this could represent a form of injustice. If *different* terms are used, this could be a way to create new meaning and categories in the law, which could be quite useful, or it could be another way to diminish Indigenous rights. In either case, it is necessary for Indigenous advocates to be very intentional in their use of terminology (for example, with respect to "data" or "information", as well as "ownership", "governance" and "sovereignty"), and to pay careful attention to how the settler Nations and their institutions use this terminology.

This chapter examines the legal and policy dimensions of Indigenous Data Sovereignty, highlighting the principles and structures that inform "data governance" under US law and international law. The positive law is not fully formed in this area, but it relates to existing rights structures. Because the rights arguments differ, I will discuss the claims as they exist under US Federal Indian law, and then compare the treatment of the "rights of Indigenous peoples" under International human rights law. The policy context for both the international and domestic discussions of Indigenous Data Sovereignty includes the policies that pertain to Indigenous Peoples and those that govern information technologies. The intersection of these disparate policy domains is complex and currently unsettled.

Importantly, the discourse of data sovereignty within domestic and international law is informed by the laws and institutions of each nation-state, and the outcome for Indigenous Peoples will depend on how they are able to locate their claims—as a matter of law or policy—within the respective national and international frameworks. The promise for the future, however, is that the world of digital data is complex and rapidly evolving. The policy structures for controlling information are antiquated, and the existing laws are clumsy and difficult to apply. In short, no one country or institution has a handle on the contours of "rights" to digital data. Nor does anyone really understand the depth of harm—to particular groups or individuals—that can result from deficiencies of data governance.[3] Indigenous Peoples possess some of the most ancient and intact knowledge systems in the world. Many Indigenous Peoples also have a powerful and nuanced understanding of how to transmit knowledge in a way that is safe and sustainable. In a world of flux and uncertainty, concerted and specific policy advocacy by Indigenous People and Native Nations can serve as a model of leadership for data sovereignty, rather than a reactive effort to control harm that has already occurred.

This chapter first probes the meaning that is attached to the various terms that are used to construct the concept of data sovereignty. Next, the chapter engages the legal framework for data sovereignty at the domestic and international levels, and then examines the emerging legal framework for Indigenous Data Sovereignty. The chapter concludes by identifying three intersecting policy themes that are at play with the concept of Indigenous Data Sovereignty.

Overcoming epistemic Injustice: articulating the meaning of "Indigenous Data Sovereignty"

The law is a social institution that broadly invokes the power relations between the US government and Native Nations. To draw on Fricker's account, social power operates through these interactions and "identity-power" is crucial to understanding how epistemic practices promote either fair or unfair outcomes (Fricker 2007). The law represents a form of social power. It can be exerted in ways that foster equity and justice for Native Nations, but historically, it has operated in very unjust ways. Native Nations and the US government do not share the same sense of identity due to their historical, cultural and political differences. In the 19th century, the United States treated Native Peoples as "wards" and effectively denied them the constitutional rights available to US citizens. Although tribal members are now US citizens, they also share in the collective right of self-determination that secures the identity of their tribal governments as distinct "Peoples". Law and policy govern the lives of tribal governments and their members in a unique manner. It is important to identify when epistemic forms of injustice curtail the power of Native Nations to exert their right to self-determination.

Indigenous Data Sovereignty has a strong link to tribal self-determination and "affirms the rights of Indigenous Peoples to control the collection, access, analysis, interpretation, management, dissemination, and reuse of Indigenous data" (Kukutai and Taylor 2016; Snipp 2016). Kukutai and Taylor use the term "Indigenous Data Sovereignty" inclusively, to describe "a wide ranging set of issues, from legal and ethical dimensions around data storage, ownership, access and consent, to intellectual property rights and practical considerations about how data are used in the context of research, policy, and practice" (Kukutai and Taylor 2016). Walter and Carroll describe "Indigenous Data Sovereignty" as "a global advocacy movement for Indigenous peoples" and identify "Indigenous data governance" as the "activating mechanism" for Indigenous Data Sovereignty (Ch. 1, this book). The term "Indigenous Data Sovereignty" is clearly being invoked in many ways, and the discussion would benefit from some initial points of clarification.

First, is the term "data sovereignty" the same as "data governance"? Some scholars believe that the terms are largely interchangeable, and this is an outgrowth of the international law notion that nation-states have the sovereignty to regulate data within their territories and that they do so under their domestic laws (Woods 2018). As Walter and Carroll observe, however, it might be productive to draw a distinction for purposes of Indigenous Data Sovereignty. Native Nations, like nation-states, ought to have the sovereign right to "govern the collection, ownership and application of data" concerning the tribe or its members, and to control data housed on tribal territory (https://usindigenousdata.org/). This is a consistent usage of the term "data sovereignty" in relation to nation-states and Native Nations. This usage of "Indigenous Data Sovereignty", however, depends upon some notion of Indigenous sovereignty, territory and jurisdiction. That linkage exists in the United States with federally recognized tribal governments, but not with non-recognized Indigenous Peoples.

Some would argue that the right to self-determination identified by the UN Declaration on the Rights of Indigenous Peoples can be equated with "sovereignty". The existing scholarship on self-determination, however, indicates that there are several models of political engagement that can be used to effectuate the right to self-determination. Recognition of group "sovereignty" is one of those models. Others include co-ownership, corporate ownership, co-management, joint management and participatory access (Tsosie 2011). None of those models of self-determination requires acknowledgment of sovereignty or territory.

Data governance concerns not only the collection of data, but the Native Nation's right to control the use or reuse of "tribal data" by third parties, even if the data was gathered in the context of earlier research studies (Tsosie 2019). In this case, Indigenous governance must depend upon the creation of a new term, such as "tribal data", that demarcates categories of information that are *owned* by the Tribal government or Indigenous People. The information may not be under the jurisdiction of a tribal government, yet the tribal government's ownership interest would require a third party to comply with tribal requirements that could include or exclude persons from being able to access, use or transmit the data to others. Obviously, the term would require definition, but it is consistent with the claim of collective ownership that Indigenous Peoples are making under international human rights law, and in this sense, it does not depend upon an acknowledgment of sovereignty, territory or jurisdiction.

The next issue involves the definition of the term "data". The proponents of Indigenous Data Sovereignty define the term broadly to include "information or knowledge, in any format or medium, which is about and may affect Indigenous Peoples both collectively and individually".[4] The norms of Indigenous Data Sovereignty prescribe Indigenous ownership and control of their data, and specify that Indigenous Peoples should have the right to "opt into data structures" that support their aspirations, priorities and values, and decline to participate in data processes that do not. This broad definition of "data" in relation to "data structures" and "data processes" is what distinguishes the claims of Indigenous Data Sovereignty from those of any other nation or group. The proponents of Indigenous Data Sovereignty are particularly concerned with the need for corrective justice after several centuries of "Indigenous policies" that ensued from the colonial governments and their successors in interest and were designed to marginalize and diminish the rights of Indigenous Peoples. Today, the policy dynamic often replicates the mistakes and failures of the past, which seems at first glance to be completely counterintuitive to the notion of "progress".

As Walter observes, however, the consistent theme is that data are not neutral: "Statistics are human artefacts and in colonizing nation states such numbers applied to Indigenous Peoples have a raced reality" (Ch.1, this book). The data gathered by the nation-state identifies the "Indigenous problem" in terms of the disparity or disadvantage suffered by the Indigenous Peoples, and then it generates a narrative about what is needed to "rehabilitate" them, and then it issues another policy. The policy generally serves the broader interests of the nation-state. Indigenous policies are expected to fail, so no one is remotely troubled when they do. It is a constant cycle. Indigenous Data Sovereignty advocates are making a statement about what has gone wrong with national data practices regarding Indigenous Peoples and they are also making a proactive statement about how data can be gathered and used by Indigenous Peoples themselves to promote the goal of "nation-building". This is the positive construction of Indigenous Data Sovereignty that resonates with the state-specific cultural, political and social values that drive the international dialog about "data sovereignty". The current situation involves "data dependence" upon the national government, which is not meeting the needs of Indigenous communities and may in fact be harmful because it replicates the racism and inequity of the national data practices.

In summary, level one of the policy discussion about Indigenous Data Sovereignty is premised on the need to overcome "data inequity, racism, and marginalization" (Tsosie 2019). Current data practices often promote epistemic injustice because they reinscribe the features of the historic practices. Level two concerns "Indigenous Data Sovereignty as nation-building", which requires the capacity to produce relevant data, as well as the ability to design, interpret, validate, own and use data sets. This is a proactive way to reshape data practices to promote social justice for Indigenous Peoples. Indigenous Data Sovereignty proponents assert that Indigenous Peoples should develop their own data resources, using Indigenous research methodologies. In the meantime, the national governments should improve their data practices and involve Indigenous Peoples in the systems and structures to ensure that the data statistics are of maximum utility to Indigenous Peoples. Building Indigenous data capacity will require governing protocols and the ability to negotiate Indigenous Data Sovereignty with the entities that control national or provincial/state data sets. To the extent that data sets are combined, there could be issues around data storage or access, potentially requiring negotiated intergovernmental agreements.

A current example is occurring in the United States with respect to the policy crisis about "missing and murdered" Native women. The statistics indicate that in the United States, Canada and Mexico, Indigenous women go "missing" or are found "murdered" in much higher percentages than women of other ethnicities. In the United States, Indigenous women are a relatively small percentage of the national population, and yet they are disproportionately represented in the "victims of violent crime" statistics. The "problem" turns out to be quite complicated because the federal and tribal governments have criminal jurisdiction over the reservations, and state governments have jurisdiction outside the reservation. Each jurisdictional authority keeps its own data. State murder investigations are likely to mistakenly identify Native women (on the basis of phenotype) as "Caucasian" if they are light skinned or as "Hispanic" if they have darker skin. The federal government and state governments do not routinely share information with each other, and tribal police may not share information with either the federal or state governments. After several recent cases involving missing and/or murdered Native women hit the national news media, the issue gained the attention of federal and state policymakers, leading to interjurisdictional task forces and data-sharing protocols. The US Department of Justice created opportunities for tribal governments to opt into data sharing protocols that they perceive as helpful, but tribal governments can also make a sovereign decision not to participate (Chaney 2018a, 2018b). There are many national crime databases that can assist tribal governments, but tribal participation is optional (Chaney 2018a, 2018b; Tsosie 2019). The federal policy structure is based on the federal government's trust responsibility to tribal governments, as well as its obligation to support tribal self-governance (Chaney 2018b). The net result is an increase in tribal data capacity and a stated respect for tribal data sovereignty.

In order to achieve these goals, tribal governments must be aware of the legal framework for data sovereignty at both the international and domestic levels. The next section of this chapter discusses that framework.

The legal framework for data sovereignty at the international and domestic levels

At the international level, data sovereignty is tied to the territorial sovereignty that each nation-state exerts within its borders. Every nation-state has the authority to manage information in a way that fits with its own laws, practices and customs (Snipp 2016). Nation-states exercise data sovereignty in various ways, including censoring offensive content, monitoring online activity, issuing take-down orders for material that violates copyright laws and barring access by other sovereigns (Woods 2018). Increasingly, data sovereignty is tied to surveillance goals and to controlling the conduct of private corporations that do business within the nation. For example, China requires companies to abide by its laws as a condition of doing business in its markets. If a company fails to do so, China can bar the company from doing business within its borders.

At the international level, there are considerable differences among the policies of the respective countries. The laws governing data within one jurisdiction are likely to conflict with the laws that apply in other jurisdictions. In this case, courts must respect each set of laws and draw on other principles to resolve disputes, perhaps by balancing interests or applying the doctrine of comity. The doctrine of comity calls for a domestic court to give effect to foreign laws and judgments so long as they do not violate domestic principles of public policy (Woods 2018). In general, the nation-states tend to embed their social, cultural and political values into their laws governing data. For example, the United States favors data policy norms promoting free speech, privacy and entrepreneurship (Woods 2018). Other countries have strong policies precluding hate speech or speech that violates norms of public decency. The United States sees these foreign policies as imposing undue restrictions on "freedom of speech", but they are important to the social, cultural and political values of the respective nations.

In summary, under international law, every nation-state has the right to define data sovereignty under its domestic law, and to apply that law within its territory and potentially to international disputes that arise out of transactions with the nation-state or its citizens. The nation-state also has the authority to identify categories of data that are tied to national interests, such as census data, and can set the terms for *gathering, using and accessing* this data. In the United States, the government's authority is limited where there are contrary principles that are protective of individual rights. For example, individuals have privacy interests protected by the US Constitution and Bill of Rights, as well as applicable federal and state statutes. Personal identities must be protected from public disclosure, even if the data has been collected for public use (as census data and associated demographic information often are). Moreover, some forms of data, such as health-related data, are subject to specific legal restrictions, designed to protect individuals from coercive exercises of state authority that would jeopardize privacy rights (such as being forced to give blood or tissue samples, or to participate in a medical study).

It is much more difficult to determine whether and when the nation-state is *using* data in ways that advantage or disadvantage a specific group. Contemporary national governments among the "CANZUS countries" designate Indigenous Peoples as citizens of the nation-state, though the Indigenous Nations also maintain their collective political identity. This may lead to the assumption that Indigenous Peoples have equal status and the same rights as other citizens, but that would be a mistake. As Walter and Carroll document, "data produced by nation states and their administrative entities as the evidence base for Indigenous related policy are narrowly focused around Indigenous disadvantage and disparity" (Walter & Carroll, Ch. 1). The nation-state deploys a statistical narrative of "Indigenous deficit" that both emphasizes the differences between the dominant society and Indigenous Peoples, but also purports to be built on a premise of "equal citizenship". Because Indigenous Peoples are lagging behind, the narrative goes, the nation-state must adopt "special policies" to "rehabilitate" them. Consequently, each country identifies an agenda for its "Indigenous policy" according to the perceived needs of the Indigenous Peoples. The applicable domestic policy, whether it is focused on health, education or economic or social development, is often justified by the "data" the nation-state has collected and then shaped by policymakers to serve the favored ends of the nation-state.

In the United States, for example, Congress enacted the *Indian Gaming Regulatory Act in 1988* (IGRA) purportedly to promote the worthy goals of "tribal economic development, self-sufficiency, and strong tribal governments".[5] As of 1988, there were ample data showing the rampant poverty on Indian reservations, as well as the lack of adequate infrastructure to draw other forms of economic development to many reservations. Of course, Tribal governments already had the sovereign authority to engage in gaming, free from state regulation, as a form of economic development on the reservation.[6] However, this legal right was perceived as a threat to the billion-dollar gaming enterprises in states such as New Jersey and Nevada. A secondary purpose of IGRA then emerged: the need to "protect" Indian gaming enterprises from "organized crime and other corrupting influences". The net result of this policy was to develop a federal/tribal regulatory structure for tribal gaming operations, but also to require tribal governments to enter compacts with the relevant state government to ensure that the *state's interests* were protected. Often this entailed some form of revenue sharing, transferring wealth from the tribal gaming operation to the state. So, while Indian gaming operations have succeeded in bringing considerable economic development to many Indian reservations, the states have also been beneficiaries of the federal legislation. There is now a backlash against federal spending for tribal programs on the theory that American Indian nations have now become "wealthy" from their gaming enterprises and no longer need their federal "welfare" programs. Of course, under US Federal Indian law and policy, the programs and services available to American Indian and Alaska Native Nations are based on the government's history of treaty-making with Native Nations and the federal government's "trust responsibility", and they are not public welfare programs.

In recognition that the US model of Indigenous rights is not applicable in other countries, the next section of this chapter constructs Indigenous Data Sovereignty in two ways. First, I describe a composite of tribal rights under US domestic law, in furtherance of the existing legal framework that governs federally recognized American Indian and Alaska Native governments. Second, I discuss the rights as they might exist for all Indigenous Peoples, in furtherance of the human rights norms embedded within the United Nations Declaration on the Rights of Indigenous Peoples. The ordering is intentional. Due to the international construction of data sovereignty, the laws of each respective country will govern many of the issues, and it will be important to assess the political and legal rights of Indigenous Peoples under national law. However, as a human rights construct, Indigenous Data Sovereignty can build upon a "universal" notion of rights that ought to be recognized as a matter of justice for Indigenous Peoples wherever they are located.

The legal framework for Indigenous Data Sovereignty

The international model of data sovereignty provides a good foundation for understanding how Indigenous Data Sovereignty might work within the United States. In the United States, federally recognized tribal governments are sovereign nations with the right to exercise legal authority over their reservation and other "trust" lands. This territorial sovereignty provides the basis for a conception of data sovereignty that would require respect for tribal laws on this topic. Moreover, many Native Nations in the United States have a treaty relationship with the US government that provides enduring guarantees for the protection of tribal self-governance within tribal territory. Even today, reservation lands are not considered to be part of the "state", although each reservation is surrounded by state land. Rather, tribal reservations are jurisdictionally distinct, and governed primarily by tribal and federal law.

The Internet and digital data are intangible resources and therefore difficult to govern using standard jurisdictional principles. It is worth noting, however, that Indigenous Peoples' claims to data sovereignty share some similarity with the values and norms of countries that seek to protect their cultures from intrusion and appropriation by outside entities. Many countries in Africa, Asia and Latin America share a similar experience of cultural appropriation by European nations during the colonial era. At that time, these countries served as colonies for the European nations. Today, they have distinct national identities and some also have Indigenous Peoples or minority groups within their boundaries that have unique cultures.

UNESCO is the primary body within the United Nations that formulates principles and instruments to regulate cultural rights as a special category of international human rights law (Graber et al. 2012; Coombe and Turcotte 2012: 279). There are several international instruments concerning tangible and intangible cultural heritage. As Rosemary Coombe and Joseph Turcotte observe, minorities and Indigenous Peoples throughout the world have been the ones "whose cultural rights have historically been violated, often through state sanctioned initiatives" designed to assimilate them and "relegate their culture to a form of historical information" (Graber et al. 2012; Coombe and Turcotte 2012: 279) Today, the data collected about Indigenous cultures is often housed in archives or libraries maintained by the colonial nations or their successors.

UNESCO treats intangible cultural heritage as a cultural right, but there are not robust protections for "traditional cultural expressions" because they lack the qualities necessary to sustain a private property right under intellectual property law. The World Intellectual Property Organization (WIPO) treats aspects of intangible cultural heritage as an "economic right" to the extent that the data becomes the subject of intellectual property law (Graber et al. 2012; Coombe and Turcotte 2012: 279). For example, data regarding traditional knowledge about medicinal qualities of plants can be entered into a database or written archive. Thereafter, if a pharmaceutical company uses the information to manufacture a drug, the company gets the patent on the product, but the group that possessed the traditional knowledge does not share in the benefit unless the company made a specific agreement to do so.

Tribal governments in the United States have continuing concerns about placing sensitive information into databases that are accessible to the public. Their understanding of whether images and information are appropriate to share or relate to their distinctive histories, legal systems and customary norms. Tribal legal systems often embody very different understandings of "ownership" and how tangible and intangible aspects of cultural heritage should be treated. In sum, tribal governments within the United States have the sovereign authority to enact laws to protect their data and interests, and the United States has a legal and political obligation to protect tribal self-governance under its trust responsibility. Because the legal claims of federally recognized tribal governments in the United States differ from those of non-recognized groups, I will first describe the nature of tribal sovereignty within the US federal system and then explore the nature of Indigenous rights to self-determination under international human rights law.[7]

The nature of tribal sovereignty under US law

Under US Federal Indian law, federally recognized American Indian and Alaska Native Nations are designated as "domestic dependent nations" (Pevar 2012).

Native Nations that are in a trust relationship with the United States are treated as sovereign governments that have the right to make their own laws and be ruled by them within their own territory, which generally includes Indian reservations and other "trust" lands.[8] Tribal sovereignty is "inherent" and preexists the formation of the United States. For that reason, tribal sovereignty is both "pre-Constitutional" and "extra-Constitutional". Tribal governments entered treaties with Great Britain and then with the United States as separate sovereigns. They are not parties to the US Constitution, and their powers are not limited by the US Constitution's Bill of Rights. However, the federal government has the exclusive authority, under the US Constitution's Commerce Clause to regulate interactions with Indian Nations. This political authority is described as "plenary power", similar to the US foreign affairs power and immigration authority. The federal authority over Indian affairs is not shared with the state governments, although the federal government may, and sometimes has, delegated aspects of its authority to the state governments.[9] As a general matter, if the federal government has not acted in this area, the state lacks jurisdiction over tribal governments, Indian reservations and other tribal trust lands. The state does have jurisdiction over tribal members in their capacity as citizens of the state. So, for example, to the extent that a tribal member applies for a state driver's license, or resident tuition at a state university, state law will govern the transaction.

The primary governments with jurisdiction to regulate tribal lands, resources and the activities of persons on tribal lands are the tribal governments. Most contemporary tribal governments have executive, legislative and judicial branches that exercise broad authority over the reservation. Because the authority of tribal governments is similar to that of foreign governments, state courts will often invoke the principle of comity to determine whether to recognize tribal laws or judgments, for example, an order of protection. State courts do not have a Constitutional obligation under the Full Faith and Credit clause to recognize tribal court judgments because tribal governments predate the Constitution and are not parties to the Constitution. The reverse is also true. Tribal courts do not have a Constitutional obligation to recognize state court judgments. Both Tribal and State courts may recognize the judgment, using the doctrine of comity, but they are not obliged to do so.

Tribal governments also can enter into intergovernmental agreements with the state government or federal agencies in order to manage their mutual interests, for example, with respect to environmental quality or public safety. Intergovernmental agreements draw on the sovereign authority of the tribe, the state and the federal government, and they are validated under the laws of each respective sovereign. So, for example, a gaming compact between a Tribal government and a State government must be signed by a qualified official (e.g., the state Governor or tribal President) and ratified in accordance with the relevant law of each jurisdiction, as well as comply with the federal law that pertains to Tribal/State gaming compacts. In that respect, intergovernmental agreements bind the respective governments and are unlike private contracts, which are regulated by the common law of contracts with respect to validity and remedies for breach. A Tribal government can sign a contract with a business or third-party vendor to purchase goods or to secure services. Those agreements will be governed by tribal law, or alternatively, by another source of law, such as state law, if this is clearly specified in the contract as being applicable to the transaction.

These principles support the idea that tribal governments have the authority to exercise sovereignty over data stored within their territory, as well as data about their members, lands or resources. To the extent that "tribal data" becomes a "shared resource" because the interests of the federal or state governments are also implicated, then tribal governments could request a negotiated co-management agreement for the database, which offers any relevant limitations on access or use of tribal data. If a tribal government chooses to create its own archive or data base, the Tribe can contract with a third-party vendor to manage the database and condition access accordingly. In these respects, the tribal government can control access to data that is currently within its control. That will be more difficult if the data is already housed outside the reservation and is part of a historic archive or database repository.

There are several challenges that tribal governments in the United States are likely to encounter with respect to Indigenous Data Sovereignty. First, the federal government's plenary power contains the power to limit or remove tribal sovereignty. This happened with the passage of the *Indian Gaming Regulatory Act*, when Congress conditioned certain forms of tribal gaming by requiring the consent of state governments through a legal "compact". So, to the extent that Congress perceives a larger interest that is in tension with an inherent power of tribal governments to regulate tribal data, it can act to condition or remove that power. Secondly, tribal sovereignty, like the sovereignty of foreign nations, generally does not extend beyond its territorial boundaries. So, to the extent that tribal data is in the possession of third parties, off the reservation, the Tribe does not necessarily have a right to govern that party's use of the data, absent some additional legal authority, such as a binding contractual agreement between the Tribe and the third party.

Another challenge is that third parties may affirmatively request tribal data from a federal agency through the provisions of the *Federal Freedom of Information Act* (FOIA). Third parties can access information even if it was gathered in the course of required federal-tribal relations, for example, consultations between the agency and the tribe. There is no categorical exclusion under federal law for information that the federal government obtains through the federal-tribal trust relationship.[10] The federal agency will have a legal duty to release the information unless it is explicitly protected by one of the FOIA exemptions (for example, as a trade secret or protected commercial or financial information) or a withholding provision in another federal statute (Tsosie 2019). For example, tribal governments lobbied for statutory amendments to protect the sensitive information that is shared with federal land managers when they engage in the required tribal consultation process under the *National Historic Preservation Act* for federal undertakings on public lands that house Native American sacred sites and burials.[11]

Finally, the principles of Federal Indian law are only applicable to federally recognized Native Nations. If a tribe lacks federal recognition or if its trust relationship has been "terminated" by federal law and not restored, then the tribe will not enjoy the rights and privileges that are secured to federally recognized tribal governments. Some states have extended political recognition to tribal groups within state boundaries, but this act does not confer federal protection for the sovereign rights of the Indigenous Nation. Therefore, it is necessary to look beyond the rights of federally recognized tribal governments to assess the rights of Indigenous Peoples, more broadly.

Indigenous Peoples and the UN Declaration on the Rights of Indigenous Peoples: The Human Rights Framework

The concept of human rights gained traction within the international community after the Second World War, and in the aftermath of the genocidal conduct of Nazi Germany. Human rights are "universal" in the sense that they extend to every living person, and they do not depend upon governmental recognition through positive law (Nickel 2007). Human rights norms describe the "minimum standards" that governments ought to adhere to in order to protect the dignity of human beings. They do not describe an "ideal world". While, some scholars argue that human rights ought to equally protect all persons, foreclosing the need for specific provisions on the rights of groups, such as women, children, ethnic or religious minorities or Indigenous Peoples, the practice has been to recognize that certain groups have particularly complex histories or vulnerabilities that require specific human rights instruments. It is in this regard that the human rights of Indigenous Peoples have secured recognition (Anaya 2004).

Within the United Nations system, human rights instruments often start with a "Declaration" which is a charter of principle, promulgated for nation-states to consider and adopt. The Universal Declaration of Human Rights, for example, was adopted in 1948 as the general consensus of nation-states on the need for a "Universal bill of rights". The terms of the Declaration are prescriptive, but are then enfolded into treaties or "Covenants", which are the mechanism for binding action by the signatory nation-states. Following the Universal Declaration of Human Rights by the UN General Assembly, for example, the United Nations promulgated the 1966 International Covenant on Civil and Political Rights, and the International Covenant on Economic, Social and Cultural Rights. Both treaties were put out for signature, although some nations, such as the United States, disclaimed the need for "economic, social and cultural rights".

Nation-states have the sovereign authority to sign onto a treaty or refuse to do so. They may also sign human rights treaties with specific reservations, for example, because a particular treaty provision would conflict with domestic law or policy. International treaties may or may not be "self-executing". This depends upon the domestic law of each nation. In the United States, international treaties require ratification in accordance with Constitutional requirements, and then Congress must pass domestic legislation to effectuate the terms of the treaty. Only then will the terms be binding, as a matter of domestic law. The United States typically does not submit itself to the Optional Protocols to international treaties that would allow for international tribunals to adjudicate its conduct in specific cases. Rather, international mechanisms for "enforcement" are much more subtle, such as a report by a Commission or Special Rapporteur, or a set of "recommendations" to consider.

The rights of Indigenous Peoples are not specifically mentioned by the 1948 Declaration, nor by the Covenant on Civil and Political Rights, nor the Covenant on Economic, Social and Cultural Rights. For the most part, Indigenous human rights were identified as a specific concern of the International Labor Organization (ILO), which as early as the 1950s, recognized that Indigenous Peoples were often exploited, marginalized and discriminated against by nation-states and private actors engaged in development (Anaya 2004; Tsosie 2011). The ILO developed two instruments for nation-states to consider. ILO 107, issued in 1957, was directed toward achieving recognition for the basic human rights of Indigenous Peoples on an equal basis to other state citizens. The goal of this document was the "full integration" of Indigenous People as citizens within the national community. It was not until 1989 that the ILO recognized the "collective rights" of Indigenous Peoples in ILO 169, as well as their right to engage in consultation before development could take place on their traditional lands. The document specified that Indigenous "self-determination" was not the same as the right that exists under the International Covenant on Civil and Political Rights for all "peoples". Indigenous Peoples were not "peoples" in that special sense, but they did merit unique forms of protection and consideration. Many governments in Latin America signed onto ILO 169. The United States did not.

It was not until 2007 that the United Nations General Assembly adopted, by majority consensus, the Declaration on the Rights of Indigenous Peoples. That document specifies that Indigenous Peoples are "peoples" with the same right to self-determination as all other Peoples. They have the right to "freely determine their political status and freely pursue their economic, social and cultural development" (UNDRIP, Art. 3). They do not have access to the extraordinary remedy of "secession" that other "peoples" have because this would dismantle the "territorial integrity or political unity" of the nation-states, contravening Art. 46 of the Declaration. Thus, to the extent that a nation-state deprives Indigenous Peoples of their human rights under the UN Declaration in a way that causes "extreme injustice", the group will likely be restricted to domestic remedies, if there are any, and to international "grievance" petitions intended to raise awareness and promote a UN "recommendation" to the offending nation-state. In the United States, an example of this occurred in 2016 with the Dakota Access Pipeline Project that jeopardized the sole water source for the Standing Rock Sioux Tribe, violating the Tribe's treaty rights, federal statutory rights and human rights. The domestic causes of action were ultimately unsuccessful in stopping the construction of the pipeline, but the Standing Rock Sioux Tribe gained national and international support on the human rights violation, and this ultimately inspired a strong statement from the UN Special Rapporteur on the Rights of Indigenous Peoples, as well as other UN officials, who criticized the United States for its failure to consult with the Tribe or mitigate the cultural, environmental and social justice harms.

There are various provisions of the UN Declaration that are oriented toward the protection of Indigenous cultures, their spiritual rights and their ability to transmit their cultures to future generations. The most relevant provision with respect to the issue of data sovereignty is Article 31, which provides that: "Indigenous peoples have the right to maintain, control, protect and develop their cultural heritage, traditional knowledge and traditional cultural expressions, as well as the manifestations of their sciences, technologies and cultures, including human and genetic resources, seeds, medicine, knowledge". This substantive right is accompanied by the right to "maintain, control, protect and develop their intellectual property over such cultural heritage", a concept that would appear to encompass various claims related to "Indigenous Data Sovereignty". In fact, Victoria Tauli-Corpuz, the United Nations' Special Rapporteur on the Rights of Indigenous Peoples has stated that Article 31 ought to be linked to the concept of "data sovereignty" and discussions about "tribal data" (Kukatai and Taylor 2016). Although there is not an explicit reference, this can be inferred from the text defining Indigenous Peoples' right to their knowledge and technologies, as well as their need to transfer their knowledge and cultural heritage to future generations (Tsosie 2019).

The Declaration on the Rights of Indigenous Peoples is prescriptive and there is not yet a treaty that has distilled the provisions into a form that nation-states could sign onto for binding effect. The various norms are important, however, because they illustrate international consensus on the fact that Indigenous Peoples are "peoples" with an "equal right" to self-determination, as well as demonstrating the different cultural rights that are necessary to accord "equal respect" to Indigenous Peoples.

Summary of rights frameworks

The rights framework for Indigenous Data Sovereignty will be informed by international law and domestic law. Each nation-state will have laws defining the status of Indigenous Peoples and their rights under domestic law. The nation-state will also have laws regarding data governance. Both sets of laws will require deference under international law. However, the UN Declaration on the Rights of Indigenous Peoples serves as a normative counterweight to domestic law. Within this text are the human rights provisions that are most directly tailored to the historical circumstances and contemporary identities of Indigenous Peoples. The right to self-determination is a moral right and a political right. It is a powerful statement to nation-states that the distinctive identities of Indigenous Peoples carry currency in today's world, and their collective rights must be respected under domestic law. The right of self-determination supports the growth and development of Indigenous laws and institutions. Indigenous Peoples' understanding of "data sovereignty" merits attention, respect and consideration. This is the essence of the political and legal engagement with nation-states that must occur for Indigenous Data Sovereignty to be realized.

The policy contours of Indigenous Data Sovereignty

This chapter has discussed the legal frameworks for data sovereignty and for Indigenous rights, within the international and United States context. Other chapters in this book provide detailed comparative case studies from other countries. I will conclude the chapter by summarizing the broader policy discourse that is being used to evaluate the claims made by proponents of Indigenous Data Sovereignty. Legal scholars tend to focus on the specifics of a particular issue, say who has rights to "own" or access a database. The issues raised by Indigenous Data Sovereignty, however, are much more powerfully related to broader justice themes. That is, who decides what the "rules" are and how are those decisions made? I will explore three potential policy pathways for that broader discussion: decolonization, human rights and development policy. These themes are highlighted in recent scholarly work on Indigenous Data Sovereignty and should be given careful consideration.

International policy, epistemic injustice and the legacy of colonialism

As the chapters within this book demonstrate, the harms of colonialism continue to be present in the lives of Indigenous Peoples. The UN human rights framework represents a policy response to some of these harms. The UN Declaration on the Rights of Indigenous Peoples calls upon nation-states to remediate past harms, for example, by repatriating cultural items and ancestral remains, and also to create new and equitable structures for current and future relationships between the nation-state and Indigenous Peoples. According to the Declaration's Preamble, nation-states should support Indigenous Peoples in "maintaining and strengthening their institutions, cultures and traditions", and also "promote their development in accordance with their aspirations and needs".

Some things remain consistent, such as the paramount position of nation-states. International law is, and always has been, the "law of nations". The nation-states have the power to enter treaties with one another and prescribe the domestic laws that are applicable within their jurisdiction. Indigenous Peoples are not able to make international treaties with nation-states. Rather, they must depend upon their domestic encompassing nation-state to work cooperatively to further their human right to "self-determination". This human rights framework is the most powerful current positioning for Indigenous rights within the international sphere. At this juncture, however, Indigenous Peoples' human rights are prescriptive because there is not yet a binding international treaty reflecting the principles enshrined in the Declaration on the Rights of Indigenous Peoples.

Epistemic injustice is a continuing reality for Indigenous Peoples because they do not share the ability of the nation-states to define the relevant terminology that controls rights to sovereignty, property and cultural heritage. Current policy calls for the interests of Indigenous Peoples to be "accommodated" by domestic governments and international organizations, but this is often done as a matter of equity and not as a matter of right. Therefore, although current policy is arguably more than just colonial policy, the hierarchies and inequities of colonialism persist due to the dominant structures and practices, which have always excluded Indigenous Peoples as equal partners in shaping national or international policy.

The human rights structure and impact of international development policy

The United Nations has several adjunct arms, such as the World Bank, UNESCO and the World Intellectual Property Organization. Each of these entities has its own mandate. The United Nations General Assembly is composed of nation-states who define the conditions for world governance through Conventions. UNESCO focuses on protecting cultural rights, again through Conventions and instruments developed by the nation-states, in consultation with other groups and organizations. WIPO strives to create coherent international frameworks for intellectual property rights in order to maximize the "creative commons" (the "public domain"), recognize and protect the property rights of individual artists and creators to benefit from their endeavors, and protect the economic interests of nation-states that possess systems of intellectual property law, including copyright, patent and trademark. Although all of these entities should care about "human rights", the United Nations structure bifurcates cultural rights from economic rights. WIPO is not structured to consider the harms to Indigenous cultures that arise when third parties commodify aspects of Indigenous cultural heritage. If the third party creates a song based on Indigenous cultural expression, for example, it may earn a "copyright" in the "new" creation. This type of exploitation is commonplace, and it is the driver for WIPO's current effort to draft treaties that outline the "equitable" interests of "Indigenous and local communities" to their traditional knowledge, traditional expressions and genetic resources.[12] These treaties will be "legally binding" if they are finalized and issued for signature, and they will impact the political, cultural and economic rights of Indigenous Peoples.

The United Nations separates political, cultural and economic rights into separate spheres. This promotes control by nation-states and limits the access of Indigenous Peoples to governance mechanisms. In comparison, the right to self-determination outlined by the UN Declaration on the Rights of Indigenous Peoples conjoins political, economic, social and cultural rights as fundamental components of Indigenous governance. Think back to Article 31 of the UN Declaration on the Rights of Indigenous Peoples, which describes the rights of Indigenous Peoples to all aspects of their cultural heritage and their intellectual property in that heritage. Is WIPO governed by Article 31? According to WIPO's mandate, the conventional intellectual property rights (IPR) frameworks protect *property* rights and everything else should be in the public domain. However, the organization favors considering the interests of "Indigenous and local communities" to their traditional knowledge, traditional cultural expressions and genetic resources to the extent that there is an equitable need to recognize them as "beneficiaries" of these "resources". To be a "beneficiary" is not the same as being an "owner". To have an "equitable interest" is not the same as having a "legal right". Furthermore, the term "Indigenous or local communities" can include a host of groups and entities (such as the Amish people) that are not recognized as "Indigenous Peoples" for the purposes of international human rights law. The WIPO treaties could definitely impact the rights of Indigenous Peoples by associating their rights with the "beneficial interests" of a vast array of cultural communities. This is the type of slippage that can result without close attention to the actors and the terminology that is being used.

Similarly, international "development policy" includes many of the same assumptions about "deficit" and "lagging behind" as domestic Indigenous-based policies. From the 1940s to 2000, for example, US policymakers advocated themes of tribal self-governance and economic development that were strikingly similar to those of international development policy ("USAID"). The policies may have been well intentioned, but they were also paternalistic (Miller 2012). The idea was to train tribal communities to behave like American communities as they "developed" their economic, social and political infrastructure. Federal grant funding was conditioned upon adherence to federal standards, for example, with respect to soil management or agricultural development. These policies did not examine or value the traditional knowledge or traditional economies of the Native Nations. Rather, the federal policies were designed to teach Native peoples how to be better "Americans".

How do these themes intersect with Indigenous Data Sovereignty?

Indigenous Data Sovereignty presents an opportunity to consider the intersection between international development policy and intellectual property rights. In recent work, Professor Chidi Oguamanam described Indigenous Data Sovereignty as a "critical tool to advance the Indigenous vision of self-determined development as part of the logic of broader self-determination" (Oguamanam 2019). This sounds promising, but what does it really mean? Oguamanam asserts that the term "self-determination" within international policy is linked to political identity and using this term "distances" Indigenous Peoples from the "direct pursuit of economic, social, cultural and cumulative development imperatives". According to Oguamanam, the human rights construct of "self-determination" is too abstract and contested to be useful. Instead, Indigenous Data Sovereignty should be read as encompassing informational communication technologies (ICT). Under this framing, Indigenous Peoples can gain capacity over ICT in the project of "Indigenous resurgence".

The usage of the terms "ICT" and "Indigenous resurgence" tips the calculus of Indigenous Data Sovereignty into the realm of economic, social and cultural rights. Oguamanam claims that we, as a global society, are transitioning from the traditional economic model driven by the Industrial Revolution to an economy driven by ICT. Information is now the greatest factor in promoting "production and wealth creation". New models of generation and deployment of data allow information to be used to promote "diversity of research, social networking momentum, biotechnology, artificial intelligence, and service delivery". This data capacity is then linked to a "global economic complex in which the multiple phenomena of big data, open data and data sovereignty shape the dynamics of the control of vital information". Oguamanam makes a very valuable observation about the nature of digital data as a new "resource" that serves the global information technology complex. He acknowledges that data has typically been under the control of the colonial nations, their agents, as well as researchers and corporations. He says that Indigenous Peoples are "late to the table" in the conversation about data sovereignty and that their claims are made "as a result of their resurgence and part of the broader decolonization project".

Drawing on work by Indigenous Data Sovereignty proponents, Oguamanam finds that Indigenous Peoples are essentially protesting the acts of appropriation of data that worked against their claims for sovereignty and self-determination. However, he shares the concern "there is no law or concept in Western society that recognizes inherent community rights and interests in data and information". If there is no recognized legal right to control data, then what is at the heart of this claim? According to Oguamanam, "Indigenous resurgence refers to Indigenous peoples' concerted and persistent struggle for decolonization". Data sovereignty is part of "decolonization", and one of those "everyday acts that resist the structures and effects of colonialism" and assert control over a resource that is of vital importance to Indigenous Peoples.

There is a technical sense in which "decolonization" works to liberate Peoples from unjust political control, but this is not the argument that Oguamanam is making. Political responses occur in the arena of civil and political rights. Indigenous Peoples are not "Peoples" for the purposes of the UN Convention on Civil and Political Rights, although they certainly can argue that they ought to be, in light of the prescriptive provisions of the UN Declaration. Therefore, "Indigenous resurgence" is tied to the "development" indicators associated with "economic, social, and cultural rights". The United States does not recognize these as "human rights", and to date, has not signed on to the UN Covenant on Economic, Social and Cultural Rights. The United States does support the UN's "development goals", including the Millenium Development goals and subsequent Sustainable Development goals, as a matter of policy, and is committed to voluntary assistance, under appropriate conditions. How does this line up with the mandate of the UN entities that promote the rights of Indigenous peoples? Oguamanam's article makes the key observation that the UN Permanent Forum on Indigenous Issues (UNPFII), which is the advisory body on Indigenous issues to the UN Economic and Social Council (ECOSOC), has made "data sovereignty" part of its "progressive policy approach to Indigenous issues". The UNPFII has a mandate to assist with social and economic development, and "culture, the environment, human health" are located within its human rights mandate. Self-determination as a political right or sovereignty as a political power do not fall within this mandate.

Thus, Indigenous Data Sovereignty as a tool for "development" fits within the scope of UN actors such as the World Bank and the International Finance Corporation. Information and data in this world have profound economic value.

Consequently, "Data is thus a core thematic of international development and the policy framework for engaging with Indigenous peoples".

Oguamanam's assertions raise various issues for consideration. A primary point made by this article appears to be that Indigenous Peoples would be better off not associating their right to data sovereignty with that of the nation-states. The notion of an *inherent* right to self-determination as "sovereignty" appears to be too controversial for most nation-states. Instead, Indigenous Data Sovereignty will be better received if it is seen as a necessary *tool* for their economic and social "development". This is an instrumental value, devoid of the moral authority of "inherent rights". The development theory also fits nicely within the comfort zone of conventional domestic Indigenous policies that aspire to move Indigenous Peoples "forward", given the disabilities that they have suffered as a result of past policies.

Compare this view with the logic of Federal Indian law. The doctrines of Federal Indian law are rooted in a colonial past that diminished tribal sovereignty into a form consistent with the hierarchy of colonial power. Today, however, the political sovereignty of federally recognized tribal governments and their control over their reservation and other trust lands and resources is premised on a political model of sovereignty that validates the ability of tribal governments to make their own laws and apply them to their territories and members, as well as third parties who consent to their governance. In the United States, the political sovereignty of tribal governments and their trust relationship with the federal government also justifies a set of "sui generis" rights under federal law that protect tribal rights to sovereignty and property. Indigenous Data Sovereignty shares resonance with international data sovereignty as the domain where politics, economics and culture intersect. This model can be adapted to the needs and requirements of Indigenous Peoples in other countries under the rubric of "self-determination". However, that construct must embody all of the parameters necessary to ensure Indigenous data governance.

Oguamanam suggests that Indigenous data governance could occur through partnerships between Indigenous Peoples and "states and other development actors", and he asserts that this is the intended meaning behind provisions such as Article 31 of the UN Declaration on the Rights of Indigenous Peoples. In this respect, Indigenous rights to cultural heritage are properly within the contemplation of an entity such as WIPO, because the issue really isn't "ownership" of data (governance per se). Rather, it is how to equitably accommodate Indigenous Peoples (and potentially other cultural communities) in a sui generis "tiered" system of protection that respects their beneficial interest in traditional knowledge and cultural expressions as a matter of equity. Oguamanam's partnership model may be quite appropriate for a number of marginalized cultural communities and perhaps even for many Indigenous Peoples. It also presents the risk of developing another convenient category that attempts to side-step the messy nature of how Indigenous Peoples were colonized. Indigenous Peoples were colonized by physical harm initially, including outright genocide. They were then colonized by various forms of forcible cultural "assimilation", which involved dislocation from lands and lifeways, coercive regulation of Indigenous social institutions (reshaping Native families, educational systems, legal systems), and various forms of shaming. Boarding schools prohibited speaking Native languages and criticized Native children as "primitive" if they wanted to dress and wear their hair in their customary way. The harms were still physical, in many cases, and the literature on historical trauma increasingly draws linkages between physical and behavioral health issues and this history.

Today, colonization is occurring at the level of consciousness, which is profoundly associated with knowledge practices (Tsosie 2015). What do we believe and why? The rationalist epistemology of Western European nations trains us to rely on tangible facts or "data". We see the statistics and then believe we are impoverished, incarcerated, unhealthy or otherwise tainted in some tangible way that justifies what we now see as being "reality". In fact, we *create* our reality, but we might do so in an unreflective way because we have been trained to focus on the rationalist approach of Western knowledge systems. What if the distinction between "civil and political rights" and "social, economic and cultural rights" is merely another form of colonial domination and use of power? What if self-determination really is the freedom to think, to make our own categories and apply them, using our own laws and philosophies, whether or not they are recognized by the United States or any other colonial power? What if we already have the mechanisms to measure the truth embedded within the knowledge systems that have been in place for generations? Those knowledge systems are ancient, powerful and they contain the knowledge of survival.

In the first chapter of this book, the authors state that:

> The denial of Indigenous rights extends to the denial of Indigenous data rights. The rapid pace of the global data revolution, epitomized through Big Data and the state and policy enthusiasm for Open Data, operate to further distance lived social and cultural realities from their database embodiment.

There is considerable wisdom in that insight. The potential for confusion and uncertainty is unprecedented as we move to a world where digital data can be manipulated to reveal "social understandings" that masquerade as 'fact'. We must be cautious of who our "partners" are and consider what actions will be necessary to protect Indigenous Peoples against the latest form of colonialism.

Conclusion

Colonialism is an on-going process and the world of digital data is the latest site for engagement. Indigenous Peoples require strong legal frameworks to enable data capacity and data governance. Indigenous Data Sovereignty advocates have revealed a powerful set of insights to guide the collective project, and their work is already engaging an international discourse that is robust, complex and will be the subject of productive debate for many years to come.

Notes

1 In this essay, I use the term "Native Nations" to refer to the federally recognized American Indian and Alaska Native Nations that possess inherent sovereign powers as sovereign Nations that preexisted the United States and are now in a "trust relationship" with the United States. I use "Indigenous Peoples" to refer to the original, land-based Peoples of the territories now under the political control of the European-derived settler nations now known as the United States, Canada, New Zealand and Australia, and whether or not they are officially "recognized" by the nation-state. There is clearly overlap between the two categories, but they are not coextensive. In the United States, for example, the Native Hawaiian People are clearly "Indigenous" and yet they lack the same type of political recognition as the federally recognized tribal governments.
2 The Doctrine of discovery served as the charter for European colonialism under International law, providing that the first Christian European nation to "discover" and "settle" lands inhabited by non-Christian and "uncivilized" Peoples could claim "Title" to these lands. The Doctrine dates back to the Crusades, but it was resurrected under US Federal Indian law in *Johnson* v. *McIntosh*, which held that the United States assumed Great Britain's "Title by Discovery", and that the American Indian nations held only the "right of occupancy" until the United States decided to extinguish that right, by "purchase" or by "conquest". *Johnson* v. *McIntosh*, 21 U.S. (8 Wheat.) 543 (1823). The right of occupancy is now associated with "Aboriginal Title".
3 For example, news reports increasingly document that artificial intelligence (AI) can encode biases abstracted from "machine learning", and the algorithms are far from "neutral". Other uses of AI are more overtly discriminatory. For example, China is among the countries that have actively exploited "facial recognition" software to profile and exercise surveillance over minority ethnic groups.
4 Statement of Principles adopted at Indigenous Data Sovereignty Summit, June 2018.
5 25 U.S.C. 2702(1).
6 See *California* v. *Cabazon Band of Mission Indians*, 480 U.S. 202 (1987) (holding that state could not regulate gaming enterprise of Tribal government on its trust land).
7 See Rebecca Tsosie, "Tribal Data Governance and Informational Privacy: Constructing 'Indigenous Data Sovereignty'", 80 Mont. L. Rev. 229 (2019).
8 See *Worcester* v. *Georgia*, 31 U.S. (6 Pet.) 515 (1832).
9 See, e.g., Public Law 280 (1953) (giving certain states the authority to exercise civil and criminal adjudicatory jurisdiction over Indian Country cases).
10 See *Dept. of Interior* v. *Klamath Water Users Protective Ass'n*, 121 S.Ct. 1060, 1065 (2001).
11 See, e.g., 25 U.S.C. 3056 (exempting specific categories of information from disclosure under FOIA in the context of activities on lands under the jurisdiction of the National Forest Service).
12 I discuss the draft WIPO treaties in "Indigenous Peoples and Cultural Sustainability: The Role of Law and Traditional Knowledge", chapter in Melissa Nelson & Dan Shilling (eds), *Traditional Ecological Knowledge: Learning from Indigenous Practices for Environmental Sustainability* (2018).

References

Anaya, S.J. (2004). *Indigenous Peoples in International Law*, 2nd ed. Oxford University Press.
Chaney, C. (2018a). Data sovereignty in tribal governance: is the law keeping pace with technology? *Tribal Net Magazine*, 12, Fall 2018.
Chaney, C. (2018b). Data sovereignty and the tribal law and order act. *The Federal Lawyer*, 24, April 2018.

Coombe, R.J. and Turcotte, J.F. (2012). Indigenous cultural heritage in development and trade chapter. In C.B. Graber, K. Kuprecht and J.C. Lai (eds.), *International Trade in Indigenous Cultural Heritage: Legal and Policy Issues (2012)*, pp. 272–305. Edward Elgar Publishing Limited.

Fricker, M. (2007). *Epistemic Injustice: Power and the Ethics of Knowing*. Oxford University Press.

Graber, C., Kuprecht, K. and Lai, J. eds. (2012). *International Trade in Indigenous Cultural Heritage: Legal and Policy Issues*. Edward Elgar Publishing.

Kukutai, T. and Taylor, J. (2016) Data sovereignty for indigenous peoples: current practice and future needs. In T. Kukutai and J. Taylor (eds.), *Indigenous Data Sovereignty: Towards an Agenda*, 1–24. CAEPR Research Monograph, 2016/34. Canberra: ANU Press

Miller, R. (2012). *Reservation Capitalism*. University of Minnesota Press.

Nelson, M. and Shilling, D. (2018). *Traditional Ecological Knowledge: Learning from Indigenous Practices for Environmental Sustainability*. Cambridge University Press.

Nickel, J. (2007). *Making Sense of Human Rights*, pp. 7–8. University of California Press.

Oguamanam, C. (2019). Indigenous data sovereignty: retooling indigenous resurgence for development. *CIGI Papers No. 234—December 2019*.

Pevar, S. (2012). *The Rights of Indian Tribes*, 4th ed. Oxford Press.

Snipp, M. (2016). What does data sovereignty imply: what does it look like? In T. Kukutai and J. Taylor (eds.), *Indigenous Data Sovereignty: Towards An Agenda: CAEPR Research Monography, 2016/34*, pp. 39–56. ANU Press, Canberra.

Tsosie, R. (2011). Reconceptualizing tribal rights: can self-determination be actualized within the U.S. constitutional structure? *Lewis & Clark Law Review*, 15, 923.

Tsosie, R. (2012). Indigenous peoples and epistemic injustice: science, ethics, and human rights. *Washington Law Review*, 87, 1133.

Tsosie, R. (2015). Just governance or just war?: native artists, cultural production, and the challenge of super-diversity. *Cybaris: An Intellectual Property Law Review*, 6(2), 63.

Tsosie, R. (2019). Tribal data governance and informational privacy: constructing 'indigenous data sovereignty'. *Montana Law Review*, 80, 229.

Woods, A. (2018). Litigating data sovereignty. *Yale Law Journal*, 128, 328.

15 Embedding systemic change—opportunities and challenges

Maggie Walter, Stephanie Russo Carroll, Tahu Kukutai and Desi Rodriguez-Lonebear

Introduction

Data and policy have a symbiotic relationship. Data without policy is just a collection of numbers or information about a given topic or issue. Even if the data analysis demonstrates an incontrovertible statistical link between two factors, such as schools with stronger positive relationships with the Indigenous community in their region and higher Indigenous student school attendance, on its own, that link has limited impact. Without policy action such as adding incentives for school leadership to build relationships with the Indigenous community or supporting Indigenous communities to develop their own schooling options and relationships, it remains just a research finding, important, but ultimately without practical outcome. Policy without data to support its design and implementation is potentially much worse than non-productive. As theorized in the work of Scott (1998) unevidenced policy is policy that is substantially at risk of going disastrously awry. Regardless of the beneficence of the policy intent, without data to evidence its efficacy such policy action is unlikely to produce the intended result.

To return to one of our central concepts, in the Indigenous realm, the connection between data and policy is not always positive. With a significant power imbalance between those determining policy and those who are its subject a long-standing feature of nation state Indigenous policy, value within the data/policy nexus and to whom that value accrues depends on whose purposes the data serve and how and why those data are deployed. The outcome has been, and continues to be, policy prescriptions that reproduce, largely unfettered and unreflexively, the pejorative presumptions of contemporary colonial race relations. As shown in many of the chapters in this book, inclusive of Chapter 1 on Indigenous data governance and policy, Chapter 3 examining data and the Closing the Gap policy framework in Australia, Chapter 7 on the challenge of Indigenous data in Sweden, Chapter 9 on Indigenous policy and data in Mexico and Chapter 12 on the data challenges in Columbia's transitional setting, the result is rarely benign. Other contributions such as Chapter 6 on the Indigenous-led health and data initiatives in Canada and the continuance policy and bureaucratic hindrances, Chapter 8 on the role of data in the contested narratives of victimhood in the Basque Country, Chapter 11 on the clash of values on data that draw on Indigenous knowledge

Systemic change—opportunities & challenges 227

within US universities and Chapter 14 which explores Indigenous data governance's role in effectuating self-determination despite the legacy of colonialism and epistemic injustice, highlight the centrality of power dynamics and often bitter contestation occurring within the Indigenous Data Sovereignty/policy nexus.

Conversely, chapters included in this collection also provide multiple examples of the value and validity of Indigenous Data Sovereignty and governance in supporting the transformative potential of data. These include Chapter 2, on the contribution of Indigenous Data Sovereignty to Māori aspirations for self-determination, Chapter 4 on the practical implementation of Indigenous Data Sovereignty for Pueblo Peoples, Chapter 5 on the role of the Te Mana Raraunga Māori Data Sovereignty Network in establishing Māori Data Sovereignty as a legitimate policy discourse, Chapter 10 on the active work of embedding Quechan Indigenous Data Sovereignty practices and Chapter 13 on Kaupapa Māori epidemiology grounded in Māori values, knowledge systems and ontologies. In these examples, data provide the policy evidence for the benefit of those to whom it relates—Indigenous Peoples.

Changing the relationship between policy and data is neither a simple task, nor for the fainthearted. Data and policy infrastructures are large and complicated with many interacting features and processes. The enabling foundations of both are also structural. Achieving actual change, rather than cosmetic tweaks and piecemeal progress, requires a paradigm shift on how Indigenous data and policy, and the connection between them, are understood. Such paradigmatic change will not come easily. Systems, and the people that facilitate and inhabit those systems, resist change, and resist change ferociously when that change is seen as de-privileging their position under the existing paradigm. As articulated by Kuhn (1970: 122) "the normal practice of science is to 'refine, extend, and articulate a paradigm that is already in existence'". It is only when the anomalies in the established paradigm become too many to ignore that "scientific revolution", shifting from the existing dominant paradigm to a new dominant paradigm, can occur. Such revolutions are more than an adjustment in practices or knowledge. Paradigm shifts both require, and result in, nothing less than a permanent change in world view. Thus, in Kuhn's (1970: 112) words, "the scientist's perception of his environment must be re-educated ... the world of his research will seem ... incommensurable with the one he had inhabited before". This is not an orderly process. Paradigm change must overcome the established interests of the existing dominant paradigm: "the proponents of competing paradigms are always at least slightly at cross purposes" (Kuhn, 1970: 148).

Being "at cross purposes" is a relatively benign way of describing the current state of play between advocates of Indigenous Data Sovereignty and those still within the old paradigm of data dependence. While, as shown by the chapters in this book, the pace of the Indigenous data revolution varies by nation state, disrupting the existing Indigenous data and policy paradigm through Indigenous Data Sovereignty and Indigenous data governance remains a mammoth task. Such a shift is more than data agencies, commissioners and users taking a different approach to Indigenous data. It requires a re-ordering of data infrastructure, prioritizing, mostly for the first time, the data interests of Indigenous Peoples. This re-ordering must be achieved on multiple levels, across the many and varied processes and practices of the complex data and policy infrastructure of the modern nation state. This shift must also be driven by Indigenous Peoples for Indigenous Peoples. It depends on developing and enriching relationships between Indigenous Peoples and external data holders to produce data stewardship that is built on mutual trust and aligned with Indigenous values and priorities. Above all, if lasting change is to be achieved, changes must also be systemic and involve power sharing with Indigenous communities and Native Nations.

Genuine power sharing has long been a barrier to the realization of effective Indigenous policy. Non-Indigenous policy-makers routinely ignore or override the deep and varied forms of local intelligence and networks that exist within Indigenous Nations and communities. The refusal of the State to recognize, respond to and support local knowledge and leadership as valid have been amplified in the Covid-19 global pandemic. In Canada, Australia, Aotearoa New Zealand and the United States, the policy response has been a universal "one size fits all" approach. For Indigenous Peoples this means "top down" policy designed by and for mainstream constituencies. The technology that is developed—such as ICU prioritization algorithms or contact tracing apps—is layered on top of existing structures that reinforce rather than unwind biases and inequities. Set against this, Indigenous communities have demonstrated a remarkable capacity to anticipate and rapidly respond to the needs of their people—from setting up community checkpoints in remote communities to providing online cultural support for grieving families holding solitary funerals to delivering elder and family care packages. Indigenous communities have demonstrated powerful forms of distributed leadership—whether tribal leaders, "aunties" or youth—and a deep capacity to care for each other, empowered by the strength of their connections and knowledge of kin and kin-like relations. Incredibly, they have been able to do so without the timely support of state information and data systems which have routinely neglected to provide accurate, relevant and high-quality data to assist with their on-the-ground responses. The missed opportunity is thus twofold: policy-makers at the "center" fail to recognize and connect with local forms of knowledge to develop more dynamic, granular pandemic planning that works in situ, and communities fail to receive the right data, in the right way, at the right time to increase the success of their response.

Clearly, there are significant challenges to generating systemic change for Indigenous data and policy and there are no easy fixes. Indeed, for some contributors in this book, the substance of Indigenous Data Sovereignty can only be truly realized in contexts where Indigenous sovereignty is prioritized and empowered. However, all contributors agree that a "do nothing" approach is untenable. With the vast majority of Indigenous data in the possession of governments and private corporations, and the rapid development of powerful digital and data surveillance technologies, the risk of data harm and the opportunity costs of not engaging are too high. Thus, in this final chapter, we describe on-the-ground activity, inter and intra nationally, to introduce Indigenous Data Sovereignty into the policy realm.

Operationalizing Indigenous rights in the global open data movement

Internationally, the United Nations Special Rapporteur on the right to privacy has called for member governments to recognize Indigenous Data Sovereignty in the context of big and open data (Cannataci, 2018) and the protection and use of health-related data (Cannataci, 2019). As the availability and use of big and open data accelerates, the expression of Indigenous rights and interests in data reveals flaws in mainstream assumptions of ownership, representation and control in these data communities (Rainie et al., 2019). Open data and big data magnify Indigenous invisibility and bias against Indigenous Peoples in data use and resultant policy. Without Indigenous data governance within open data communities, the current policy paradigm reigns, and data access, use and interpretation, in general, are left to those who claim power, such as nation states. These data hold great promise for Indigenous Peoples for our own social, political and economic development, yet Indigenous Peoples are often erased from the systems that steward these data.

Recognizing the critical relationship between data and policy for Indigenous self-determination and the need to protect and control Indigenous data within open data communities, the CARE Principles for Indigenous data governance (Collective benefit, Authority to control, Responsibility, Ethics) provide external data stakeholders with guidance on stewardship responsibilities for Indigenous data (RDA IG, 2019). The CARE Principles complement mainstream principles focused on data attributes by centering people and purpose in data policies and practices. For example, the FAIR scientific data principles (Findable, Accessible, Interoperable, Reusable) seek to transform data for machine readability and other secondary use applications within open science (Wilkinson et al., 2016). Engagement with Indigenous data requires enacting FAIR with CARE. As Indigenous and mainstream data practitioners advance standards and practices for data reuse via mechanisms that align with the FAIR Principles, implementing the CARE Principles expands that work by addressing historical and current power imbalances through the creation of policies and practices for Indigenous data that are grounded in Indigenous worldviews (Carroll et al., forthcoming).

Equitable data, data practices and policies necessitate a CARE-full process. Operationalizing the CARE Principles requires policy and practice actions by data stakeholders guided by Indigenous Peoples that impact activities across the data lifecycle, both before and after making data FAIR. Currently, a number of projects are underway to identify and create tools for a CARE-full process across research, government and foundation data environments (Carroll et al., forthcoming). These tools include Indigenous data standards; artificial intelligence protocols; metadata that adhere provenance, transparency and accountability to data throughout data lifecycles; tribal and institutional guidelines; tribal codes and research review boards; data access protocols and more. Additionally, collaborators at the Global Indigenous Data Alliance (gida-global.org) and the Research Data Alliance International Indigenous Data Sovereignty Interest Group (rd-alliance.org) are developing CARE criteria for operationalizing each principle. The criteria will provide guidance on the CARE Principles in action for policy and practice.

Implementing CARE with FAIR leads to data that reflect Indigenous realities, and shifts power differentials, ultimately rendering data to inform policies that affirm Indigenous rights to self-determination. Internally, for Indigenous Nations these data become useful for governance, decision-making, and meeting the needs of the community. Externally, the Indigenous leadership and governance in data governance alters the existing data and policy paradigm by leading with Indigenous values, goals and control.

Data about the research that produces the data

In Australia and Aotearoa New Zealand, as in most other developed nations, policy-makers frequently proclaim evidence-based policy making as at the heart of policy planning. Defined by Banks (2018: 1) as "an approach to policymaking that makes systematic provision for evidence and analysis", the evidence for evidence-based policy making is largely drawn from publicly funded research. Government-supported entities in both nation states administer a broad range of grant programs. While a small number of programs are Indigenous researcher specific, most Indigenous-related research is undertaken via the mainstream programs grants.

Knowing the breadth and impact of a field of research is a prerequisite of a robust evidence base for evidence-based policy making. But although the primary research data collection mechanism, the Australian and New Zealand Standard Research Classification (ANZSRC) states its purpose as to ensure research statistics "are useful to governments, educational institutions ... community groups and private individuals in Australia and New Zealand" (ANZSRC, 2019a) this purpose is not deliverable for Indigenous research because of coding linked lack of measurability. Aligned to the OECDs Fields of Science 2007, the ANZSRC has three measures: (1) type of activity (i.e., applied research); (2) field of research (FoR) which categorizes by area (i.e., history); and (3) socio-economic objective (SEO code) which classifies by intended purpose (i.e., economic development). The most commonly used classification, FoR Codes, are divided into 22 broad discipline divisions, each represented by a two-digit code (e.g., 21—History and Archaeology). Each division contains a set of groups which share similar methodology, represented by a four-digit code (e.g., 2101—Archaeology). Under each group is a set of fields represented by a six-digit code (e.g., 210103—Archaeology of Asia, Africa and the Americas). Indigenous-related research is coded at the six-digit level.

Relegation of Indigenous research to the six-digit level poses severe barriers to measurability. The first is that Indigenous research is currently classified as a field subset within other research disciplines such as education or health. Subsumed within mainstream discipline (two-digit) and groups (four-digit), Indigenous research is presented therefore as a type of health or education research, not as its own broad discipline. More damagingly, ANZSRC data is only analyzed and reported at the two-digit division and four-digit group level. This means that Indigenous research is neither counted nor countable, making it invisible. There are therefore, no "useful statistics" generated to indicate the level of Indigenous research activity or output in Australia or Aotearoa. Even from a raw fiscal outlook, this data gap is deeply problematic. Public monies expended on Indigenous research are substantial. Yet, there is no capability for measuring the location or outcomes of that expenditure and whether this investment is value for money for taxpayers, government or, more importantly, for Indigenous Peoples.

The lack of data on the breadth or depth of Indigenous research also has Indigenous Data Sovereignty and policy implications. Indigenous Peoples, in Australia and Aotearoa, increasingly look to research to inform nation rebuilding and development programs. Yet the current system does not have the analytical functionality to support Indigenous ambitions. Without visibility, the conduct and outcomes of Indigenous research are neither accountable to the People/s who are its subject or knowledge base nor amenable to Indigenous data governance protocols. From an Indigenous policy perspective, the implications are even more dire. The nation state relies on research to support its Indigenous policy platform yet, the current system has little capacity to track what Indigenous research is being done, in which academic, public or private settings, and less capacity to identify research gaps.

In 2019, the ANZSRC was formally reviewed by the Australian Bureau of Statistics (ABS) and Statistics New Zealand, the Australian Research Council (ARC) and the New Zealand Ministry of Business, Innovation and Employment. The aim was to ensure that the ANZSRC reflected current research practice and was sufficiently robust to allow for long-term data analysis. A special consideration was Aboriginal and Torres Strait Islander, Māori and Pacific Peoples studies (ANZSRC, 2019a). Wide public consultations were undertaken and for the first time Indigenous researchers and peak bodies were explicitly included (ANZSRC, 2019c).

The Maiam nayri Wingara and the Te Mana Raraunga Indigenous Data Sovereignty networks, based in Australia and Aotearoa, respectively, were prominent in advocating for broadscale change within the ANZSRC (ANZSRC, 2019c). The *Consultation Draft: Indigenous Research, Australian and New Zealand Standard Research Classification Review 2019* (ANZSRC, 2019b) came to a range of conclusions. Acknowledging the growth in the field, the report stated that current classifications significantly under-represented the breadth and scope of Aboriginal and Torres Strait Islander, Māori and Pacific Peoples research. The report recognized under-representation results in an impeding of: the ability of government and others to report and analyze data; the ability of Indigenous Peoples and communities to identify and access research and data; and the ability to measure the funding and participation of Indigenous Peoples in research and development and the ability to measure the influence of research on Indigenous well-being and development.

The ANZSRC review is now completed and the new Classification released (ARC 2020). But despite some resistance from within the higher education system the revised code will include a new FoR and SEO Indigenous research division (two-digit). This division will position Indigenous research, for the first time in Aotearoa or Australia, as its own knowledge domain based on its shared methodologies and approaches. This domain will also recognize the diversity of Aboriginal and Torres Strait Islander, Māori and Pacific Peoples research. The result of this systemic change will be widespread, probably in ways not yet fully realized. At a minimum, it will make Indigenous research visible and therefore measurable and analyzable. The recognition of Indigenous research as its own knowledge domain will also alter how Indigenous data and other research outputs are understood. Most critically, over time, being able to measure and analyze Indigenous research scope and output will reshape the Indigenous data that is produced and available as evidence for use in policy making.

Data for tribal governance

Policy doesn't just emanate from the state or its institutions, but also from tribal nations whose authority and responsibility to plan and care for the collective well-being of their communities pre-dates colonial structures and regulations. Neither is data-driven policy foreign to tribal nations. Since time immemorial, Indigenous Peoples have drawn on the data all around them to inform decision-making for survival. Like all other nation states, modern tribal governments are actively engaged in the policy world. Policy action at the tribal level can take many forms, from official resolutions and agreements to visiting elders and recording oral histories. Accurate and relevant data are critical to effective tribal governance. These include data on everything from tribal citizens to lands, resources and cultural ways of knowing, doing and being. As tribal nations continue to rebuild their governance structures, they are also reclaiming processes of "doing data" by them for them.

Tribal population data is one area in which tribal nations in the United States are challenging existing settler-colonial data systems and carving their own path toward data for tribal governance. Demographic methods to count, classify and measure populations have long served the settler-colonial state (Kertzer & Arel, 2002; Rowse, 2017). The enumeration of American Indians and Alaska Natives (AIANs) in the US official statistics system, through instruments like the US Census and national surveys, is directly tied to millions of dollars in federal funding on which AIAN communities depend. Yet, tribal nations have little control over those data. Moreover, national statistics on AIANs have a long history of being incomplete due to census undercounts, misclassification and problematic tribal identifiers. Given these limitations, there is a growing movement among tribal nations to challenge official statistics by developing their own systems of tribal demography.

Tribal nations are strengthening their data capability and fighting back against hundreds of years of data dependence so that they no longer rely on the colonizer's data about their citizens. One area of development is the tribal census, which is becoming a priority for tribal nations because effective governance requires data that speak to the size, characteristics, conditions and realities of one's citizenry. Examples include the Ho-Chunk Nation Census in 2015, the "K'awaika YOU Count!" Laguna Pueblo Census in 2016, and the Sault Ste. Marie Tribe of Chippewa Indians' Census collected in 2014 and 2019. Another emerging area of tribal demography involves efforts to evaluate the sustainability of tribal nations in the United States amidst colonial blood quantum standards that have controlled the boundaries of tribal belonging for decades. It must be underscored that minimum blood quantum is not a traditional means of conferring tribal citizenship; it was introduced by the federal government to hasten Indigenous assimilation (Snipp, 1992). Results from a large multi-tribal research project reveal that the most common metric to qualify for tribal citizenship is one-quarter tribal blood, meaning individuals must have at least one "full-blooded" grandparent (Rodriguez-Lonebear, forthcoming).

Tribal nations are urgently realizing that demographic realities, like high rates of intermarriage and urbanization, combined with strict blood quantum minimums, effectively threaten the future of their nations. In response, tribal nations are pursuing critical data for governance. By using their tribal citizenship data to project the future size of their tribal populations under different citizenship criteria, tribal nations are exploring how to develop citizenship policies that future proof their nations. The Minnesota Chippewa Tribe embarked on a tribal population projections initiative in 2015, which has since become the model for other tribal nations. Most recently, the Northern Cheyenne Nation is engaged in a tribal demography research project in which they have found significant differences in the size and composition of their tribal population when comparing tribal citizenship records to those of the US Census. They have also conducted population projections comparing the demographic outcomes of different citizenship criteria, which they are currently considering as they evaluate a new tribal citizenship policy. This is what tribally controlled, future-focused, and data-driven policy looks like in action.

Conclusion

Data are a resource with a tangible and rapidly increasing policy-related value. The centrality of data to Indigenous policy has been discussed across many of its multiple dimensions in this edited collection. All authors are actively engaged in asserting Indigenous data rights through Indigenous Data Sovereignty scholarship and data advocacy. But the Indigenous data/policy nexus is complex and complicated. As shown in the chapters, the recognition and acceptance of Indigenous demands, nationally and internationally, for the right to control the collection, use, ownership and application of our data remains limited and highly contested. Yet, these data rights are foundational to the realization of Indigenous social, political and economic rights and nation rebuilding with policy, whether emerging from nation states or Tribal and First Nations, the intervening mechanism. Good Indigenous policy is reliant on good Indigenous data, and both must be conceptualized through the lens of Indigenous rights, needs, and aspirations.

References

ARC. (2020). *Revised Australian and New Zealand Standard Research Classification (ANZSRC 2020)* https://www.arc.gov.au/news-publications/media/network-messages/revised-australian-and-new-zealand-standard-research-classification-anzsrc-2020.

ANZSRC. (2019a). *Discussion Paper: Australian and New Zealand Standard Research Classification Review 2019*. Australian Bureau of Statistics, Stats NZ, Tatauranga Aotearoa, Australian Research Council, Ministry of Business, Innovation & Employment, Hikina Whatatutuki, Canberra and Auckland.

ANZSRC. (2019b). *Consultation Draft: Indigenous Research, Australian and New Zealand Standard Research Classification Review 2019*. Australian Bureau of Statistics, Stats NZ, Tatauranga Aotearoa, Australian Research Council, Ministry of Business, Innovation & Employment, Hikina Whatatutuki, Canberra and Auckland.

ANZSRC. (2019c). *Submission 160 Maiam nayri Wingara Indigenous Sovereignty Collective (Australia) and the Te Mana Raraunga Māori Data Sovereignty Network submission to ANZSRC Review2019*. ANZSRC.

Banks, G. (2018). Whatever happened to evidence base policy making. *The Mandarin*. https://www.themandarin.com.au/102083-whatever-happened-to-evidence-based-policymaking/.

Cannataci, J. (2018). *Report of the Special Rapporteur on the Right to Privacy*, October 17, A/73/45712. Retrieved from https://www.ohchr.org.

Cannataci, J. (2019). *Mandate of the United Nations Special Rapporteur on the Right to Privacy—Task Force on Privacy and the Protection of Health-Related Data*. Retrieved from https://www.ohchr.org/Documents/Issues/Privacy/SR_Privacy/DraftRecommendationProtectionUseHealthRelatedData.pdf.

Carroll, S.R., Hudson, M. et al. (forthcoming). CARE principles for the governance of indigenous data. Under review at the *Data Science Journal*.

Kertzer, D. I., & Arel, D. (2002). *Census and identity: The politics of race, ethnicity, and language in national censuses.* Cambridge, UK: Cambridge University Press.

Kuhn, T.S. (1970). *The Structure of Scientific Revolutions*, 2nd Edition. University of Chicago.

Rainie, S.C., Kukutai, T., Walter, M., Figueroa-Rodriguez, O.L., Walker, J., & Axelsson, P. (2019). Issues in open data: indigenous data sovereignty. In T. Davies, S. Walker, M. Rubinstein, & F. Perini (Eds.), *The State of Open Data: Histories and Horizons* (pp. 300–319). African Minds and International Development Research Centre, Cape Town and Ottawa.

Research Data Alliance International Indigenous Data Sovereignty Interest Group. (September 2019). *CARE Principles for Indigenous Data Governance.* The Global Indigenous Data Alliance. GIDA-global.org.

Rodriguez-Lonebear, D. (Forthcoming). The blood line: racialized boundary making and citizenship among native nations. Revise and resubmit at the *Sociology of Race and Ethnicity*.

Rowse, Tim. (2017). The Statistical Table as Colonial Knowledge. *Itinerario* 41(1):51–73.

Scott, J.C. (1998). *Seeing Like a State: How Certain Schemes to Improve the Human Condition Have Failed*. New Haven, CT: Yale University Press

Snipp, C. Matthew. 1992. "Sociological Perspectives on American Indians." *Annual Review of Sociology* 18:351–71.

Wilkinson, M., Dumontier, M., Aalbersberg, I. et al. (2016). The FAIR guiding principles for scientific data management and stewardship. *Scientific Data*, March 15, 2016. doi:10.1038/sdata.2016.18.

Index

Page numbers in *italics* reference figures.

5D data 9
1967 referendum (Australia) 36–37
2005 Social Justice Report 41

AASTEC (Albuquerque Area Southwest Tribal Epidemiology Center) 51, 54–55
Aboriginal Community Controlled Health Organizations (ACCHOs) 43
Aboriginal people 3; legislation and policy 36–40; school attendance 7
ABS (Australian Bureau of Statistics) 231
Access to Information Act, Canada 89
ACCHOs (Aboriginal Community Controlled Health Organizations) 43
Acoma Nation 157
Act 4/2008 of June 19, 2008, Spain 122
Act 4/2014, Spain 126
Act 5/2019 of April 4, Spain 122
Act 29/2011 of the Spanish Parliament on the Recognition and Comprehensive Protection of Victims of Terrorism, Spain 124
Act 29/2011 on the Recognition and Comprehensive Protection of Victims of Terrorism, Spain 121
Act of Historical Memory (2007), Spain 113
Act on Historical Memory 52/2007, Spain 121
Act to Encourage the Gradual Civilization of the Indian Tribes in Canada of 1857 82–83
advocacy, Māori Data Sovereignty (MDS) 65–67
agency responses to Māori Data Sovereignty (MDS) 69–74

age-standardization, Māori 196
Ahmed, S. 26
AIAN (American Indians and Alaska Natives) 157, 232; cultural sovereignty 159–160; political sovereignty 158; qualitative data 158–159; research mechanisms 160–162; tribal sovereignty 212–215
Albuquerque Area Southwest Tribal Epidemiology Center (AASTEC) 51, 54–55, 60n3
Amazon, rubber industry 173
American Indian Higher Education Consortium Native Research and Scholarship Symposium 161
Amnesty Act (1977), Spain 121
Andersen, C. 148, 187, 198
Anderson, I. 99
Anderson, J. 83
ANZSRC (Australian and New Zealand Standard Research Classification) 230–232
Aotearoa New Zealand: data colonialism 25 data self-determination 28–31; data policy structure 62–64; Kaupapa Māori 191 197; Māori *see* Māori; Māori Data Sovereignty (MDS) 64–65; Māori policy 25–28; self-determination 23–24; Te Puni Kōkiri Ministry of Māori Development 1
Apache tribes 161
Aponte, J. 175
Arizona Board of Regents 157, 162
Arizona State University 157, 162
assimilation policy, Aotearoa New Zealand 25–26
Attaching Your Heart 55

236 Index

AUC (United Self-Defenders of Colombia) 175
Australia: Aboriginal people *see* Aboriginal people; CTG (Closing the Gap), Australia 40–7; legislation and policy 36–40; Maiam nayri Wingara Aboriginal and Torres Strait Islander Data Sovereignty Collective 12–13; National Indigenous Australians Agency 1; school attendance 7–8
Australian and New Zealand Standard Research Classification (ANZSRC) 230–232
Australian Bureau of Statistics (ABS) 231
Australian Constitution 36–40
Australian National Audit Office 43
Australian Productivity Commission 3
authoritarian state 6
Autodefensas Unidas de Colombia (United Self-Defenders of Colombia AUC) 175
autonomous consultation, Colombia 181–182
autonomous data governance, Basque Country 120–121
Avilés, W. 180
awareness raising, Māori Data Sovereignty (MDS) 69–71

Bahia Portete massacre 179–180
Banks, G. 230
Bargh, M. 26
Basque Act 12/2016 of July 28 122
Basque Autonomous Community 120
Basque conflict (1968-2011) 112–114, 123; Gogora Institute 125–127; Memorial Centre for Victims of Terrorism 124–125; memorial data 123–124
Basque Country 112; data colonialism 117–121; data on memory and conflicting narratives 121–127
Basque People 114–115
Basque Society of Studies 120
Belmont Report 163
belonging, Pueblo People 55
Bengoetxea, J. 171–172
Big Data technologies 5
Bishop, R. 191
Boege, E. 141
Bonilla-Silva, E. 2, 190–191
Boston, J. 25
Browne, S. 31
"The Building Blocks" 41

Calls to Action (Canada) 81
Canada 81; assessing Indigenous data quality 90–91; Data Governance Agreement 43; First Nations *see* First Nations; governance 91–92; history of policy in 82–84; Indigenous Data Sovereignty 92–94; Indigenous Services Canada 1; Métis 81–84; OCAP (ownership, control, access, possession) principles 12, 29, 43, 87–90; privacy 29; reconciliation 85–87
Canada Health Act (1984), Canada 83
Canadian Public Health Association (CPHA) 87
CANZUS (United States, Aotearoa New Zealand, Canada and Australia) 1, 15; emphasizing differences 9
CARE (Collective benefit, Authority to control, Responsibility, Ethics) principles 106–107, 229–230
CARE Principles 13
Carolina Herrera 141–142
Carroll, S. 29, 206, 210
Caso, A. 131
Castillo, V. 173
Catalan process (2014) 112
CCC Order 04/09, Colombia 176
CCC order 004/2009, Colombia 177
CDI (National Commission for the Development of Indigenous Communities) 135, 143
CEMR (Community Electronic Medical Record) 91
census 99, 119, 197, 210, 232–233; Mexico 131–133; New Zealand 25, 27, 30, 63–64, 66–67
Centro Memorial de Victimas del Terrorismo 124
Cerrejon mine 178–179
Chief Data Steward, Aotearoa New Zealand 63
Chief Digital Officer, Aotearoa New Zealand 63
children: removal of 4; Wayuu (Colombia) 179
China 209
Chomsky, A. 180
Chosa, C.T. 55
Closing the Gap (CTG), Australia 39–47
Cloudry, N. 31
COAG (Council of Australian Governments) 41
Coaltion of the Peaks 48

Index 237

Coffey, W. 160
Collective benefit, Authority to control, Responsibility, Ethics (CARE) principles 106–107
collective rights 29
Colombia 169; autonomous consultation 181–182; Bahia Portete massacre 179–180; Cerrejon mine 178–179; Constitutional order 004/2009 170; historical presentation of Indigenous peoples 172–175; periodization 172; TJ framework 175–177; Wayuu 178; Wayuu safeguard plan 180–181
colonialism 84; Māori 197; Pueblo People 53
coloniality 174
colonization 28, 83, 114, 130, 144, 178, 188, 193, 223; Anglo colonization 10, 15; decolonization 24, 218, 221
commodity food 149–150
Common Rule 162–163
communal lands, Mexico 140–141
community engagement, Pueblo Data Sovereignty 55
Community Institute, Pueblo People 54
community values, Quechan Nation 150–152
CONAPO (National Population Council) 134
CONEVAL (National Evaluation Council) 135
conflicting narratives, Basque Country 121–127
Constitution Act (1867), Canada 83
Constitutional order 004/2009 170
Coombe, R. 212
Cossins, D. 5
Coulthard, G. 28
Council of Australian Governments (COAG) 41
Council of Europe 116
CPHA (Canadian Public Health Association) 87
Crown, monitoring (Māori) 193–194
Crown policy, Aotearoa New Zealand 25–26
CTG (Closing the Gap), Australia 39–47
cultural genocide 82–84, 173
cultural heritage, Mexico 141–142
cultural license 64
cultural property 161
cultural sovereignty, AIAN (American Indians and Alaska Natives) 159–160

Dakota Access Pipeline Project 216
Data Act, Sweden 101
data collection: Pueblo People 57; Quechan Nation 152–153
data colonialism 24–25, 31
data dependence 28, 208
data development, United Nations Permanent Forum on Indigenous Issues 43
Data Futures Partnership, Aotearoa New Zealand 63–64
data governance 206–207; Australia 42–47; Basque Country 117–121; *see also* governance
Data Governance Agreement, Canada 43
Data Iwi Leaders Group 65–67
data policy structure, Aotearoa New Zealand 62–64
datafication 118
decolonization 218, 221; self-determination 24
decolonizing epidemiology 199
Decree 4633/2011, Colombia 176
deep sovereignty, Pueblo data sovereignty 58
demography, tribal demography 233
Department of Interior, Indian Affairs, United States 1
Department of International Affairs (DIA), Aotearoa New Zealand 27
development policy 220
DIA (Department of International Affairs), Aotearoa New Zealand 27
differences, emphasizing/disguising 8–9
digital data 211
disguising our differences 8–9
disruptive staring 31
distributed leadership 228
domestic violence, Mexico 143
Dozier Enos, A. 58
Draft Algorithm Charter (Stats NZ) 27

ECOSOC (UN Economic and Social Council) 221
education, kohanga reo (Māori language preschools) 26
emphasizing differences 8–9
ENADID (National Demographic Dynamic Poll) 133
epidemiology: decolonizing 199; Māori 189–197
epistemic injustice 204, 218; overcoming 206–209

equal explanatory power (Mana Whakamārama) 195–197
ETA (Euskadi Ta Askatasuna) 112–113, 126, 128; Basque conflict (1968–2011) 113–114; terrorism 122
ethnic profiling 117
ethnicity index, Mexico *134*
EU General Regulation on Data Protection 118
European Convention of Human Rights 117, 122
Euskaltzaindia 120
Eusko Ikaskuntza 120
extractive activities, Mexico 141

failed policy, Indigenous policy 6–8
FAIR (findable, accessible, interoperable, reusable) 13, 229–230
FARC (Fuerzas Armadas Revolucionarias de Colombia) 169
FCAA (Federal Council for Aboriginal Advancement) 36
FCMVT (*Fundación Centro para la Memoria de las Víctimas del Terrorismo*) 124–125
Federal Council for Aboriginal Advancement (FCAA) 36
Federal Freedom of Information Act (FOIA), United States 214
Federal Indian law, United States 221
Final Report of the National Inquiry into Missing and Murdered Women Indigenous Women and Girls (MMIWG)87
First Nations, Canada 10–11, 81; history of policy in 82–84; OCAP (ownership, control, access, possession) principles 12, 87–90
First Nations Center, Canada 88
First Nations Health and Social Secretariat of Manitoba (FNHSSM), Canada 92
First Nations Information Governance Center, Canada 21, 89; OCAP (ownership, control, access, possession) principles 29
Floridi, L. 29
FNHSSM (First Nations Health and Social Secretariat of Manitoba), Canada 92
FOIA (*Federal Freedom of Information Act*) 214
fracasomania 6–8
Framework Convention for the Protection of National Minorities 116

freedom of speech, United States 209
Fricker, M. 206
Fundación Centro para la Memoria de las Víctimas del Terrorismo (FCMVT) 124–125

Gamio, M. 131
GIDA (Global Indigenous Data Alliance) 13, 21, 229
Gill, D. 25
giving back, Quechan Nation 150–3
Global Indigenous Data Alliance (GIDA), 13, 21, 229
Gogora Institute, Spain 124–7
governance 15; Canada 91–92; data for 10–11
Gradual Civilization Act (1857) 83
Gray-Sharp, K. 26
guidelines for research, universities 162–165

Haldi project, Sweden 100–101
hapū 30
Havana Accords 170
"Havasupai Blood Case" 162
Havasupai Nation 157
He Korowai Oranga 26
health data: First Nations, Canada 83–84; Māori 191–192, 198–199; Sami people 101–105
health disparities, Canada 86–87
healthcare authorities, Sami people, perspectives on health data 103
Hereditary Chiefs (Canada) 81
hermeneutical injustice 204
higher education, Quechan Nation 149–155
high-modernist ideology 5
Hirschman, A.O. 6 7
Historical Memory Act, Spain 122
homegrown models 55
Hongoeka Declaration 192
Hudson, M. 68
human rights 215–220
Hunn report (1961) 26

ICT (Information and Communications Technology) 63, 220
identifying resources, Quechan Nation 149–150
IDGov (Indigenous data governance) 15, 22, 28
IDI (Integrated Data Infrastructure) 62

IDN (Indigenous Data Network) 40; see also networks
IDS networks see networks
IGRA (Indian Gaming Regulatory Act 1988) 210
ILG (Iwi Leaders' Group) 65–67
Indian Act (1985), Canada 82–83
Indian Gaming Regulatory Act (1988) (IGRA) 210
Indian Health Policy (1979), Canada 83
indigeneity 130–131, 133–135
Indigenous Administrative Data Identifier Standard 92
Indigenous communities: Colombia 169; Mexico 135–138
Indigenous data gaps, Canada 88
Indigenous data governance (IDGov) 15, 22, 28
Indigenous Data Network (IDN) 40; see also networks
Indigenous data quality, assessing (Canada) 90–91
Indigenous economies, recommendations for strengthening 143
Indigenous leadership 11
Indigenous Peoples, seeing like a state 4–6
Indigenous policy, fracasomania 6–8
Indigenous resurgence 220
Indigenous Services Canada 1
Indigenous social policy 3–4
INEGI (National Institute of Geography, Statistics and Informatics) 133
Information and Communications Technology (ICT) 220. 63
injustice 204
INPI (National Institute for the Indigenous Communities) 135
institutional responsiveness, Maori Data Sovereignty (MDS) 71
Institutional Review Board (IRB): AIAN (American Indians and Alaska Natives) 161; Quechan Nation 152
Integrated Data Infrastructure (IDI) 62
intellectual property 157
intellectual property rights (IPR) 219
Inter-Apache Policy on Repatriation and the Protection of Apache Cultures 161
inter-legality, TJ framework (Colombia) 175–177
International Convention on Economic Social and Cultural Rights 23
International Covenant on Civil and Political Rights (1966) 23

international development policy, human rights 219–220
International Indigenous Data Sovereignty Interest Group 13
international law 218
Internet 211
interracial marriage 25
Inuit (Canada) 81–84
Inuit Qaujisarvingat 88
Inuit Tapiriit Kanatami (ITK) 88
Inuit Tuttarvignat, Canada 88
IPR (intellectual property rights) 219
IRB (Institutional Review Board): AIAN (American Indians and Alaska Natives) 161; Quechan Nation 152; universities 162–165
isolationist approach to truth 176
ITK (Inuit Tapiriit Kanatami) 88
iwi 30–31

Jackson, M. 23, 28
JEP (Special Jurisdiction for Peace) 169, 177
Jordan's Principle 83

Kaupapa Māori 187–188; health data 198–199; research and epidemiology 191–197
Keres Children's Learning Center (KCLC) 59, 61
King, T. 9
knowledge, Māori 189
knowledge economy 24
kohanga reo (Māori language preschools) 26
Krieger, N. 189
Kuhn, T.S. 227
Kukutai, T. 24, 119–120, 198, 206
Kwet, M. 30

labeling data 127–128
Landa, J. 122
Language Charter for Regional or Minority Languages 116
Law 21/1991, Colombia 180
law of nations 218
leadership 11; distributed leadership 228
legal frameworks 209–217
legal pluralism 175
legislation, Australia 36–40
LI (Sante Fe Indian School Leadership Institute) 51, 54–55
Library and Archives of Canada Act (2004), Canada 89

Lomawaima, K.T. 158
Lopez, L. 175
Luarkie, R. 59

Maiam nayri Wingara Aboriginal and Torres Strait Islander Data Sovereignty Collective, Australia 12–13, 40, 46, 231
mana motuhake 23
Mana Whakamārama (Equal Explanatory Power) 188, 195–197
mana whenua 23
Mana-Mahi Framework *66*
Manzanas, M. 114
Māori: age-standardization 196; children 5–6; collective data privacy 29–30; data colonialism 25; from data dependency to data self-determination 28–31; data policy structure 62–64; health data 191–192, 198–199; Kaupapa Māori 187–188, 191–197; knowledge 189; Mana Whakamārama (Equal Explanatory Power) 195–197; monitoring the Crown 193–194; policy 25–28; quantitative research and epidemiology 189–191; right to be counted 195–197; right to name racism and colonialism 197; right to recognition 195–197; self-determination 23–24; Te Mana Raraunga Maori Data Sovereignty Network 12
Māori Data Audit Tool 68–69, 72
Māori Data Sovereignty (MDS) 22, 64–65; advocacy 65–67; agency responses to 69–74; principles of 67–68; research 74–75
Māori language preschools 26
Māori reserve army of labour 26
Martinez, A. 29
Mataatua Declaration on Cultural and Intellectual Property Rights 65
Matheson, D. 160
MDS (Māori Data Sovereignty) 22, 64–65; advocacy 65–67; agency responses to 69–74; principles of 67–68; research 74–75
mechanisms for research, American Indians and Alaska Natives (AIAN) 160–162
Meijas, U. 31
Memorial Center for Victims of Terrorism, Spain, 124–125, 127

memorial data, Basque conflict (1968-2011) 123–124
mestizo 132
Métis, Canada 81–84
Métis Center, Canada 88–89
Mexico: CDI (National Commission for the Development of Indigenous Communities) 143; census 131–133; domestic violence 143; ethnicity index *134*; indigeneity 133–135; Indigenous communities 135–138; Indigenous data sovereignty 138–144; mestizo 132; natural resources 140–141; Political Constitution of the Mexican United States 130; rights 142–143; social conflicts 143; social deprivation 136–137
Millenium Development goals 221
mining, Mexico 141
Ministry of Social Development (MSD), Te Pae Tata 74
Minnesota Chippewa Tribe 233
minorities 116
Missing and Murdered Indigenous Women and Girls (MMIWG), Canada 87
MnW (Maiam nayri Wingara) 40–45
movement building, Pueblo data sovereignty 55–56
MSD (Ministry of Social Development), Te Pae Tata 74
Murphy, M. 28
Mustimuhw Community Electronic Medical Record (CEMR) 91

Nabokov, P. 157
NAGPRA (*Native American Graves Protection and Repatriation Act*) 157, 161
Nagy, R. 176
National Aboriginal Health Organization (NAHO) 88–89
national census 4
National Commission for the Development of Indigenous Communities (CDI) 135
National Demographic Dynamic Poll (ENADID) 133
National Evaluation Council (CONEVAL) 135
National Historic Preservation Act, United States 214
National Indigenous Australians Agency 1
National Indigenous Reform Agreement (NIRA) 41

Index   241

National Institute for the Indigenous Communities (INPI) 135
National Institute of Geography, Statistics and Informatics (INEGI) 133
National Inuit Strategy on Research (NISR) 88
National Population Council (CONAPO) 134
National Program for Indigenous People 2018-2024 139
nation-states 209–210, 218; sovereign authority 215
Native American Graves Protection and Repatriation Act (NAGPRA) 157, 161
Native Nations 206; research abuse 162–165
natural resources, Mexico 140–141
Navajo Nation Historic Preservation Department 162
Navajo Nation Human Research Review Board (NNHRRB) 161
Navajo Nation Resource Center 162
Navarre Foral Act 16/2015 of April 15 122
networks: AASTEC (Albuquerque Area Southwest Tribal Epidemiology Center) 54; Data Iwi Leaders Group 65–67; First Nations Information Governance Center 21; IDN (Indigenous Data Network) 40; IDS networks *see* IDS networks; LI (Sante Fe Indian School Leadership Institute) 54; Maiam nayri Wingara Aboriginal and Torres Strait Islander Data Sovereignty Collective 40, 46; Te Mana Raraunga Maori Data Sovereignty Network 65–67
New Mexico Summer Youth Tribal Employment 55
New South Wales Colony 3
New Zealand Ministry of Business, Innovation and Employment 231
Ngā Tikanga Paihere 72–74
NIRA (National Indigenous Reform Agreement) 41, 45
NISR (National Inuit Strategy on Research) 88
NNHRRB (Navajo Nation Human Research Review Board) 161
non-performativity 26
Northern Cheyenne Nation 233
Northern Territory Emergency Response (NTER) 40

OCAP (ownership, control, access, possession) principles 12, 29, 43, 87–90
OECD (Organization for Economic Cooperation and Development) 63, 100, 143
Office of the Privacy Commissioner, Aotearoa New Zealand 63
Oguamanam, C. 24, 220–222
Oñati Indigenous Data Sovereignty Communique 13–14
Open Data Charter, Aotearoa New Zealand 63
operationalizing Indigenous rights 229–230
Oregon State University 163
Organization for Economic Cooperation and Development (OECD) 63, 100, 143
Organization for the Advancement of Aboriginal Peoples Health 88
O'Shea, L. 30
overcoming epistemic injustice 206–209
Overcoming Indigenous Disadvantage 3

Peace and Justice Law (Colombia) 175
periodization 112; Colombia 172; Spain 122
plenary power 213
policy 207–208, 226; Australia 36–40; Canada 82–84
policy failure, Indigenous policy 6–8
Political Constitution of the Mexican United States 130
political philosophy, Australia 38–40
Pōmare, E. 192
Pool, I. 26, 170
Populations, Māori 189; right to be counted 194–195
positivism 189–190
Poverty in the Indigenous population in Mexico 2008-2018 report 136
power sharing 228
predictive risk modeling (PRM) 5
privacy: Canada 89; Māori 29–30
Privacy Act 1993, Aotearoa New Zealand 63–64
Privacy Act, Canada 89
PRM (predictive risk modeling) 5
Pueblo Convocation 56–57
Pueblo Data Sovereignty 52–54, 57–59; movement building 55–56; opportunities for 59–60; support for 56–57
Pueblo Revolt (1680) 53

qualitative data, AIAN (American Indians and Alaska Natives) 158–159
quality, of Indigenous data, Canada 90–91
quantitative research 188; in racialized, colonial contexts (Māori) 189–191
Quechan Nation: community values 150–152; data collection 152–153; identifying resources 149–150; IRB (Institutional Review Board) 152
Quijano, A. 174

Racheria River, Colombia 181–182
racherías 178
racism: Māori 197; quantitative research 189–191
RCAP (Royal Commission on Aboriginal Peoples), Canada 85–87
RDA (Research Data Alliance) 13, 21
reconciliation, Canada 81, 85–87
relational model of self-determination 28
removal of children 4
research: data about the research 230–232; Māori Data Sovereignty (MDS) 74–75; qualitative data, AIAN 158–159; quantitative research 188–191
Research Data Alliance (RDA) 13, 21
research mechanisms, AIAN (American Indians and Alaska Natives) 160–162
re-use of qualitative data 158–159
Revolutionary Armed Forces of Colombia (FARC) 169
Ricuarte, P. 25
right to recognition, Māori 195–197
rights: human rights 215–220; Mexico 142–143; operationalizing Indigenous rights 229–230
rights framework 217
Roc*Roi algorithm 6
Rodriguez-Lonebear, D. 29
Ronaki, M. 99
Royal Commission on Aboriginal Peoples (RCAP), Canada 85–87
rubber industry (Amazon) 173
Ruling 079 (Colombia) 169

Sadowski, J. 24
Sami Parliament 106; health data 103
Sami people 99; Haldi project 100–101; perspectives on ownership and governance of data 101–105
Sámiid Riikkasearvi (SSR) 106
SAMINOR study 100–101
Santa Fe Indian School Leadership Institute (LI) 51, 54, 55

SATRC (South African Truth and Reconciliation Commission) 176
school attendance, Australia 7–8
Scott, D. C. 82
Scott, J. C. 4–6
SDGs (Sustainable Development Goals) 120–221
Seeing like a State (Scott 1998) 4–6
self-determination 22–24, 31, 88, 206–207, 216–217; relational model of self-determination 28
Smith, G. H. 199
Smith, L. T. 199
social conflicts, Mexico 143
social deprivation, Mexico 136–137
social investment approach 25
social license 64
social mobilisation, Colombia 175
social power 206
Social Wellbeing Agency, Aotearoa New Zealand 63
South African Truth and Reconciliation Commission (SATRC) 176
Spain: *Act 4/2008 of June 19, 2008* 122; *Act 5/2019 of April 4* 122; *Act 29/2011 on the Recognition and Comprehensive Protection of Victims of Terrorism* 121; *Act on Historical Memory 52/2007* 121; *Amnesty Act* (1977) 121; Basque conflict (1968-2011) *see* Basque Conflict (1968-2011); ETA 112–113; *Historical Memory Act* 122; *Navarre Foral Act 16/2015 of April 15* 122
Spanish Act on Historical Memory 122
Special Jurisdiction for Peace (JEP) 169
SSR (*Sámiid Riikkasearvi*) 106
Standing Rock Sioux Tribe 216
state 4–6; emphasizing/disguising our differences 8–9
statistical analysis 190
Statistics Act, Aotearoa New Zealand 64
Statistics New Zealand 231
Stats NZ Tatauranga Aotearoa (Stats NZ) 63–64; Māori Data Sovereignty (MDS) 69–70
Suina, J. H. 58–59
support for Pueblo data sovereignty 56–57
Sustainable Development Goals (SDGs) 120, 221
suzerainty 170
Sweden: Haldi project 100–101; IDS (Indigenous Data Sovereignty) 105–107; Sami people 99–105

Tauli-Corpuz, V. 119, 217
Tawhai, V. 26
Taylor, J. 24, 119–120, 206
Taylor, L. 29
Te Ao Māori 67
Te Mana o te Raraunga model 71–72
Te Mana Raraunga Maori Data Sovereignty Network 12, 64–67, 231; awareness raising 69–71; institutional responsiveness 71
Te Pae Tata 74
Te Pou Tuatahi 74
Te Puni Kokiri Ministry of Māori Development 1
Te Ropu Wahine Maori Toko i te Ora Māori Women's Welfare League 191–192
Te Tiriti 27
terra nullius 177, 179–180
terrorism: Basque conflict (1968-2011) 123–124; ETA 122, 128
tino rangatiratanga (absolute chiefly authority) 23–24
TJ framework (Colombia) 171–172, 175–177
TMR (Te Mana Rarunga) 65–67; awareness raising 69–71; institutional responsiveness 71; Māori Data Audit Tool 69
Toki, V. 23
Torres Strait Islander Peoples 3; legislation and policy 36–40; school attendance 7
TRC (Truth and Reconciliation Commission of Canada) 86–87
Treaty of Waitangi 67
Tribal Council, AIAN (American Indians and Alaska Natives) 160
tribal governance, data for 232–233
tribal governments, United States 212–215
tribal sovereignty 160; United States, 212–215
Trudeau, J. 81, 89
Truth and Reconciliation Commission of Canada (TRC) 86–87
Tsosie, R. 160
Tuck, E. 31, 199
Tui'kn Partnership 91
Turcotte, J. 212

UM (University of Montana) 164
Unama'ki Client Registry 91
UNDRIP (United Nations Declaration on the Rights of Indigenous Peoples) 11, 13, 23, 101, 114–115, 158–159; human rights 215–217
UNESCO (United Nations Educational, Scientific, and Cultural Organization) 212, 219
unethical research practices, "Havasupai Blood Case" 162
United Nations: Covenant on Economic, Social and Cultural Rights 221; Declaration on the Rights of Indigenous Peoples (UNDRIP) 11, 13, 23, 101, 114–115, 158–159, 215–217; Economic and Social Council (ECOSOC) 221; Educational, Scientific, and Cultural Organization (UNESCO) 212, 219; Permanent Forum on Indigenous Issues 11, 43, 119, 219, 221; reports on Mexico 137–138
United Self-Defenders of Colombia (AUC) 175
United States 206; cultural sovereignty 159–160; Department of Interior, Indian Affairs 1; freedom of speech 209; IDS and qualitative data 158–159; Indian Gaming Regulatory Act (1988) (IGRA) 210; political sovereignty 158; Quechan Nation 149–155; tribal sovereignty 212–215; UN Covenant on Economic, Social and Cultural Rights 221
United States Indigenous Data Sovereignty Network (USIDSN) 12; Indigenous Governance Principles 51
universities: guidelines for research, 162–165; IRB (Institutional Review Board) 162–165; Oregon State University 163; Sami people, perspectives on health data 103; UM (University of Montana) 164; UNM (University of New Mexico) 163
UNM (University of New Mexico) 163
UNPFII (UN Permanent Forum on Indigenous Issues) 221
USIDSN (United States Indigenous Data Sovereignty Network) 12; Indigenous Governance Principles 51

van der Sloot, B. 29
Velasquez, R. 173
victims: Basque conflict (1968-2011) 123–124; of terrorism 122

Walter, M. 9, 148, 172, 187, 194, 198, 206, 210
Wayuu (Colombia) 178; autonomous consultation 181–182; Bahia Portete

massacre 179–180; Cerrejon mine 178–179
Wayuu safeguard plan (Colombia) 180–181
West, W. R. 160
WIPO (World Intellectual Property Organization) 212, 219
women: Bahia Portete massacre 179–180; Indigenous communities, Mexico 143; Missing and Murdered Indigenous Women and Girls (MMIWG), Canada 87
World Intellectual Property Organization (WIPO) 212, 219

Yang, K.W. 31
Yazzie/Martinez lawsuit 56, 60–61n6

Zuberi, T. 2, 190–191

Made in the USA
Monee, IL
21 February 2023